SINGING THE TRAIL

SINGING THE TRAIL

THE STORY OF MAPPING AOTEAROA NEW ZEALAND

—

JOHN MCCRYSTAL

ALLEN&UNWIN
SYDNEY·MELBOURNE·AUCKLAND·LONDON

CONTENTS

INTRODUCTION 6

PART ONE
COAST
11

ONE
TE ATA O TE MĀTAURANGA 13

TWO
BEACHED AS 41

THREE
DUTCH COURAGE 57

FOUR
THOROUGHLY COOKED 71

FIVE
SEALING THE DEAL 101

PART TWO
INTERIOR
129

SIX
SETTLING DOWN 131

SEVEN
ONWARDS, INWARDS 161

EIGHT
CADASTRE VS AHI KAA 187

PART THREE
CHANGING VIEWS
213

NINE
GREATER NEW ZEALAND 215

TEN
PLACES IN THE HEART 225

ELEVEN
A MOVING STORY 237

TWELVE
SCRUTINY ON THE BOUNTY 257

FURTHER READING 272

ACKNOWLEDGEMENTS 274

INTRODUCTION

Maps mean different things to different people. For me, they have meant a range of things, according to the various stages of my life.

When I was a child, my brothers and I used to explore our neighbourhood—the playing fields, the stinky creek, the big subdivision, the boundaries of the farmlet from which the subdivision had been carved. We named significant features: a glade where the foetid water of the creek pooled we named 'Minty Pools' after our dog, a constant companion on our voyages of exploration; the clay hills of the subdivision we named 'the clay hills' (James Cook, ever the prosaic namer, would have nodded in approval at that one); a thicket of woolly nightshade trees we named 'Chrysler Forge' (well, my brother did: I don't really know where that name came from, as it was many years since we'd owned a Valiant). We loved exploration, and we loved maps, which were the record of our explorations. The naming and the mapping were an act of possession, of laying claim to a larger world.

My father was a devoted boatie, and we were fortunate enough to spend many happy days cruising Auckland's Hauraki Gulf. Dad never ceased to amaze us with his ability to know exactly where we were, day or night and whatever the weather, simply by looking out for landmarks, lights and buoys and referring to the nautical charts with their spindly black lines and hieroglyphs and pale green shading. We were even more impressed—and grateful—the day we brought a boat to Auckland from Whāngārei, beyond our usual cruising grounds. She was slower through the water than we had expected, and night fell before we had rounded Cape Rodney and made familiar waters. By reading the patterns of winking lights and keeping an eye on the compass, Dad brought us surely and safely to anchor in what daylight revealed to be one of our favourite places, Mansion House Bay on Kawau Island. It seemed little short of miraculous, this business of navigation. I had always been interested in maps: now I became obsessed with charts.

I also have a nephew who has always been fascinated by maps and charts. Before he was five, he was capable of following the route we were driving on a road map, which he would keep open on his lap. This habit didn't change as he grew older, and one day, I suddenly realised that the charm of maps was different for him than it was for me. He was an anxious child, and following the route of an outward journey was less about the sense of venturing into a wider world than it was about marking the return.

For him, there was only one place of significance marked on the map, and only one cardinal direction: respectively, home and the way home.

When, in my turn, I became a parent, my days all began with me pushing my children up the hill on an arrangement of vehicles—my son on a trike in front, my daughter on her trike with the front wheel hooked in the tray behind him, me pushing using a handle attached to my daughter's trike. We called this 'bike train'. Each day, bike train would make its way from our gate up the road to their daycare, about one and a half kilometres distant—a mile in the old money. We had various stops along the way: the bank where wildflowers grew, where my daughter would pick a couple and use them to decorate her handlebars; the traffic lights, where we would impatiently wait for the 'safe to cross' buzzer; a couple of addresses where there were occasionally friendly cats; a phone box where the children would pretend to phone their grandmother to tell her about their forthcoming day; their destination. And in the afternoon, we would make the same journey in reverse. After my son had graduated to primary school, I still kept the same routine with my daughter. One day, she and I drew a map of our habitual route, with all those points of significance marked. That map was more about memorialisation than orientation: we never took it with us, or even consulted it, but I meant to keep it. Years have passed, and I have misplaced the map, or it is lost forever, but it is still printed on my heart.

―――

Maps are records of the known and, as such, they need not be made of lines on paper. Indeed, we are not the only creatures that make them: bees and birds have their own methods of geolocation, and this surely relies upon some kind of mental map. The homing faculty of pigeons is well known, but it pales by comparison with the epic wayfinding facility of migratory birds such as the sooty shearwater, which makes an annual pilgrimage from the subantarctic islands where it breeds to Siberia and then back again to tiny dots of land in the vast Southern Ocean. Bees are thought to use the sun and various landmarks to guide them to the flowering plants where they forage, and then back to the hive. The ability of cats to find their way to former territories when they run away from their owners' new homes is legendary. Anyone who has ever owned a Labrador will know the precision with which it will mentally map the location of, say, a discarded half-sausage, and find its way back unerringly many days later. The dogs that the polar explorers took to Antarctica seemed to have had a keen sense of north and south. In 1916, one sledging party, while on the return journey from 80° South, found the need to backtrack, but the dogs refused. It was necessary to drive them northward and then work them in a wide turn to point their noses south again.

Maps, then, are the means by which geographic knowledge is communicated. If you Google 'world's oldest map', the result takes you to a description of a stone tablet found in a cave in Spain that, at 14,000 years old, is supposed to be the earliest known depiction of a landscape. But maps are older than that. Human beings—perhaps even their not-quite-human ancestors—were communicating their knowledge of the world to one another long before they came to draw it. The earliest cartographic technology is story. Ancient stories contained useful information, such as the relation of changes in the night sky to the rhythms of nature; they also contained navigational and cartographic information. For posterity—or for cultural outsiders—this information can be obscure. But for those intended to hear them, they served as mnemonics. Homer's *Odyssey*, for example, is a baffling story in many ways, loosely based on history and geography. But it has been suggested that it is an ill fit to the places and people it names because the story has been constructed around a set of sailing instructions to anyone circumnavigating the isle of Sicily. The doings of gods, men and monsters are simply a vivid means of making notices to mariners memorable.

Of course, for those cultures blessed with the technology of writing and drawing, maps soon became physical objects: stone tablets, papyrus, parchment, paper. Maps might be simple line drawings, or they might be richly illuminated paintings: there were few conventions until the map-making 'schools' of the Renaissance sought to introduce them, largely to serve the needs of those using them to explore the unknown. Accuracy, too, changed radically with advances in the technology of measurement. For centuries, even maps of the known world were, to the modern eye, strangely distorted, partly because there was no standard projection method (that is, how to represent the spherical globe on a plane, i.e. a sheet of paper), but mostly because until the late eighteenth century there was no way of measuring longitude. Celestial navigation techniques enabled people to fix their latitude (their position on the globe relative to the north and south poles) with precision; but determining where you were around the globe was another matter altogether. The odd, elongated representations of familiar land masses from maps dating to the sixteenth and seventeenth centuries are illustrative of this imprecision. But once the chronometer became a standard navigational tool, cartographers began to achieve levels of accuracy that have only recently been surpassed, with the advent of satellite telemetry.

———

The Polynesian myth of the creation of New Zealand was that the demigod ancestor Māui fished it up, and the crew of his waka subsequently carved up the land. The reality is not far different. Since its discovery by humankind, Aotearoa New Zealand has been carved up many times with different kinds of knives. Like any chronological series of New Zealand maps, those in the following pages illustrate the differences that arise from the two sets of factors described above. The maps reflect the technological differences, in methods of measurement and of recording the results of that measurement. But just as significantly, they also reflect the changing agendas of those making the maps, and of those for whom the maps were made. The first European maps of Aotearoa New Zealand were works of science fiction. It wasn't until explorers actually traversed the territory these islands occupy that reality began to supplant hypothesis. And by now, much of the coastline had already been caught in the cartographic net of those greatest of all navigators, the Polynesians, who recorded what they knew in stories, some of which survive.

Once the first lines had been inked onto the blank spaces, knowledge began to spread inward, like a stain. Harbours—the first thing necessary to anyone visiting in the age of sail—were the first aspects of the coastline to be drawn in detail. Then, inevitably, it was the resources—seals, flax, timber—that drew the eye that drew the map. When the project of European settlement got under way, the distinctive straight lines and grids of the cadastre arrived, confined to the regions adjacent to commodious harbours, at first. Meanwhile, intrepid and hardy souls were pushing the bounds of knowledge inland: surveyors, adventurers, explorers and prospectors ventured into the blank white spaces and brought back more lines and shades corresponding with the focus of their interest.

Inevitably, the expansion of European interests rubbed up against those of Māori, and the heat of the friction sprang into flame. The conflict between the colonisers and the colonised is memorialised in maps, too—ordnance surveys, military route-finding, plans of pā and redoubt—as are the dismal results: maps of the massive transfer of swathes of land from Māori to the settler and colonial government.

From the latter days of the nineteenth century, maps reflected the pursuit of economic prosperity: surveys of resources, records of the construction of lines of communication, depictions of scientific study of the economic potential of land and people. This process has been progressively refined with new technologies of measurement, culminating in the latest electronic survey techniques that can pierce rock and drain oceans and measure the very air, yielding gloriously illuminated versions of continental New Zealand, seismic New Zealand, hollow New Zealand, warming New Zealand.

The following pages are divided into three parts. The first two describe the process by which Aotearoa New Zealand was put on the map: first the coast, then the inland detail, including the internal boundaries and divisions. The third part looks at the ways in which New Zealand has expanded beyond its own natural boundaries (or, in some mysterious cases, contracted to the point of vanishing altogether), and a selection of some of the ways in which changing technologies and the changing priorities of observers have produced different views of our little country.

In the end, of course, the maps presented in the following pages are a personal selection, and probably say more about what preoccupies me and catches my eye than they necessarily do about the breadth and scope of New Zealand map-making. One of my aims was to select aesthetically pleasing maps, which probably accounts for my bias towards historical maps. Another was to find maps that told a story. Sometimes, a map had a better story than appearance; sometimes, it was simply too gorgeous to pass over, however rich (or otherwise) its story. Here and there, maps that were drawn on a large scale are drastically reduced in size; you may need to keep your magnifying glass handy to make out some of the finer features. But between them, they draw a picture—idiosyncratic, even as it may be—of New Zealand, my New Zealand, and how New Zealanders came to be where and who they are.

PART ONE

COAST

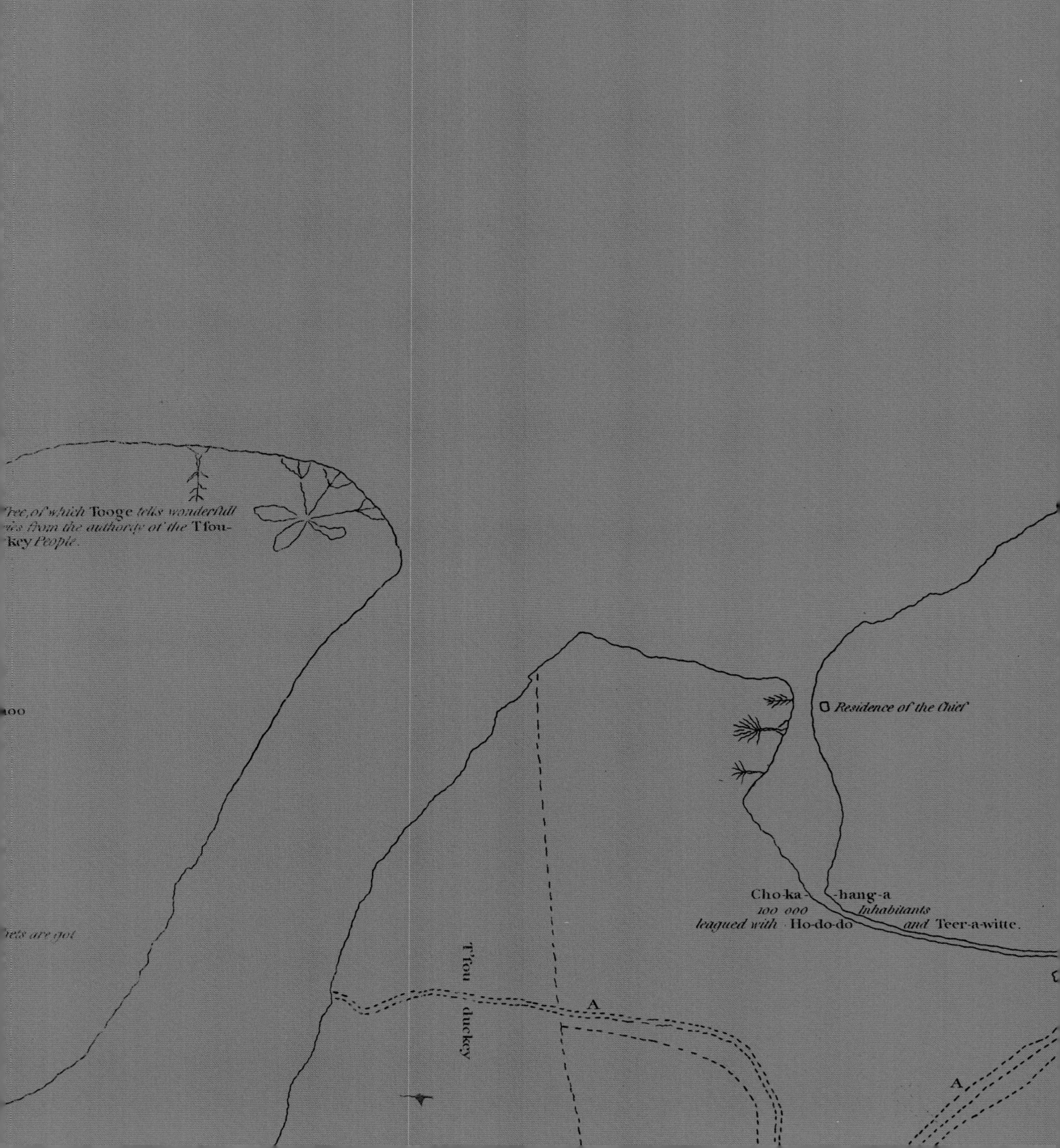

Tree, of which Tooge *tells wonderfull*
ies from the authority of the T'fou-
key People.

○ *Residence of the Chief*

Cho-ka- -hang-a
100 000 *Inhabitants*
leagued with Ho-do-do *and* Teer-a-witte.

T'fou duckey

A

ONE

TE ATA O TE MĀTAURANGA

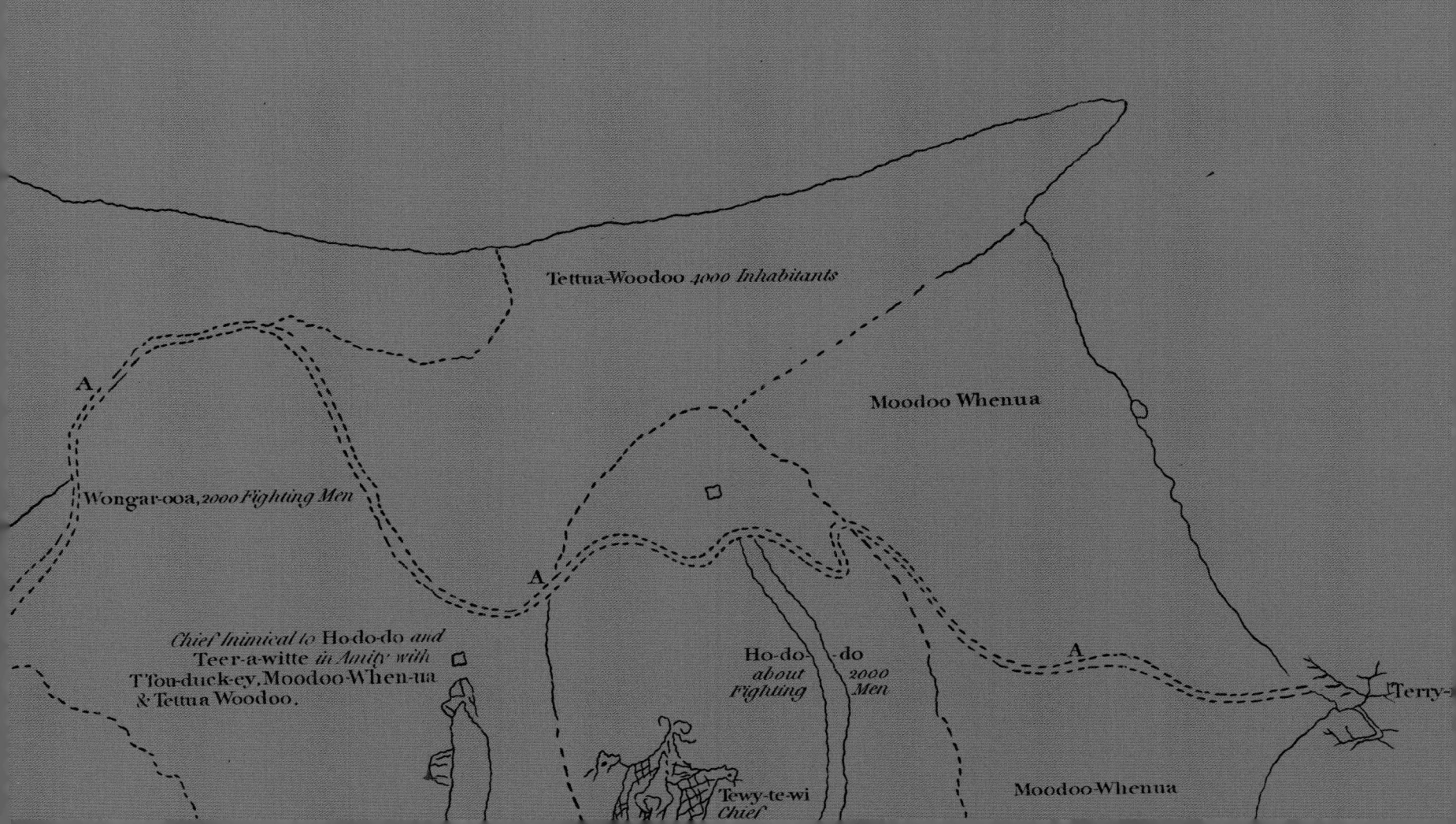

Manoui Taoai *no Water on it*

Tettua-Woodoo *4000 Inhabitants*

Moodoo Whenua

A.

Wongar-ooa, *2000 Fighting Men*

A.

Chief Inimical to Ho-do-do *and* Teer-a-witte *in Amity with* T'Tou-duck-ey, Moodoo-When-ua & Tettua Woodoo.

Ho-do-do *about Fighting* *2000 Men*

A.

Terry-

Tewy-te-wi *Chief*

Moodoo-Whenua

We have only the bleached remnant of the first map of New Zealand. It is many hundreds of years old, and while it was probably once richly figured and detailed, the colour has bled from it over time. What's more, even some of the surviving notation is arcane, which makes it all but impossible to read. Nonetheless, it is one of the oldest human objects associated with Aotearoa New Zealand and it is rightly treasured as a taonga.

It is not precisely known when New Zealand was discovered. It likely happened late in the long series of voyages of discovery begun by the Lapita people from their base in the Bismarck Archipelago region of the western Pacific. According to the archaeological evidence, these people began to move eastward into the Pacific around 3000 years ago: fragments of the highly distinctive pottery associated with their civilisation is found in successively younger sites from the Santa Cruz Islands, Vanuatu and New Caledonia in Melanesia, through Fiji and Wallis and Futuna to Tonga and Sāmoa, where it seems local materials were unsuitable for ceramic production and the tradition of its manufacture died out. But the exploration didn't end there. The Polynesians, no less intrepid than their Lapita ancestors, swept still further eastward: the Tuamotu and Marquesas groups in the central Pacific had been colonised by around 2000 years ago, and even Hawai'i and remote Rapa Nui (Easter Island) had been peopled 500 years later than that. Evidence suggests the great journey even stretched as far as South America—the bones of domestic fowl, which were native to Asia (whence the Lapita themselves are thought to have originated up to 30,000 years ago), have been found in Chile pre-dating the arrival of Europeans, and by then the sweet potato and gourds, natives of South America, had likewise spread right across the Pacific. What's more, DNA evidence indicates that the people of Rapa Nui have both Polynesian and Native American heritage: given the voyaging prowess of the Polynesians, the strongly inferred conclusion is that it was Polynesians who contacted South America and returned to Rapa Nui with Native American women.

Who knows what stone was cast in order to set the ripples of Lapita migration going in the first place. It could be that they were displaced by pressure from other peoples to their west. It could be that their own isles were becoming overpopulated. Or that a technological advance—the development of the double-hulled canoe would seem the most likely—made it possible, and then restless human inquisitiveness did the rest. But what can't be doubted is that the ancestors of the Polynesians swiftly became expert fishers for islands. The pattern of settlement was against the prevailing trade winds (which blow from the east in the region), so it is supposed that the modus operandi was to sail upwind as far as one dared, and then to turn around and be borne home by the favourable breeze at the expedition's end. By reading signs in the oceans and the air, early navigators could deduce the proximity of land even as it still lay over the horizon.

Disruptions to the regular swell pattern might hint at the presence of an island; the appearance of seaweed or parts of terrestrial plants would confirm it, as would sightings of seabirds and certain distinctive cloud forms. It helped that many of the island groups of the Pacific lie in chains: these, together with the halo of indications of their proximity, formed a 'screen', a much larger target than their individually insignificant land masses. Each landfall was noted, along with sets of sailing instructions for subsequent navigators to follow. Positions were fixed with reference to the natural world—the patterns of wind and waves and, of course, the movement of the sun, moon and stars overhead and relative to the horizon.

Then it was the turn of the people who served as cartographers in this oral culture, the storytellers. Information gathered by the navigators was encoded in stories: thrilling, spellbinding epics full of the deeds and misdeeds of gods, men and women and monsters, all designed to help detailed information stick in the memory. And discoveries were recorded. One Sāmoan legend described a god moving over the ocean and scattering sand: wherever a grain fell, an island emerged. This must have been a comforting story for those out of sight of land in the vast Pacific! European nautical language describes the sighting of a landmark as 'raising' it, which makes sense to anyone who has ever watched land emerge from over the horizon as one approaches it. In much the same way, the act of discovering an island seemed to the early Polynesians to be perfectly analogous to hauling a fish from the depths.

Most of the expeditions that resulted in the discoveries of the main island groups of Polynesia are memorialised in the fishing yarns of a demigod by the name of Māui Tikitiki-a-Taranga, the youngest of four brothers all named Māui. According to these stories, Māui Tikitiki was the figure who 'caught' most of the islands of Polynesia. New Zealand was no exception, and the story of how Māui caught his great fish—'Te Ika-a-Māui', the North Island of New Zealand—is the oldest surviving record of the discovery of Aotearoa New Zealand.

According to the story (there are variations, but the main elements are common across versions), Māui was not permitted to accompany his brothers on their fishing expeditions beyond the reef. But one day, equipping himself with the jawbone of his grandmother as a fish-hook, he stowed away in their waka, remaining concealed until they were too far out to return. They weren't happy when he revealed himself. They got on with their fishing, but when they had caught enough and were ready to return, Māui argued that they should venture a little further. His brothers taunted him, asking what he intended using for bait, since they would not give him some of their own. He replied by delivering a blow to his own nose and using the blood that flowed from his nostrils to bait his hook. No sooner had he lowered his hook to the bottom of the sea than he caught something, and it was immediately obvious that this was no ordinary fish. In one version of the story, Māui wonders aloud which of the three rumoured fishes he might have caught: Seek the Sea God, Seek the West Wind or Seek the Land. It took all his might and demi-divine magic, and the straining sinews of his brothers paddling the waka, to bring his catch to the surface. When it finally broke the water, it was vast. Māui recognised it as Seek the Land. Some stories record that Māui's hook was snagged in the gable of the house belonging to the great goddess of the night, Hine-Nui-te-Pō; others that there were many houses and they had fires burning in their hearths.

Māui set off on foot to examine this leviathan, warning his brothers not to damage it. But contrary to his instructions, they began cutting it up in order to bring some of it home with them. According to some versions of the story, the creature stirred under their knives and shook itself, casting several of them to their deaths. When it finally settled, it still bore the scars—the high mountains and deep valleys where previously there was only flat land.

This local story of the discovery of New Zealand is similar to its counterparts in the mythologies of other Polynesian lands, but differs in some key respects. In the Tahitian version, Māui baits his hook with the wing of a sacred bird. And while his brothers are furiously paddling and he is hauling up the fish that will become Tahiti, he becomes distracted by a calabash floating on the water. When he picks this up, it transforms into the shape of his beautiful sister. His brothers can't resist sneaking a peek at her, even though Māui has told them not to look back. Because of their disobedience, the land he is hauling from the depths breaks into pieces—which is why Tahiti is a chain of islands, rather than one single land mass.

Māui's fishing exploits are a record of the discovery of Polynesia. The fishing expedition of Māui's brothers can be read as the voyages of exploration of the ancestors. Māui's bold urging that they should try fishing further than before records the proposal to explore deeper into the Pacific Ocean than previously, and the legendary three fishes represent the three possible outcomes: the expeditioners might meet the sea god, or find the source of the west wind, or they might find land.

And more than this, they are the first maps of the region, albeit faded, and impossible to read with any precision without the key. It is likely that Māui's fish-hook and unconventional bait are a clue to the direction that the successful voyage of discovery sailed: the curved tail of the constellation Scorpius is named Te Matau-a-Māui, the Fish-hook of Māui, but without a grasp of ancient Polynesian astronomy, the significance of baiting the hook with blood is obscure (as is the significance of the red wing of the alae bird in the Tahitian equivalent). It's possible that the reference to Māui's hook lodging in the gable of the goddess's house records the first sighting, perhaps of a prominent coastal peak of Aotearoa. The name Te Matau-a-Māui is also given to Māhia Peninsula in Hawke's Bay, which perhaps commemorates a landfall in this vicinity. The cutting up of the fish describes the land they had found— vast and rugged in a way that most of the Polynesian island homelands were not. And the death of some of Māui's brothers suggests that exploration of the new country was a dangerous business.

The awe with which these feats of navigation were held in Polynesian society is easily inferred from the fact that they were attributed in the stories to a demigod—human, but blessed with superhuman powers. Navigation was a superpower; the stories that imparted its secrets were disseminated and kept amongst a select few, a sanctified elite.

———

It was popularly believed until quite recently that it was a Polynesian navigator by the name of Kupe who rediscovered New Zealand, while chasing a monstrous octopus across the ocean around AD 950. He reported the landfall upon his return to his homeland, which subsequently sparked the wave (or waves) of migration that was accomplished in a 'great fleet' of waka. It's a neat, tidy story, to the point where it seems a great shame that it isn't authentic. Indeed, so beguiling is this story that, even though it was altogether debunked by an academic working in the 1970s, it still enjoys a wide currency among those who believe they know the ancient history of New Zealand (and is repeated in no less an authority than the *New Zealand Historical Atlas*, published in 1998). The late ethnologist David Simmons showed that while there are, in fact, many traditions of a navigator named Kupe (and many place names that record his progress around the coastline), few of these stories credit him with the first rediscovery. Indeed, some place him amongst the first or even subsequent waves of settlers. An octopus does feature in a handful, but the traditional Māori source for the story of an epic chase into high latitudes has proved elusive. The romantic version of Kupe's story that Simmons called 'the great New Zealand myth' seems to have originated with Stephenson Percy Smith, a polymathic English early settler with a passion for ethnography and, apparently, a facility for invention. (We will meet Smith again in a different capacity in subsequent pages.) All that can be claimed of Kupe is that he has the status of an early explorer amongst several iwi and hapū. Enough of the stories (such as this one, collected by Sir George Grey and reflecting the eccentricities of his spelling) agree to indicate that it was he who proved that the North Island of New Zealand was separate from the south (and that there were two islands, Kapiti and Mana, lying off the southwestern coastline):

Ka tito au
Ka tito au
Ka tito au ki a Kupe
Te tangata
Nana i topetope
Te wenua
Tu ke Kapiti
Tu ke Mana
Tau ke Arapaoa
Ko nga tohu, tena
O taku tupuna
O Kupe
Nana i waka tomene
Titapua
Ka toreke i au te whenua nei

I sing,
I sing,
I sing of Kupe,
The man who sliced up the land
Kapiti stands away
Mana stands away
Arapaoa separated
These are the signs
Of my ancestor
Of Kupe
Who explored Titapua
This land was thrust apart by me.

Stories from the Taranaki and Whanganui regions add that one of Kupe's daughters, Taipua, killed herself in the region of Cook Strait. Kupe was so grieved by this that he cut his forehead, and the blood stained the rocks. There is an area on the Wellington South Coast named Red Rocks. And several of the Kupe stories record that he cast his girdle into the water of the Tasman Sea to cause it to become rough and prevent one of his companions (whom he had left ashore) from following him. In this way—adding landmarks, passing on knowledge of hazards such as sea conditions—traditional stories served as maps.

Another tradition links the rediscovery of New Zealand to pounamu, or greenstone, which was said to have been discovered by Ngāhue, who brought a block of it (significantly called Te Ika-o-Ngāhue, Ngāhue's fish) back to the ancestral homeland Hawaiki. Here, it was fashioned into a number of articles, including personal ornaments and two adzes, which were used to build some of the great waka used to carry migrants to Aotearoa. Partly, this tradition is likely to have served as an oral map to the sources of pounamu (more on this below). Partly, it may well commemorate an early exploration.

―――

Being an oral culture, the Polynesians stored all of their cartographical information—along with their knowledge of the seasons, the natural world, the history of their people—in their own memories. Stories were the principal way in which this information was transmitted from one person to another. From time to time, they doubtless used different methods to assist in the transmission: Marshall Islanders, for example, used elaborately woven arrays of wands made from coconut fronds to represent the complicated patterns of oceanic swells that sailors might encounter en route from one island to another. These weren't carried aboard voyaging canoes: they were simply a tool to aid in the work of committing the information to memory. The marae (or malae) in which budding Tahitian or

Hawaiian navigators learned their art may well have been arranged and decorated in a way that helped students orient themselves in relation to the night sky. And some methods will have been improvised. A master navigator explaining a sea route to a novice would almost certainly have picked up a stick and traced lines in the sand or dust, placing objects to represent islands or guiding stars. But it was the stories, chants and incantations containing the information that most closely approximated the paper maps on which Western cartographers relied.

Needless to say, when the two cultures encountered one another, there was considerable mutual curiosity about the very different technologies used to accomplish the same task. The most dramatic examples of this transaction—illustrative of the cultural divide between Europeans and Polynesians—date from 1769, when a remarkable symposium occurred between master European mariners and a highly skilled arioi, or Tahitian navigator priest. The Europeans were the scientists and ranking officers aboard James Cook's *Endeavour*, on the first of his three voyages to the Pacific; the Tahitian was a young noble named Tupaia.

Tupaia was already known to a number of Cook's company, as he had been prominent in Tahitian society when another British vessel, the *Dolphin*, under Captain Samuel Wallis, had visited two years previously. His fortunes had suffered somewhat in the interim, but he remained a high priest and thus an important figure in the entourage of Tutaha, who ruled as paramount chief. Tupaia assumed an intermediary role between the Tahitians and the British, and grew to be not only trusted but also liked and admired by Cook and his officers. He particularly hit it off with Joseph Banks, the wealthy young gentleman-scientist who had shipped with Cook. It was Banks who persuaded a reluctant Cook to take Tupaia aboard for the onward journey. Banks wrote in his journal of Tupaia that

> he is certainly a most proper man, well born, chief Tahowa [*sic*] or preist of this Island, consequently skilled in the mysteries of their religion; but what makes him more than any thing else desirable is his experience in the navigation of these people and knowledge of the Islands in these seas; he has told us the names of above 70, the most of which he has been at.

Cook recorded his equally favourable impression of the Tahitian in his own journal:

> This man had been with us most part of the time we had been upon the Island which gave us an opportunity to know something of him. We found him to be a very intelligent person and to know more of the Geography of the Islands situated in these seas, their produce and the religion laws and customs of the inhabitants than any one we had met with.

Although Cook was charged, upon departing Tahiti, with sailing south in search of new lands, he delayed long enough to chart the Society Islands, as he named the group (according to his journal, to commemorate the fact they all lay within such cosy proximity to one another, but likely also as a compliment to his sponsors, the Royal Society). In this work he was ably assisted by Tupaia, who piloted them from island to island and directed them to safe passages through dangerous coral fringe reefs. And when they laid a course southwards, Tupaia was able to predict the appearance of the Austral Group.

The second task to which Tupaia was put was very much more ambitious. He had made it plain to Cook and his officers that he had knowledge—some of it at first hand, some of it from others and, presumably, from information bequeathed from antiquity—of anywhere up to 130 islands stretching from the area to the immediate east of Ra'iātea far across to the western Pacific. Excited to learn that here was a short cut in the tedious business of exploration, Cook and his officers promptly asked Tupaia to list the islands and then to map them.

Tupaia's map of the Pacific is a remarkable object, even if it has baffled, frustrated and defeated generations of academics who have sought to understand it. It was an attempt to communicate across a linguistic divide: the names that appear on the map, and which feature in the lists that Tupaia compiled, were written down as his European audience heard them, which accounts for their obscurity. (Many of the names by which Tupaia knew these places have likely changed in the two centuries since he dictated them—and might even have changed *before* he came to speak them, in the cases of places he had learned of from tradition.) Far more fundamentally, it was an attempt to communicate across culturally different conceptions of the world and, as such, there was a kind of radical incompatibility between the information and the medium in which it was being transmitted. Western cartography was executed according to centuries-old conventions, which in turn derived from principles of mathematics and geometry. It used precise measurements to produce the kind of objective view of the world a bird would have—if the world it was viewing had been converted from a sphere to a two-dimensional plane. To assist in depicting it, maps conventionally featured reference grids: lines of latitude representing distance from the poles, and lines of longitude, describing distance from an arbitrarily chosen prime meridian (that is, the zero point from which degrees around the circumference of the Earth were counted). On British maps, of course, this prime meridian was the line of longitude that passed through Greenwich, home of the Royal Observatory since the seventeenth century.

Polynesian navigators, by contrast, had a subjective view of the world. Their sense of time, space and distance was fluid, and subject to the vicissitudes of wind and tide. There are no words for measurements of distance in te reo Māori, which is typical of Polynesian languages: instead, journeys were described in terms of the time it would take to accomplish them. In sea voyages, needless to say, this depended upon whether you were sailing upwind or down. Tupaia told Cook that it took around ten days to sail the 2000 kilometres from Ra'iātea to what are now known as Boscawen and Keppel islands in the Tongan archipelago (much faster than the *Endeavour* could have managed it at her stately top speed), but that it took close to thirty to make the return journey (unless you waited for the favourable winds that summer brought). Furthermore, a Polynesian navigator fixed his position on the face of the Earth by referring to landmarks when they were visible, and a combination of the patterns of wind, waves and the movement of the stars when they were not. His (so far as we know, it was always a he) reference point was always himself, sitting in his vaka, observing the

Following page
TUPAIA'S MAP OF THE PACIFIC, CIRCA 1770

Strictly speaking, this isn't a New Zealand map at all, as New Zealand doesn't feature and none of the people involved in its creation were New Zealanders. But it's a kind of Rosetta Stone for those seeking to reconcile Māori mapping techniques with the Cartesian system used by Europeans.

In all the history of all the encounters between cultures that make up the story of humankind, there are very few moments to rival the meeting of European and Polynesian minds that is commemorated in this document. It defies easy explanation: it is almost certain that Cook and his officers invited Tupaia, the forty-something-year-old arioi from Raʻiātea, to chart the numerous Pacific islands (up to 130, according to Cook) of which he claimed knowledge.

Doubtless Tupaia had paid great attention to the techniques he saw the *Endeavour*'s people using to navigate: compass, sextant, log line and nautical chart. But even people who grow up familiar with European cartological conventions—north at the top (since mediaeval times), east to the right, west left and south at the bottom, and depicted according to a mathematical transformation of the precisely measured distances from a prime meridian and from the equator—won't all at once grasp the use of a magnetic compass, let alone the esoteric business of celestial navigation. There is no reason to suppose (as some have) that Tupaia did, either. He will have perceived more or less how charts worked, but he was confronted with the task of placing islands that he located according to the movement of the sun, moon and stars; the patterns of wind and water and of marine life; and the distance travelled from his starting point, which varied from one vessel to the next. It has often baffled would-be interpreters of his map that, for example, his map depicts Rurutu northwest of Tahiti, whereas it ought to be southwest.

Being hazy on the details of the cardinal points of the magnetic compass, and on distance as an objectively measurable quantity, the chart is impressionistic, and depicts the relations of islands to one another, more as a modern, schematic subway map depicts stations on a line rather than in strict geodetic relation. What's more, Tupaia's map is drawn to what we might call a 'parochial' projection, where the familiar is drawn larger and in more detail than the distant and little-known.

The fact that New Zealand is altogether absent from this map suggests that the Society Islanders had long ago lost contact with this ancient colony. This squares with what is known about the pattern of migration, too: while many of the stories of the Polynesian settlement of Aotearoa mention return journeys to the Pacific homeland, these are placed in the distant past. And by the time Europeans contacted Māori, enough time had elapsed for the technology of building bluewater voyaging craft to have been completely forgotten.

21,593.c

Opatoerow
N

Oahourou
Oryvavai Olematerea
Orarathoa   Oateeu   Orurutu
                    Oahoo-ahoo
                                        Ooureu   Maatăah   Oo-
Toutepa   Oweha   Motuhea
                                Whennua ouda   Oanhu
toe miti no terara te rietea   Opopotea   Tupia tata ve pahei matte
            Orivavie   Mau- Tupi
                                            -rua
Tinuna   Orotuma   Bola-bola
                                        Opoopooa   Otahah
                                                Ulietea
                                                Tuboona no Tupea pahei tayo
Tereati W   Eavatea
Toottera   Huaheine
        Ohetepoto   Tetupatupa eahow
                                Moenatayo
        Ohetetoutou-atu   Imao
                                                Tapooa-mannu   Meduah no te t
        Ohetetoutou-mi
                        Teerrepooopomathehei Oheavie

        Ohetetoutoureva   Opooroo   Oheteroa

                                Teorooromatiwa- Oottow
                                -tea   Itonue

        Ohetetaiteare
                                        Otootooera
                                                    Mannua

                Teamoorohete Teatowhete
                                        Onowhea   Mou

S
Opatoa

Ohevapoto	Oheva roa		Tebooi	
	Ootto	Whatterreero	Terouuhah	
	Temanno			
ra.			Whaterretuah	
Teoheow		Tetineoheva		
Oryroa			Whaneanea	
Otaah				
		Oremaroa	Ohevatoutouai	

Maa te tata pahei rahie ete
re pahei no Brittane

E. Tatahieta
Ohetoottera

Whaow

Mytea
Tupia pahei tea   Ohevanue

Oirotah

Tometoaroaro

Ohete maruiru

Ouropoe

Tenewhammeatane

shifting patterns of the natural world, and his map was the store of wisdom distilled by generations of his predecessors and imparted to him in words. Navigation was less of a science than an art, based not upon precise measurement and depiction but on a kind of deep, instinctive, empathetic understanding of the world.

Consequently, when Tupaia was asked to draw a map of the places of which he spoke, there was little chance he would produce anything resembling a nautical chart on the standard Mercator projection (that is, the spherical world flattened onto a sheet of paper, as was done by Gerardus Mercator in 1569, in such a way that a line drawn between two points would be straight—and very handy for navigators). It would be like asking legendary cricketer Sir Richard Hadlee to explain swing bowling using Lego.

In a sense, it is inaccurate to talk of Tupaia's map as though there were only one of them. Neither of the versions that remain to us is actually his map at all: both are copies, and there is a case to be made that there was more than one draft. Whichever of the two versions of the map you view, the first thing that strikes you is how peculiar it is, viewed as a map. The Society Islands are relatively accurately drawn, and this is supposed to be because the group was drawn by one of Cook's navigators—perhaps even by Cook himself—as a starting point. The piece of paper was then presumably passed to Tupaia along with the instruction to fill in the blanks. Even such places as can be positively identified are not drawn to scale, and are out of position (in some cases, in completely the wrong quadrants). Various ingenious explanations for these apparent discrepancies have been attempted down the years, with all kinds of quasi-numerological jiggery-pokery applied to try to resolve the system according to which Tupaia was working. The latest of these, by two German scholars, claims to have identified an entirely novel cartographic system, pioneered for the occasion by Tupaia himself, in order to overcome the incompatibility of the Polynesian and European operating systems. It seems plausible, but does rely upon a towering card-house of assumptions, the failure of any one of which would bring it all crashing to the ground. According to the theory, the key to the map is the term *e avatea* in the centre, close to the intersection of the two meridians. This, the learned Germans assert, represents the position of the sun at noon, a reference point relative to which bearings from the observer's position and to their intended destination can be reckoned.

It is early days for this theory, which has only recently been published. If, after critical scrutiny, it is pronounced to be correct, the sad historical fact of the matter is that its genius was quite lost on the worthies of the *Endeavour*, who hardly refer to the map at all in their journals. It's likely Cook and his officers dismissed it as a mere curiosity, which would place them at the head of a long tradition of doing just that. Georg Forster, the son of Johann, the dour malcontent who sailed as Cook's naturalist on his second voyage to the Pacific, had a copy of the map, in which he rapidly lost confidence, pronouncing Tupaia to have been nothing more than a blowhard:

> if his drawing had been exact, our ships must have sailed over a number of these islands which he [Tupaia] had set down. It is therefore very probable that the vanity of appearing more intelligent than he really was, had prompted him to produce this

fancied chart of the South Sea, and perhaps to invent many of the names of islands in it.

Many more recent historians have agreed with Forster, and have argued that what appear to be inaccuracies at best and apparent guesswork at worst indicate the Polynesians muddled their way across the Pacific through good luck and as the beneficiaries of the law of averages. In the same vein, the fact that the map did not depict New Zealand at all was taken by an influential New Zealand historian to prove his theory that the settlement of Aotearoa was by accident rather than by purposeful migration. It's only in recent years that due allowance has been made for the profound cultural barriers that Tupaia would have needed to surmount in order to communicate his knowledge to his audience. The seamen aboard the *Endeavour* who kept secret diaries marvelled at Tupaia's ability to point in the direction of Tahiti after days, weeks, even months of voyaging. What's more, it's plain that Cook believed in Tupaia: there is no way he would have entrusted his vessel to the pilotage of someone whom he suspected of not knowing what they were doing. But whether during the drafting of the map, before or shortly after it, Cook's focus had shifted from the islands of the central Pacific to the principal purpose of his mission, which was to explore south beyond the ken even of the Tahitian arioi. We will never know what he made of it.

So what do *we* make of it? Tupaia's map is best considered a map of the Pacific on what might be called a parochial projection, which places the subject (and that which is best-known and dearest to the subject) at the centre, with other, less well-known places arranged in a rough spiral outwards. It seems unlikely Tupaia had much regard for the cardinal directions on a Western compass when he was drafting his map (which accounts for the fact that Rurutu (Orurutu, as transcribed) lies to the northwest of Ra'iātea on his map, when it is in fact to the southwest). It's more likely that islands were juxtaposed according to where they occurred along the path of one's journey. Polynesian voyages were likely to have been island-hopping exercises. Each stop on the way was an important source of fresh water and food, to say nothing of being a comforting waypoint. Perhaps Tupaia's map is better interpreted as a schematic diagram of routes than as a nautical chart—that is, it has more in common with the famous map of the London Underground than it does with the average Admiralty nautical chart.

———

When East Polynesians arrived and settled in Aotearoa, they brought with them the same mapping techniques and applied them to the slightly different business of finding their way over and around Aotearoa, the land masses of which were far larger than their Pacific homelands. Many of the local myths, legends and waiata thus contain cartographic information. A fine example is the legend that describes te ara pounamu, the greenstone trail. According to this, there lived in the waters off the West Coast of the South Island a taniwha named Poutini. Being an adventurous sort of water spirit, Poutini was accustomed to roaming far and wide from his coastal home. One day, he happened to be near the island of Tūhua in the Bay of Plenty (now also known as Mayor Island) when he saw a beautiful young woman named Waitaiki swimming. Instantly infatuated with her, he abducted her and set off for home. Her husband, Tamaahua, realising she had been kidnapped, consulted a magic wherawhera (a ceremonial dart) that pointed in the direction in which she had been taken. He set off in pursuit.

At each point on the main islands of Aotearoa where Poutini stopped to rest, he built a fire to warm his captive. Each fireplace contained tell-tale deposits of precious and useful stones, and also served as a trail marker not only for Tamaahua, but also for those who came after him. Poutini sensed he was being chased. He carried Waitaiki as far south as remote Piopiotahi (Milford Sound), where he hoped he would be safe. But, cold and bereft, Waitaiki implored him to return to more hospitable climes. Poutini bore her to the Arahura River and climbed the stony bed of the river high into the mountains. Tamaahua, meanwhile, had found the tears of his wife at Piopiotahi (in the form of tangiwai, bowenite, which is a lovely and useful form of green serpentine). This evidence of his wife's distress enraged him and spurred him on. His wherawhera pointed the way, and he turned towards the Arahura River, where he knew he would bring the taniwha to bay.

As Tamaahua closed in on him, Poutini considered his options. He could flee no further, and he doubted that his strength and magical resources would equal those of Tamaahua, who was giving very few indications that he was looking to forget and forgive. So, in a final, spiteful act, Poutini decided to deprive Tamaahua of his wife. He laid Waitaiki in the riverbed and changed her to his own essence, slipping away downstream past Tamaahua to his home in the sea. When Tamaahua found Waitaiki the following morning, she was cold, hard and lifeless. He tangied for his lost wife, and returned, grieving, to the north.

Poutini still swims to and fro along the coast (which is named Te Tai o Poutini, the tides of Poutini, in his honour), guarding his captive. Parts of Waitaiki—her children—occasionally break off and roll down the river. And the valley in which Waitaiki, the motherlode of the entire pounamu resource, lies still echoes with the lament of Tamaahua.

This, a version of the surviving tale of Poutini, is likely a highly abridged version of the more detailed story, which would have provided useful descriptors of routes and landmarks, but it gives the gist. The fact that the taniwha still guards the resource was a notice to mariners: taniwha were often signifiers of natural hazards, in this case the dangerous conjunction of the Tasman Sea and the West Coast, with its dearth of safe havens.

———

A different taniwha, Taniwha Horeta, who was a young man at the time of Cook's first visit, recalled in much later life that the local (Whitianga) chiefs drew a map in charcoal on the *Endeavour*'s deck, some time between the fourth and fifteenth of November 1769. The reason we can't be clear as to the date and time is that none of the *Endeavour*'s luminaries recorded this event in their journals. Phil Barton, sometime curator of the Alexander Turnbull Library's cartographic collection and someone who made a particular study of Māori mapping, has claimed that Māori were probably accustomed to making physical maps in impermanent media, such as with charcoal on stone, or even simply using a stick to draw lines in the sand. This claim is controversial, as no examples of pre-European maps have survived. In order to defend his hypothesis, Barton collected references in early literature to Māori showing their aptitude in drawing maps for Europeans. In 1793, a young man named Tuki sketched a map of Aotearoa for the commandant of the penal colony on Norfolk Island (see page 28). In 1815, a chief referred to as 'Korra-Korra' drew a map for missionaries. In 1840, a man probably named Pomare drew a map of the Chathams for the New Zealand Company's naturalist, Ernst Dieffenbach. A year later, an unknown Ngāi Tahu obliged the new Protector of Aborigines and Commissioner of Native Reserves, Edmund Halswell, with a sketch of the South Island (see page 34). In 1843, Hone Tuhawaiki (picturesquely known as 'Bloody Jack', owing to his affection for the expletive) collaborated with Colonel E. L. Godfrey in a series of maps of the south coast of the South Island. In 1844, a chief named Huruhuru drew a map of the lakes of Central Otago for William Shortland, and maps of the same district were drawn by Rakiraki for J. W. Barnicoat in 1844. A sketch of the course and catchment of the Waitaki River was made by Reko (aka Te Wharekorari) in 1848 for Walter Mantell (see page 32), and the same man prepared a sketch of the Clutha and central lakes for John Turnbull Thomson in 1856. In 1859, Ferdinand von Hochstetter reported that a Māori man (whose name he failed to record) made a rough map of Lake Wakatipu and its environs using the blade of a knife. Julius von Haast mentioned a map of the same district that was in his possession (but has not survived), which may well have been a copy of Hochstetter's.

For all his diligence, however, Barton has not proved his case. Each of these maps was likely to have been an effort to translate knowledge learned and retained orally for an audience accustomed to physical, visual representation, much like Tupaia's map for Cook and company. Like Tupaia, the Māori involved in the transaction in each case would have had the occasion to observe Europeans interacting with maps, and while (like Tupaia) they didn't immediately grasp the niceties of spherical geometry and plane figure projections, they grasped enough of what was depicted and how to present their knowledge on paper.

The earliest of the surviving maps drawn by Māori for Europeans is that roughed out in chalk on the floor of a room on Norfolk Island in 1793 by Tuki Tahua for Governor Philip King, on whose orders Tuki and another man, Ngahuruhuru, were abducted (see page 28). King was keen to learn how flax was dressed, and so when HMS *Daedalus* visited the Cavalli Islands (off the east coast of Northland), Tuki and Ngahuruhuru were lured aboard and distracted until the vessel was far enough offshore to prevent their escape. The hapless pair were taken first to Port Jackson and then to Norfolk, where King did all he could to induce them to share their secrets. It was some time before they were mollified to the point where they deigned to cooperate, but their collective knowledge of the art of flax dressing was soon found wanting. Tuki was a tohunga, and Ngahuruhuru a toa, or warrior: dressing harakeke was women's work.

However, on an inspiration, King asked Tuki to describe Aotearoa for him, and Tuki was happy to oblige. His map is a remarkable artefact, standing alongside Tupaia's map as an authentic crystallisation of a world view (albeit mangled by the same kind of losses in cultural translation) that would never be accessible in such pure form again. To the eye accustomed to viewing a conventional map of New Zealand, it is grossly distorted to the point of being unrecognisable. But it is fully intelligible if viewed as a parochial projection: the areas drawn

Continued on p. 36

TUKI'S MAP OF AOTEAROA, 1793

In 1793, two chiefs from the Doubtless Bay region accepted an invitation to inspect the *Daedalus*, visiting from Australia. While Tuki Tahua and Ngahuruhuru were being entertained below, the order was given to make sail. By the time they had woken up to the trick, they were many miles offshore.

After touching at Port Jackson (Sydney), the pair were taken to Norfolk Island, where the governor of the British penal colony, Philip King, upon whose orders they had been abducted, was anxious to learn how to dress flax. Neither Tuki nor Ngahuruhuru was inclined to help him on this point. But rather than waste the opportunity to extract some useful knowledge from them, King persuaded them to describe their homeland to him. While neither would have had any experience with European maps, they did consent to trace something approximating a map of Aotearoa in chalk on the floor of a room. This was copied onto paper and (in 1798) published.

Like Tupaia's map, Tuki's sketch is a parochial view of New Zealand, with Northland drawn both larger and in more detail than the rest, which recedes to the margins. Traces of the questions King asked can be made out: trees (representing kauri) are drawn at Hokianga (which King heard as Cho-ka-hang-a). The numbers of inhabitants (and fighting men) are noted here and there, as are the relations—whether 'in league' with Tuki's people or in enmity—between iwi. The South Island is amorphous in outline and lacking in detail, but four significant features are drawn: the Marlborough Sounds, a harbour or river system on the West Coast, a 'Lake, where Stone for Hatchets are got' and a 'Tree, of which Tooge [sic] tells wonderful stories from the authority of the Tsou-duckey People'. This last detail suggests that Tuki's knowledge of Te Wai Pounamu came second-hand from the Hauraki people, who seem to have had a monopoly on the pounamu resource for some period of history, as their own stories record. Marked on the map is 'The Road which goes the length of E-a-hei-no-maue' (Te Ika-a-Māui, the North Island), finishing at 'Terry-inga' (Te Rēinga), the leaping-off place from which the souls of the dead began their long journey back to Hawaiki.

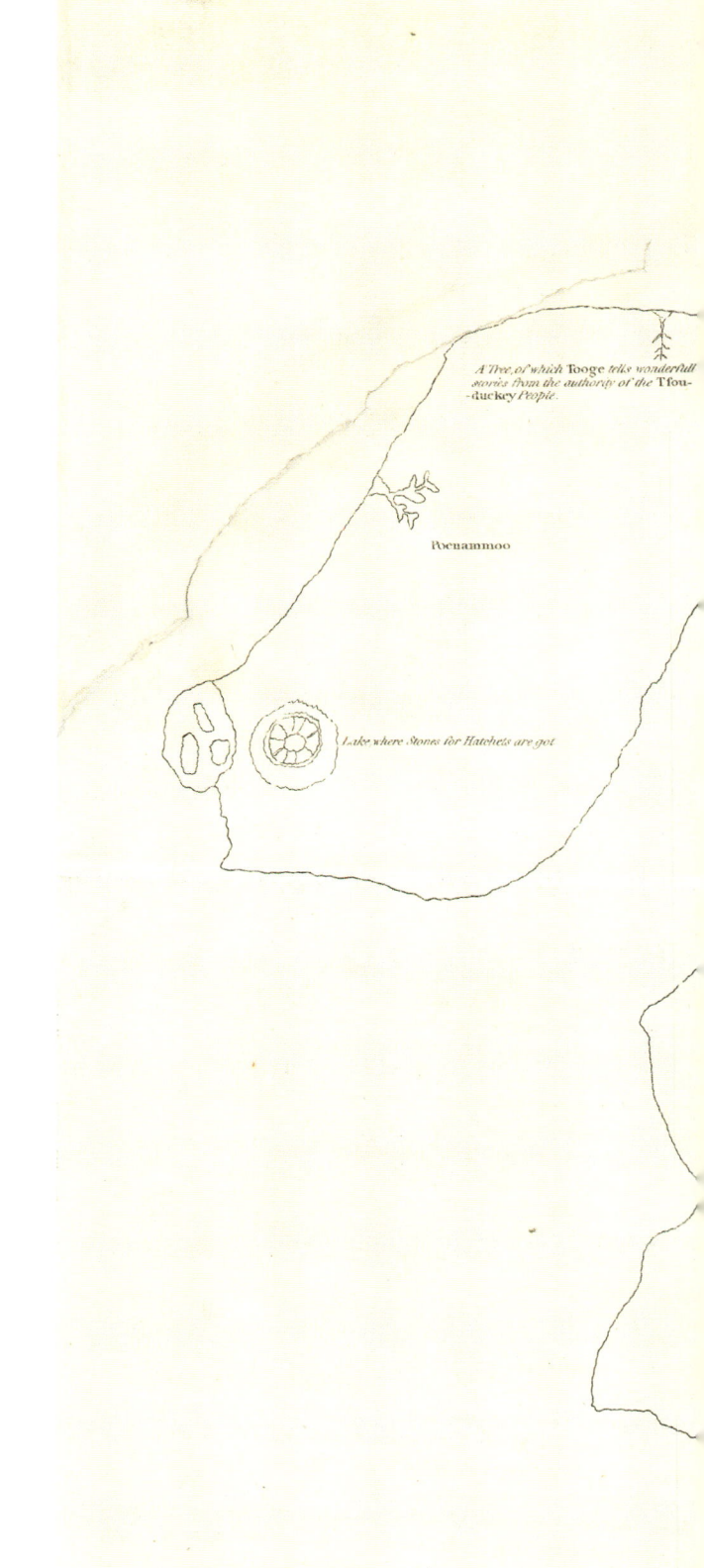

Manoui Taoai
no Water on it

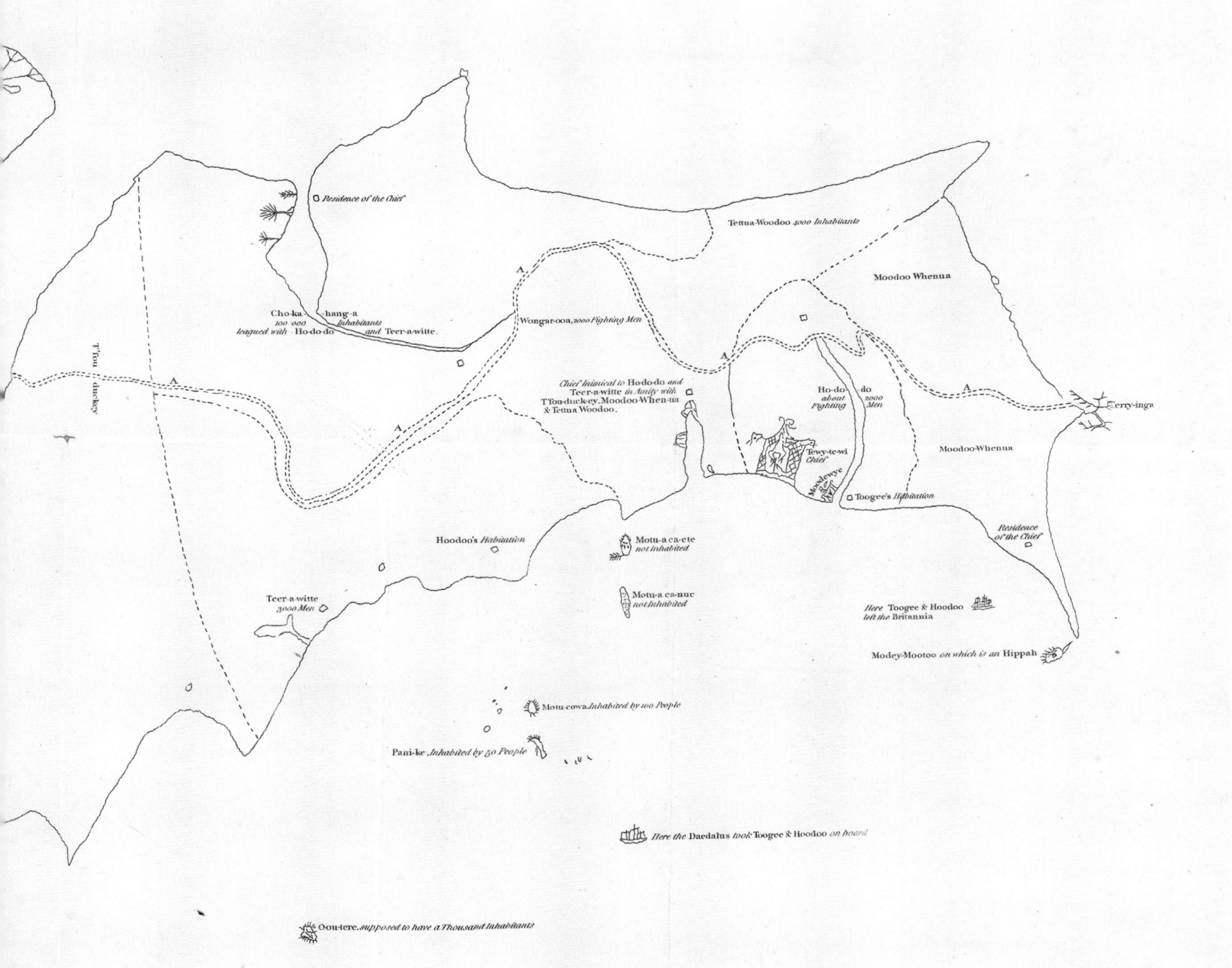

Residence of the Chief

Tettua-Woodoo *4000 Inhabitants*

Moodoo Whenua

Cho-ka-hang-a
*100 000 Inhabitants
leagued with Ho-do-do and Teer-a-witte.*

Wongar-ooa, *2000 Fighting Men*

T'fou duckey

Chief Inimical to Ho-do-do and Teer-a-witte in Amity with T'fou-duck-ey, Moodoo-When-ua & Tettua Woodoo.

Ho-do-do *about 2000 Men fighting*

Tewy-te-wi *Chief*

Moodoo-Whenua

Ferry-inga

Moodewye

Toogee's *Habitation*

Residence of the Chief

Hoodoo's *Habitation*

Motu-a ca-ete *not Inhabited*

Motu-a ca-nuc *not Inhabited*

Here Toogee & Hoodoo left the Britannia

Teer-a-witte *3000 Men*

Modey-Mootoo *on which is an Hippah*

Motu-cowa *Inhabited by 100 People*

Pani-ke *Inhabited by 50 People*

Here the Daedalus took Toogee & Hoodoo on board

Oou-tere, *supposed to have a Thousand Inhabitants*

A.A.A. *The Road which goes the length of the Ea-hei-no-maue — see the Vocabulary.*

Published May 25th 1798, by Cadell & Davies, Strand.

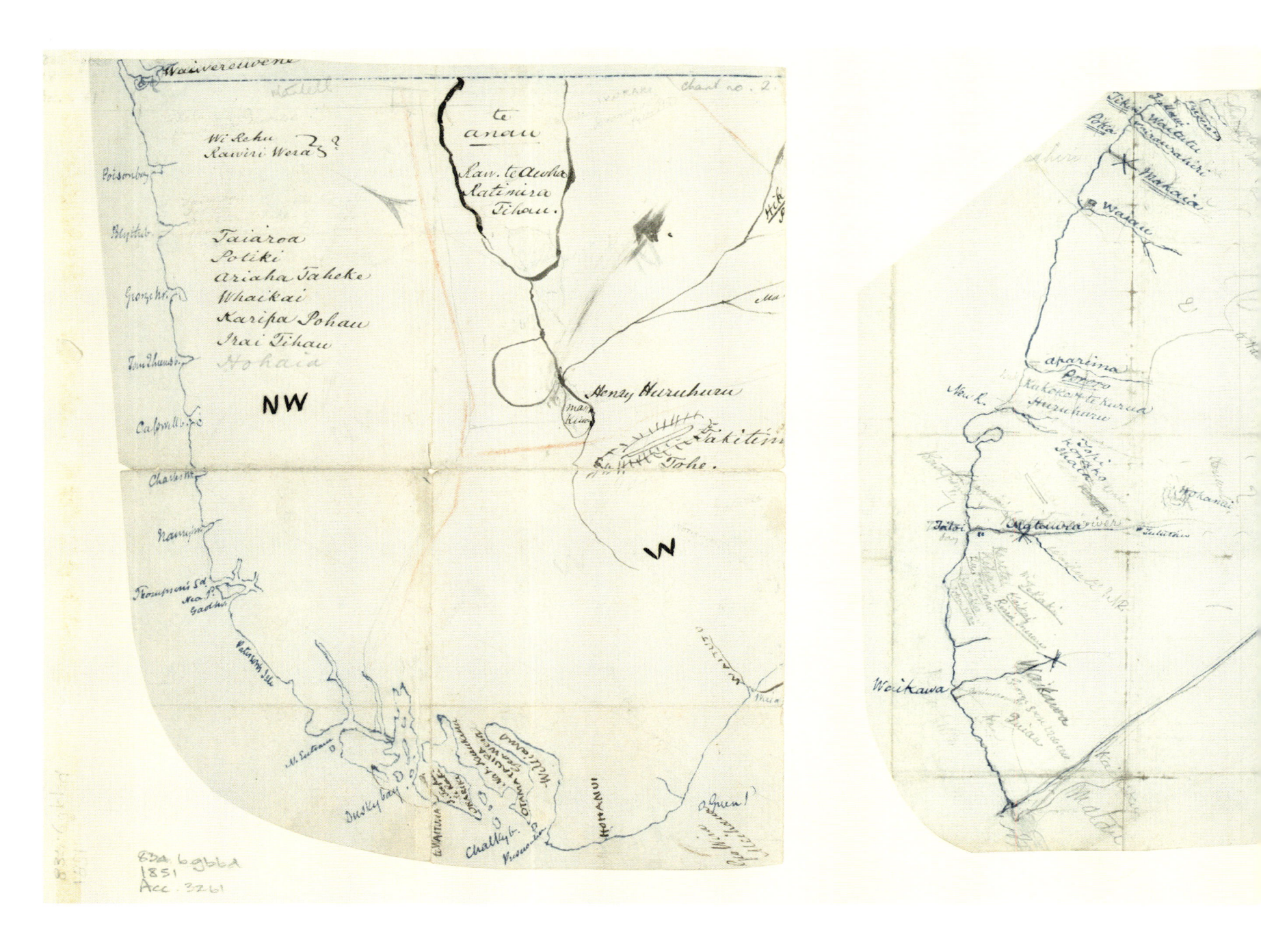

MANTELL'S KŌRERO MAPS OF SOUTHLAND, 1851

As he went about his business enquiring into who amongst the Māori of Murihuku (the far south of the South Island) laid claim to what territory, Walter Mantell compiled these 'kōrero charts': sketch maps of the countryside upon which he pencilled the names of claimants and which he used to get a picture in his own mind of who belonged where. The map on the left depicts the coastline from the Waitutu River, which drains Lake Poteriteri in Fiordland, around to Milford Sound. Interestingly, while a succession of European explorers had regarded this area as uninhabited, Mantell was given quite a list of names of those who 'owned' it (that is, travelled it and exploited it). The middle sheet covers the coast from Waitutu around to Waikawa in the Catlins: once again, there are the pencilled names of those with mana whenua. The right-hand sheet carries the coast around to just south of the mouth of the Clutha. The lists of names grow longer as the coast becomes more hospitable. Mantell used the information he gathered to inform the Crown who it was that they needed to treat with to alienate the land. But by now, he was already disheartened at the extent to which the transactions the Crown concluded fell short of the promises made to the vendors—namely, the tangata whenua.

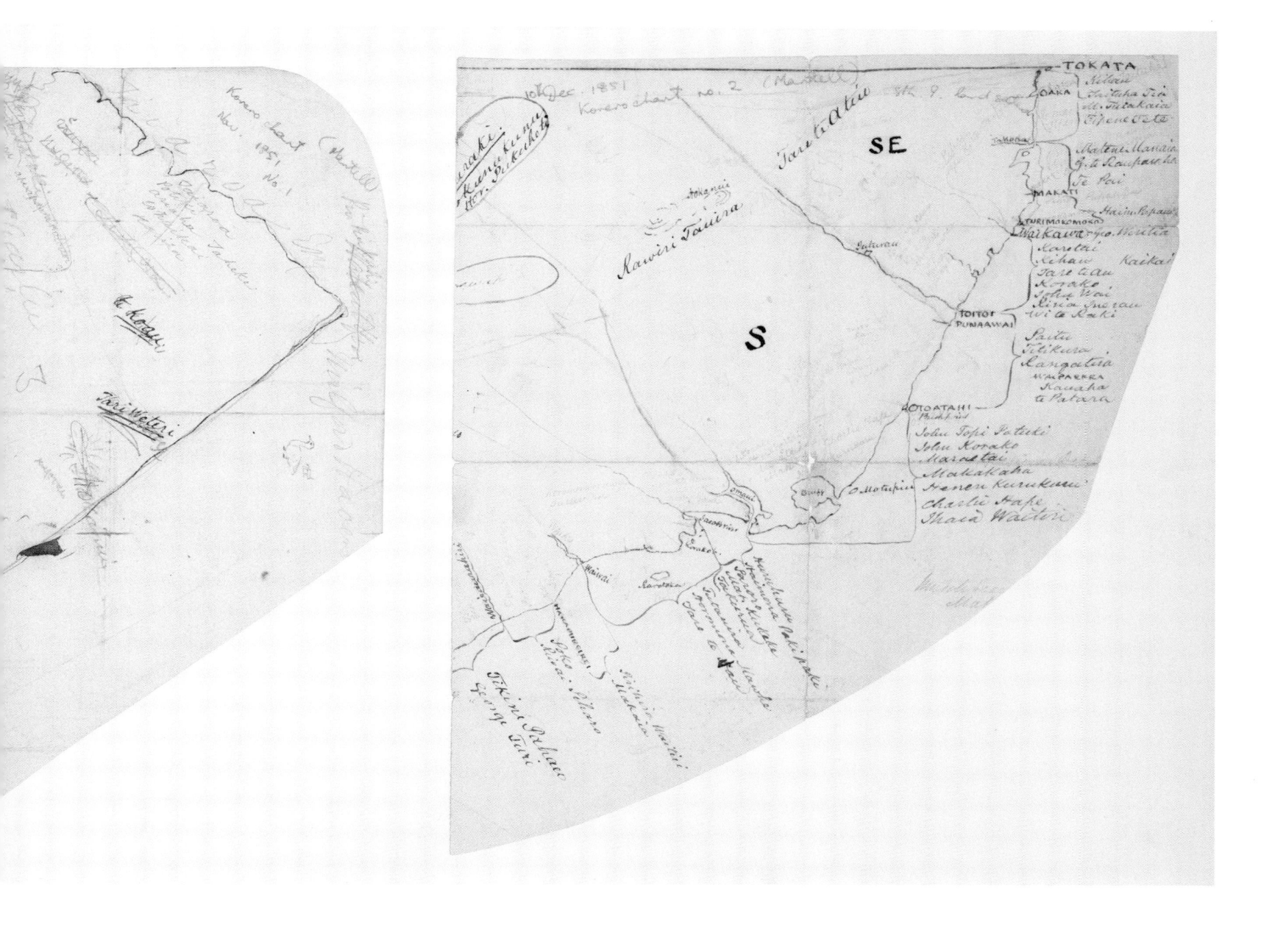

TE WHAREKORARI'S MAP OF
THE WAITAKI RIVER, 1848

A written document representing Māori knowledge of the land would look far more like this map of the Waitaki River, drawn in Walter Mantell's sketchbook either by, or at the direction of, Te Wharekorari (whom Mantell and his travelling companion, Alfred Wills, knew as Reko). First drawn in pencil, it was later inked over, presumably by Mantell. The sketch depicts a simplified Waitaki River, and names each of the major tributaries feeding from the true right. There are numbers between the names, representing days' travel, the way in which Māori measured distance. This kind of knowledge would have been transmitted from one person to another much as it was to Mantell, in a recitation of the place names, the 'singing of the trail'. Arriving at Otiaki (Oteake, as Mantell has it) at the end of four days' march, you would know that you had thirteen days' journey ahead of you to the headwaters. Of course, much of the landscape in the vicinity of Ōtemātātā has changed beyond recognition with the drowning of the river valleys by the Benmore and Aviemore hydro dams, both commissioned in the 1960s.

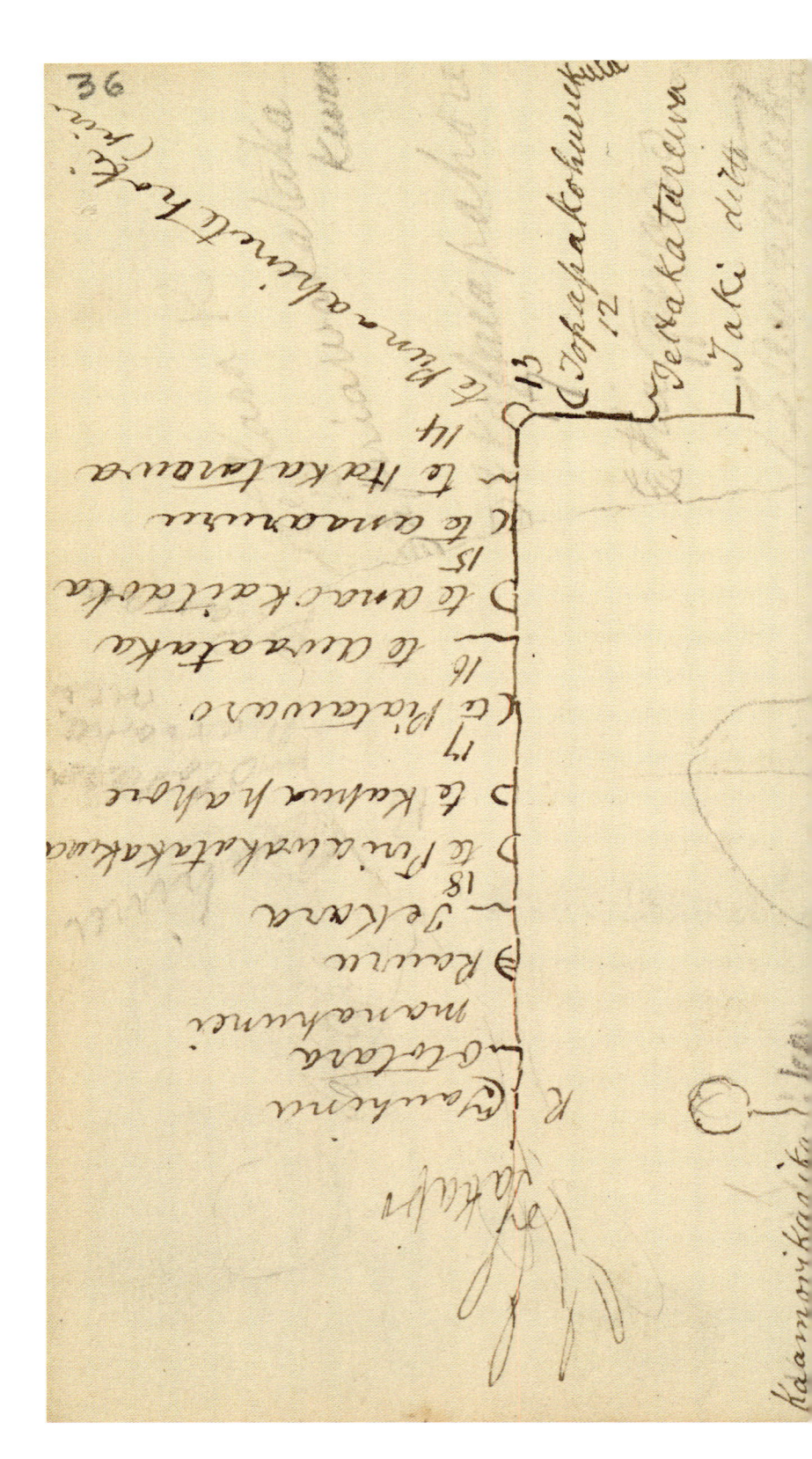

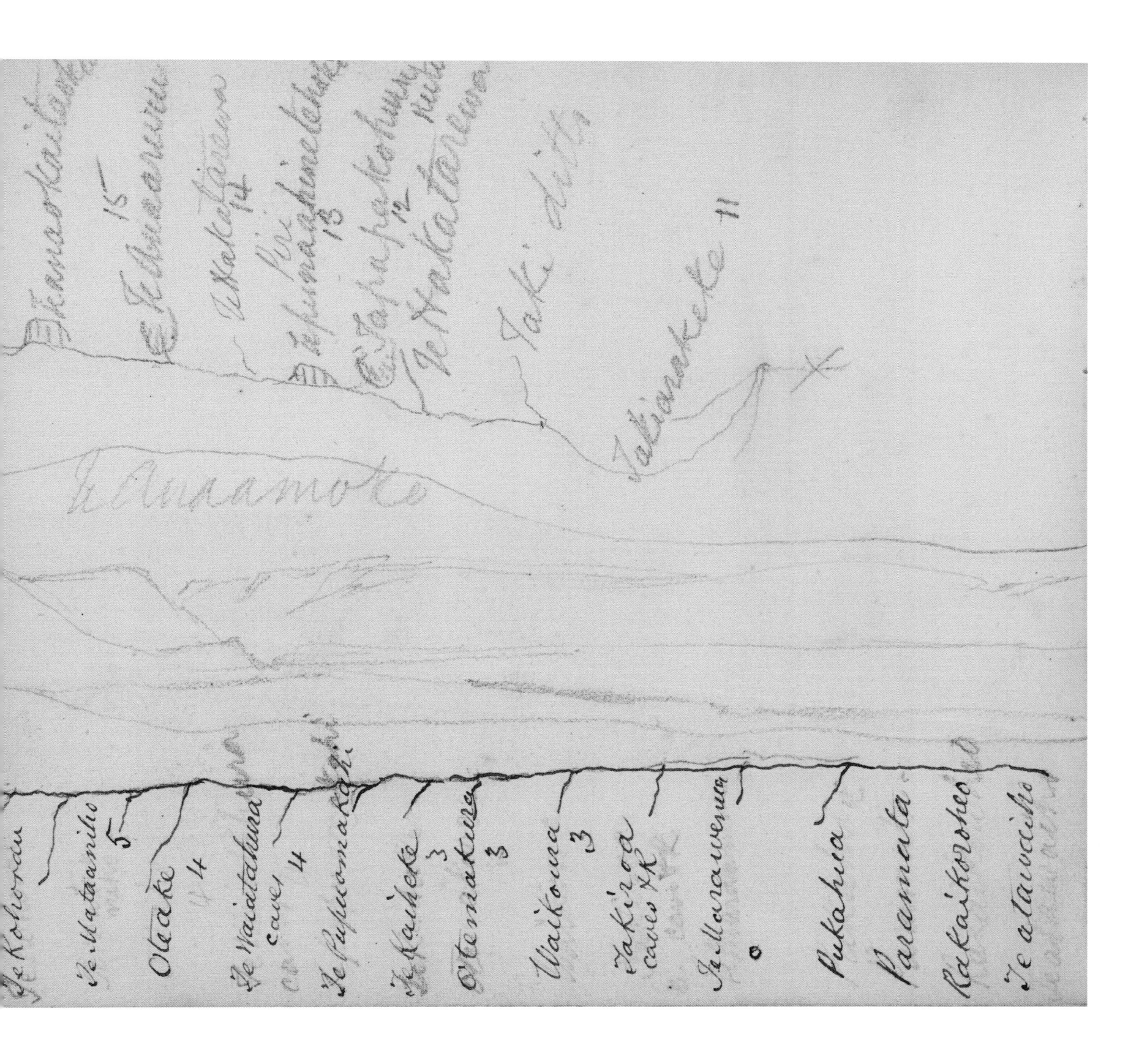

Top labels (left to right):
- Ekinsokaitau...
- Ehuareru 15
- EWakatauwa
- Piu
- Epungahinetaha 13
- Etahahakohuru
- Te Wakataurua
- Taki ditts
- Takinakeke 11

Middle:
Te Anamote

Bottom labels (left to right):
- Te Kohioau
- Te Mataaniho 5
- Otaake 1/4
- Te Waiatahuna caves 4
- Te Pupuanaahi
- Te Kaiheke 3
- Otaiakura 3
- Waikoua 3
- Takiroa caves XX
- Te Manawuna
- Pukahua
- Paranata
- Kakaikoroko
- Te atawaiho

SKETCH OF THE MIDDLE ISLAND (CREATOR UNKNOWN), CIRCA 1841

When young British lawyer Edmund Storr Halswell arrived, bright-eyed and bushy-tailed, in New Zealand in early 1841, it was to take up the position of Protector of Aborigines and Commissioner of Native Reserves, charged with 'protecting the natives' rights from the dangers of colonialism'. He duly travelled the country, talking with the tangata whenua and learning about their lives and customs. Somewhere in the vicinity of Banks Peninsula, he plainly sat down with one or more Ngāi Tahu, who either drew this map for him or advised him as he drew it himself.

At first glance, it doesn't look like the South Island as known to us, or to anyone who had seen James Cook's charts. But those who informed it might have seen maps only once or twice in their lives (if at all), and had rarely if ever considered what Te Wai Pounamu would look like from the eye of a bird at extreme altitude. Some may never have visited some of the places they depicted, and were perhaps relying on second-hand knowledge. All things considered, this is a creditable effort.

We know the informant or informants were of Ngāi Tahu because the metropolis of that iwi—Banks Peninsula—is drawn in far more detail and with far greater accuracy than any other part of the coastline. Similarly, the east and south coasts are more detailed than the northern and, especially, the west, suggesting diminishing familiarity. There are some mistakes: a place named Ohakea on Stewart Island is described as 'the good harbour of Captain Cook', but if James Cook is intended by this, it is wrong, as he never approached, let alone anchored, here. Some places are well out of position: Rangitoto ki te Tonga (D'Urville Island) is depicted on the West Coast, rather than to the north of the Marlborough Sounds. But perhaps the most striking aspect of the map is what it reveals about the interrogator (Halswell himself). The quality of harbours is noted, many locations have commentary such as 'plenty of seals' or 'good timber', and substantial tracts of flat land are marked. A sense of humour on the part of Halswell's informants is also captured: while the answer to the question 'what is there at Dusky Bay?' was 'plenty of seals', the answer to 'what is there at Aretoka Point (apparently the name for Cape Providence, the western headland of Chalky Inlet)?' was 'plenty of rocks'. A whaling settlement near the mouth of the Molyneux (Clutha River) is noted, as is the danger to vessels anchored there in southeast winds. One schooner, the map reports, has been lost there (probably the *Sydney Packet*, driven ashore after dragging her anchors in a sou'easterly gale in 1837).

Map of 934ap
Date [1841-2?]
Compiler
Drawer Acc. 527

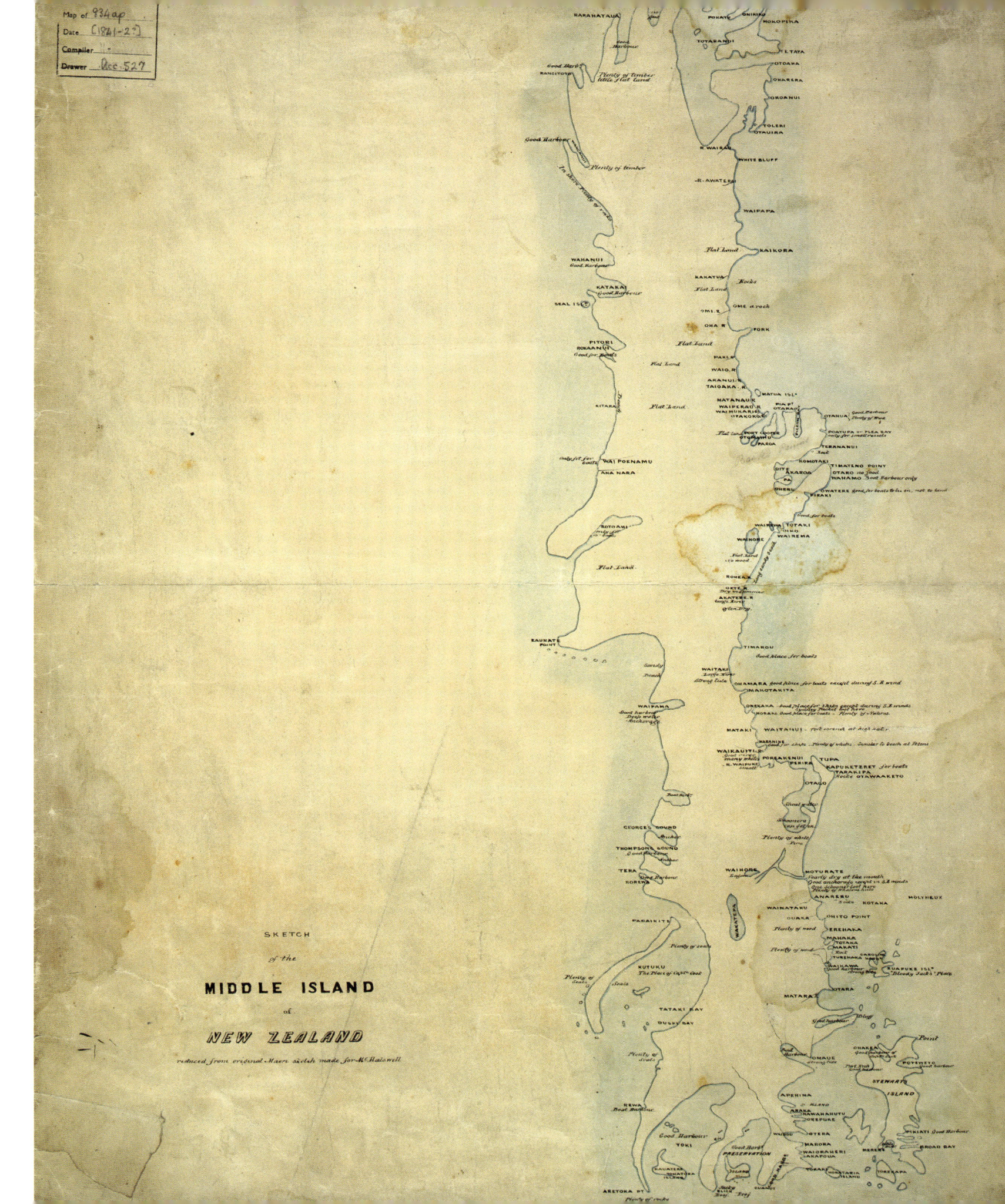

SKETCH

of the

MIDDLE ISLAND

of

NEW ZEALAND

reduced from original Maori sketch made for Mr Halswell

Place names (east coast, north to south)

KARAHATAUA
POHATU
ONIRING
MOKOPIKA
TOTARANUI
TE TATA
OTOAHA
OHARERA
ORONUI
TOLERI
OTAUIRA
WHITE BLUFF
R. WAIRAU
R. AWATERE
WAIPAPA
KAIKORA
Flat Land
KAHATUA
Rocks
OMI. R.
OME a rock
ONA R.
FORK
PAKE
WAIG. R.
ARANUI. R.
TAIGAKA. R.
MATUA ISLD
HATANAU R.
WAIPERAU R.
PIA PT
OTAKOU
WAIMUKARIRI
OTAKOKO
OTANUA
PORT COOPER
POATUPA or PLEA BAY only for small vessels
PAROA
TERANANUI
KOMOTARI
TIMATENO POINT
AKAROA
OTARO no food
WAHAMO Boat Harbour only
OHERU
WAIRAKI
MAWATERE good for boats to lie in, not to land
Good for boats
WAIRAU
TOTAKI
WAIHORE
TIHO
WAIREMA
Flat land no wood
ROREAE
OREY R Dry in summer
ALATERE R large Bay
Glen Bay
TIMAROU
Good place for boats
WAITAKI large River
ONAMARA Good place for boats except during S.E. wind
MAKOTAKITA
OREKAKA Good place for ships except during S.E. winds
MORARI Good place for boats
NARAIRE
WAITAIHUI rock covered at high water
MATAKI Plenty of whales similar to beach at Patani
WAIKAUTI R.
PORAKANUI many mills
KAPURETEREKI for boats
N. WAIPURE
PERIRA
TUPA
TARAKIPA
OTAGO
Nooks
OTAWAAKETO
Shooners can sit fast
Plenty of whales
WAIHORE
MOTURATE Nearly dry at the mouth. Good anchorage except in S.E. winds. Give shelter for any. Plenty of Natives.
ANARERU
KOTAKA
WAINATANU
OUAKA
OHITO POINT
MOLYNEUX
Plenty of wood
EREHAKA
MANARA
TOTARA
MARATI
Rock
TUREIMA
KAROWA
Good Harbour
RUAPUKE ISL Nooks
"Bloody Jack's" Place
MATARA
KOTARA
Bluff
CHARKA
Good Harbour
POTEWETO
Point
STEWARTS ISLAND
TOMAUE
APERIMA
ARAKA
KAWAHARUTU
OREPUKE
HUGOI
OTERA
BROAD BAY
MAKORA
MERENE
WAIORAHERI
SARAPUA
PRESERVATION
PINIATI Good Harbour
ORAKI
HONATARIA
CHANUI
ARETORA PT

Place names (west coast, north to south)

Good Harbour
Sandy Harbour
RANGITOTO
Plenty of timber
little flat land
Good Harbour
Plenty of timber
Te River Plenty of fish
WAHANUI Good Harbour
KATAKAI Good harbour
SEAL ISLD
PITORI
ROKAANUI Good for boats
KITARA
Flat Land
Flat Land
Flat Land
WAI POENAMU
Unfit for boats
ANA NARA
ROTOAHI
Flat Land
RAUNATE POINT
D SOUND
Sandy beach
WAIPARA Good Harbour
Deep water anchorage
GEORGES SOUND
THOMPSONS SOUND Good Harbour
TERA Good Harbour
KORENU
PARAIKITE
Plenty of seals
KUTUKU The Place of light wood
Seals
Plenty of seals
TATAKI BAY
DUSKY BAY
Plenty of Seals
SEWA Boat harbour
Good Harbours
TOKI
Kauater Islands

largest and in the most detail are those areas most familiar to Tuki. Both detail and accuracy fall away as the reach of the draughtsman's depiction exceeds the grasp of his knowledge. Some key elements from beyond the area of his expertise are there: te ara o te wairua tapu—the spirit road leading from the southern extremity of the North Island to te rerenga o te wairua tapu, the leaping-off place of the souls of the newly dead who are beginning their journey to their homeland—is shown, terminating in the pōhutukawa tree that grows from the headland of Cape Rēinga. Tuki's map acknowledges that his knowledge of the South Island is on the authority of 'the Tsou-dacky [Hauraki] people': he himself had never visited. But the Marlborough Sounds are shown, as are a West Coast harbour (possibly Milford Sound, possibly Little Whanganui) and 'the lake where stones for hatchets are got'.

Similarly, the map of the South Island drawn for Halswell is, for all its weirdness to the modern eye, a remarkably detailed and accurate attempt at a bird's-eye depiction of a territory that has only ever been contemplated from on foot or from the water.

———

For practical purposes, Māori used a version of the kind of map known as an itinerarium, which, as the name suggests, was the kind of information the Romans relied on to get from place to place. This was essentially a list of waypoints culminating in your destination, made possible by the orderly system of Roman roads. Māori, too, made lists of waypoints along traditional routes: practically every feature in the landscape was named, sometimes for a striking visible characteristic, sometimes after some exploit of an ancestor there. These place names served as 'survey pegs of memory', as Ngāi Tahu elder Tipene O'Regan put it. And the lists were cast in songs, chants, karakia and stories, so that in order to give directions, one 'sang the trail'. Learning the song (or chant, etc.) committed the route and its survey pegs to memory. These were learned by rote in whare kura, one of the three kinds of schools in which knowledge was passed from one generation to the next. In his 1948 book *Maori Place Names in Buller County*, Gilbert Mitchell recalled:

> Tama Mokau te Rangihaeata informed me that when he was a mere lad living on D'Urville Island (Rangitoto) he had heard elders describing their journeys when visiting the Maori residents at Mawhera [Greymouth], Kumara, Arahura and Hokitika. Feature name after feature name would be mentioned during the recital and so vividly were they described that Mokau himself was able to identify many localities and recall their names when he made his first visit to the land of the greenstone when as a young man.

Likewise, according to Mitchell, explorer and artist Charles Heaphy was astonished at how accurately his Māori guide Kehu described the route they were to take with Thomas Brunner down the West Coast of the South Island:

> [Kehu's] description of the country the party would be required to traverse as recited to the two explorers before they set out on their journey, amazed them as they progressed southward and recognised mountains, hills,

rivers, streams, headlands and other natural features from E Kehu's prior description.

Another good example of an oral map, conveniently graphically depicted, is the sketch of the course of the Waitaki River prepared by Reko for the explorer and surveyor Walter Mantell. Whether the drawing itself is accurate is quite unimportant, as it is the blizzard of place names along it that is the real map. Every hapū in Aotearoa will have a collection of stories that relate to the deeds of their tīpuna (ancestors) in the landscape, and which will have served as the description of a route to some place or another. This is how it was done. It was an ancient Polynesian (and, more broadly, human) technique: in a chart of the coast of Tahiti that Tupaia helped to prepare, every nook and cove, every cave and headland is named. There will have been stories and songs that wove these together: a voyage around the coast will have been accomplished much as many car journeys are with GPS these days—not with a chart but with a soundtrack.

BANKS PENINSULA MĀORI NAMES (UNKNOWN CREATOR), 1894

While this is not strictly speaking a Māori map, it is worthy of inclusion as a document that shows the transition that Aotearoa New Zealand was undergoing at the turn of the twentieth century, and as a foreshadow for the maps in chapter eight. The map-maker is unknown, but when he drew it in 1894 he was clearly engaged in the business of enquiring into the justice (or otherwise) of Māori claims to land that had been alienated since settlement. The map depicts a Māori view of the land—the inked outline of the peninsula is furred with names, all of which would have been mentally ticked off by the paddlers of waka as they proceeded around the coast. Old—some ancient—pā sites are named, as are burial grounds: one is noted as the resting place of Tangatahara, a Ngāi Tahu rangatira who distinguished himself in battle when a raiding party of the North Island iwi Ngāti Toa attacked their pā. Also noted is 'the place where [Te] Ake stuck his walking stick when he took possession': Otokotoko, in present-day Robinson's Bay. The land that the investigator is principally interested in is marked in yellow—little enough, given Ngāi Tahu once occupied all of it. As you gaze into this map, you sense that te ao Māori is being steadily submerged: some Māori place names are accompanied by European (some English, some French) in parentheses: Tuhiraki is parenthetically known as Mount Bossu. But other place names are given in English, with their names in te reo relegated to the brackets, and it is significant that the information upon which the cartographer relied was supplied by Europeans, principally Canon James Stack. It was becoming harder to hear the names in the land which, under the feet of the surveyors and the settlers, was falling silent.

An inset in the map shows the area around Birdlings Flat; another depicts the farm of William Deans, patriarch of that Christchurch (and rugby union) dynasty, shown as Deans himself drew it in 1845.

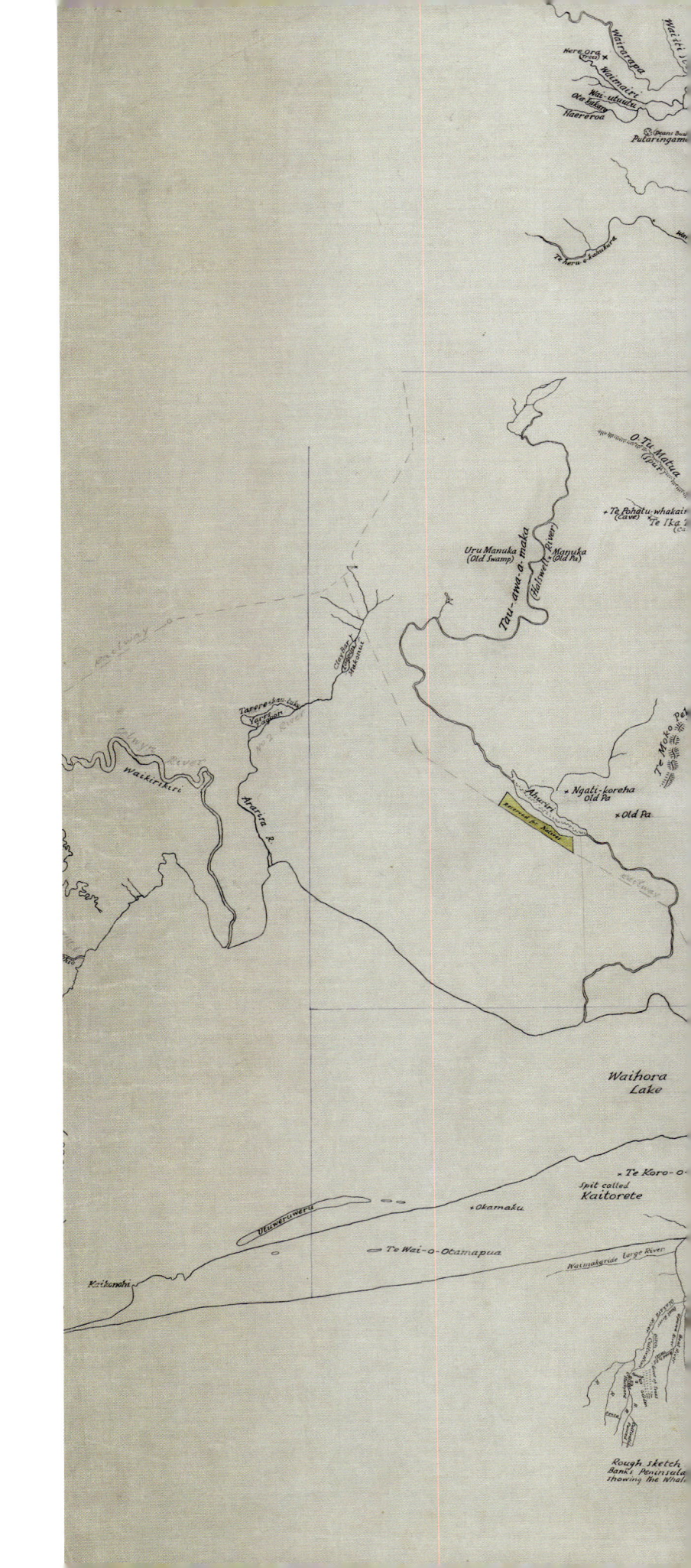

For description of positions of names see
Place Names - Banks Peninsula - J.C. Andersen.

Maori names from sketch plans
supplied by Canon James W. Stack 19.11.94 (thus
see File L 26 folios 87&88
Additional names by
(W.H.S. Roberts & Others)   W.A. Taylor
Scale 80 Chains to an Inch

FAICTE A ARQVES
PAR PIERRES DESCELIERS
PBRE LAN 1550

AVSTRALLE

LA MER DES INDES
ORIENTALLES

LA ZONA TORRIDA
TROPIQUE DE

REGION
TEMPEREE

TWO

BEACHED AS

Every so often, some diehard enthusiast will claim to have detected cartographic evidence that New Zealand was found and charted by Europeans before its official discovery by Abel Tasman in 1642. Many early maps of the world tantalisingly depict land masses in the zone of the globe where real-life New Zealand appears on modern maps. Partly, these were inspired by the ancient theory that there simply had to be land in the southern hemisphere to balance the heft of the known land masses in the northern. Partly, they were the cartographic reflection of rumours reported by such early travellers as Marco Polo, who described a country south of the regions with which he was familiar that went by the name of Locach (which, due to the kind of error that could never happen in a modern publishing house, became corrupted to 'Boeach', or even 'Beach', when his stories came to be told).

This place really caught the European imagination, as the great Venetian described it as doubly blessed—once with an abundance of natural resources, including gold, and again with a native population who, while hostile to visitors, were altogether ignorant of the value of the first. This notion that there was an undiscovered land filthy with gold somewhere to the south of South-East Asia aligned well with accounts in Indian literature (incorporated into Greek geographies at the time of Alexander the Great) of a land or lands south of Sumatra named variously the Gold and Silver Isles, or the Golden Peninsula. Where there was so much glister, to the European mind, there simply had to be gold.

Similarly, some maps (such as Gerardus Mercator's 1569 map of the world) show a promontory of the fabled southern continent (Terra Australis Incognita, or 'unknown southern land') named Psittacorum Regio, or Land of Parrots. The discovery of this in 1500 by the Portuguese navigator Pedro Álvares Cabral, who was taking a fleet of ships to India, was described by a contemporary report of his expedition thus:

> Above the Cape of Good Hope, to the south-west, they [Cabral and his crew] have discovered a new land; they call it the Land of Parrots, because they are an arm and a half tall and multi-coloured; we have seen two of them . . . they think this territory is mainland . . . good-looking, native people live there.

The directions to this new land were worse than vague: anything 'above' the Cape of Good Hope could not also be to the southwest of it, although the writer may have meant that the land was 'above the Cape of Good Hope and south-west of his place of writing', namely Portugal. There are, of course, many theories as to which parrot-infested coast Cabral happened upon. Australia has been suggested, as has (most plausibly) South America, and in particular Brazil. But if we indulge the fantasy, with its once-abundant populations of kākāpō (the largest parrot in the world), kākā, kea and smaller relatives such as the kākāriki, New Zealand's South Island must surely also be a candidate.

Marco Polo—or rather, his careless readers and sloppy publishers—can also be held responsible for the cartographic persistence of a land mass to the south of Java that acquired the name Jave la Grande. Two sets of errors gave rise to this phantom: one was the common misperception that a list of places that he gave was a record of land masses you would strike if you journeyed southwards from the place he was writing (Champa, or modern-day Vietnam). Two of the names on the list (in order) are Java Minor and Java Major, which seemed to place Java Major to the south of ordinary, workaday Java. Because Marco Polo extravagantly described Java Major (or Jave la Grande, as some preferred to call it) as 'the largest island in the world', many sixteenth-century map-makers felt obliged to slap a large land mass to the south of Java. The most influential of these were several who were associated with the Dieppe cartographic school in France, and it just so happens that at least one version of their Jave la Grande more or less occupies the region of Australia and also resembles Australia, supposing the east coast of New Zealand's North Island were appended to it. Looking at this map, you will notice that the eastern extremity is even given a name, Cap de Fremose, apparently a French translation of the Portuguese Capo Formosa, or 'lovely cape'.

The notion that Australia was first 'discovered' (not counting, as was the custom, the fact that the Australian Aboriginals had occupied it for millennia) by the Portuguese was first postulated in 1786 by the Scottish head of the Admiralty, Alexander Dalrymple

Continued on p. 50

CANADA

EVROPPE

AFFRICQVE

LA TERRE DV BRESIL
CANIBALLES

EQVINOCTIAL
LE PERU

LA MER PACIFICQVE

LA TERRE AVSTRALLE

ASIE LA GRANDE

MER DES INDES

IAVE

IAVE LA GRANDE

Previous page
DAUPHIN (OR HARLEIAN) MAP (CIRCA 1547)

> The notion that sixteenth-century maps might depict parts of the coasts of Australia and New Zealand was first postulated by Alexander Dalrymple, a rival and detractor of James Cook, who believed he ought to have been given Cook's job as explorer of the Pacific. It was a member of the company of the *Endeavour*, the naturalist Daniel Solander, who loaned Dalrymple a library copy of the beautiful 'Dauphin' map, drawn on the orders of King Francois I of France for his son, known as the Dauphin. Like other maps of the day, the Dauphin map reflected the mediaeval belief that there must be a vast land mass in the nether regions of the globe to balance the land masses in the north, as refined with a graphic depiction of the rumours of lands to the south of Java. Dalrymple noticed that the portion of Jave la Grande, the land mass immediately to the south of Java, featured a southeasterly trending coast with a distinct, triangular projection. There was, he decided, a striking similarity between this piece of coastline and what you would get if you imagined the northeast coast of present-day Queensland was continuous with the East Cape of New Zealand's North Island. This proved, he concluded, the rumours that the French makers of the map had information from the Portuguese, who were supposed to have discovered land in this part of the world. While it is not impossible, no concrete evidence (cartological or archaeological) has ever emerged to support this theory, but that hasn't stopped it from surfacing again and again in the intervening two centuries.
>
> While it is not likely to show New Zealand, the Dauphin map is a useful place to start a description of what Europeans imagined to lie in these parts. It includes many features that sixteenth-century map-makers received without question from their mediaeval forerunners: the existence of the continent, to start with, and the cartographical tradition of filling blank spaces ('the horror of the void', as it has been well put) sees the unknown southern land forested and peopled, with the figures of dusky natives interacting with animals resembling deer and camels.

Following page
DESCELIERS' MAP OF THE WORLD, 1550

While no one knows who drew the Dauphin map, it is plain that they were either part of, or heavily influenced by, the great cartography school in the northern French port town of Dieppe, represented here by a map of the world drawn by Pierre Desceliers for King Henry II of France (which is what the Dauphin of Dauphin map fame became when he was all grown up). Desceliers was a vastly influential map-maker and has been called 'the father of French hydrography', but while he was connected with a number of explorers, he was unlikely to have done the hard yards of discovery himself. Instead, he was a collator of information gleaned by others.

The source of the geography of Australasia as shown in the Dauphin map is plain to see here: Jave la Grande is shown in roughly the same proportions and as part of what Desceliers tantalisingly terms 'Terra Australis Recenter Inventa sed nondum plene cognita'—'the southern land that was recently discovered but which is not yet fully known'. Just how little it was known, if indeed it had been discovered, is revealed by its fauna: elephants and swan-necked dromedaries.

REGION FROIDE
CANADA
MER DE FRANCE
MER DESPAIGNE
MER OCCEANE
MER DES ENTILLES
LE PERV
MER DV SV
AMERIQVE
LA LIGNE
LA ZONA TORRID
TROPIQVE
MER AVSTRALLE
MER DE MAGELLAN
LA TERRE

LA MER GLACIALLE

ASIE

REGION TEMPERÉE

LA ZONA TORRIDA
TROPIQUE DE

LA MER DES INDES ORIENTALLES

CAPRI CORNE

AUSTRALLE

FAICTE A ARQUES
PAR PIERRES DESCELIERS
PBRE LAN 1550

(the Royal Society's pick for the post of leader of an expedition to search for the great southern continent, which in the event was given to an obscure officer named James Cook). The idea has gained quite a following down the years and, besides the flimsy cartographic evidence, a smattering of archaeological finds has been adduced to prove it—some cannon, a set of keys, the rumours of an ancient shipwreck made of mahogany, the remains of what appears to be an old defensive blockhouse constructed using European stoneworking techniques, which can be seen in Bittangabee Bay on the coast of southern New South Wales.

Not to be outdone, there is a small but fervent coterie of Kiwis who believe that the Portuguese also happened upon New Zealand in the sixteenth century. Besides the 'lovely cape' marked on some of the Dieppe maps (and see the intriguing legends appearing on the British Admiralty chart on p. 96), a similar litany of archaeological finds is usually produced as evidence: a Spanish helmet reputedly dredged from Wellington Harbour some time prior to 1904; rumours of a shipwreck, possibly made of mahogany, buried in sand in Northland; a 300-year-old skull, apparently of a European woman, washed from a riverbank in the Wairarapa; a 300-odd-year-old pōhutukawa growing in La Coruña in Spain; a 500-year-old bell from a Tamil vessel that was in the possession of Māori 'for generations' before it was collected by an early British missionary to New Zealand in 1836; a small stone bird, carved with metal tools and of a form quite unlike other Polynesian workmanship, which was found in 1878 (according to one story) in the earth under the roots of an old tree; the remains of ancient stone walls in the Kaimanawa Ranges . . .

Anticlimactically as it seems, the evidence for the theory of the Portuguese discovery of Australia has been rigorously debunked—the supposed Spanish or Portuguese carronades have been shown to be of South-East Asian origin; the keys collected from a silt stratum in Geelong in 1847 probably belonged to a lime-burner who was working on the same beach at the time, and were, in any case, swiftly lost again so that they have never been subjected to rigorous scrutiny; the 'mahogany ship' has not been sighted since the nineteenth century (despite any number of searches), and many of the original sightings are now supposed to have been of the wrecks of relatively recent, Australian-built ships in the general area; the blockhouse was actually a storehouse built by a pair of British traders (the beginning of construction was even reported in an Australian newspaper). Similarly, the Jave la Grande of the Dieppe maps has been convincingly shown to have originated in a misunderstanding of descriptions of the South China Sea.

Likewise, while it is perfectly plausible to suppose that the Portuguese or others (it has been suggested with a straight face that everyone from the Phoenicians and the Chinese to the Celts found New Zealand long before Tasman) *may* have stumbled across these islands, there is no convincing evidence that it *did* happen. There is nothing distinctively Spanish about the Spanish helmet, and if it did lie at the bottom of Wellington Harbour for any significant period of time before being found (the story of its provenance is highly doubtful), it is mysteriously free of corrosion for an iron artefact; our own 'mahogany ship' has proved as elusive as Australia's (although searchers claim to have found a post-Tasman, pre-Cook wreck in Northland that appears to have been constructed using European techniques and timber indigenous to Dutch-controlled Indonesia); the Kaimanawa Wall proved to be a natural geological formation that just happened to resemble dressed stone . . . Some items, such as the Korotangi (the stone bird), the Tamil bell and the Ruamahānga skull defy easy explanation, but nor do they point in any particular direction, such as landfall by the Spanish, Celts or Chinese. And if Portuguese explorers ever did reach and chart the New Zealand coast, in order for the Dieppe map-makers to include their discoveries, no trace of the Portuguese originals for these charts (or the Chinese originals, from which the Portuguese are alleged to have copied *their* charts) has ever been found.

At the risk of digressing, many of the claims for pre-Tasman European discovery of New Zealand want to go much further, and to claim that there were people living here before Māori. There are, in fact, plenty of Māori stories that hint at this, including the one cited above, where Māui fished the North Island from the depths and found it to be peopled. So do the many, many stories about pale, sprite-like folk, the pakepakehā and patupaiarehe, who haunted forests and mountain heights. Many iwi have traditions of an older people than themselves known as Waitaha inhabiting Aotearoa. These have been used as evidence for the (frankly fantastic) claim that these islands were settled by a Celtic race long before the coming of the Māori. But almost without exception, such claims can be ascribed to political agendas. If Māori were *not* the first inhabitants of New Zealand, this line of argument runs, then surely the 'privileged' status they claim as tangata whenua under successive sickly white liberal governments is baseless?

In fact, New Zealand's constitutional arrangements are founded in British common law, which had contemplated the situation where British subjects might encounter peoples living in non-British jurisdictions long before Cook sailed. Its principles recognised and protected the land tenure of aboriginal people, based not on the assumption that they were there first, but on the fact that they were there, in charge, *at the time*. Even if a sixteenth-century Portuguese map were to come to light clearly showing something resembling the New Zealand coast and with the legend 'here be stroppie, eight-foote fowle', it would do nothing to undermine the Treaty of Waitangi. Nor would anything change if it were established that Māori had, indeed, arrived only to find New Zealand had been populated by the descendants of (say) bands of Morris dancers who had gone badly out of their way in ancient times. Either would be fascinating from a historical perspective, but altogether lacking in jurisprudential significance.

JOHN ROTZ MAP OF THE WORLD, 1542

The most striking resemblance of the coastline of The Lande of Beach, as it is here described, to the northeast coast of Australia is in the so-called John Rotz map. Part-French, part-Scottish, Jean Rotz was a member of the Dieppe school of map-makers. He had more hands-on experience than most, as he seems to have travelled to at least some of the places he drew on his beautifully illuminated maps. It is not known for certain whether he accompanied French explorer Jean Parmentier on his 1529 voyage to Sumatra, intended to break the Portuguese monopoly over the spice trade: no maps made on that expedition survived (and nor did its leader), but the knowledge of South-East Asia that was gained was transmitted to the cartographers of Dieppe and it is distilled here in a map that is refreshingly free of the embellishments—the sea monsters, the imaginary forests, the grass huts, the fabulous fauna—that so burden its contemporaries.

One feature of the elegantly spare Rotz map that adds considerable authority to its depictions is that it shows discontinuities, as though the map-maker were following the nautical convention that it was irresponsible to chart anything that was not known for certain. If it weren't for the anomalous, roughly triangular projection from the coastline below 45° South, you could be fairly confident that this was a depiction of Australia. But what has excited believers in a sixteenth-century (or earlier) discovery of Australasia is that the projection itself is a relatively good match (albeit well out of scale) of the North Island's East Cape.

EIST NEST

The Indies of orient

ORTELIUS' MAP OF THE PACIFIC OCEAN, 1589

The idea that the Spanish might have had anything to do with the discovery of Australia and/or New Zealand before Abel Tasman can be dispelled by the very first map of the Pacific Ocean, namely this 1589 chart by the Dutch cartographer Abraham Wortels (who adopted the Latinised name Ortelius). Any blushes arising from European ignorance of everything to the south of New Guinea are covered with the large, decorative cartouche that holds the map's dedication and maker's name. While the Dieppe map-makers depicted the coast trending sharply southeast from the point at which Terra Australis most closely approaches New Guinea, here it has been changed to slope gently to be continuous with Tierra del Fuego, which Magellan passed to the north of when he became the first European to penetrate the straits that bear his name and to sail into the Pacific Ocean. The significance of this is that Ortelius was the royal geographer to the Spanish court. If the Spanish knew of the existence of New Zealand or its big brother to the west, they weren't letting on, nor were they admitting anything they might have learned from the Portuguese.

This map, amongst others, first appeared in a revision of Ortelius' collection of equally gorgeous maps named *Theatrum Orbis Terrarum* (Theatre of the World), first published in 1570—the first modern atlas.

1589

MARIS PACIFICI,
(quod vulgò Mar del Zur)
cum regionibus circumiacentibus, insulisque in eodem
passim sparsis, novissima descriptio.

SEPTEMTRIO

AMERICAE SEPTEM-
TRIONALIOR PARS.
Quivira.

MARIS ATLANTICI,
SIVE MAR DEL NORT
PARS.

Noua Hispania.
Florida.
Bermuda
Cuba
Spagnola
Iamaica
S. Ioan
La Trinidad

MARE PACIFICUM, QUOD VULGO NOMINANT MAR DEL ZUR.

Californi.
Yucatan
Cartagena
Caribana
Quito
Peru
AMERICAE
MERIDIONA-
LIOR PARS.
Charcas
Chili
Patagones
Archipelagus insularum
Fretum Magellanicum
Mar del Nort
Tierra del Fuego

Circulus Aequinoctialis.
Circulus Capricorni.

Insulae Salomonis.
Isabella
Nombre de Jesus
Los Martas
S. Catalina
S. Anna
Los Tuberones
S. Petri

Prima ego velivolis ambivi cursibus Orbem,
Magellane novo te duce ducta freto.
Ambivi, meritoq́ vocor VICTORIA: sunt mi
Vela, alæ; præcium, gloria; pugna, mare.

TERRA AVSTRALIS,
SIVE MAGELLANICA, NON-
DUM DETECTA.

Cum privilegiis Imp. & Reg. Maiestatum,
nec non Cancellariæ Brabantiæ, ad decennium.

MERIDIES.

Cabo Maria van Diemen

Drie Koningh Eijlant

Januario 1643

THREE

DUTCH COURAGE

It's a curiosity that the first printed map of New Zealand (or at least, out of deference to those who will have objected to the previous chapter, the first map *known* to have been printed) was Italian. It appeared in the 1690s, nearly half a century after the Dutch explorer Abel Janzsoon Tasman saw the lofty peaks of the Main Divide soaring from behind the breakers from the deck of his vessel, the *Heemskerck*, on 13 December 1642, as he approached the coast of South Westland from Van Diemen's Land (the name he had given Tasmania). Tasman had set sail from Batavia—now known as Jakarta—in August of that year with two ships, the *Zeehaen* and *Heemskerck*, under orders from his employer, the VOC (Vereenigde Oostindische Compagnie, or Dutch East India Company) to nail down the truth about this unknown southern land that kept cropping up in high latitudes on maps of the world. The company's primary motive was, of course, financial: the VOC didn't really do anything for any other reason, as is signified by the fact that one of the senior officers aboard company vessels held the rank of merchant. The VOC was keen for Tasman to find the land that was rumoured to lie south of Indonesia. If the rumours proved to be true and it was filthy with gold, so much the better. He was warned it was likely to be inhabited by hostile natives.

If so, he was to exercise caution both in dealing with them and in letting on about what it was that he was keen to find in their homeland: he was instructed to observe 'what they esteem and to what goods they are most attracted, particularly finding out what wares are among them, likewise about gold and silver . . . representing yourself to be not eager for it in order to keep them unaware of the value of the same'. But if there were neither gold nor even a country there, intelligence of the existence of a useful sea lane from the Indies to South America would do.

That, at any rate, was the motivation of the company itself. But the expedition was likely to have been the brainchild of some combination of Tasman, Isaac Gilsemans (who sailed as the merchant of the *Zeehaen*) and Francoijs Visscher (pilot-major or navigator): it has been convincingly argued that the three were associated with one another in earlier expeditions in the vicinity of Japan, and that Tasman and Gilsemans are likely to have had a hand in the 'Memoir Concerning the Discovery of the Southland', which was submitted to the company under Visscher's name on 22 January 1642. Who knows what their individual or collective motivations were—whether the seaman's hunger to know what lay over the horizon, the cartographer's abhorrence of blank space or the fairly general Dutch lust for personal fortune—but the venture (or a version of their rather more ambitious proposal, at least) was given the green light.

The *Heemskerck* and *Zeehaen* sailed first for Mauritius, where they were provisioned for the real business of the voyage, a dip to high latitudes, whereupon they were supposed to track eastwards until they fell in with the coast of the fabled southern land. In the event, it was too cold by the time they reached their farthest south of 49°, so they steered north again, before heading east on the forty-fourth parallel, more or less the latitude of Jackson Bay on the South Island of New Zealand, or the southern extremity of Tasmania. Imagine their excitement when, at about 4 p.m. on 24 November, seven weeks after leaving Mauritius, land was sighted. The officers and crew could be reasonably well assured that no one (or at least, no one who counted in their world view) had clapped eyes on this shore before. They could also be perfectly certain that if they messed up their approach and stacked a ship up upon some shoal or the unnamed rocky coastline before them, no one was coming to their rescue.

There has been a long, mainly British tradition of disparaging Tasman for what is regarded as his rather irresolute habits as an explorer, but it's unlikely any of the men who depended upon his decision-making for their survival shared this view. The two vessels crept their way along the shoreline of the newly christened Van Diemen's Land (named after Anthony, the governor of Batavia) until they found a safe anchorage. A landing was made, and further along, a flagstaff inscribed with the company's insignia was swum ashore by the *Heemskerck*'s carpenter to claim the territory for the VOC. After that, Tasman directed his ships far enough north to be certain that Van Diemen's Land was an island and not part of his quarry, Terra Australis, and then turned east again to continue the search.

Eight days later, he hailed the west coast of the South Island of New Zealand in the vicinity of Ōkarito, believing (or hoping) it to be part of the same land mass spotted to the south of Tierra del Fuego by another pair of Dutch navigators in 1615, which they had christened Staten Landt (after the Dutch parliament, the Staten-Generaal, or States

VISSCHER'S CHART OF NEW ZEALAND, 1665

Francoijs Visscher was the pilot-major (sailing master) of the *Heemskerck*, the principal of Tasman's two-ship fleet. He had demonstrated to the VOC (the Dutch East India Company) that he was a capable cartographer, and that was likely why he was chosen to accompany Tasman on his search for the rumoured southern continent. Indeed, he may well have been instrumental in putting the proposal for the expedition together in the first place.

Tasman and his officers have copped quite a lot of bad press in their historiography, but let's just consider the limitations they were working under: they had no reliable means of fixing longitude, and even the measurement of latitude was performed using a backstaff or a Jacob's staff. This was a fairly crude if ingenious method of measuring the height of a heavenly body (usually the sun) above the horizon; using the resultant angles and distances and the time of day, a navigator could consult his almanac (a series of tables) for the figures with which he could calculate his distance from the equator.

Note that Visscher's chart—this is a copy, published in the 1665 *Atlas Stosch*—shows a gap in the coastline between what we now know to be the South and North islands. This indicates that Visscher, at least, thought there was a fair probability that what Tasman himself called the Bight of Zeehaen was a strait.

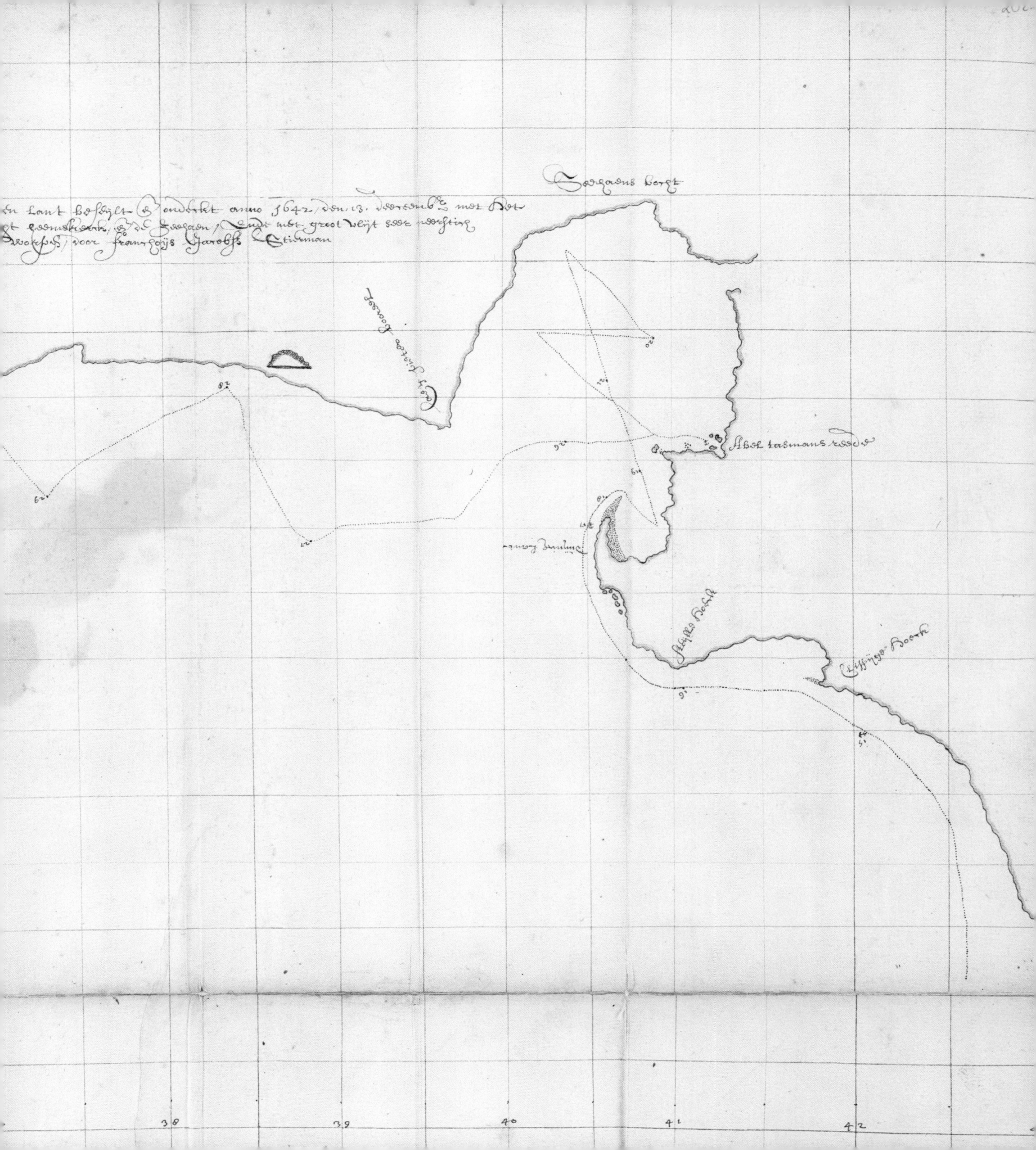

't Lant beseijlt ende ondekt anno 1642 den 13 decemb: met het
jacht heemskerk, ende de Zeehaen, ende met groot vlijt seer neerstig
bekeken door Francoijs Jacobsz: Visscher

Saagaens bergt

Abel tasmans reede

Moordenaers baeij

Zeehaens hoeck

Vlissinge hoeck

General). Tasman believed he might be looking at the northern extremity of the unknown southern supercontinent which stretched all the way to the tip of South America. He gave the same name to his discovery: Staten Landt. The name reflected his hope that the land he had now discovered was continuous with it. Rather surprisingly, instead of following the coast south (as you would if you meant to determine whether this was an island or part of a greater land mass lying to the south), Tasman steered north, intent upon finding a secure anchorage. Nothing presented itself until he rounded Cape Farewell and entered the beautiful, wide sweep of the waterway known to Māori as Taitapu. Here, they anchored, well off the beach. An exploratory party of Māori—almost certainly of the Tūmatakōkiri people—visited in a pair of waka, keeping their distance but calling out 'in gruff voices' and sounding a call on a conch. A Dutch crewman was sent below to fetch his trumpet, and he blew a few retorts. No one on either side seemed to know quite what to make of the others.

The following, fateful day, the *Zeehaen*'s cock-boat (a small rowboat) was intercepted by a waka taua while plying between the Dutch ships, and four of its crewmen were killed. Apparently emboldened by the success of this attack, a larger force put off from the shore as Tasman's crews readied their ships for a hasty departure. The flotilla of waka was engaged with musketry and cannon fire and an unknown number of tangata whenua were killed or wounded.

After 'this enormous event and detestable affair', as Tasman put it, any appetite he may have had for more intrepid and exhaustive exploration of the interior of the new land was gone. He sailed to the northeast and anchored on the far side of Rangitoto ki te Tonga (now known as D'Urville Island), where he was pinned down by poor weather for a few days, doubtless scanning the land anxiously all the time. When the weather relented, he pressed on. He correctly guessed from the current that he was anchored at the entrance to a strait which would lead him to the southeast, but decided it wouldn't be prudent to investigate, in case the wind changed and embayed him. So he sailed northward along the west coast of the North Island as far as the point where the land seemed to end, as here it trended sharply east. He named the headland Cape Maria van Diemen, after the VOC principal's wife, and left 'Staten Landt' behind. En route to warmer and—as it proved—more hospitable climes, he encountered and investigated the Three Kings Islands, where he was keen to water the ship but nervous about his crewmen's reports of uncommonly tall natives inhospitably waving spears. He chose not to risk a landfall and proceeded north, home, via Tonga.

―――

Tasman's voyage received mixed reviews. The VOC were distinctly unhappy with him, due to the expedition's disappointing bottom line: no gold, no intelligence of gold or prospects of useful trade of any other description, nor even a satisfactory answer to the question regarding the existence of a great southern land. Nevertheless, a couple of years later, Tasman was considered able enough to be entrusted with another exploratory mission, this time charting the coasts of New Guinea and the northern coast of Australia, stopping (if he would) to pick up a box of cash and a big gun that the company had lost when its vessel *Batavia* was wrecked on a collection of rocks off western Australia. (Its complement had been cast ashore and turned upon one another in an orgy of cannibalistic sadism whilst awaiting rescue.) Tasman made a poor fist of the exploration (he didn't land, didn't press on as far as Australia's western seaboard) and never even attempted the salvage. The VOC swallowed this disappointment, too, and gave him another job to do. Tasman's last appointment was to the position of pirate, with key performance indicators around preying on Spanish silver galleons. The company's return on this investment never amounted to a single piece of eight. Tasman was disciplined, ironically, for being too harsh in administering discipline, but soon reinstated and put on whatever early modern Dutch for gardening leave was. He lived out his days in relative prosperity in Batavia, dying there in 1659. His two cartographic collaborators weren't so lucky: Visscher died in 1645 after sustaining wounds in a naval scrap with the Portuguese, and Gilsemans within a year of him, his cause of death unknown.

Nor did Ngāti Tūmatakōkiri fare so well, in the long run. They were recent migrants from the North Island, and it has been speculated that Tasman's two vessels hove in view while they were still feeling jittery and insecure. There is archaeological evidence of major agricultural development in the vicinity of Taupō Point, from which the attack upon the Europeans was mounted: it is surmised that the iwi was merely taking a front-foot defensive stance when it launched its pre-emptive attack. There is little or no oral history on the subject: as if in vindication of their fears, Ngāti Tūmatakōkiri were all but wiped out by encroaching iwi in the musket wars of the early nineteenth century.

———

The records of Tasman's voyage to New Zealand, including his charts, remained unpublished for centuries (and the originals are now lost), but the information contained within them became relatively common knowledge soon after his voyage. A manuscript map, known as the Bonaparte map (because it was at one time owned by Napoleon's grand-nephew), is conventionally dated 1644. There is no agreement as to who drew it, or where (whether in Batavia or in Amsterdam or in some combination of the two), or even that it was done in 1644: it seems unlikely to have been the work of Tasman himself, but it has been plausibly attributed to some combination of Visscher and Gilsemans, perhaps supplemented by a VOC functionary in Amsterdam. It depicts Tasman's discoveries to the south and east of the Dutch East Indies—Van Diemen's Land, Staten Landt, Tonga, Fiji and some portion of the southern and northern coasts of New Guinea and Australia respectively. It is the blank white spaces on this map that will have haunted Tasman and irked his superiors: despite his brief to settle the question as to the existence of a southern continent, everything to the south of Tasmania and the charted portion of New Zealand is as empty as ever. And despite his orders to establish whether there was a channel between New Guinea and Australia, only a question mark as to the reality of Torres Strait exists in the shape of a discontinuity of the coastline between the tip of Land van Carpentarie and the east-west trending coast of New Guinea above it. This chart shows a large bay, Zeehaens Bogt (Zeehaen's Bight), where a manuscript map by Visscher showed the probability of a strait (in fact, Cook Strait).

This brings us back to the first printed version of Tasman's discoveries, which appeared on page 150 of an atlas published in Venice some time during the 1690s by a Franciscan priest named Vincenzo Coronelli. Like many learned men of his age, the good friar Coronelli was something of a polymath, being accomplished not only in cartography but also in maths and theology. He published an encyclopaedia—the first in the world to be arranged alphabetically—and was the founder of a geographical society, Accademia Cosmografica degli Argonauti.

The fact that his atlas entry relies upon Tasman's charts and reports of his voyage can be gleaned from the place names, which appear in both Italian and Dutch (Baia degli Assassini is also Moordenaars Bay, for example). Tasman's superiors preferred the name 'Niew Zelandt' to 'Staten Landt', hence the entry in Coronelli's atlas is the first reference on a chart or in an atlas to 'New Zealand'.

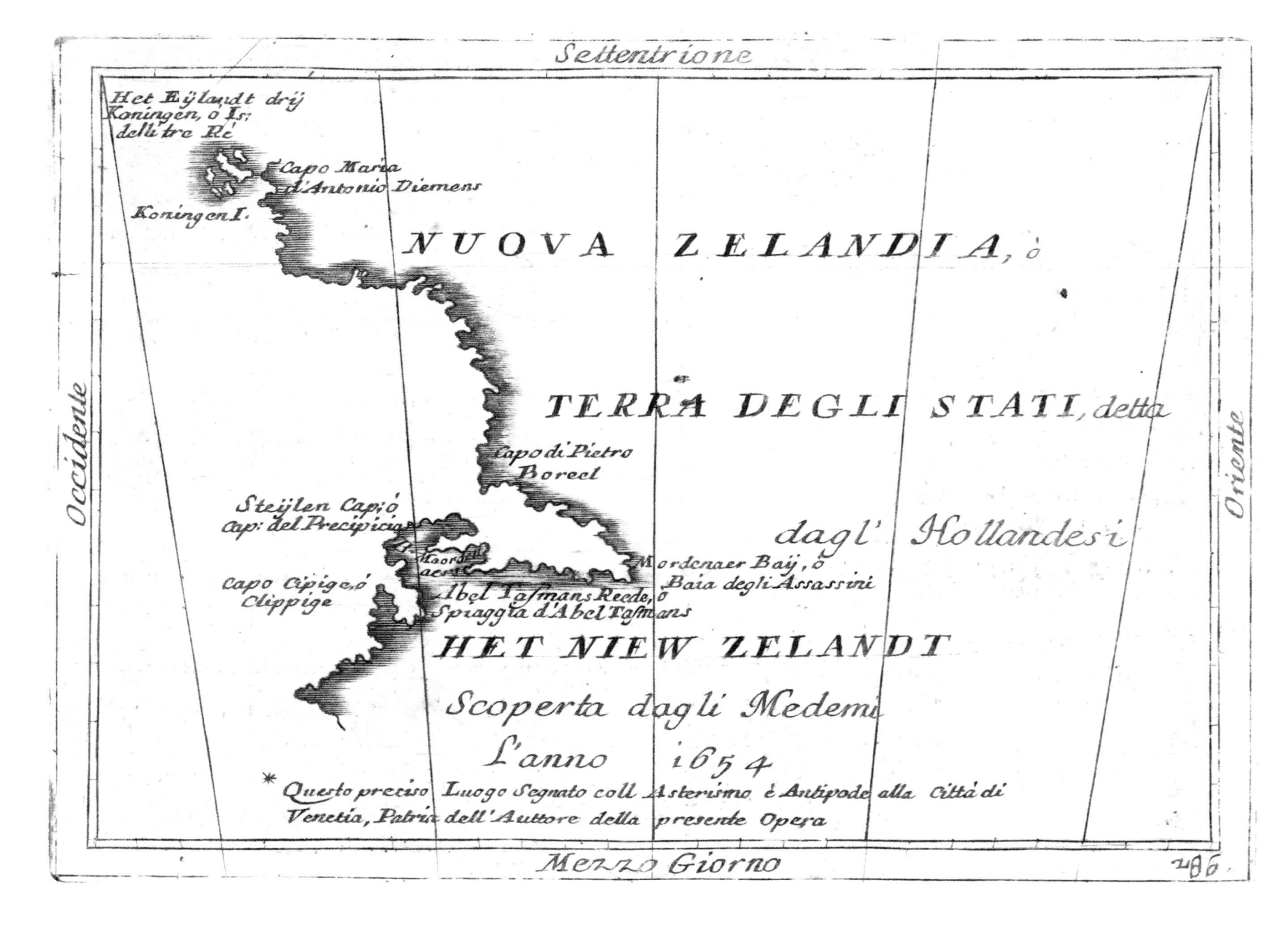

Opposite page
CORONELLI'S MAP OF NEW ZEALAND, 1696

The fact that Abel Tasman's discoveries were an open secret by the end of the seventeenth century can be established beyond doubt by their appearance in an atlas by Vincenzo Coronelli, a polymathic Franciscan priest who published what is widely reckoned to have been the first modern encyclopaedia. And while Tasman and Visscher had both dubbed the land they had encountered in the remote South Pacific 'Staten Landt', reflecting their wistful conviction that this was part of the same land mass that had been spotted by a compatriot south of Cape Horn, by the time Coronelli came to include a copy of the expedition's map in his encyclopaedia, it had come to be known, translating from the Dutch, as Nuova Zealandia (or Nuova Zealanda, depending on whether you went with the text entry or the cartographic label). This makes this map the first to mention the name 'New Zealand'.

Following page
BONAPARTE MAP OF TASMAN'S DISCOVERIES, 1726

None of Abel Tasman's own maps were published in his lifetime, or for some time after that. But versions filtered out, such as the one attributed to Visscher on page 60. Another is commonly called the Bonaparte map, on account of the fact that it once belonged to Roland Bonaparte, the more famous Napoleon Bonaparte's grand-nephew. The map itself, which is in the collection of the State Library of New South Wales, is difficult to make out, faded and yellowed as it is. But it depicts Tasman's discoveries and the path his expedition took and is dated 1644, so is thought to have been a close copy made of an original chart very shortly after Tasman's return to Batavia. It was probably drafted in Amsterdam from original documents supplied by the VOC's offices in the Dutch East Indies, perhaps the work of Francoijs Visscher and the merchant of the *Zeehaen*, Isaac Gilsemans: it has a number of spelling errors that indicate the final draughtsman was unfamiliar with the proper spellings of place names. When it is cleaned up, it looks much like this 1726 map, drawn by François Valentijn in a history of the East Indies. When it is cleaned up, the Bonaparte map looks a lot like this chart redrawn in 1666 by Françoijs Jacobsen, and reprinted in an atlas named *Monumenta Cartographica* in 1933.

Pages 68–69
BELLIN'S CHART OF THE PACIFIC OCEAN, 1753

The European understanding of the geography of the Pacific on the eve of the voyages of James Cook is summarised in this map. The discoveries of Tasman are reflected, but a fair bit of imagination has gone into relating them to other bits of the known world. Tasmania, the east coast of Australia and New Guinea have all been conflated to create a tentacular New Holland that reaches far up into the South China Sea and far down into the Southern Ocean, and resembles nothing so much as the south end of a north-going terrier. A slight hiatus in the west coast of the monstrous Carpentaria (Cape York) peninsula reflects Tasman's suspicion that there was a waterway there (which others showed to be Torres Strait). But the remainder of the fabrication was rendered with complete assurance.

New Zealand, meanwhile, has swelled somewhat away from the landfall that Tasman made, and hovers at the margin of all that white space occupying the southern Pacific, beyond the limit of human knowledge. It's not known whether its draughtsman, Jacques-Nicolas Bellin, the first Ingénieur de la Marine de France, was relying on others for these flights of fancy, or whether they were his own work.

OCEANVS,

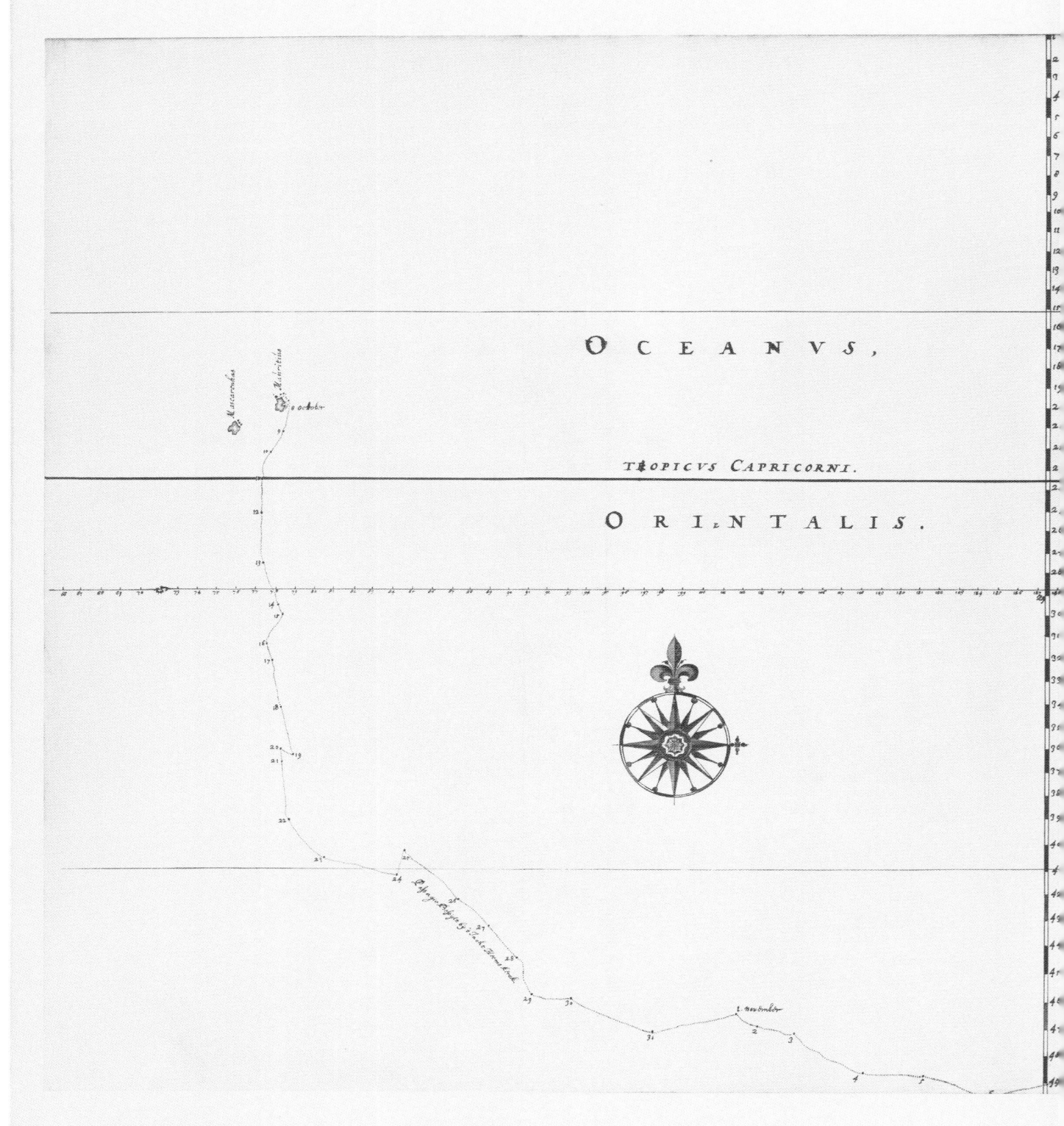

TROPICVS CAPRICORNI.

ORIENTALIS.

FRANÇOIJS JACOBSEN, CHART OF TASMAN'S VOYAGES, 1642—43 AND 1644. REDRAWN c. 1666. (3 sheets)

THE HAGUE — MARTINUS NIJHOFF

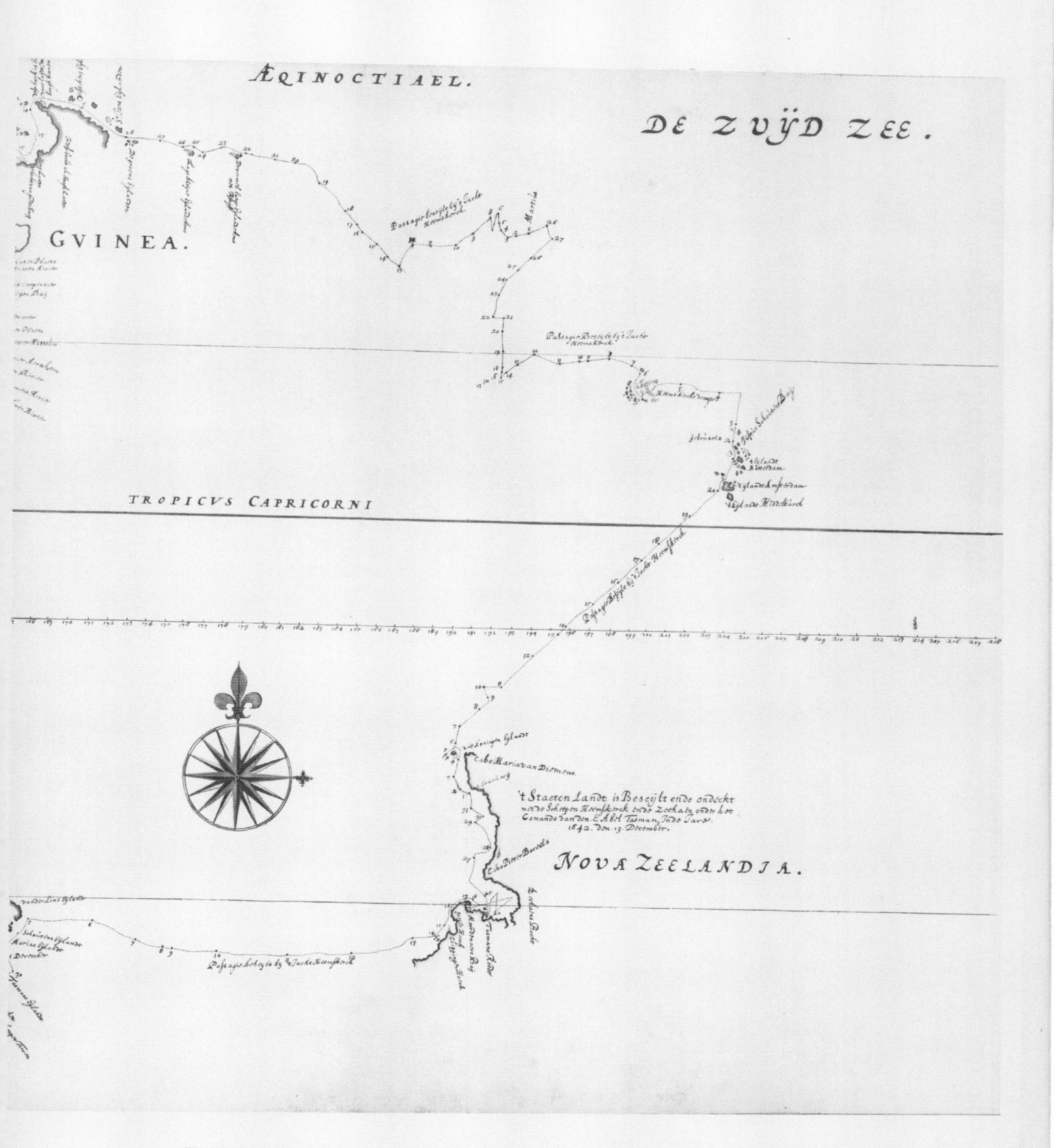

FRANÇOIJS JACOBSEN, CHART OF TASMAN'S VOYAGES, 1642—43 AND 1644. REDRAWN c. 1666. (3 sheets)

I. Matbare

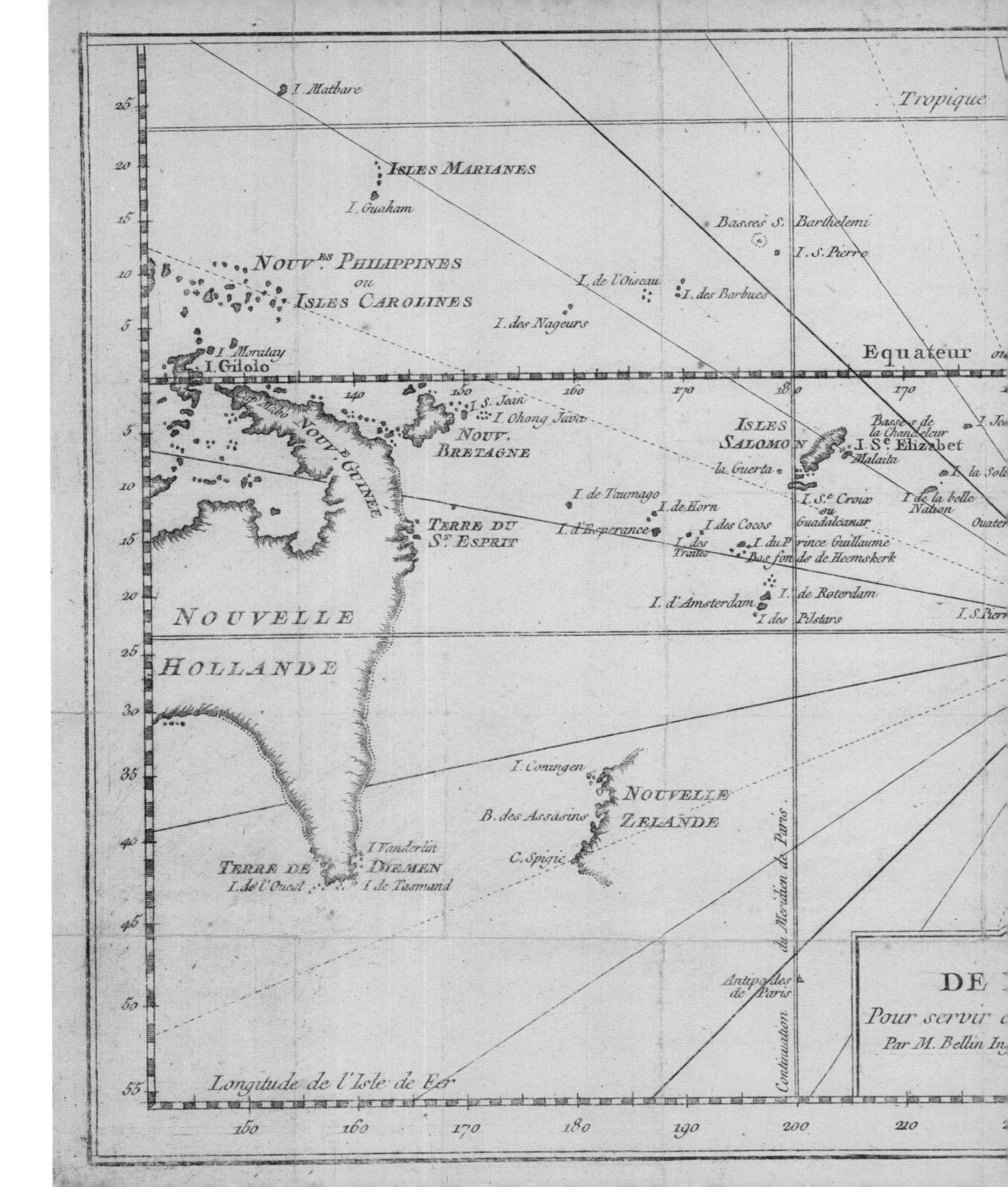

ISLES MARIANES

I. Guaham

Basses S. Barthelemi

I. S. Pierre

NOUV.ᴱˢ PHILIPPINES
ou
ISLES CAROLINES

I. de l'Oiseau

I. des Barbues

I. des Nageurs

Equateur

I. Moratay
I. Gilolo

Cap Mabo

NOUV.ᴱ GUINEE

I. S. Jean
I. Ohong Java

NOUV.
BRETAGNE

ISLES
SALOMON

Basses de
la Chandeleur

I. S.ᵉ Elizabet
Malaita

la Guerta

I. la Sol

TERRE DU
S.ᵗ ESPRIT

I. de Taumago
I. de Horn
I. d'Esperance
I. des Cocos
I. des Traites

I. S.ᵉ Croix
ou
Guadalcanar

I. de la belle
Nation

I. du Prince Guillaume
Bas fonds de Heemskerk

Ouate

NOUVELLE

HOLLANDE

I. d'Amsterdam
I. des Pilstars

I. de Roterdam

I. S. Pier

I. Coningen
B. des Assasins

NOUVELLE
ZELANDE

I. Vanderlin
TERRE DE DIEMEN
I. de l'Ouest I. de Tasmand

C. Spigie

Antipodes
de Paris

Continuation du Meridien de Paris

DE

Pour servir

Par M. Bellin Ing

Longitude de l'Isle de Fer

150   160   170   180   190   200   210

CARTE RÉDUITE DE LA MER DU SUD

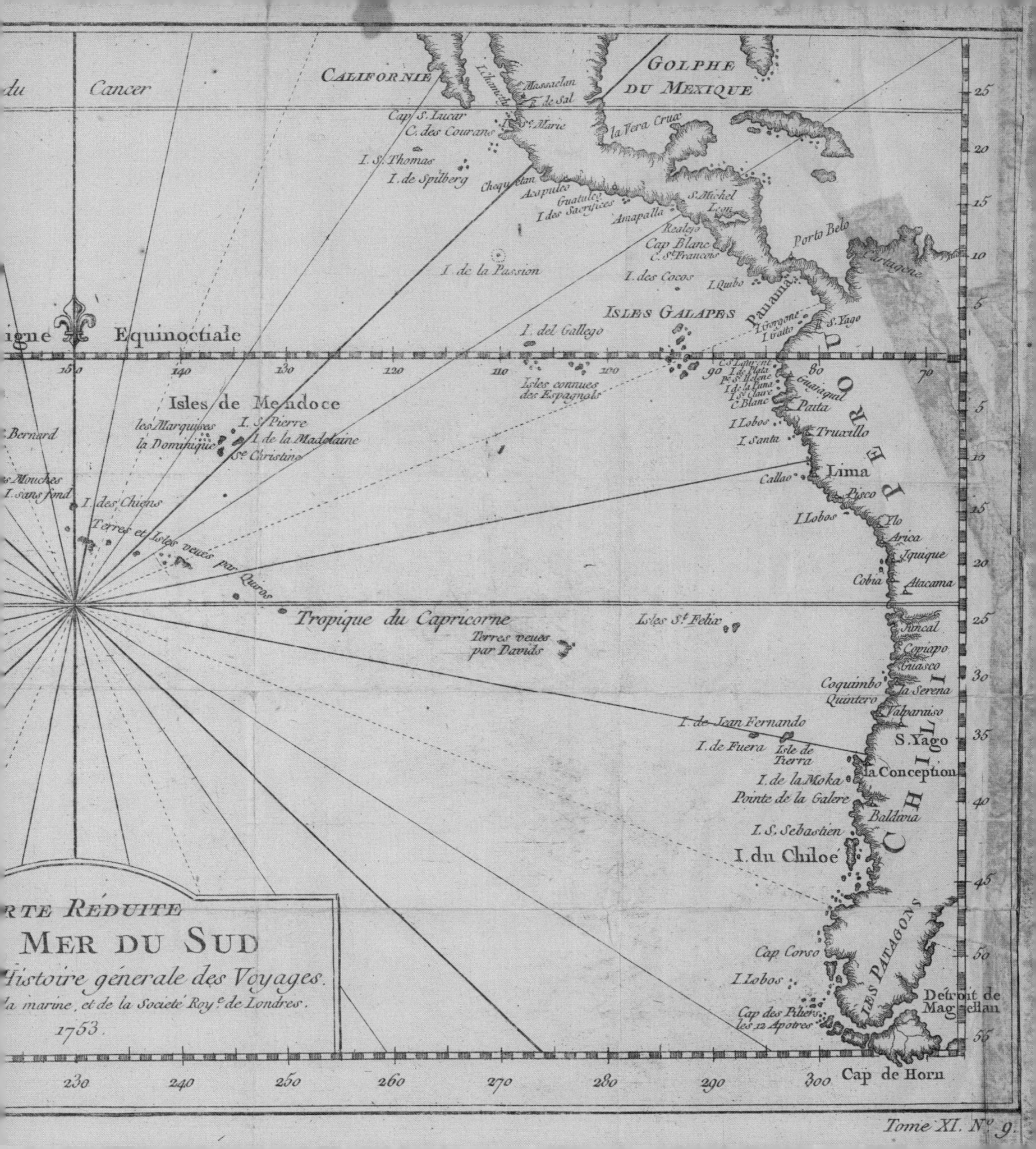

Pour l'Histoire générale des Voyages.
... la marine, et de la Société Roy.e de Londres.
1753.

Tome XI. N° 9.

CALIFORNIE — **Golphe du Mexique**

- du Cancer
- Cap S. Lucar
- C. des Courans
- I. S.te Marie
- Massaclan
- I. de Sal
- la Vera Cruz
- I. S. Thomas
- I. de Spilberg
- Choquitlan
- Acapulco
- Guatulco
- I. des Sacrifices
- Amapalla
- S. Michel
- Realejo
- Cap Blanc
- C. S.t Francois
- Porto Belo
- Cartagène
- I. de la Passion
- I. des Cocos
- I. Quibo
- Panama
- **ISLES GALAPES**
- I. Gorgone
- I. Gallo
- S. Yago

Ligne Equinoctiale

- I. del Gallego
- Isles connues des Espagnols
- C.S. Laurent
- I. de Plata
- p.e S.te Helene
- I. de la Puna
- I. S.te Claire
- C. Blanc
- Guayaquil
- Patta
- **PEROU**
- **Isles de Mendoce**
- les Marquises
- la Dominique
- I. S.t Pierre
- I. de la Madelaine
- S.te Christine
- I. Lobos
- I. Santa
- Truxillo
- Bernard
- s Mouches
- I. sans fond
- I. des Chiens
- Terres et Isles veues par Quiros
- Callao
- Lima
- Pisco
- I. Lobos
- Ylo
- Arica
- Iquique
- Cobia
- Atacama

Tropique du Capricorne

- Isles S.t Felix
- Terres veues par Davids
- Juncal
- Copiapo
- Guasco
- Coquimbo
- Quintero
- la Serena
- Valparaiso
- I. de Jean Fernando
- I. de Fuera
- Isle de Tierra
- S. Yago
- **CHILI**
- I. de la Moka
- Pointe de la Galere
- la Conception
- Baldivia
- I. S. Sebastien
- I. du Chiloe
- **LES PATAGONS**
- Cap Corso
- I. Lobos
- Cap des Piliers
- les 12 Apotres
- Détroit de Magellan
- Cap de Horn

Moudi-W
Pa-reinga-reinga
Sandy - Bay
Dunes
de
Sables
M.t Ohoura
7 midi   9 midi
10 midi
P.te Kari-kari
6 midi   Rou
11 m
Baie Nanga-onnou
Baie Oudou-Oudou
P.te Surville

District de Poro

NGATEPO

CARTE

Pina

IE SEPTENTRIONALE

Tepapa

MAOURE-OURE

Mangouniga   Ware-hou

UVELLE ZÉLANDE

Horeke Houta-Koura
Karaka

Lac Ma

SHOUKI-ANGA

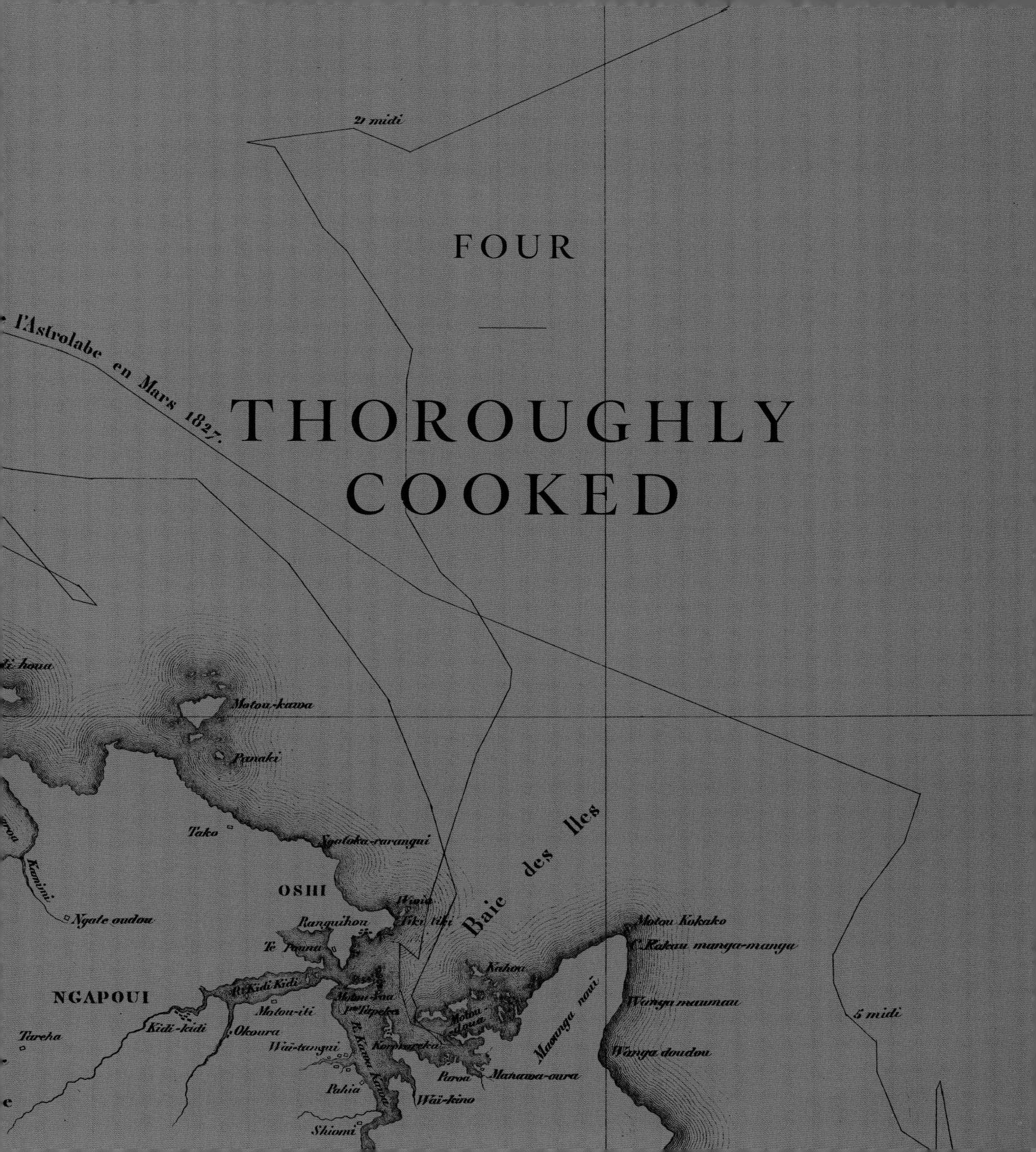

FOUR

THOROUGHLY COOKED

As I write, it is nearing the two hundred and fiftieth anniversary of the arrival within eyeshot of New Zealand, a little after two on the afternoon of 8 October 1769, of Lieutenant James Cook in His Majesty's Bark *Endeavour*. It is somewhat to be regretted that whereas Cook was once a heroic figure in New Zealand history, the mood on the eve of the sestercentennial is slightly queasy. Since the Māori renaissance kicked off in the 1970s, Cook's standing has gathered aspersions as rapidly as any timber hull will gather barnacles. Strictly in accordance with the law that historiographical perspectives swing from one extreme position to another like a pendulum, there has been a tendency in recent years to devalue his achievements and to freight him with the entire weight of the wrongs done during the colonial enterprise. This is not entirely fair.

There was undeniably an imperialist impetus to his voyage to the South Pacific: the sealed orders he opened in August 1769 specifically directed him to perform what Tasman had failed to do and determine once and for all whether there was a continent lurking in the globe's nether regions. In the event he found any new territories, he was to claim them for Britain. But his principal mission was scientific—to observe the transits of the planets Venus and Mercury across the sun's disc (which would enable calculations to be done to determine the Earth's circumference): geography was an opportunistically added sideshow.

In the five months that Cook spent poking about the New Zealand coast, he had several encounters with the tangata whenua. Some of these—particularly the early ones, when everyone was an unknown quantity to everyone else—went badly, and, given the superiority of European weaponry, it was the tangata whenua who suffered. But once Cook had realised that Tupaia could understand te reo Māori and make himself understood, things went rather better. The existence of linguistically conclusive proof that the ancestors of Tupaia had spread across the Pacific, even so far south as New Zealand, must have been a revelation to Cook: any doubts he had about Polynesian seafaring and wayfinding prowess were put to rest. As he subsequently became better acquainted with the wide sweep of the Pacific and the populations of Polynesian people upon its far-flung atolls and islands, his admiration only deepened.

The choice of Cook as commander of this expedition into the deep south had come as a surprise to many in England, where few would have bet against Alexander Dalrymple. It may have been Cook's comparative youth and vigour (he was thirty-nine at the time), or his seamanship, or the skill he had demonstrated as a hydrographer in his surveys of Newfoundland and the North Atlantic coast of Canada during Britain's Seven Years' War with France, or his interest in astronomy (which he demonstrated to the Royal Society in a paper on a solar eclipse he observed while in North America), or his progressive sociological ideas, or it may have been some combination. Whatever the case, he was a happy choice, because he performed all of his key roles with distinction. He had time on his first voyage to perform only a running survey—that is, to sketch a chart of his discoveries based upon bearings and estimated distance from his vessel's known locations—yet the charts that were published based upon his reports and sketches after his return to England were remarkably accurate. But it is the relatively enlightened approach he took to the indigenous people he met upon his voyages—especially this first one—which singles him out as an unusual figure, somewhat at odds with the temper of his times. He seems to have had no difficulty in dealing with the Pacific peoples he met as human beings, fully equal with any Englishman in terms of their capacities even if rather deprived (as he doubtless saw it) of the benefits of civilisation. This might have been born of a religious or intellectual conviction: it might have arisen under field conditions from his respect for the Polynesians he met, especially Tupaia. Either way, he took care, where he could, to be scrupulously fair in his dealings with Pasifika people, and to see that his crew (who didn't all share his views) maintained the same high standards.

While it is impossible to read motives and ideologies back into the past, you can't help but wonder what Cook would have made of the impact of British colonialism. As the man who put New Zealand 'on the map', he was instrumental in bringing it about (even if it was likely to have been, for him, an unintended consequence): but it's hard to imagine that he would have approved of much of what was subsequently done in the name of the colours that flew on *Endeavour*'s stern.

———

Continued on p. 80

COOK'S CHART OF COOK'S STRAIT, 1770

James Cook's Christmas present to himself in 1769 was that, for the first time in many months, *Endeavour* would sail in charted waters. After a measure of trouble with contrary winds off North Cape, he doubled what he identified as Tasman's Cape Maria van Diemen and began battling the sou'wester down the west coast of the North Island. He was abreast Tasman's Cap Pieter Boerel on 3 January (he discreetly renamed it Cape Egmont) and, giving a wide berth to the unpropitiously named Moordenaars Bay (Murderers Bay), he sailed into what Frans Visscher had followed Tasman in naming Zeehaen's Bight but which he had surmised was the entrance to a strait. Cook had a copy of Visscher's chart with him, with the tantalising gap indicating where the Dutchman strongly suspected a strait to lie. But Cook was the first European to sail through the strait that now bears his name—narrowly missing running aground on The Brothers—and in so doing, he accomplished for Englishmen what Kupe had done for Polynesians: cutting off the North Island from whatever it was that lay to the south. He carried on around Cape Palliser and up the east coast of the North Island to Cape Turnagain, which he'd named after approaching from the north, where he turned yet again and sailed south on a mission to chisel the South Island out from the unknown, too. He was back in the vicinity of Cook Strait a little under two months later, but on neither of these first two visits did he spot Wellington Harbour, or bother to chart the western side of the strait in detail.

A version of this chart of his discoveries was first printed in 1773 in a book by John Hawkesworth, who was commissioned by the Admiralty to ghost-write a compendium of the journals of Cook and four other British explorers. Cook saw the book while he was at anchor in Cape Town on his second voyage: he was appalled at the liberties Hawkesworth had taken. Nevertheless, it was a runaway bestseller and was translated into French and German. This hand-coloured version is from the French edition.

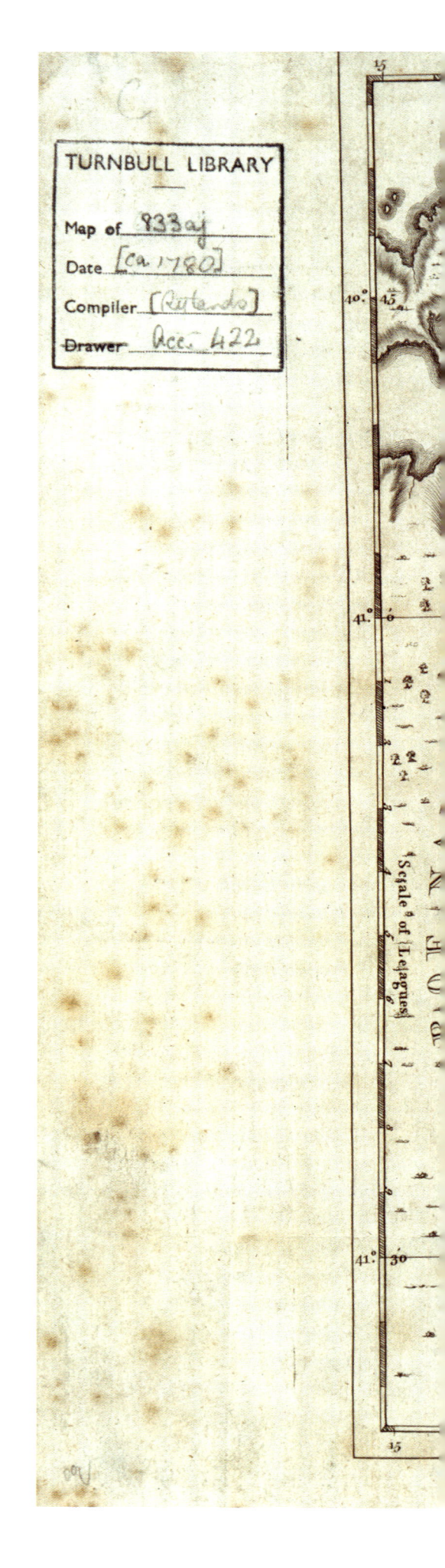

CHART of Cook's Strait in NEW ZEALAND

PICKERSGILL'S MAP OF EAST CAPE, 1769

While James Cook receives pretty much all of the credit for the excellent chartwork that came out of the *Endeavour* voyage, he had at least two other, very capable hydrographers aboard as well, who produced their own suite of charts. One was Robert Molyneux, the *Endeavour*'s navigator (whom Cook wrote he had to keep busy, to keep him away from the bottle) and the other was Richard Pickersgill, a Yorkshireman like Cook, who was similarly described as 'a good officer and astronomer, but liking the grog'.

As the *Endeavour* ran down the coast from the expedition's initial landfall in Poverty Bay (her track is marked by the soundings they took roughly every ten nautical miles), opinion was still divided as to whether this was a continent or an island that they had fallen in with. Pickersgill's chart of the first portion of their circumnavigation reflects this: the title in the cartouche proclaims it 'A Chart of Part of the SO: CONTIT. between Poverty Bay and the Court of the Aldermen discovered by His Majs. BARK ENDEAVOUR', but beneath it Pickersgill (or another) has added in hand: 'NB This Chart was taken before this Country was found to be an island.' Pickersgill notes intensive cultivation and habitation along the northern coast of East Cape, and especially in the vicinity of East Cape itself, where he describes '[m]any Indian Towns and Cultivated Lands here'.

PLENTY BAY

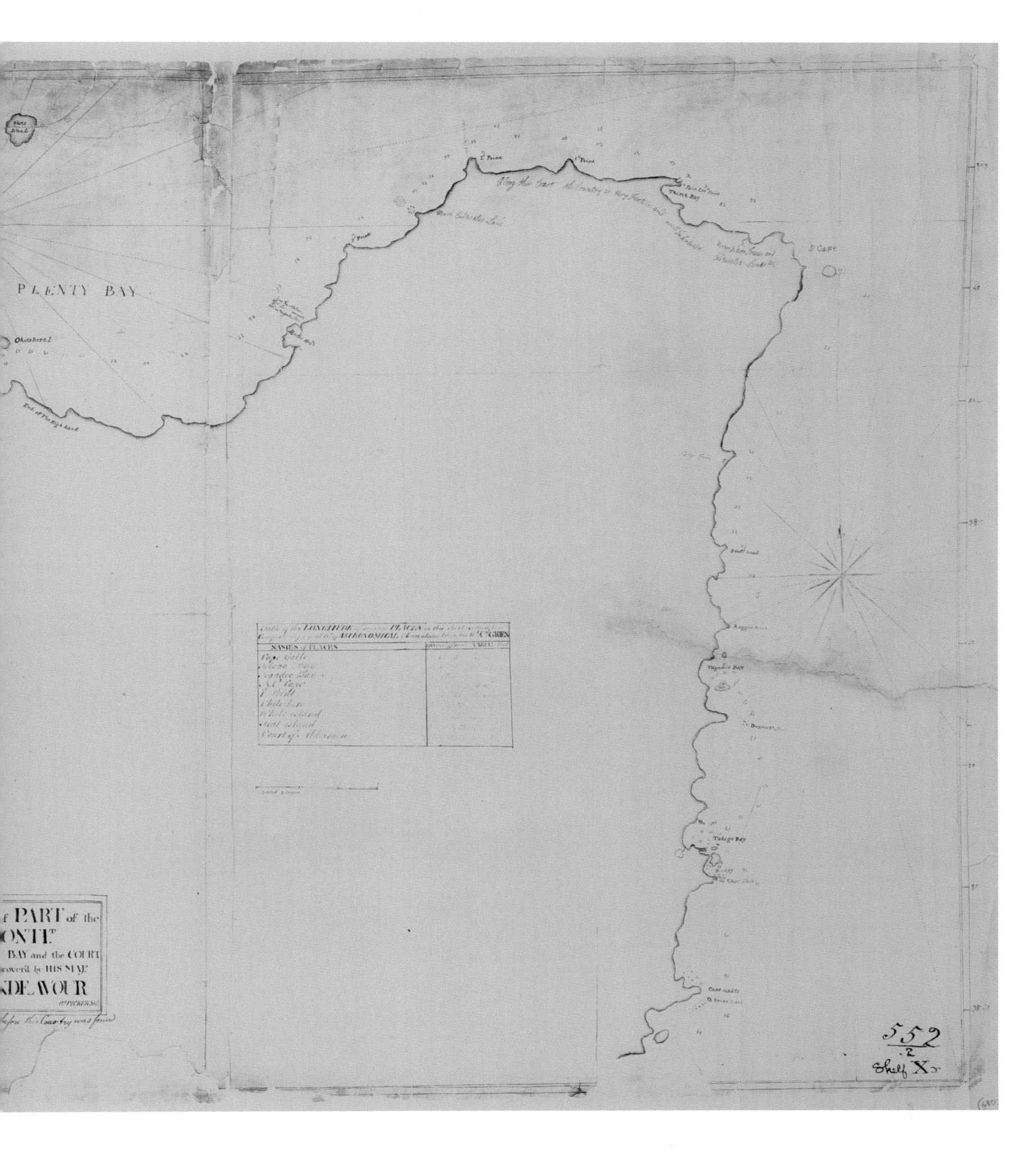

Ohitehoro I.

End of the High land

Sketch of the LONGITUDE ... PLACES on the ...
... ASTRONOMICAL ... taken by M.ᵣ C. GREEN

NAMES of PLACES		
Cape Gable		
Wood Bay		
Tangee Bay		
E. Cape		
Portland		
Hitehero		
White Island		
Flat Island		
Court of Aldermen		

Scale of Degrees

PART of the
... ONTI...
... BAY and the COURT
...overd by HIS MAJ.ᵗʸ
...DEAVOUR
M.ʳ PICKERSG...
...fore this Country was found

E. Point   C. Point
Along this Coast the Country is very Fertile ...
Town Ledi Point
Third Bay
Main Catholic Land
E. Cape

Tugudu Bay

Tatugo Bay

Cape Gable

552
2
Shelf X

882.15aj
1769
Dec 2014

Point Mercury

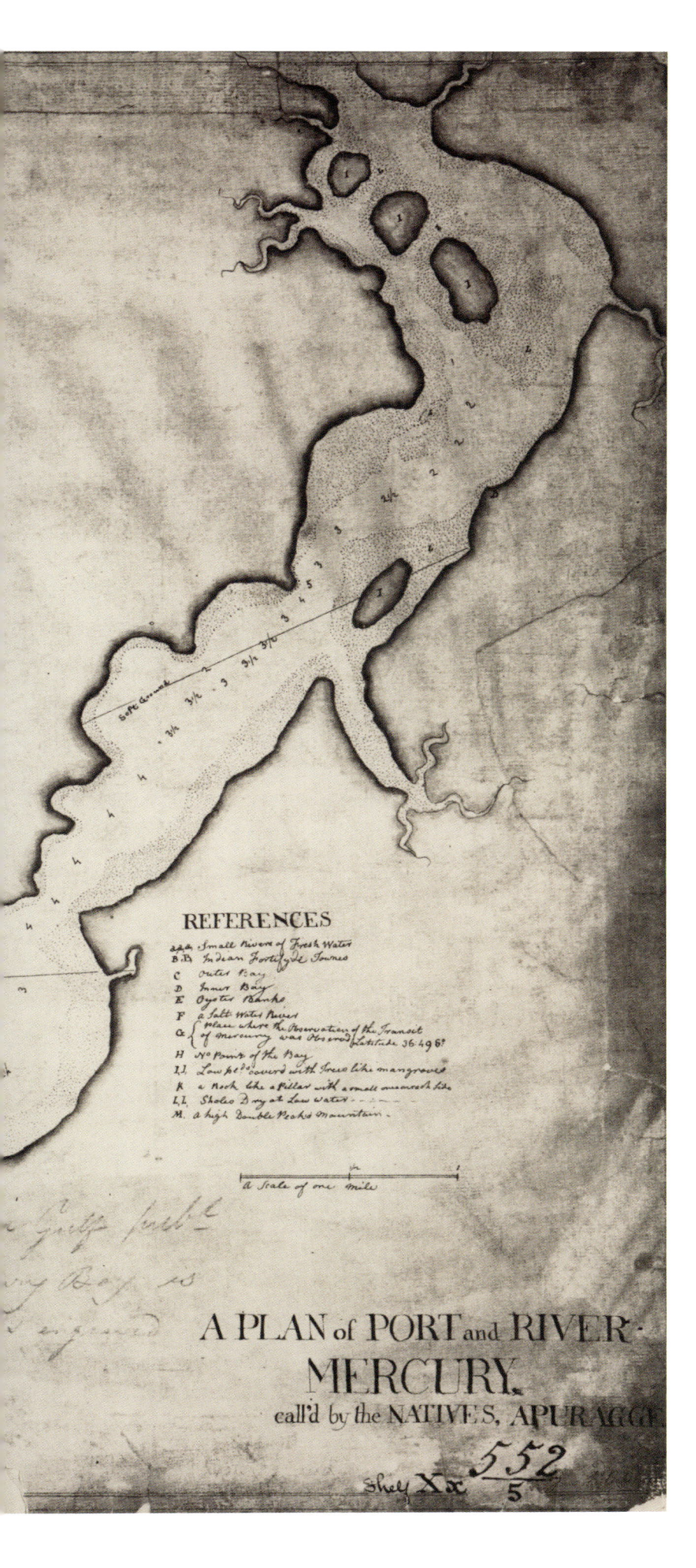

PICKERSGILL'S CHART OF MERCURY BAY, 1769

One of the only genuinely detailed explorations the *Endeavour*'s crew was able to make of the North Island was at Mercury Bay (in the vicinity of present-day Whitianga), where Cook paused in his voyage to make an observation of the transit of Mercury (hence the name he gave it) on 9 November 1769. Pickersgill was able to take one of the ship's boats several miles up the river at the head of the bay, noting the various features—fresh water, oyster banks and 'indian fortified towns' (marked 'B' on two of the islets and a headland). He has also rendered a coastal view of the distinctive rock at the entrance to the bay that Cook named 'Tower Rock'.

While Cook's reputation has suffered somewhat, his legacy is everywhere on modern-day maps. After his first landfall at the mouth of the Tūranganui River, the site of present-day Gisborne, he meandered down, up, over and around the New Zealand coastline, exercising the prerogative of explorers and naming its features—never mind, of course, that they already had names. Cook's nomenclature style seems to have been rather mood-dependent. Because the locality didn't afford him what he wanted—fresh water was the top of his list—Tūranganui became Poverty Bay. Further up the coast, where he saw lots of settlements and economic activity, he labelled the area the Bay of Plenty. Some features he named for events: Cape Kidnappers was where Tupaia's Tahitian companion, Taiata, was snatched by Māori (he was soon returned, after guns were fired as a warning); Cape Turnagain, where he ceased southing at 40° latitude and steered north again; Cape Runaway, where several waka approached the *Endeavour* but ran away when a gun was fired; Mercury Bay, where an observatory was established so as to record the transit of Mercury. Sometimes, he attempted to preserve Māori names, although results varied: how he got 'Tegadoo' out of Anaura, and 'Tolaga' out of Uawa is anyone's guess. Some places were named for crewmen of the *Endeavour*: Young Nick's Head, after Nicholas Young, the cabin boy who won a gallon of rum for reporting the first sight of land from the maintop; Hicks Bay, after Lieutenant Zachary Hicks; Banks' Island (actually a peninsula), after supernumerary Joseph Banks; the Molyneux River, after the *Endeavour*'s sailing master (it is now named the Clutha). Apparently trying to keep with the theme of Tasman's naming of offshore islets, he gave the names of minor court officials to Mayor Island, the Court of Aldermen and the Poor Knights (to go with Tasman's Three Kings). Some features were named rather prosaically for their appearance: Table Cape, because it was flat; Flat Island, because it also was flat; White Island, for the plume of white steam it produced; Doubtless Bay, because it was 'doubtless a bay'; East Cape, because it lay farthest east; North Cape, because it was farthest north; the Bay of Islands, because it was a bay, with islands. The Hen and Chickens were named for the resemblance of the silhouette of the main island to a stretched-out chook, attended by a cluster of smaller islets (the chickens). Other, more significant features were rather sycophantically named after patrons of the voyage: Cape Palliser, for Admiral Hugh Palliser, under whom Cook had served in Newfoundland; Cape Egmont, for the Earl of Egmont, First Lord of the Admiralty; Hawke's Bay, for Edward Hawke, Admiral of the Fleet; Cape Brett, for Admiral Sir Piercy Brett, Senior Naval Lord at the time of Cook's appointment. Every now and then, even a Yorkshireman will allow himself a bit of fun: off the tip of Cape Brett lies the small island he named Piercy Island in honour of the Hole in the Rock, a natural archway that pierces it. And on rare occasions, he waxed poetic: as he sailed along beneath them, he named the serried ranks of the Seaward and Inland Kaikōura ranges 'the Lookers-On', as if the land stood solemnly marking his passage.

―――

Once Cook had rounded Cape Maria van Diemen, he found himself in charted waters. He was carrying a copy of Visscher's chart (see page 60), and he matched features as he sailed south along the North Island's inhospitable coast. He was unable to make landfall until January 1770, when he sailed into Queen Charlotte Sound (which he named for the wife of the reigning monarch, George III). Here, he found a safe anchorage in Ship Cove, which was to become one of his favourite places in the South Pacific. Climbing a hill on Arapawa Island, he was able to make a significant advance on Tasman's exploration, eyeballing the waterway that the Dutchman had only suspected to exist: Cook (not Tasman) Strait. When his ship and crew were patched up and refreshed in early February, he resumed his voyage, somehow managing to miss Wellington Harbour. Sailing up the east coast of what he had now determined to be an island, he recognised Cape Turnagain and turned again, running south this time to try to detach the more southerly land mass from the mythical continent, too. This took two months, during which time the *Endeavour* remained at sea, sometimes close to the land, sometimes standing further off. For this reason, his chart of the southern regions of the South Island isn't his best work. Not only did he mistake Banks Peninsula for an island, but also, because he pushed due south to investigate something that his lieutenant, John Gore, thought to be land, he could only pencil in the tract of South Canterbury that lay to the north of where he fell in again with the coastline. Gales forced him off the Otago coast, too, and when he regained the land in early March, visibility was poor enough for him to imagine that what is now known as Rakiura/Stewart Island was part of the mainland.

By the time he arrived at what he named Admiralty Bay to the east of D'Urville Island (which he didn't recognise as an island) on 27 March 1770, he had circumnavigated Te Wai Pounamu, the South Island, and he knew that if there really was a great south continent, it was well south of South Cape (which is what he named the southernmost extremity of Stewart Island).

By now, the *Endeavour* was creaking at the seams. She badly needed repairs and remedial work if Cook and his crew were to be sure of seeing the English Channel again. So it was decided that rather than risk the fearsome waters off Cape Horn, he would instead sail to Batavia via the uncharted east coast of New Holland. After an eventful seven months—one brush with the Great Barrier Reef north of present-day Cairns nearly saw the vessel lost—the battered little collier made Batavia on 10 October 1770. She was in that pestilential port for only eight days, but it was long enough for disease to take hold and for seven hands to be lost. The ship's surgeon, William Monkhouse, was the first. Next was Taiata, on 9 November, and around two days later (the precise date is doubtful), his relative and mentor Tupaia, that giant of the Pacific, fell victim to a likely combination of scurvy and typhoid fever.

It was a sad end to such an unusual and illustrious life, halfway between the life he had left behind and the future he was so eagerly imagining and anticipating in Europe, and Batavia was an ignominious resting place. But if ever there was a spirit that would find its way home, it was Tupaia's.

―――

Some time on or around 10 December 1769, there had nearly been a close encounter of the Anglo-French kind. As Cook tacked to and fro off the east coast of the Far North, French explorer Jean-François-Marie

DE BLOSSEVILLE'S CHART OF BAY OF ISLANDS, 1824

In 1822, an expedition set off from Toulon in France to explore the Pacific Ocean and add, if it could, to the store of knowledge from Cook's voyages. It was under the command of naval officer Louis Isidore Duperry, and comprised a single corvette by the name of *La Coquille*. The vessel reached New Zealand in April 1824 and anchored in the Bay of Islands (which they understood from Māori to be named Port Manawa), where Duperry's midshipman Jules Poret de Blosseville busied himself surveying the bay and environs; his meticulous work was later published as this chart. When the expedition returned to France, it was celebrated not only for the advances in scientific and geographical knowledge that it had brought about, but also for the fact that not a single member of Duperry's crew had died in its execution. When Jules Dumont d'Urville, who had been Duperry's second-in-command, was seeking to mount an expedition of his own, he asked for de Blosseville to be assigned to him. This was declined. Instead, de Blosseville settled down to write reports about New Zealand and its prospects as a French colony. He came, in time, to be allowed to command an expedition of his own, this time to the Arctic. Soon after charting some of the Greenland coast (which bears his name), he and his ship disappeared, some time in 1833.

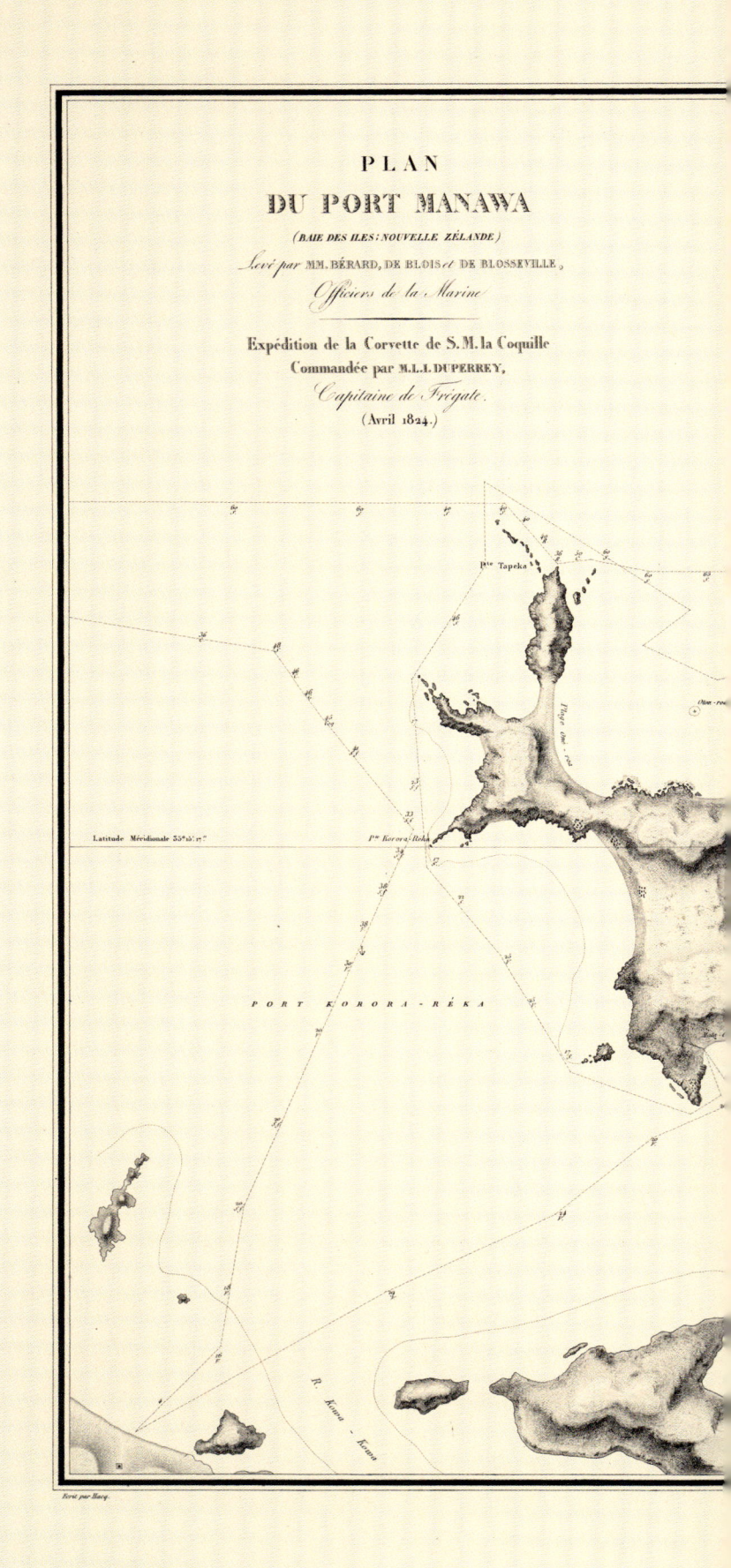

HYD. FR. N.º 702. N.º 20.

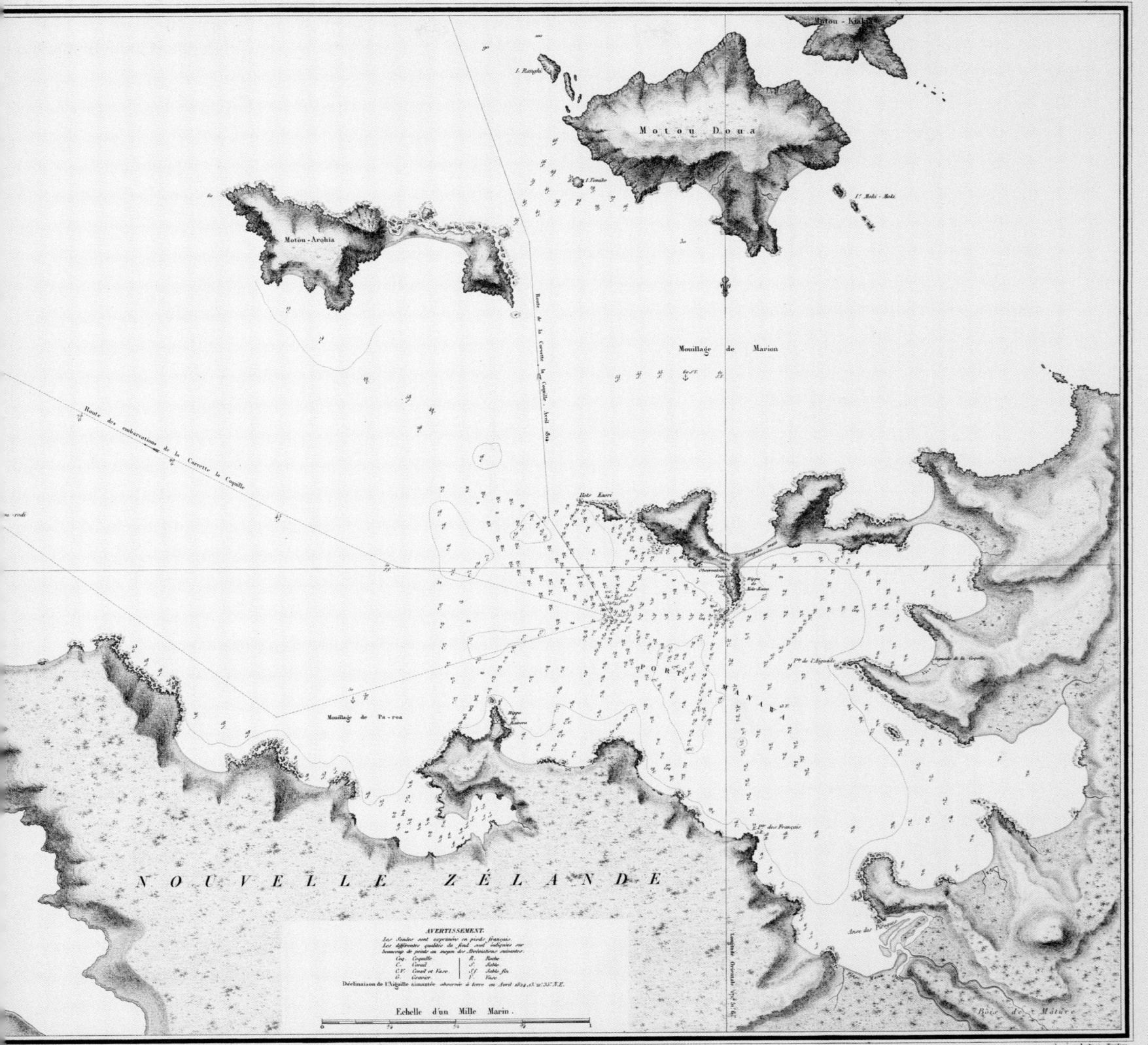

Motou-Kiakiao

Motou Doua

I. Rangki

I. Tonako

I.º Moki-Moki

Motou-Arohia

Route de la Corvette la Coquille Avril 1824

Mouillage de Marion

Route des embarcations de la Corvette la Coquille

Baie Kauri

Observatoire

P.te de l'Aiguade

PORT MANARA

Mouillage de Pa-roa

P.te des Français

NOUVELLE ZÉLANDE

Anse des Pirogues

Baie de Mature

AVERTISSEMENT.
Les Sondes sont exprimées en pieds français.
Les différentes qualités du fond sont indiquées sur
beaucoup de points au moyen des Abréviations suivantes.
Coq. Coquille   R. Roche
C. Corail   S. Sable
C.V. Corail et Vase   Sf. Sable fin
G. Gravier   V. Vase
Déclinaison de l'Aiguille aimantée observée à terre en Avril 1824, 13° 21' 35" N.E.

Echelle d'un Mille Marin.

Gravé par Ambroise Tardieu

PRIX. 1.ᶠ 50.ᶜ

de Surville was approaching from the west, having sought the south from the vicinity of Dutch Indonesia and coming so close to the east coast of Australia that some of his crew claimed to be able to smell land. The two vessels likely missed each other only by a couple of hundred nautical miles and two or three days: the exact synchronicity is hard to determine, as the log books of the *Endeavour* and de Surville's *Saint Jean-Baptiste* were on slightly different time frames: Cook, sailing from the east, was travelling against the direction of the earth's rotation, whereas de Surville was sailing with it, causing the kind of chronological complications that the International Dateline was created to resolve in 1884. Cook's time was kept with each day starting at noon; de Surville's days began at midnight.

De Surville sailed as far south as what he named Lauriston Bay (not knowing that Cook had beaten him to the punch by a matter of a week in naming it Doubtless Bay). He anchored off Tokerau Bay and preached the first Christian service on New Zealand waters there. He enjoyed more or less cordial relations with the tangata whenua, but a series of misunderstandings culminated in the kidnapping of a chief in retaliation for the supposed theft of one of the ship's boats. Poor Ranginui, the captive, died of scurvy just before the *Saint Jean-Baptiste* reached South America. The French commander fared little better, drowning when a ship's boat overturned in heavy surf at Chilca in Peru. De Surville's visit to New Zealand is commemorated by the name of the Surville Cliffs, the northern face of North Cape and the most northerly point of mainland New Zealand.

De Surville was the first of a handful of French explorers who visited shortly after Cook. Marc-Joseph Marion du Fresne arrived in 1772, supposedly on a mission to return Ahutoru, a Tahitian uplifted to France by yet another French explorer of the Pacific, Louis Antoine de Bougainville, to his homeland. Du Fresne's real mission was to seek the great southern land, and he probably thought he'd found it when he raised a lofty, snow-capped peak that he named Pic Mascarin (after his vessel) on 25 March 1772, unaware that this already had a couple of names: Taranaki and Mount Egmont. He sailed north around North Cape and anchored in the Bay of Islands (or Port Marion, as he named it). Relations with the local Māori were cordial at first, but then went drastically wrong, with du Fresne and 26 of his crew killed and cannibalised for reasons that are the subject of enduring debate. Hundreds of Māori died when the French retaliated by sacking a pā. After all the excitement, Jean Roux, who assumed command of the expedition, buried two bottles containing papers officially claiming 'France Australe' for la belle France.

Next in the French procession was Antoine Bruni d'Entrecasteaux, who was searching the South Pacific for news of the fate of Jean-François de La Pérouse, yet another French explorer, who had vanished apparently without trace on his own voyage of discovery in the late 1780s. D'Entrecasteaux arrived in September 1791, found no trace of La Pérouse (who was later found to have been shipwrecked in the Solomon Islands), but lingered long enough to prepare several fine charts of the New Zealand coastline, along with a group of islands he named after Jean-Michel Huon de Kermadec, the master of his consort vessel, *L'Espérance*. It was an ill-fated expedition, as Kermadec died of tuberculosis and d'Entrecasteaux himself died of scurvy in 1793; and when the remnant arrived in Surabaya, it learned that there had been a revolution in France and a republic had been established instead of the monarchy.

Next was Jules Sébastien César Dumont d'Urville, who visited three times: once as an officer aboard a frigate named *La Coquille* under the command of Louis Isidore Duperry, then twice more as her commander, after her name had been changed to *L'Astrolabe* in honour of the vessel belonging to the vanished La Pérouse. In the course of his circumnavigations, d'Urville managed to detach the island that bears his name from the northern tip of the South Island (Cook and Tasman had both supposed it to be part of the mainland: d'Urville discovered the narrow strait that is known as French Pass).

———

Cook himself was back on a second voyage in March 1773, this time in command of a pair of vessels: the *Resolution* (his flagship), and *Adventure* under Tobias Furneaux. Approaching from the west after performing a sweep of the southern Indian Ocean in an effort to verify or disprove the existence of Terra Australis Incognita, he entered Dusky Sound (which he hadn't been game to do on his first voyage). In the month they were anchored there to effect repairs to the ships and to give his crew time to recover from the chilly sojourn in the deep south, he performed his first proper hydrographical survey of any part of New Zealand. In the estimation of P. B. Maling, an expert on New Zealand maps, the chart that resulted really showed what Cook could do. He had the time and the instruments, as this time around he was carrying a version of a chronometer designed by John Harrison, which made it possible to fix longitude for the first time. K1, as this piece of machinery was known, far exceeded everyone's expectations, including Cook's.

He was back twice more on this, his second voyage, in between sweeps of the central and southern Pacific Ocean, basing himself each time at Ship Cove. Early on, the *Resolution* lost track of the *Adventure*: she spent some time alone in Queen Charlotte Sound in November and December 1773, during which time Peter Fannin, her master, explored and charted much of the head of Dusky Sound and the Tory Channel, which Cook had suspected to exist but had not proved. The *Adventure* had an adventure on 17 December, when a party sent ashore to cut grass did not return. Upon enquiry, Furneaux discovered they had been ambushed and cannibalised. After this incident, he needed little encouragement to sail for home.

By the time Cook had completed his second voyage, he had proved to his own satisfaction that if any land did exist in the deep south, it was too cold and inhospitable to be doing with. He'd also criss-crossed the Pacific in a way that left very little possibility that there might be any major land masses left for Europeans to discover. It was a monumental contribution to European geographical knowledge, and one that would never be surpassed.

Cook was back yet again, on his third, final and fatal voyage in February 1777. He based himself at Ship Cove yet again, where he found the local Māori had a tendency to fail to meet his eye and to shoot nervous glances at the *Resolution*'s ordnance. Both codes of justice, Māori and European alike, indicated some action should be taken in retribution for the massacre of the *Adventure*'s boat crew. Everyone—Māori and Pākehā—watched him to see what form his utu would take. To universal surprise, mixed with indignation and relief (depending upon whose side you were on), he took no action at all. Many historians have taken this as a certain sign that Cook's

Continued on p. 94

DE SURVILLE'S CHART OF LAURISTON BAY, 1769

By the time his expedition sighted the Northland coast in the vicinity of Hokianga on 12 December 1769, many in Jean-François-Marie de Surville's crew were suffering from scurvy, a deficiency of vitamin C. They'd had a rough time in the Solomon Islands, where hostile natives had intervened whenever they attempted to land for food and fresh water. De Surville was carrying charts from Tasman's voyage, and judged that his best chance of resupplying was to head to the vaguely known New Zealand. As they battled a gale off North Cape, they narrowly missed crossing tracks with James Cook, who was battling the same gale a couple of hundred nautical miles away. When finally they spotted a commodious anchorage, it was in what Cook had already named Doubtless Bay. De Surville named it Lauriston Bay, and anchored at a spot he named Chevalier Bay on 17 December. In the two weeks they were there, he and his crew made a full recovery from the effects of scurvy (thanks to the greens that he was able to trade with Ngāti Kahu), to celebrate the first Christian service on New Zealand waters (which his ship's chaplain, Paul-Antoine Léonard de Villefeix, is believed to have given on Christmas Day), to make this elegant chart, and to thoroughly alienate the locals. A misunderstanding over the status of the ship's yawl, which drifted ashore in a storm, saw de Surville kidnap the local chief, Ranginui, and bear him off when they continued their onward journey. The chief died aboard the *Saint Jean-Baptiste* shortly before they reached the coast of Chile, where de Surville himself lost his life in the surf while trying to land.

This version of his chart was published in English on the orders of Alexander Dalrymple, as the footer states, in 1781. This, a few sketches and descriptions of Māori life and customs, and a sole place name—the Surville Cliffs, at the North Island's northernmost extremity—were the Frenchman's only legacy.

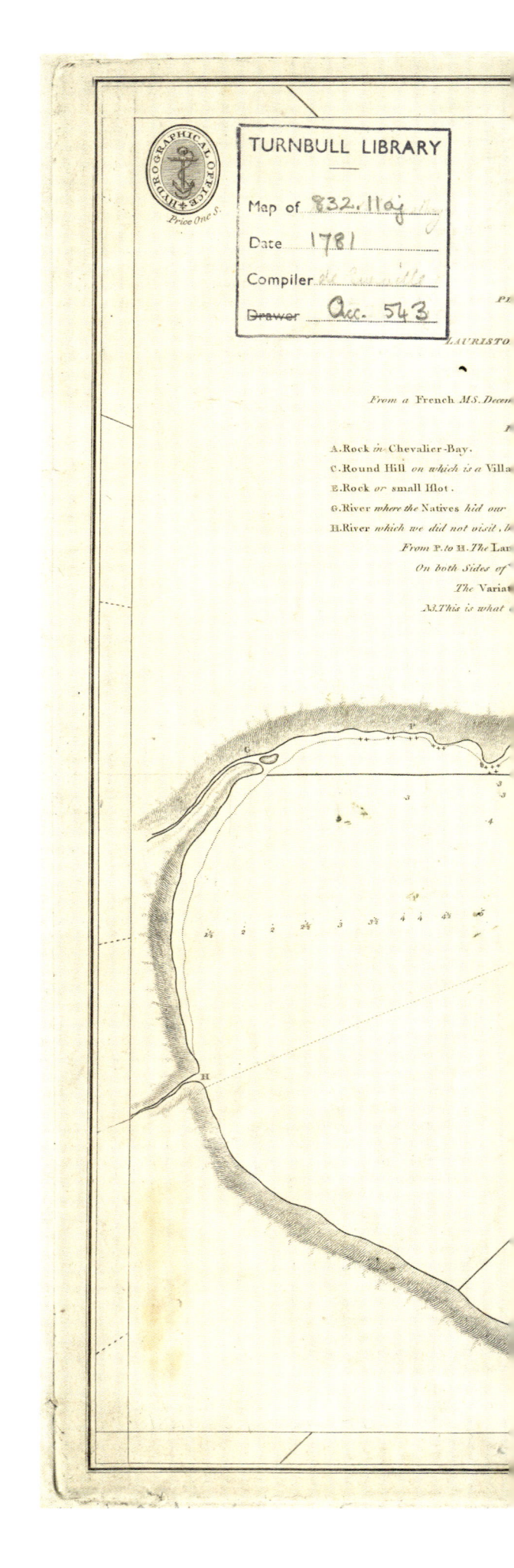

BAY

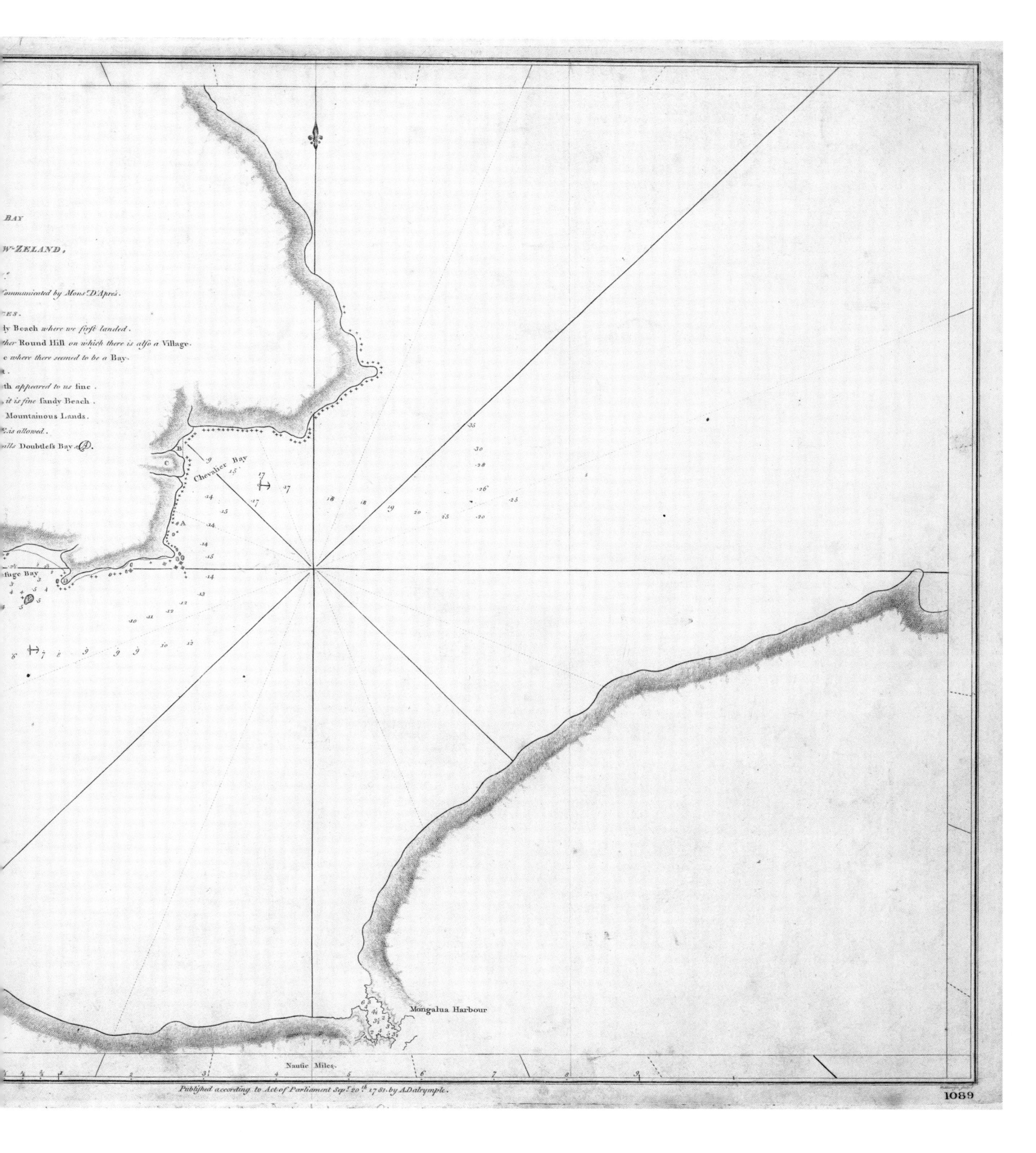

Wn ZELAND,

Communicated by Monsr D'Apres.

ly Beach where we first landed.
ther Round Hill on which there is also a Village.
where there seemed to be a Bay.
th appeared to us fine.
, it is fine sandy Beach.
Mountainous Lands.
is allowed.
alls Doubtless Bay. A.

Chevalier Bay

fuge Bay

Mongalua Harbour

Nautic Miles.

Published according to Act of Parliament Sepr. 20th 1781. by A. Dalrymple.

1089

COOK'S CHART OF DUSKY SOUND, 1773

Cook was loath to attempt to enter Dusky Sound on his first voyage in the *Endeavour* in 1770, despite the urgings of Joseph Banks, who was desperate to do some botanising. As the prevailing wind was from the southwest and the entrance was narrow, Cook feared he would not be able to sail out again. But when he visited again in March 1773 on his second voyage to the Pacific, he took the chance. Once inside the magnificent, sheltered waterway, he despatched boats to investigate the chances of anchoring. Richard Pickersgill, who had offered a vote of confidence in Cook by electing to ship with him again on this, his second voyage, took one of the boats to the southern end of the inlet, where he found a snug anchorage, protected from winds from every direction, in the lee of an islet. Cook was pleased— and named Pickersgill Harbour after his lieutenant. The ship secured, Cook then set out to perform a survey of the sound (actually a fiord), and whereas his other work on the hydrography of New Zealand had been done on the hoof (a running survey), he was able to pull out all stops during the month and a half he was anchored in Dusky. This wonderful chart—little different from charts made with better technology in far more recent times— was the result.

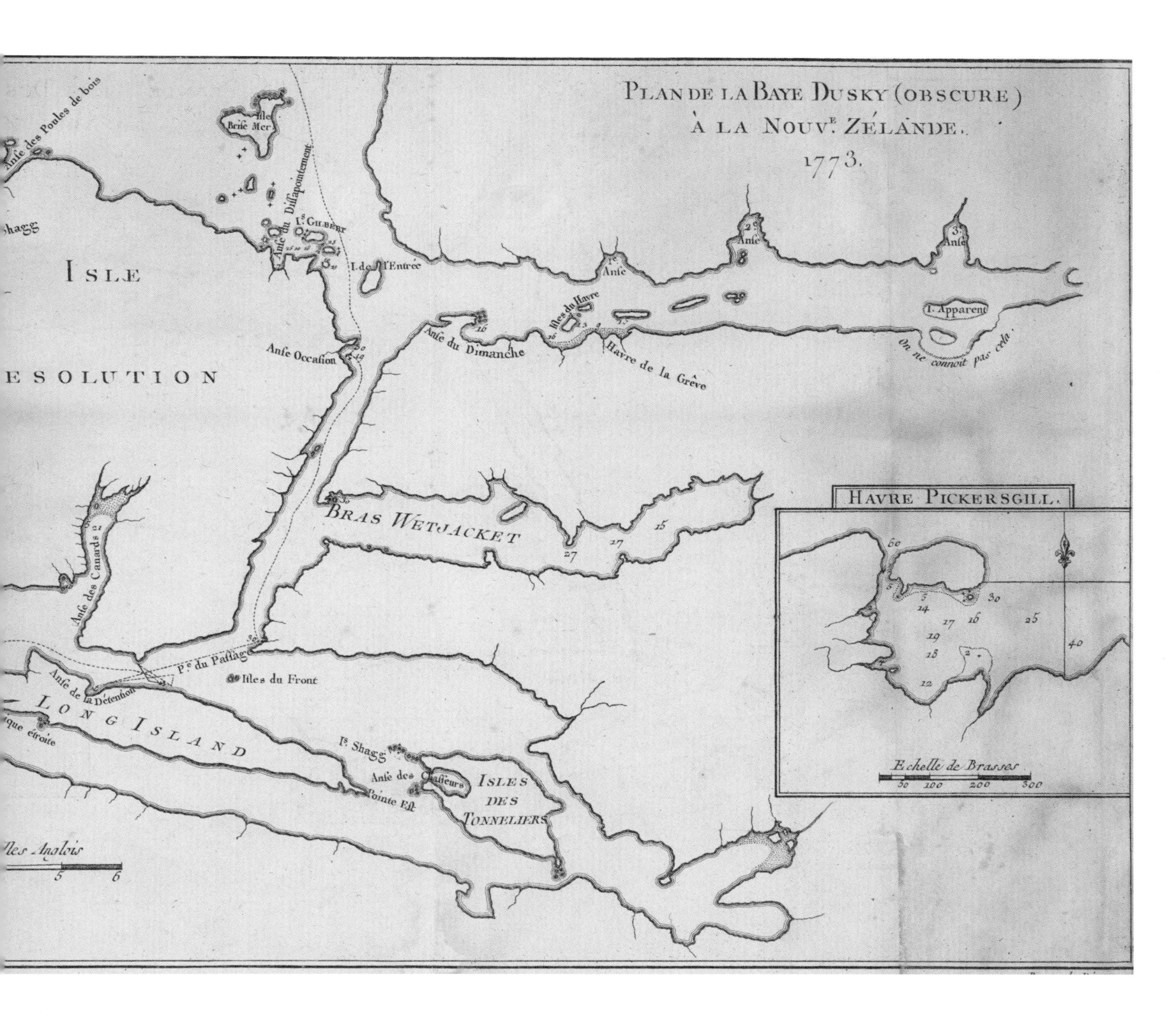

PLAN DE LA BAYE DUSKY (OBSCURE)
À LA NOUVᴱ ZÉLANDE.
1773.

HAVRE PICKERSGILL.

Echelle de Brasses
50 100 200 300

VUES DES ILES KERMADEC, tirées des Cahiers de l'Ingr. Hydrogr. Beautemps-Beaupré

L'Ile Raoul à 4ʰ 55ᵐ

L'Ile Raoul à 3ʰ 40ᵐ

L'Ile Raoul à 1ʰ 42ᵐ

L'Ile Raoul à Midi

L'Ile Raoul à 7ʰ 33ᵐ instant des Observations

1ʳᵉ Vue de l'Ile Raoul le 1ᵉʳ Mars au matin

L'Ile Macaulay le 16 à Midi

Les Iles Curtis et Macaulay à 8ʰ 34ᵐ

Les Iles Curtis et Macaulay à 6ʰ 34ᵐ le milieu de l'Ile Curtis restant à l'O.

1ʳᵉ Vue des Iles Curtis et Macaulay le 16 Mars à 3ʰ 52ᵐ du matin

Le Rocher l'Espérance restant à l'O. ¼ Mille de distance.

Le Rocher l'Espérance restant au N. à ¼ Mille de distance

Vue du Rocher l'Espérance restant au N. 3¼ E. à 6ʰ 23ᵐ

Le 15 Mars à 4ʰ 33ᵐ instant des Observ. le Rocher l'Espérance fut découvert et relevé du haut des Mâts au N. 19° 24' E. du Monde à 10 M. de distance

CARTE DES ILES KERMADEC,

Situées dans le Grand Océan Austral, entre la Nᴸᴸᵉ Zéelande et les Iles des Amis,
Levée et Dressée
dans le Voyage du Contre-Amiral
BRUNY-DENTRECASTEAUX
Par C.F. Beautemps-Beaupré
Ingénieur-Hydrographe
en 1793 (An 1ᵉʳ)

Rocher l'Espérance

PLAN PARTICULIER de L'ILE RAOUL

Milles Marins

Gravé par E. Collin.

D'ENTRECASTEAUX'S MAP OF THE KERMADEC ISLANDS, 1793

It was common for hydrographers to supplement charts—the two-dimensional representation of land masses and waterways from a bird's-eye perspective—with coastal views, just as architects will supply elevations along with floor plans. These beautiful little sketches of the scattered islands and islets of New Zealand's Kermadec group were made by Charles-François Beautemps-Beaupré, the hydrographer-engineer attached to the expedition of Rear-Admiral Antoine Bruni d'Entrecasteaux, which passed the islands en route from Australia to Tonga in February 1793. D'Entrecasteaux had been charged with determining the fate of Jean-François de La Pérouse, who had disappeared in the South Pacific in 1788. He named the Kermadecs after Jean-Michel Huon de Kermadec, the master of his consort vessel, *L'Espérance* (which gave its own name to L'Espérance Rock in the south of the group). The Kermadec Islands belong to New Zealand, but are not part of an administrative district, being designated an 'Area Outside Territorial Authority'. A permanent meteorological and scientific base is maintained on Raoul Island, the largest of the group.

Following page
LOTTIN'S MAP OF NORTHLAND, 1826

Having already visited New Zealand as an officer aboard *La Coquille* under Capitaine Louis Isidore Duperry, Jules Dumont d'Urville was his own boss when he next arrived in the same vessel at the end of 1826, having changed her name to *L'Astrolabe* in honour of the ship of the great (and presumed late) Jean-François de La Pérouse. The results of the survey of the northern part of the North Island that he and his officers (especially Lieutenant Victor Lottin) conducted were published upon his return in the shape of fourteen rather beautiful charts, of which this is one. As it was a coastwise exploration, little interior detail is shown and is, as stated in the note under the title, supplied by the accounts of missionaries. Of the landward features, the most significant (as it would be to many Europeans after d'Urville) is the vicinity of Shouki-Anga (the Hokianga), described as '*populeux et riche en bois de construction*'—'populous and rich in construction timbers'.

D'Urville returned to New Zealand for another three-month sojourn in 1840, and is commemorated in the name of D'Urville Island (and French Pass, which he found divided it from the mainland) at the top of the South Island.

VOYAGE DE L'ASTROLABE.

CARTE
DE LA PARTIE SEPTENTRIONALE
DE LA NOUVELLE ZÉLANDE
par M.M. DURVILLE et LOTTIN.
1831.

N.B. Pour le littoral, cette Carte est dressée d'après l'exploration de l'Astrolabe, et pour l'intérieur d'après les mesures conjecturales déduites des relations des Missionnaires.

Gravé par Laurent.

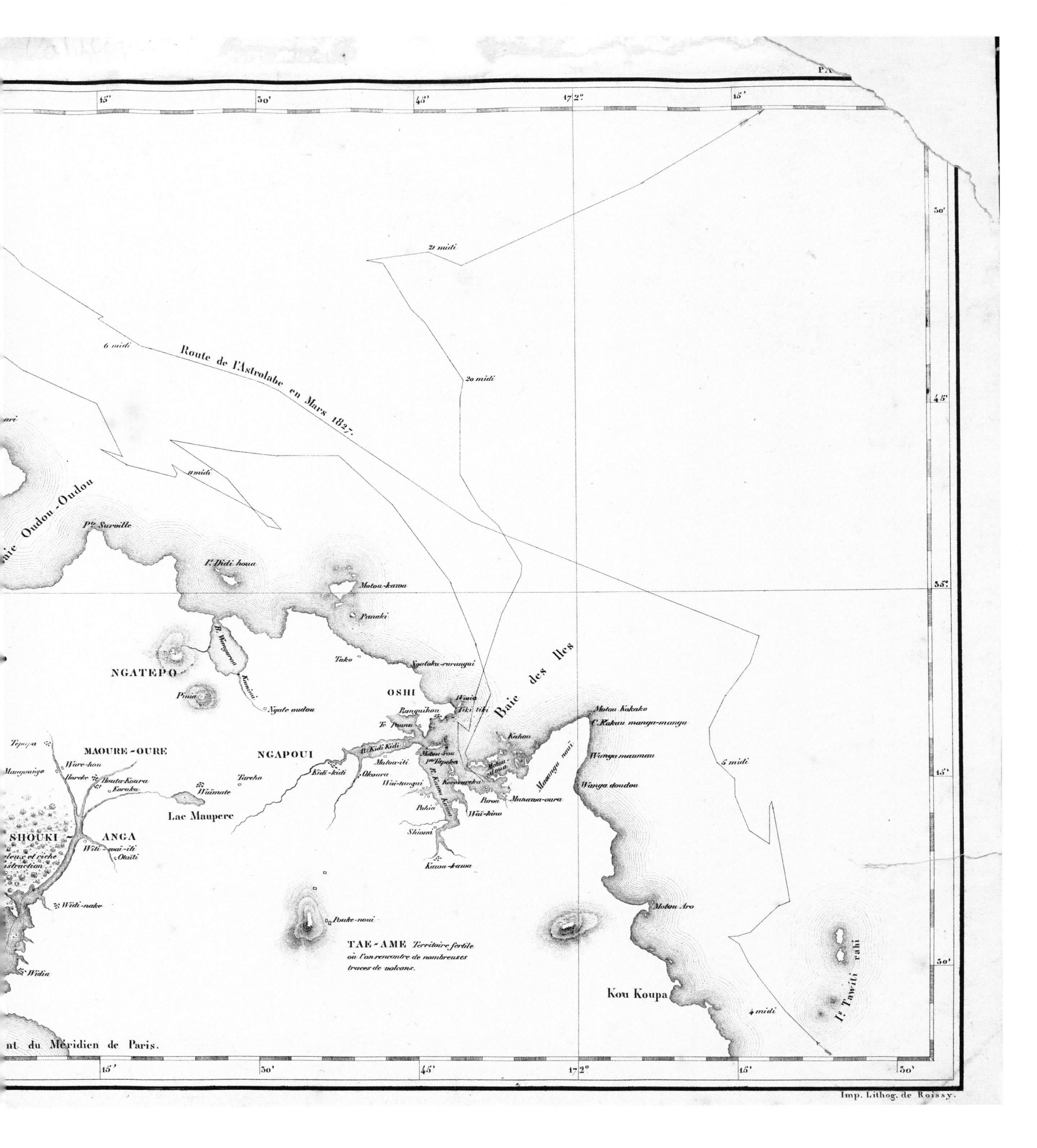

Route de l'Astrolabe en Mars 1827.

Baie Oudou-Oudou
Pte Surville
I. Didi houu
Motou-kawa
B. Wangaroa
Panaki
NGATEPO
Kawini
Tako
Ngatoka-rarangui
Pina
OSHI
Waia
Ngate oudou
Ranguihou
Tiki tiki
Baie des Iles
Tepupa
F. Toawa
Motou Kakako
MAOURE-OURE
NGAPOUI
Kahou
C. Rakau manga-manga
Ware-hou
R. Kidi-Kidi
Motou Sou
Mangounga
Hareke
Tareha
Motou-iti
I. Papoka
Motou
Wanga maumau
Houta-Koara
Kareka
Kidi-kidi
Okoura
R. Kawa Kawa Korovareka
Koua
Masunga noui
Waïmate
Wai-tangui
Paroa
Manawa-oura
Wanga doudou
Lac Maupere
Pahia
Waï-kino
5 midi
SHOUKI- ANGA
Wili-wai-iti
Shioui
Otaïti
Kawa-kawa
Widi-nake
Pouke-noui
Motou Aro
TAE-AME Territoire fertile
où l'on rencontre de nombreuses
traces de volcans.
Widia
I. Tawiti rahi
Kou Koupa
4 midi

nt du Méridien de Paris.

Imp. Lithog. de Roissy.

previously sure instinct for intercultural relations was suffering, and that this was indicative of a deeper loss of judgement. He had travelled many thousands of miles in the difficult shipboard conditions of the eighteenth century. He had contracted diseases and endured the food and the constant, nagging strain of risking his and others' lives pushing ever further into the unknown. Little wonder he was burnt out. When he departed Queen Charlotte Sound and Aotearoa slipped below the horizon for the last time on 27 February 1778, Cook had seen his last of a place he had come to know and love.

A year later, on 14 February 1779, soon after he and the crews of his vessels *Resolution* and *Discovery* had come to anchor in Kealakekua Bay on the island of Hawai'i, he was killed in a brawl that broke out onshore and which also claimed the lives of four of his marines and seventeen Hawaiians. Speculation on what led to his death has been constant since the news of it reached England in January 1780. We'll never know. But believe what you like about the impact of colonialism, it is hard to read accounts of Cook's voyages of discovery—the greatest in European history—without feeling profound admiration. And while it is poignant that he never made it back to his wife and children in England, it seems somehow fitting that he died on a Pacific beach, a symbolic, liminal zone like the paepae of a marae, where challenges are issued, welcomes are negotiated, and the tangata whenua and strangers lock eyes, trying to read one another's intentions. That is where James Cook distinguished himself, where he spent the best years of his life, standing on the brink of one of the tipping points of history.

FOUR | THOROUGHLY COOKED

Following page
DE LA ROCHETTE CHART OF THE PACIFIC, 1817
When James Cook was appointed to lead his expedition in search of the great southern land in the late 1760s, it raised a few bushy eyebrows in Whitehall. The honour, it was widely felt, should have gone to Alexander Dalrymple, the chief hydrographer of the British East India Company and, despite his cantankerous nature, a darling of the Admiralty and Royal Society alike. It's likely that Dalrymple himself, or his supporters, therefore mounted a concerted campaign to diminish the scale of Cook's achievements. This chart—the first Admiralty chart to feature Cook's work—reflects that effort.

It was Dalrymple who had postulated that the Dauphin map (see pp. 44–46) depicted a coastline discovered by the Portuguese to the south of New Guinea. This chart, prepared by French-born draughtsman Louis Stanislas d'Arcy Delarochette, who worked for the British Royal Geographer William Faden, goes a step further, naming Cook's East Cape 'Cabo Fermoso' ('lovely cape' in Portuguese: a name that the strange protrusion from the Australia-like coast of Jave la Grande has on certain maps), and labelling the eastern reach of Cook Strait with the notation 'Gulf of the Portuguese, 1550'. The country's label reads: 'New Zeeland: Discovered and named by Tasman, 1642, but whose eastern coast was known to the Portuguese about the year 1550.' Faden effectively ran a private cartography business, but was induced to sell his sea-chart plates to the British Admiralty, the Chart Committee of which printed the charts (including this one) without serious critical examination. Thus, the unsubstantiated claim that the Portuguese had discovered New Zealand before Tasman enjoyed a brief run in the official sun.

A CHART OF THE
INDIAN OCEAN
Improved from THE CHART
OF M. D'APRES DE MANNEVILLETTE;
with the Addition of
A PART OF THE PACIFIC OCEAN,
as well as of THE ORIGINAL TRACKS
of the Principal Discoverers, or other Navigators
to India and China;
and in which it has been attempted to give
A CHRONOLOGICAL INDICATION
of the Successive Discoveries,
BY L.S. DE LA ROCHETTE.
LONDON.
Published by W. FADEN, Geographer to THE KING
and to H.R.H. the PRINCE OF WALES.
June 4th 1803.

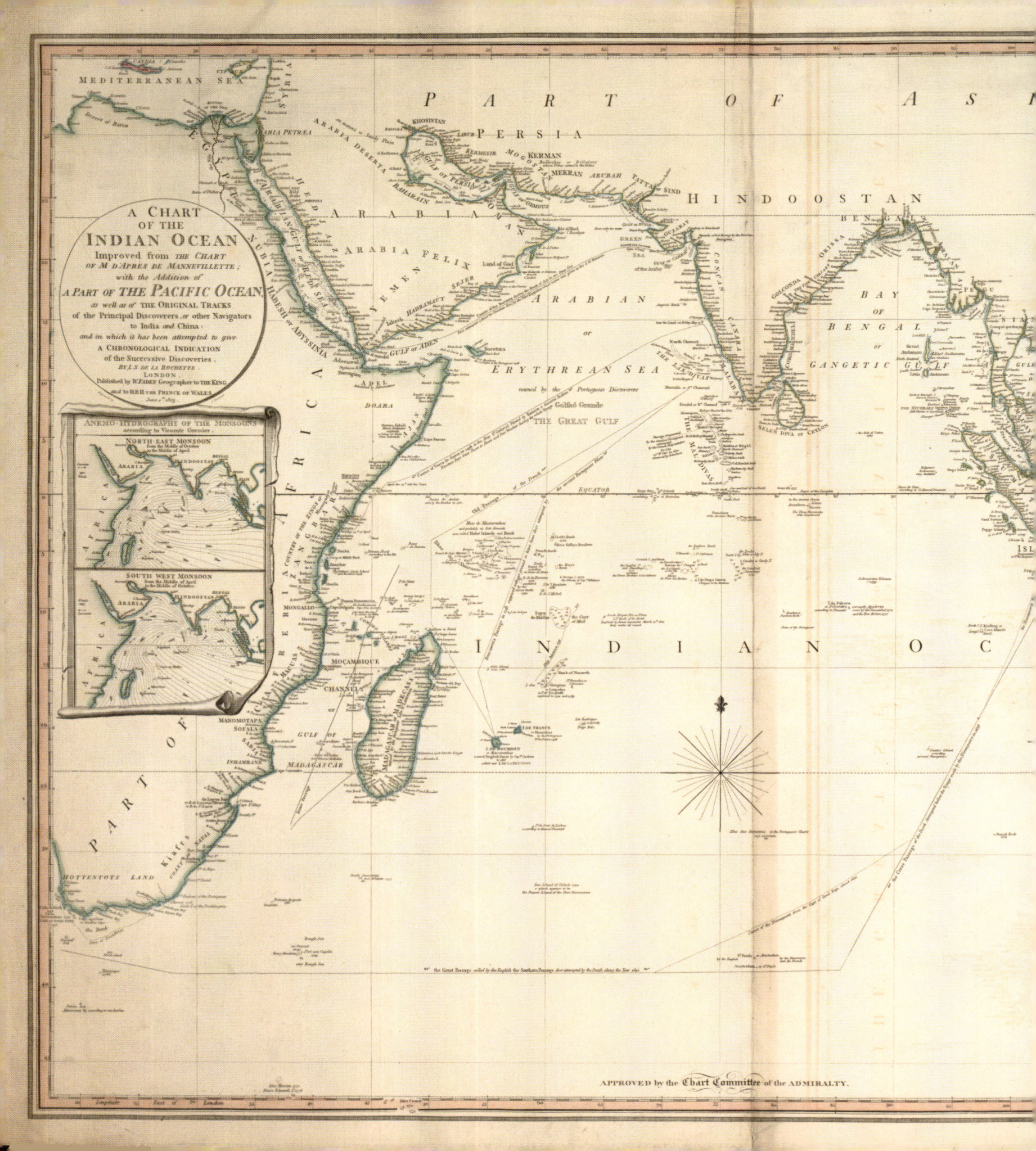

ANEMO-HYDROGRAPHY OF THE MONSOONS
according to Vicomte Grenier.

NORTH EAST MONSOON
from the Middle of October
to the Middle of April

SOUTH WEST MONSOON
from the Middle of April
to the Middle of October

APPROVED by the Chart Committee of the ADMIRALTY.

CHINA
COREA
NIPON
ISLES OF JAPAN
ISLES OF LEKEYO
FORMOSA
EASTERN SEA
GULF OF TONG-KIN
CHINESE SEA
PHILIPPIN ISLANDS
LUCON
SOOLOO SEA
CELEBEAN SEA
BORNEO
CELEBES
MOLUCCA
GILOLO
SUNDA SEA
JAVA
BANDA SEA
LAND OF THE PAPOOS
NEW GUINEA
LOUISIADE
ISLES OF SOLOMON
ISLAS MARIANAS or DE LAS VELAS
LADRONES ISLANDS
NORTHERN POLYNESIA
CAROLINE
NEW PHILIPPINE ISLANDS
EQUATOR
LANTCHIDOL SEA of Linschoten
CARPENTER'S BAY
CARPENTARIA
SOUTH LAND of the Dutch Discoverers or
AUSTRALIA INCOGNITA and TERRA AUSTRALIS
of the Ancient Cosmographers
named afterwards
NEW HOLLAND
BEACH
LUCACH
MALETUR
Dinnings Land
NEW SOUTH WALES
EXPLORED and NAMED
BY COOK 1770
Discovered by COOK 1770
VANDIEMENT LAND
Tasman's Course 1642
TERRA AUSTRAL DEL ESPIRITU SANTO
NEW HEBRIDES
NEW CALEDONIA
WESTERN POLYNESIA
NAVIGATORS ARCHIPELAGO
FRIENDLY ISLES
NEW ZEELAND
EAHEI NOMAUWE
TAVAI POENAMMOO
THE GREAT SEA or PACIFIC OCEAN

ZATTA CHART OF THE PACIFIC, 1775

When the news of Cook's discoveries in the South Pacific burst upon the world, there were plenty who were quick to capitalise on it. One of these was the Venetian cartographer Antonio Zatta, whose attractive *Atlante Novissimo* (New Atlas) was published between 1775 and 1784 and featured two plates depicting New Zealand. The first was a relatively accurate reproduction of Cook's famous chart. The second was a smaller-scale map of the Nuovo Scoperte ('new discoveries') in the South Pacific more generally, showing the path Cook sailed on his first voyage but rather hilariously having the *Endeavour* shoot the gap between the Canterbury coast and what Cook had mistakenly identified as an island (Banks Peninsula).

Nonetheless, when Zatta's view of the South Pacific is compared with Ortelius' (see p. 54), the leap forward in European knowledge is plain to see.

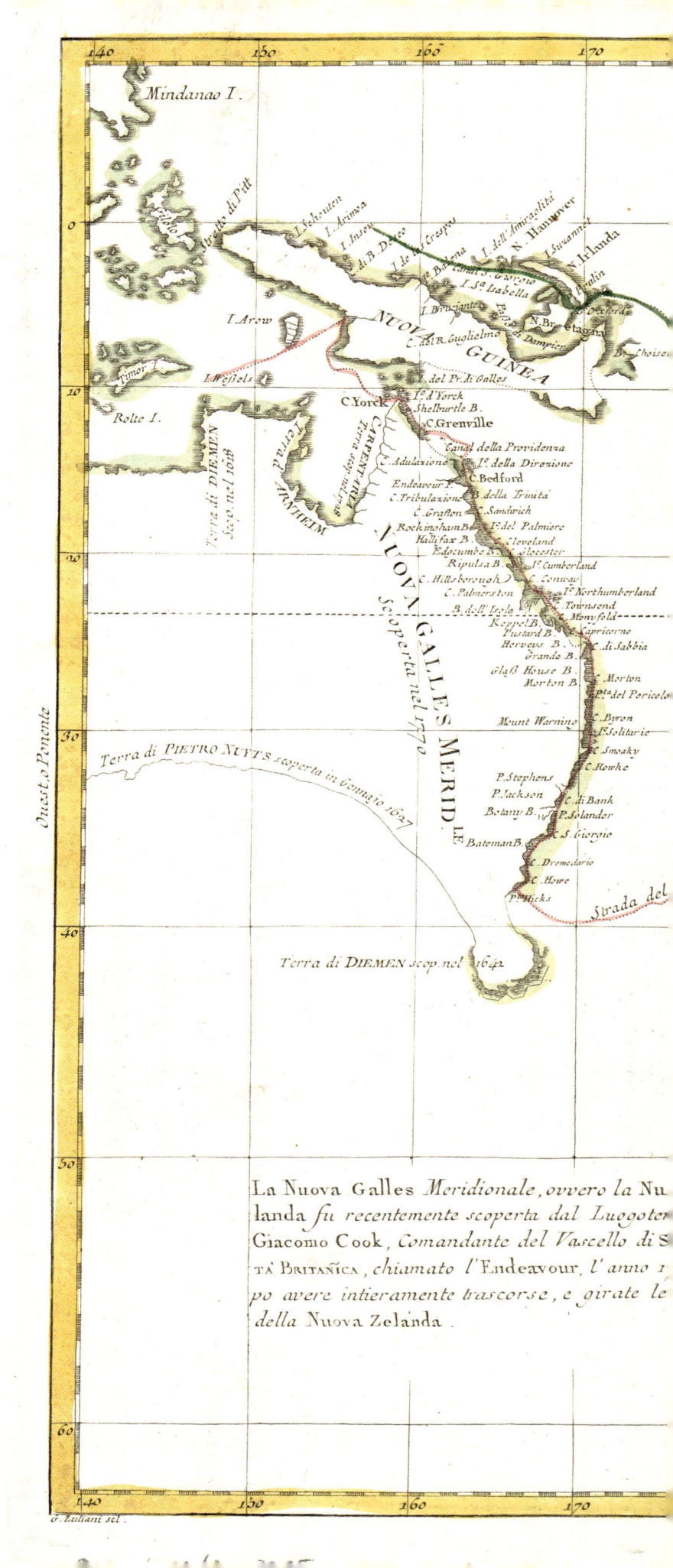

Nord, o Tramontana

Linea Equinoziale

LES MARQUISES DE MENDOZE

I. di Byron
Strada del Byron, e Mouats
Strada del Wallis
Strada del Carteret

I. Jesus
I. S. Bernardo
I. la Dominique   I. S. Pierre
I. Magdeleine
I. Christine

I.ͣ del Pericolo
I. Solitaria
ola o Terra dello Spirito Sᵗᵒ di Quiros
Pͤ dell'Averdy
I. l'Enfant perdu
Iˢ del Contratempo
Strada del Byron, e Mouats
Gran Cycladi
I. del Horn
I. de la Pentecote
I.ͤ del Principe Guglielmo
I. del Pr. di Galles
Iˢ del Re Giorgio
I. S. Paul
I. di Cocos
I. dei Traditori
Bassi fondi di Hoornkerk
I. Maurua
I. Scilly   I. Tubai   I. Huaheine
I. Howe   I. Ulietea   Otaha I.   I. Tethuya
SOCIETÀ
I. della Speranza
I. Taposamoa   I. Emeo   I. Taiti   Osnaburg   de la Chaine   l'Ucello   les a grouppes
ISOLE DELLA
I. Pr. Roy.   l'Arco
Cumberland   la Reine Charlotte I.
I. Anamoeha
I. Oheteroa
I. Glocester   I. Gloucester   I. Egmont   la Pentecote
Strada del Wallis
Iˢ Pylstart   I. Amsterdam

Tropico del Capricorno
Pitcairn I.
Strada del Carteret

Strada del Cook
MARE DEL SUD
Strada del Cook

I. dei 3 Re   C. Nord ov. Tasman
C. Maria di Diemen   I. di Sable
M.ᵉ del Comello   B. dell'Isole
Falsa Baja   C. Brett
C. de la Bremine
Gannet   C. Colvil
Zumet   B. di Mercurio
C.ᵖ Egmont   B. dell'Abbondanza
STRETO   Kidnap Nomare   B. della Pouerta
C. Farewel   B. di Hawke
C. del Mal Vente   C. del Ritorno
OVA   B.ͣ Amagadala   C. Pallider
B.ͣ Carlotta   C. Campel
P.ᵗᵒ delle Cascate   B. de Banck
P.ᵗᵒ Dubbioso   Tavai Poenammoo I.
C. Ouest   C. di Saunder
di Solander   ZELANDA   DI COOK
C. Sud   le Trappes

MARE DEL SUD

NUOVE SCOPERTE
Fatte nel 1765. 67. e 69 nel
MARE DEL SUD

VENEZIA 1776
Presso Antonio Zatta
Con Privilegio dell'Ecc.ᵐᵒ Senato.

Sud, o Mezzodi
G. V. Pasquali scri.

Many Islands about this Coast & perhaps

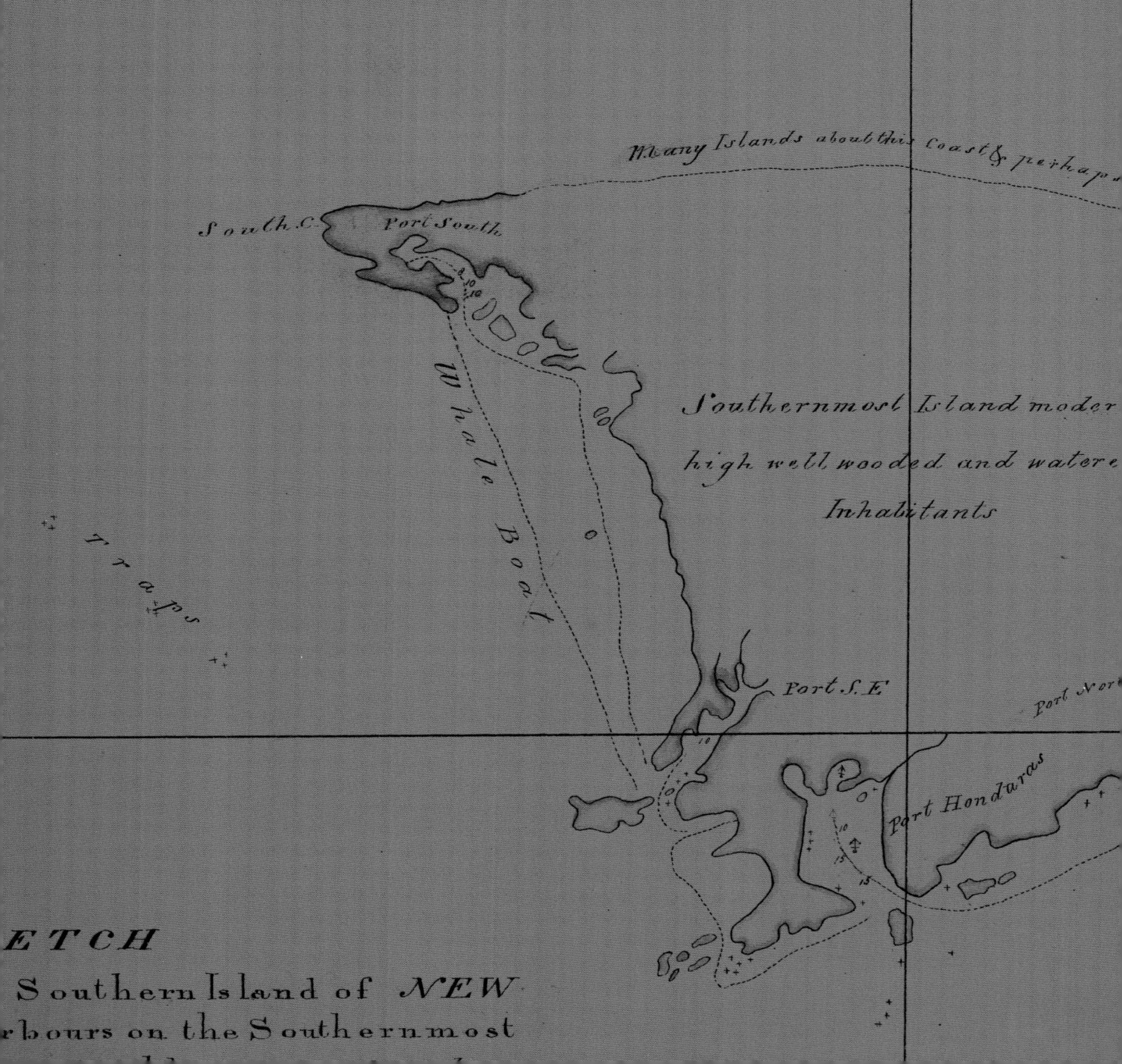

South C. Port South

Whale Boat

Southernmost Island moder
high well wooded and watere
Inhabitants

Traps

Port S.E.

Port Nor

Port Honduras

ETCH

Southern Island of NEW
rbours on the Southernmost

FIVE

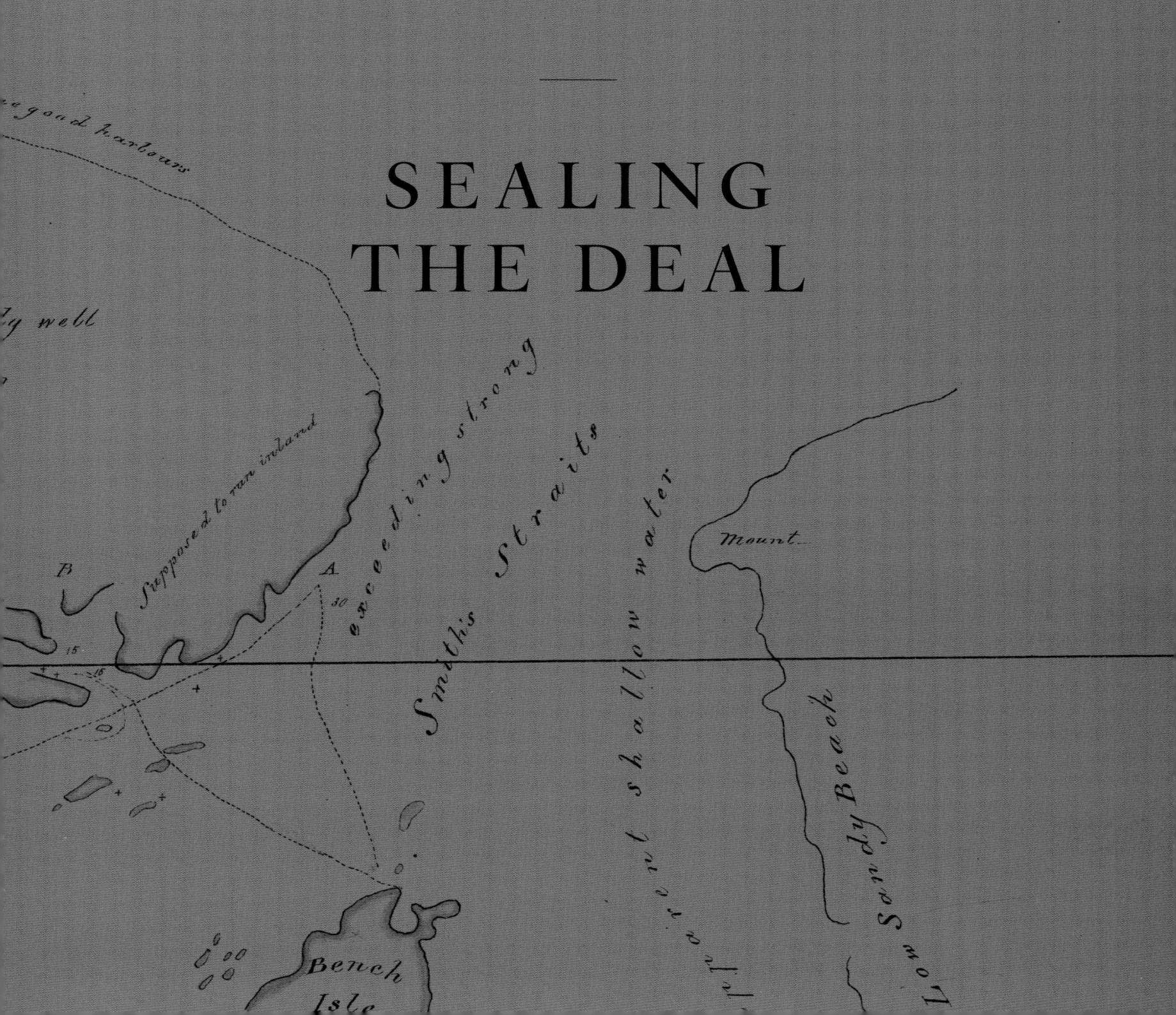

—

SEALING
THE DEAL

Cook was the first of many birds of passage to light on the New Zealand shore. Once the place was on the map, the rest soon followed, and their mission was exploitation rather than exploration. Nevertheless, it was in the pursuit of riches—in the form of seals, whales, timber and flax—that much of the detail of the coastline was filled in.

Subsequent to Cook, other voyages of discovery inked in the islands to the south of New Zealand. The Snares (named as a companion to the group of rocks south of Stewart Island that Cook had eloquently named the Traps) were sighted independently by the masters of two vessels, William Broughton aboard the *Chatham* and George Vancouver aboard the *Discovery*, in 1791. Broughton and Vancouver had both served under Cook: now they were sailing in consort on their own voyage of discovery, which Vancouver commanded. They had been separated by a storm shortly after leaving Dusky Sound, and approached the Snares from opposite directions: Vancouver named them the Snares, and Broughton named them the Knights. The skipper of yet another vessel, the *Britannia*, spotted them a year later and called them the Sunday Islands. It was only later when notes were compared that it was realised that everyone had seen the same islands. Whether because Vancouver was the boss, or because his log showed him narrowly to have priority, his name for the islands stuck. Broughton wasn't to be left out, however: soon after sighting the Snares/Knights/Sundays, he found another group to the east of the mainland in the latitude of Christchurch, and named the group and the main island after his vessel. Broughton was interested to find that the Chatham Islands were inhabited by Polynesians, but with enough differences in language and culture from Māori to suggest that they had been living in isolation from the mainland for a very long time.

Another former Cook man, William Bligh, soon to become infamous for his unpopular shipboard management style, had sighted a group of islets to the east of the southern extremity of the South Island in 1788 whilst en route to his rendezvous with destiny. He named these the Bounty Islands after his ship. In 1800, Captain Henry Waterhouse of HMS *Reliance*, which was carrying merino sheep and people with such illustrious Australian place names as Bass and Flinders, found yet another group of rocky islets that lay roughly in the region of the antipodes of England, which he commemorated by naming them the Antipodes Islands. In 1806, Abraham Bristow, master of the *Ocean*, a vessel belonging to the British whaling firm Samuel Enderby and Sons, sighted a group of islands further south again. He named the northernmost after his employer, and the main island of the group after William Eden, the first Baron Auckland. Interestingly, a centuries-old midden discovered in the late twentieth century on Enderby Island—beautiful but bleak, cold and inhospitable in the middle of one of the most turbulent tracts of ocean on Earth—established this as the southernmost point of Polynesian exploration.

On the face of it, you wouldn't have thought there was much to excite anyone about these discoveries. But the casual mention that they were crawling with seals caused something of a stir. Seals were once widespread around the New Zealand coast, but whether because of changing climate or marine conditions, or because of pressure from hunting by Māori, they were progressively pushed southwards. They were abundant in Otago, Southland, Fiordland and Westland, on the subantarctic islands and on practically every little rock and islet besides. Then: apocalypse. The first European sealing crews arrived in New Zealand waters a mere decade after Cook had last visited, and within thirty years, the New Zealand fur seal and the New Zealand sea lion were both brought to the brink of extinction.

The modus operandi was crude. You located a seal colony, landed a gang of men with minimal supplies—salt for preserving skins was the main thing they needed, along with their long wooden clubs; the meat of the seals they killed would be their staple diet—and then you buggered off, returning in a few months to collect the gang and the pile of skins they had secured, which you brought triumphantly back to port and market. Mostly, this system worked, although there were many of what would now be known as epic fails—and some great stories. A crew of four was landed on the Snares Islands in 1810 when the skipper of their ship determined he didn't have enough supplies to keep everyone alive. They were there for six years, one of them quite understandably going mad and being tipped over a cliff by his comrades before they were rescued. Another five were landed in 1808 on the Solander Islands (a group off the Southland coast, named by Cook after the

SMITH'S MAP OF SOUTHERN NEW ZEALAND, 1806

After the explorers came the exploiters, and it was these men—seeking whales, seals, flax or timber—who corrected some of the errors in the official charts and made discoveries of their own. It was probably whales that drew Owen Folger Smith to this part of the world from his home town of Nantucket in the USA, but it was seals that brought him to New Zealand.

In 1804, he, along with a gang of others, was landed on the east coast of what James Cook had supposed to be a peninsula at the bottom of the South Island; their vessel, the *Independence*, then returned to Port Jackson (Sydney). The *Independence* sailed again from Port Jackson in company with the *Favorite* in mid-1805, bound for the Antipodes Islands, where they were to pick up another gang of sealers and (they hoped) their large bundle of salted hides. The plan was then to sail on to New Zealand to uplift Smith and co.

When on 10 March 1806 the *Favorite* arrived back at Port Jackson, it was to learn that the *Independence* was overdue. It was soon surmised that she had been lost somewhere with all hands, including the Antipodes sealing gang. Smith, meanwhile, presented Captain Philip King, formerly the lieutenant-governor of Norfolk Island (see p. 27) and now the governor of New South Wales, with a chart that he had drawn of what turned out to be an island, separated from the mainland by a strait that he named after himself. This was useful information, not least to sealers, and for this reason King suppressed it, as the alarming decline in the seal population on both sides of the Tasman had induced him to impose a ban on sealing beyond latitude 43°49′S (roughly the latitude of Christchurch).

King was replaced as governor in 1806 by William Bligh, who was himself replaced in 1809 (after presiding over yet another mutiny, this one known as the Rum Rebellion) by Joseph Foveaux. It was under Foveaux's watch that the truth about Stewart Island was revealed, as William Stewart, first officer on a ship named the *Pegasus*, reported that he had circumnavigated it and (incidentally) named it after himself. Doubtless as a calculated attempt to ensure the name stuck, Stewart dubbed 'Smith's Strait' Foveaux Strait, and so it has remained ever since.

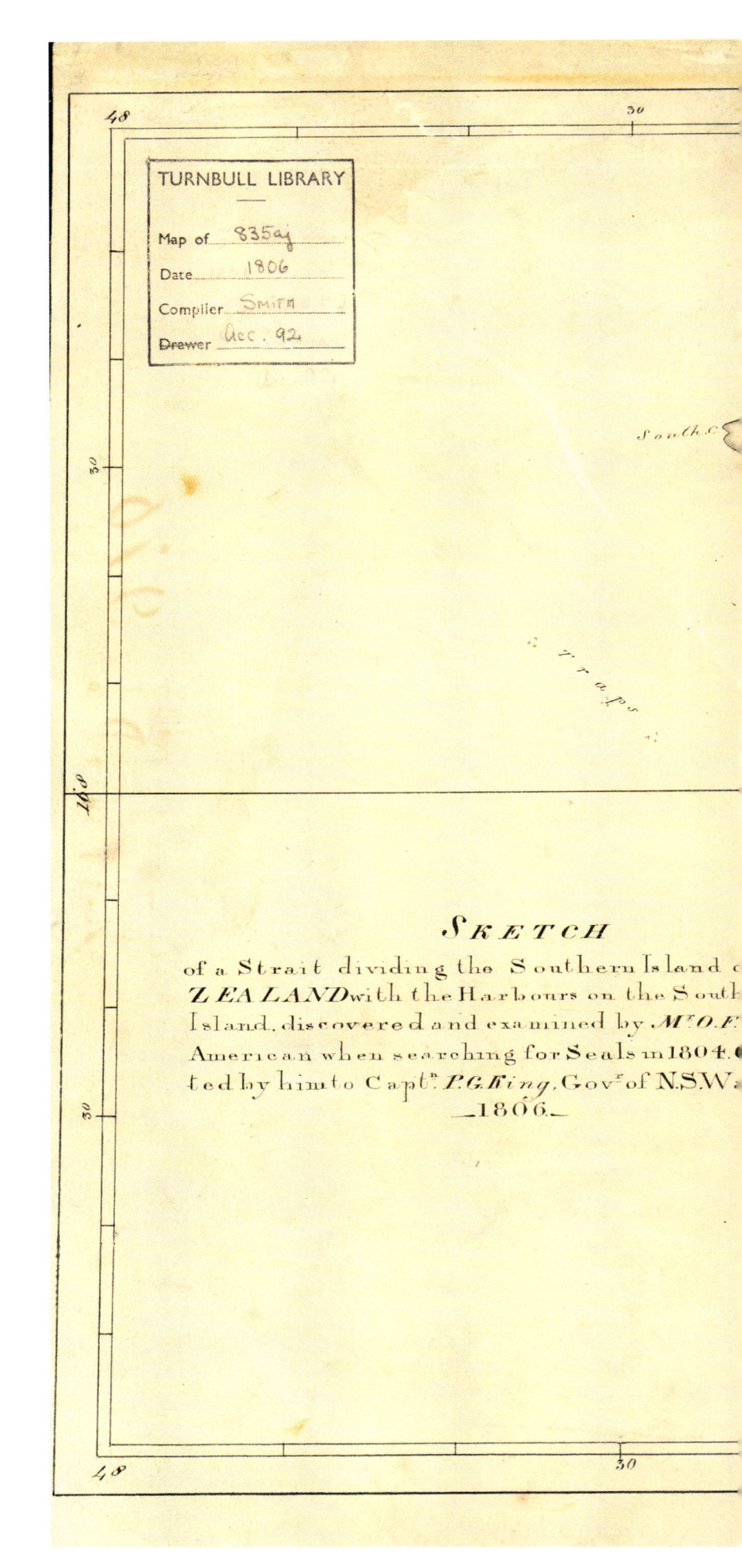

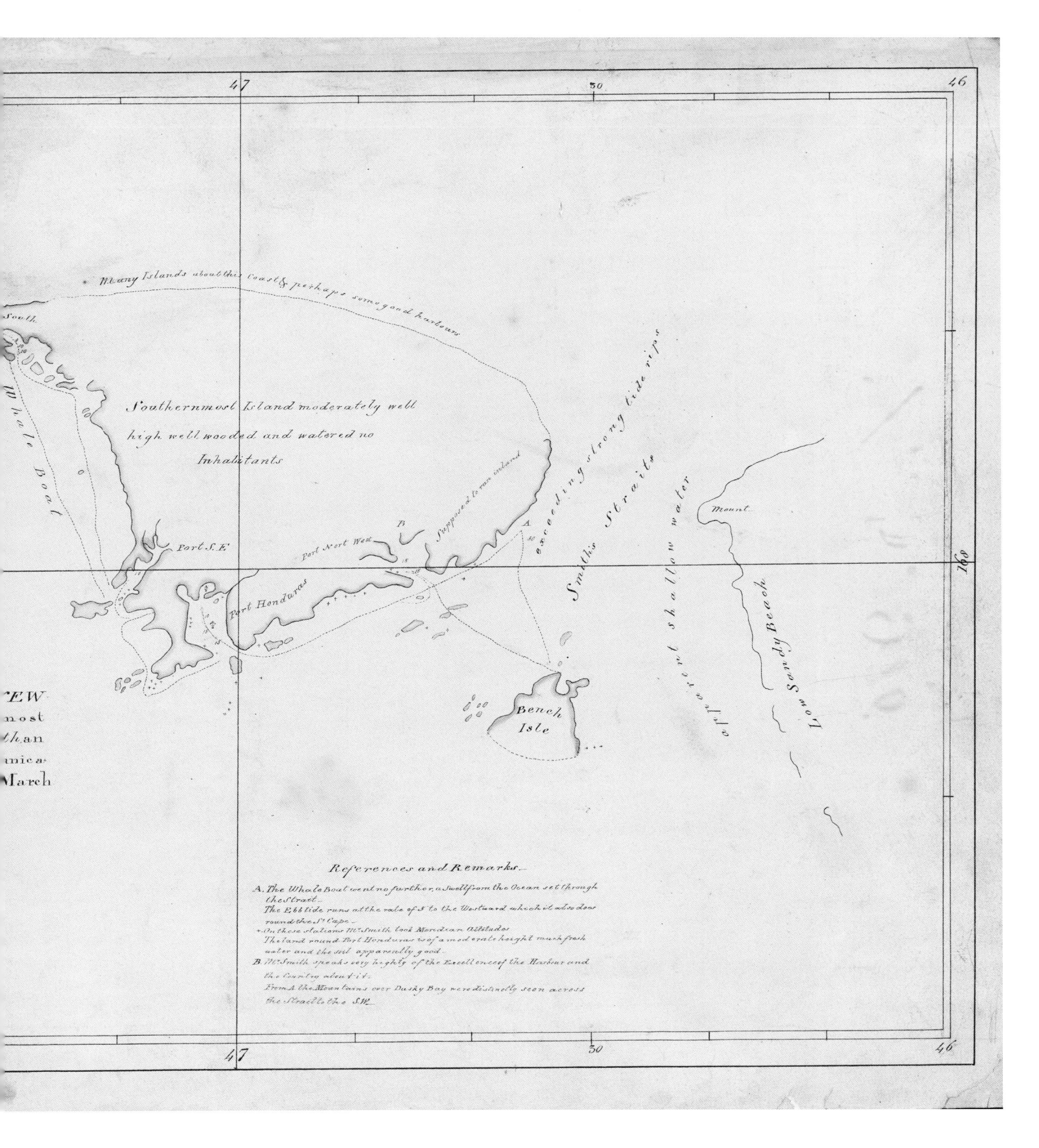

Many Islands about this coast & perhaps some good harbours

Southernmost Island moderately well high, well wooded and watered no Inhabitants

Supposed to run inland

South

Whale Boat

Port S.E.

Port North West

Port Honduras

B

A

exceeding strong tide rips

Smith's Straits

apparent shallow water

Mount

Low Sandy Beach

Bench Isle

EW
most
than
nica
March

References and Remarks

A. The Whale Boat went no farther, a Swell from the Ocean set through the Strait.
 The Ebb tide runs at the rate of 5 to the Westward which it also does round the S.t Cape.

+ On these stations M.r Smith took Meridean Altitudes
 The land round Port Honduras is of a moderate height much fresh water and the soil apparently good.

B. M.r Smith speaks very highly of the Excellence of the Harbour and the Country about it.
 From A the Mountains over Dusky Bay were distinctly seen across the Strait to the S.W.

Endeavour's naturalist) and not uplifted until 1813. Yet another gang was landed in 1810 on what were then known as the Open Bay Islands (Open Bay is now known as Jackson Bay), a few miles off the coast of South Westland. Their vessel, the brig *Active*, sailed off over the horizon and was never seen again—or at least, not afloat. The ten men survived for three years and ten months, making the five-kilometre crossing to the mainland in their little wooden boat, and then back and forth several times in a coracle after their boat was smashed by the surf, before they were picked up by another sealing ship at the end of 1813. Who knows how many other gangs never lived to tell their own tall-but-true tales?

One such gang was landed on the Antipodes Islands in 1804 by an American vessel named the *Independence*, which returned for the men two years later, sailing in consort with another American, the *Favorite*. The plan was then to sail on further to (what is now) Rakiura/Stewart Island, where the *Independence* had left another gang. The *Favorite* arrived home; the *Independence* did not, and was never heard from again.

When the *Favorite* returned to Port Jackson, and presumably after a long, hot bath and a meal of something other than seal blubber, Owen Folger Smith, the leader of the Stewart Island gang, met Philip King, governor of New South Wales, and shared his knowledge of the area in which he had been hunting these last two years. This was recorded on a map, and while the original hasn't survived, a copy made a couple of decades later has. The curious feature of this map is that it shows a strait between the South Island and the 'Southernmost Island', rather immodestly named 'Smith's Straits'. King had lately banned sealing south of 43°49' (roughly the latitude of Lake Ellesmere, at the base of Banks Peninsula), so rather than risk opening up the shores of this newly discovered waterway to a further round of slaughter, he suppressed the information. It wasn't until 1809, when a vessel named the *Pegasus* completed a circumnavigation of Rakiura and its first officer, William Stewart, renamed the island after himself, that news of the strait was released. Smith's name did not appear. Instead, perhaps as a canny means to preserve his own claim to cartographic immortality, Stewart had renamed the strait after the acting governor of New South Wales, Joseph Foveaux.

Sealers were poor sources of accurate cartographic information. They were a bit like anglers with their favourite fishing spots, and tended to keep news of any new discoveries to themselves. When in 1810 Frederick Hasselborough, commanding the brig *Perseverance* on a sealing voyage, discovered Campbell and Macquarie islands far to the south and a little to the east of New Zealand, he swore his crew to silence. Word eventually got out, however, and rival sealing gangs were soon battling each other on the rocky, bloodstained beaches of these impossibly remote places. In 1821, William Elliot of the *Emerald* reported an island to the south of Macquarie, which he named after his vessel. Over the years that followed, plenty of people sought out the island, and while none could find it in the location he named, this wasn't taken as proof of its non-existence. It was believed there was every chance it was there, somewhere, and that Elliot had either accidentally or (most likely) deliberately misreported its position. After all, while Bristow had accurately charted the Auckland Islands, others were more interested in keeping rivals for its abundant seal resource away. It's quite possible that the makers of early nineteenth-century charts of the Southern

Ocean received information from these unreliable sources: on one of these, for instance, Auckland Island appears up to forty nautical miles north of its true latitude.

There is every chance that this had tragic consequences. Shipping volumes between Australia and Great Britain increased throughout the nineteenth century, and ships increasingly sailed the 'Great Circle' route that exploited the strong westerlies in high latitudes. Vessels sailing from the Australian east coast often aimed to shoot the gap between the Snares and the Aucklands, en route to Cape Horn. The skies are often overcast, and fog is prone to descend on the face of the Southern Ocean for days on end, making fixing your position using nineteenth-century technology difficult. For this reason, the subantarctics—especially the Aucklands—took a cruel toll in the years between 1833, when the first hapless wreck is known to have smacked into the sheer cliffs on Auckland Island's west coast, and 1905, when the last wreck of a sailing vessel occurred. Improvements in marine steam engines and then the opening of the Panama Canal in 1914 meant it was no longer necessary to brave high latitudes. Who knows how many of the skippers of the eleven known wrecks on the Aucklands were relying on faulty charts?

―――

Sealers and whalers were far more likely to disseminate accurate information than to dissemble about the approaches to harbours and to anchorages in the places they frequented. For this reason, in the years before formal European settlement, the sheltered bits of the coastline were charted in far higher resolution than the rest. Once settlement gathered momentum, the volume of coastwise shipping increased and the prospect of bringing in vessels with large numbers of migrants loomed, there was a much greater need for a detailed hydrographical survey of the coast. The man chosen to lead this work was a Welshman by the name of John Lort Stokes, who had proven his hydrographical chops in a number of enterprises, including surveys of South America and of the northern parts of Australia aboard the *Beagle*—none other than the ship that carried Charles Darwin to scientific fame (it was Stokes who named Australia's Darwin River for his shipmate). Stokes was promoted to the rank of captain and appointed to the command of HMS *Acheron*, a paddle-wheeler and one of the first steam-powered vessels to arrive in New Zealand waters, on 7 November 1848.

Over the next two years, Stokes produced a series of fourteen meticulous charts of the coastline, correcting many errors in the work of his predecessors. The advantage of using a steam-powered vessel was, of course, that she was not at the mercy of the winds, and could carry on working where a vessel under sail might be forced off by adverse weather. While Stokes himself finished his work in 1851, the survey was continued in the less well-suited *Pandora*, a sailing ship, under Captain Byron Drury. By the time Drury had finished, there was little left to know about the inshore waters the length and breadth of the country. The coast, that is, was known. The white paper regions were now confined within its lines.

WILLIAMS' MAP OF BLUFF HARBOUR, 1813

This sketchy map records the first European exploration of Bluff Harbour, in April 1813, by the crew of the Sydney brig *Perseverance*, who named the harbour 'Port Macquarie', after the governor of New South Wales. On the same voyage, they managed to rescue five souls who had been marooned for years on the Solander Islands (see p. 103). The object of their interest was flax, which grew (as the newspaper report of their voyage puts it) 'in tolerable abundance' around the harbour (although the map calls it 'hemp'). The men found the local Māori to be hospitable: the map shows the point at which they took a man aboard to guide them.

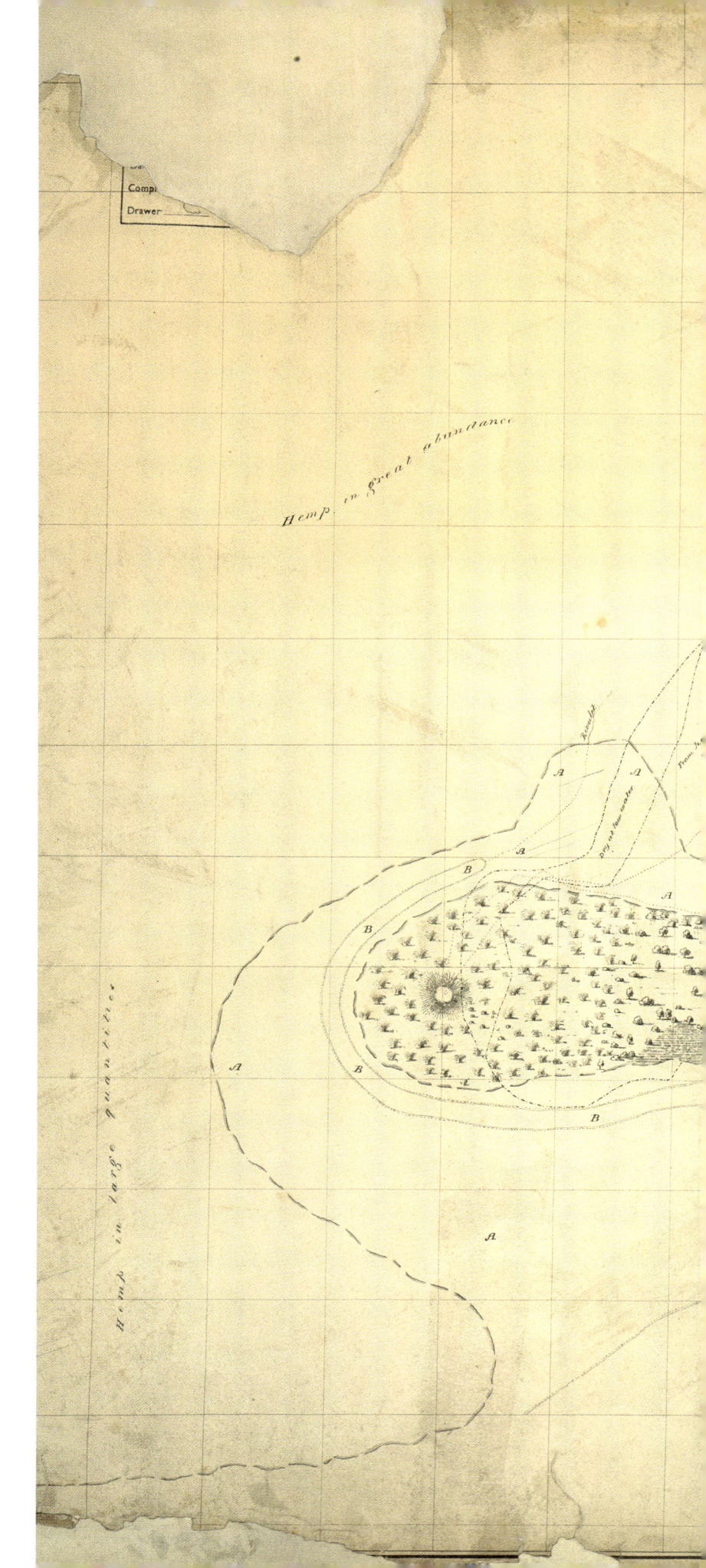

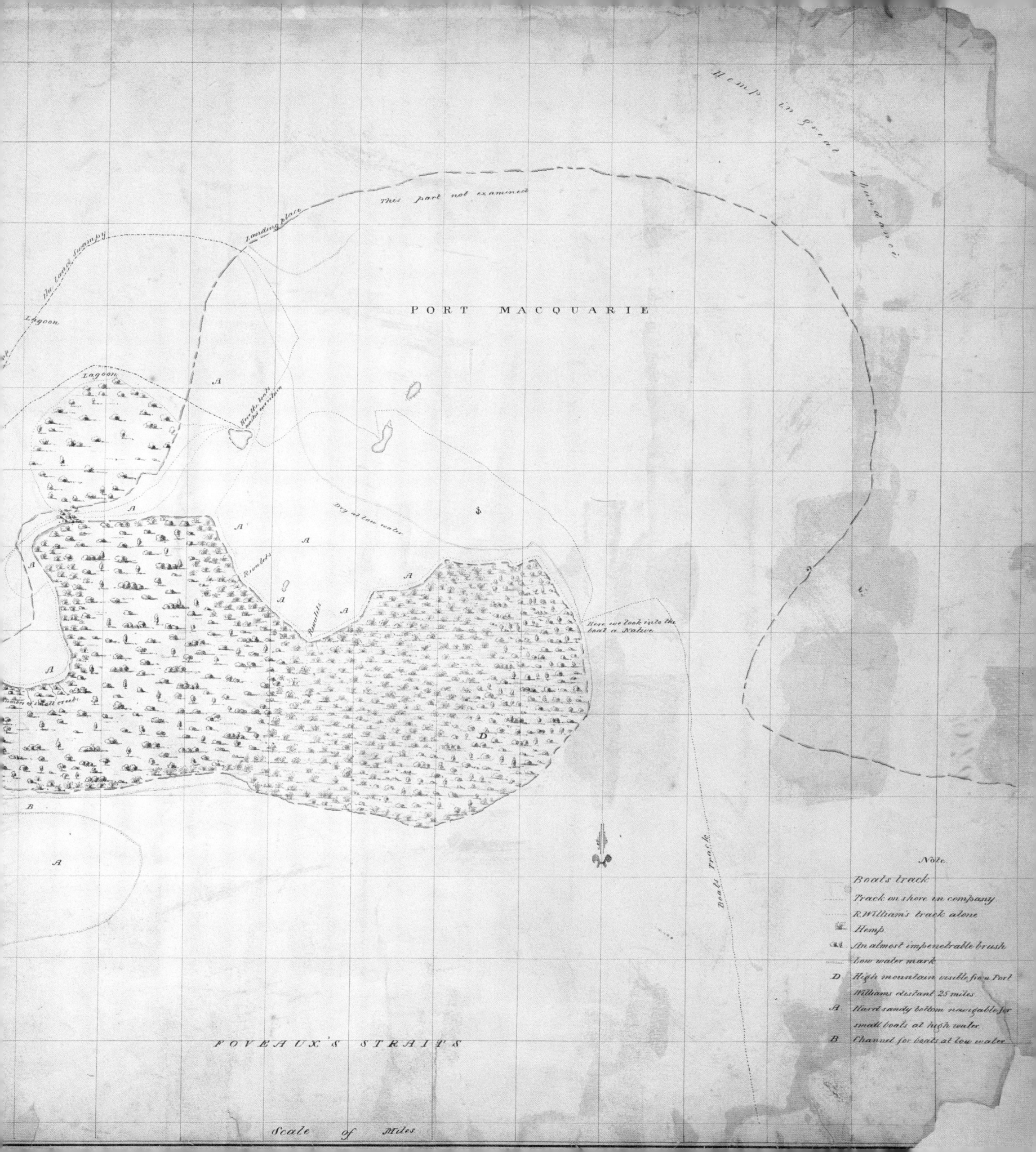

PORT MACQUARIE

This part not examined

Landing place

The Coast Swampy

Lagoon

Lagoon

Rivulets

Dry at low water

Here we took into the boat a Native

Hemp in Great abundance

Boats track

FOVEAUX'S STRAITS

Scale of Miles

Note.
- ――― Boats track
- ‒ ‒ ‒ Track on shore in company
- .... R. Williams's track alone
- ※ Hemp
- ⁂ An almost impenetrable brush
- ——— Low water mark
- D High mountain visible from Port Williams distant 25 miles
- A Hard sandy bottom navigable for small boats at high water
- B Channel for boats at low water

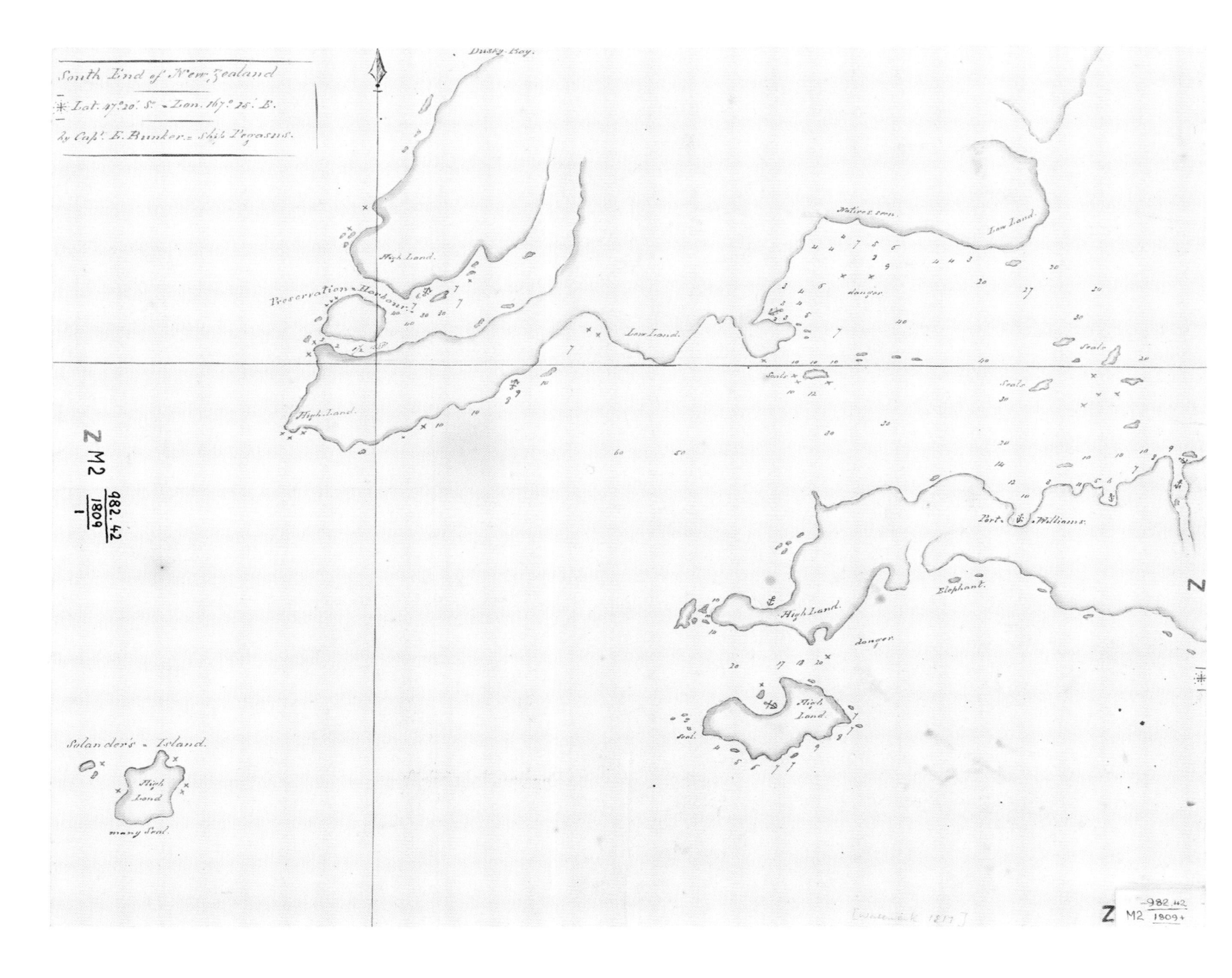

EBER BUNKER MAP OF SOUTHERN NEW ZEALAND, 1808

Despite the numbers of sealers and sealing captains who knocked about the New Zealand coast while there were still seals to knock about—and that wasn't for very long—very few of the charts they doubtless prepared have survived. Partly this will have been due to their tendency to be secretive as a breed. One that has come down to us was drawn by Eber Bunker, a Nantucket-born sealer who visited the deep south in 1808. His chart is light on details—it shows 'high land' and 'low land', 'natives seen', rocks, a few soundings and 'danger'. It also shows islets with the word 'seals'. As usual, a chart reflects the interests of its maker.

Following page
IMRAY'S CHART OF THE SOUTH PACIFIC, 1849

James Imray, the maker of this chart, never saw any of the countries he depicted. In 1826, having served an apprenticeship as a stationer, he entered into a partnership with Michael Blachford, who had taken over the chart-making interests of Robert (likely his father) and William Blachford. Imray bought out Blachford in 1846, and turned what had been a failing business around, with James Imray and Son becoming in fairly short order one of the most successful publishers of nautical charts in England. Imray, like other private nautical chart-makers, applied a backing of blue paper to his charts, and hence these are known as 'blue-backed' charts.

It seems likely that Imray got his notion of New Zealand from James Wyld, as the coastline as charted here is substantially the same as that in Wyld's chart of New Zealand (see p. 166), complete with errors. But who knows where he got his information about what lay to the south. At this point in time, the status of Macquarie Island, well to the south of New Zealand, was undetermined: it is geologically part of New Zealand, but was eventually assigned by Great Britain to the government of Tasmania. South of Macquarie, Imray depicts Emerald Island, sighted by William Elliot, the skipper of the *Emerald*, in 1821. Many subsequent voyagers to the region had failed to set eyes on Emerald Island: it became something of a joke amongst those plying the Southern Ocean that perhaps this island was blessed with the power of movement. Most had probably guessed that what Elliot had seen through the fog that regularly settles on the sea in these latitudes was an iceberg. Emerald Island was finally struck off the charts when none other than Ernest Shackleton deliberately sailed his vessel *Nimrod* over its location in 1909.

But the Imray chart is interesting for another, potentially more serious error. It depicts a fairly impressionistic silhouette of Auckland Island—copied from an Admiralty chart prepared by hydrographer John Walker in 1823, presumably working from a drawing made by whaler Abraham Bristow in 1806. Trouble is, Walker's chart does not give a position, merely stating that the Auckland Islands lie '66 leagues south by west from the South Cape of New Zealand'. Imray places them lying between 51°05' and 51°30' south, whereas they are the better part of two-thirds of a degree of latitude further north, a discrepancy of close to forty nautical miles. This in no small part accounts for the high number of ships that came to grief there, including the *General Grant*, whose last movements plainly indicate that William Loughlin, her master, expected the Auckland Islands to lie to the north of where he fatally encountered them.

Pages 114–115
WING'S CHART OF NAPIER, 1837

This elaborate and informative chart shows both Ahuriri Harbour (on the left) and the Hawke's Bay coast from Cape Kidnappers to Tolaga Bay on the right. It was drawn by Thomas Wing, skipper of the schooner *Trent*, visiting in August 1837 from the Bay of Islands. It shows a substantial pā on the island in the middle of the Ahuriri Lagoon, palisaded 'with white timber', and advises that the harbour isn't suited to vessels of more than 60 tons due to the poor holding ground for anchors around the heads. In the notes, he recommends a complicated set of manoeuvres to bring a vessel through the channel to the east of the island and to anchor against the southern shore. This landscape was transformed a century later, when the 1931 Hawke's Bay earthquake uplifted and dried the lagoon.

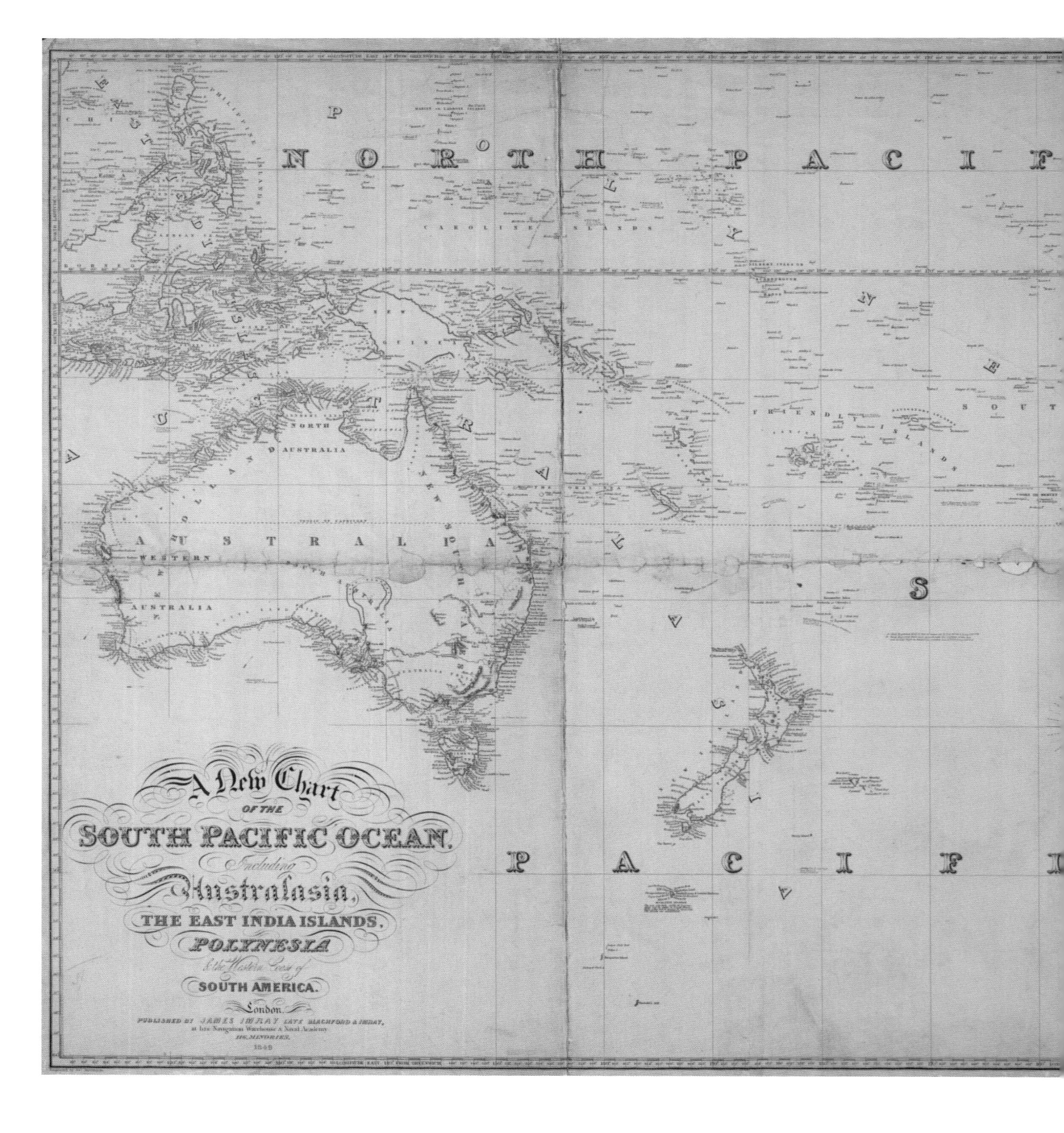

A New Chart
OF THE
SOUTH PACIFIC OCEAN,
Including
Australasia,
THE EAST INDIA ISLANDS,
POLYNESIA
& the Western Coast of
SOUTH AMERICA.

London.
PUBLISHED BY JAMES IMRAY LATE BLACHFORD & IMRAY,
at his Navigation Warehouse & Naval Academy
116, MINORIES.
1849

C O C E A N
CARIBBEAN SEA
COLUMBIA
S E A I S L A N D S
SOUTH AMERICA
U T H
PERU
PATAGONIA
C O C E A N

TURNBULL LIBRARY

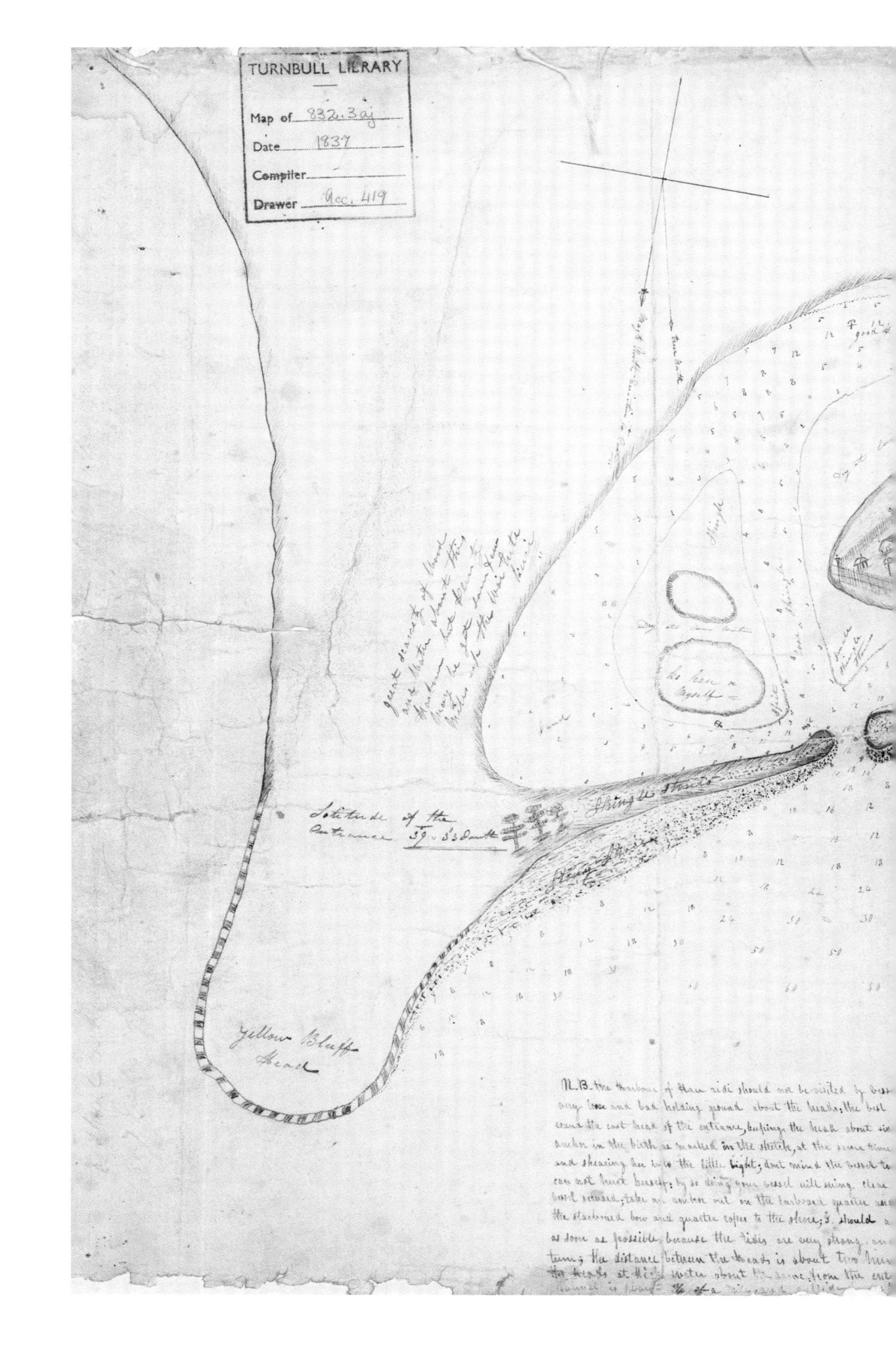

Map of 832.3aj
Date 1837
Compiler
Drawer Acc. 419

Latitude of the
Entrance 39"53'South

Yellow Bluff
Head

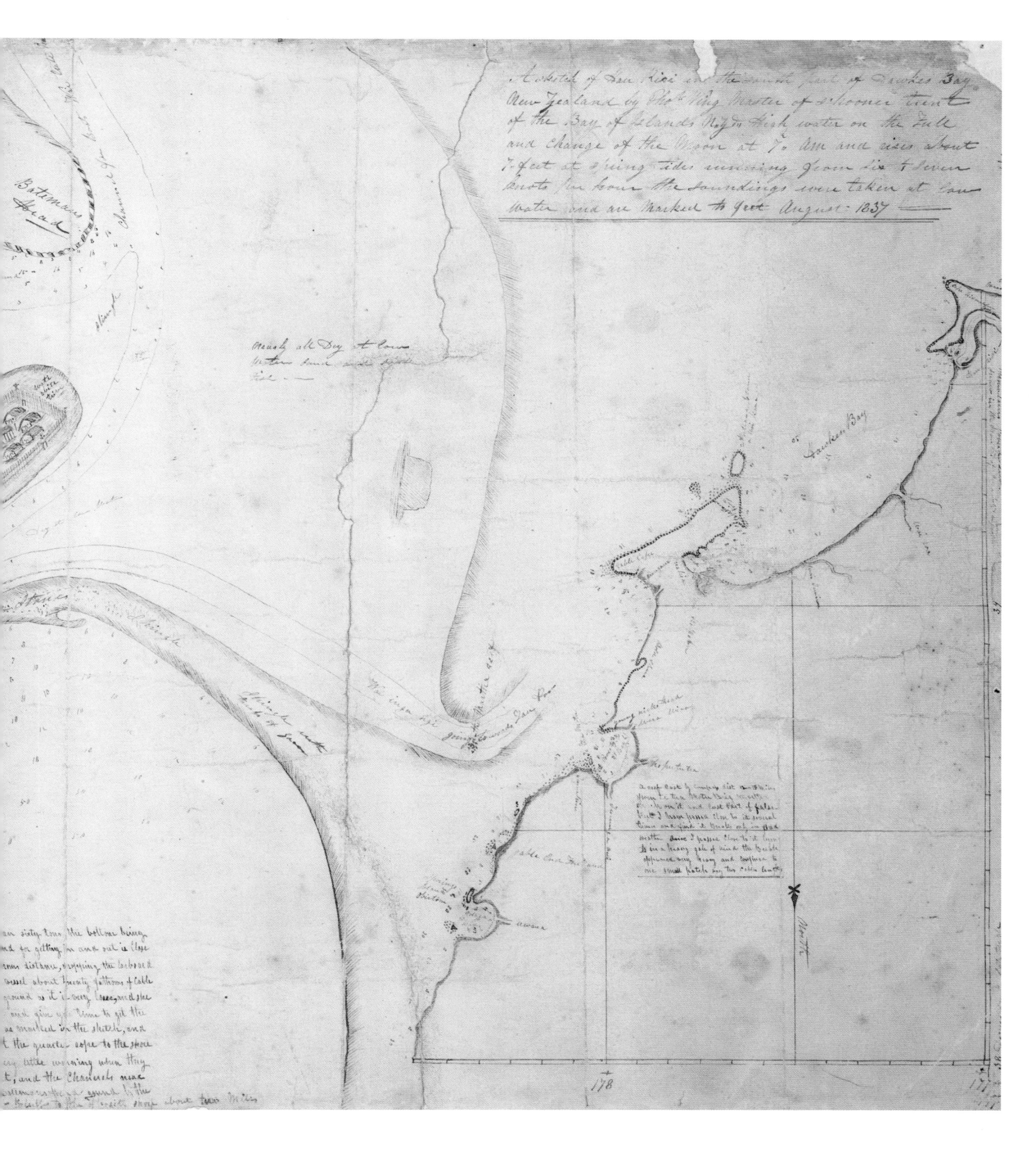

A sketch of Sea Rise in the south part of Cookes Bay New Zealand by Thos King Master of schooner trent of the Bay of Islands N.Z. the High water on the full and change of the Moon at 7h AM and rises about 7 feet at spring tides running from six to seven knots per hour the soundings were taken at low water and are marked to feet August 1837

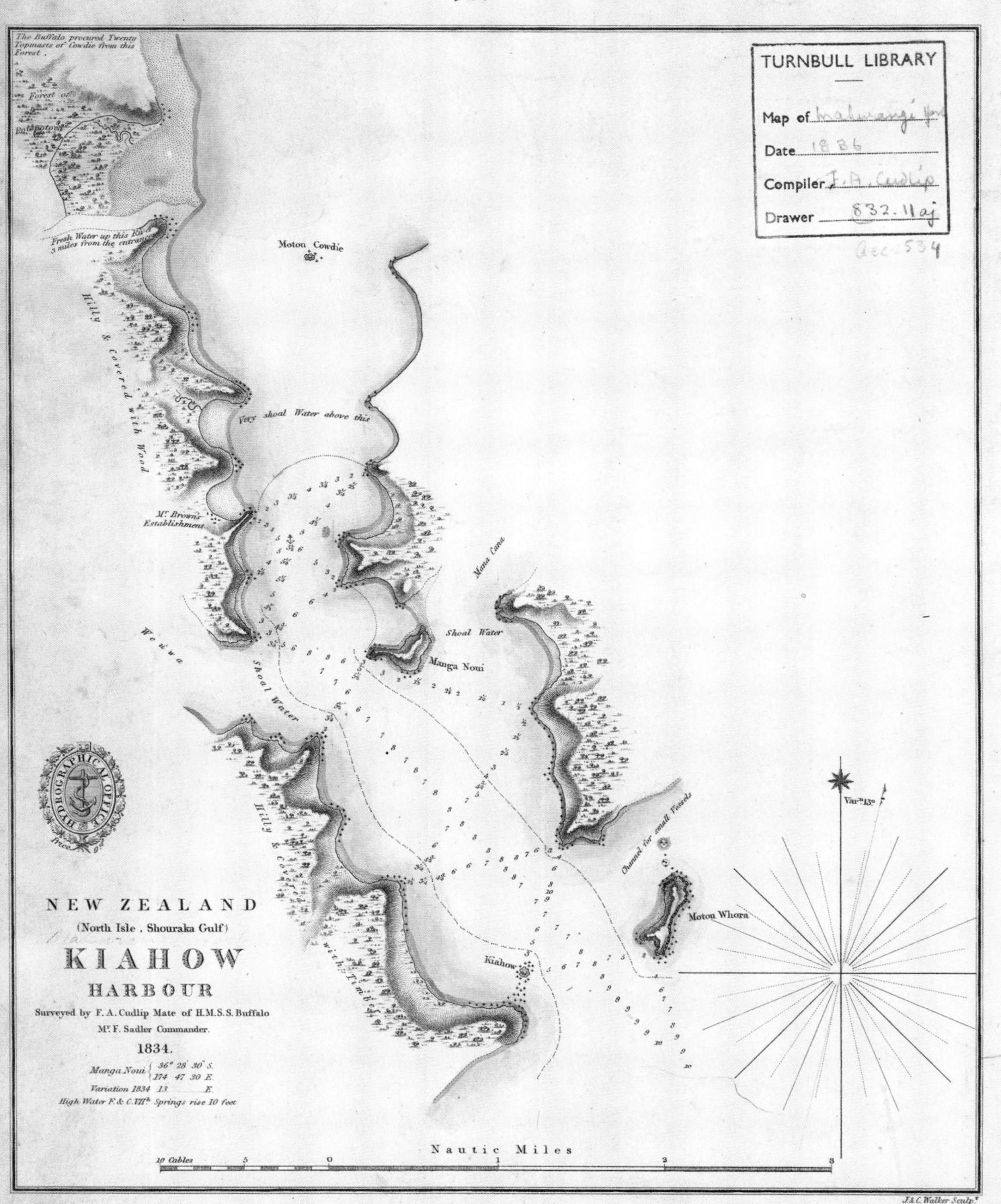

NEW ZEALAND
(North Isle, Shouraka Gulf)
KIAHOW
HARBOUR

Surveyed by F. A. Cudlip Mate of H.M.S.S. Buffalo
Mr. F. Sadler Commander.
1834.

Manga Noui { 36° 28′ 30″ S.
{ 174° 47′ 30″ E.
Variation 1834   13   E.
High Water F. & C. VIIh Springs rise 10 feet

Nautic Miles

Published according to Act of Parliament at the Hydrographical Office of the Admiralty July 1st 1836.
Sold by R. B. Bate Agent for the Admiralty Charts 21 Poultry.

J. & C. Walker Sculpt.

CUDLIP'S CHART OF MAHURANGI, 1834

His Majesty's Ship *Buffalo* was a fixture in the early days of the colonisation of Australia and the early settlement of New Zealand. She first visited this country on an expedition to cut spars in 1831, but it was as a convict vessel under the command of Captain F. W. R. Sadler that she arrived in 1834, making the return journey after delivering 179 of the 180 hapless female convicts she carried to Australia. While anchored near the mouth of the tidal Mahurangi River, her mate, F. A. Cudlip, performed the boat survey that resulted in this chart. The purpose of her visit is made plain by the notation in the top left corner, which records: 'The Buffalo procured Twenty Topmasts of Cowdie [kauri] from this Forest.' The name Kiahow Harbour (after the drastically misheard name of Te Haupa Island at the entrance) did not stick: it soon reverted to Mahurangi. The *Buffalo* is one of New Zealand's celebrity shipwrecks, having been driven ashore in a storm at Whitianga (again laden with kauri spars) on 28 July 1840. Her remains lie in shallow water and can still be seen, when conditions permit.

PORT NICHOLSON
OR
WANGENUE'TERA
IN
NEW ZEALAND.

Surveyed by T. Barnett, May 1826

Scale of ———————— 2 Miles

References
※ Latitude 41°.17'.11" South and Longitude 174°.50'.15" East
▲ Rocks above Water
× Rocks under Water
Soundings are in Fathoms

BARNETT'S CHART OF WELLINGTON, 1826

Neither Cook nor d'Urville had been game to enter the harbour that they supposed pierced the land at the eastern entrance to Cook Strait, as weather conditions didn't permit. But you famously can't beat the place on a good day, and that seems to have been how Captain James Herd and Thomas Barnett, commanding the *Rosanna* and the *Lambton* respectively, found it in 1826.

By the middle of the 1820s, the colonisation of New Zealand was (literally) on the agenda. They were investigating possible sites for settlement on behalf of the first incarnation of the New Zealand Company, and what they found in Wa'ngenue'tera (Whanganui-a-Tara) was later to draw the eye of Colonisation, Inc. The chart that Barnett drew shows a good harbour with plentiful supplies of fresh water: a lake where Miramar is now, and a pond on the neck of the isthmus; streams in Evans Bay, the site of present-day Te Aro; and, of course, the Hutt and Waiwhetū rivers. Barnett clearly indicates a flaxy swamp to occupy the site that, in their wisdom, later New Zealand Company officials would choose as the site of a new township. Herd is thought to have named the harbour Port Nicholson, after the harbourmaster at Sydney, Captain John Nicholson.

HERD'S CHART OF HOKIANGA, 1826

James Herd's expedition visited and charted four locations that he thought might fit the New Zealand Company's requirements as the site for a new settlement: Port Pegasus (on Stewart Island), Otago Harbour, Port Nicholson (later to become Wellington) and what he misheard as Jokeehangar (Hokianga). The chart of the last is beautifully illuminated with coastal views executed in watercolour, and notes such features as might appeal to would-be settlers: 'fine level ground clear of timber [that] has the appearance of once being in cultivation' on the northern side of the harbour, fresh water and, of course, the vast forests of 'cowdie' carpeting the hills inland. A 'hippah' (pā) and the residence of a chief in 'a pleasant grove' are noted on the southern shore.

Port Oxley
Zealand

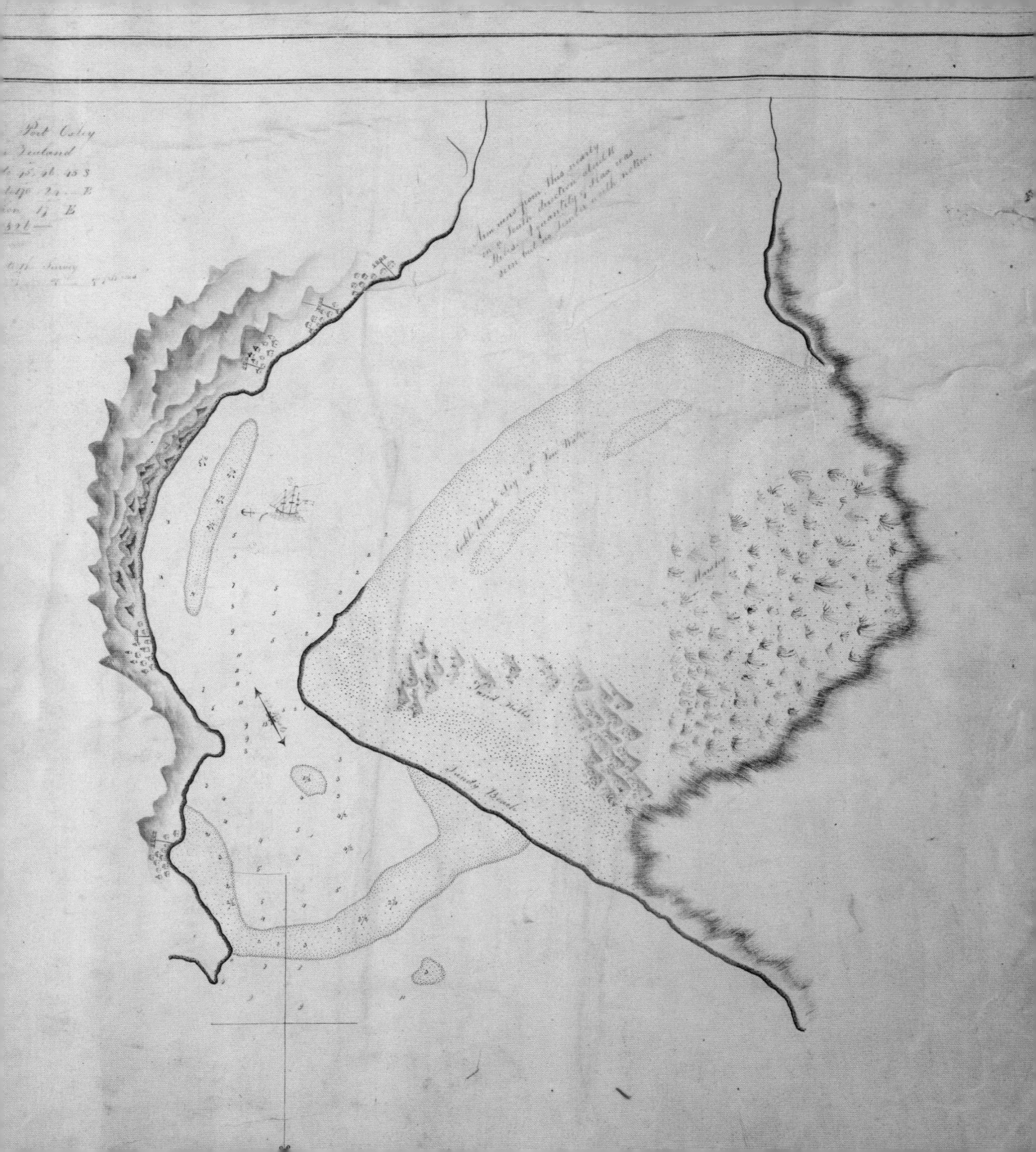

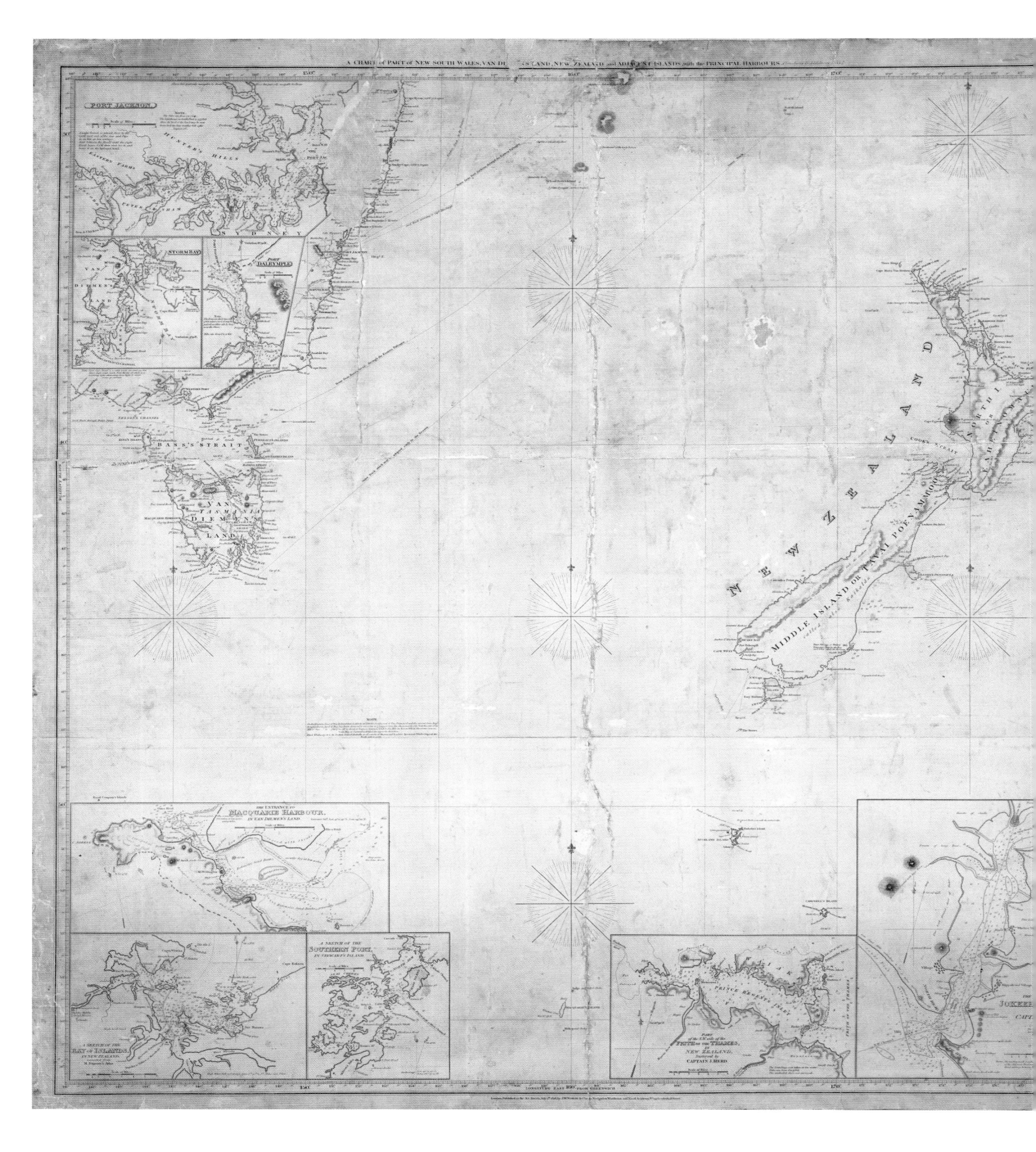

A CHART of PART of NEW SOUTH WALES, VAN DIEMEN'S LAND, NEW ZEALAND and ADJACENT ISLANDS with the PRINCIPAL HARBOURS

PORT JACKSON

STORM BAY

PORT DALRYMPLE

VAN DIEMEN'S LAND

BASS'S STRAIT

VAN DIEMEN'S LAND
TASMANIA

NEW ZEALAND

MIDDLE ISLAND OR TAVAI POENAMMOO

THE ENTRANCE TO MACQUARIE HARBOUR, IN VAN DIEMEN'S LAND

A SKETCH OF THE SOUTHERN PORT, IN STEWART'S ISLAND

A SKETCH OF THE BAY OF ISLANDS, IN NEW ZEALAND

PART of the N.W. side of the FRITH OF THE THAMES, NEW ZEALAND, Surveyed by CAPTAIN J. HERD

LONGITUDE EAST FROM GREENWICH

NORIE'S CHART OF THE SOUTH-WEST PACIFIC, 1828

James Imray's egregious mis-charting of Auckland Island (see p. 111) is harder to understand when you reflect that its discoverer, Abraham Bristow, who chanced upon it in 1806, and the maker of this fine 1828 blue-backed chart had its position just about spot on. John William Norie's career more or less mirrored that of Imray: he bought into the nautical chart business when he took over the interests of his business partner William Heather in 1813. Norie enjoyed a career as a respected chart-maker for the next thirty years. After his death in 1843, the firm became Norie and Wilson, eventually merging with Imray and Son in 1905 to become Imray, Norie, Laurie and Wilson, which (remarkably) is still in business.

You can see where Norie acquired his information: insets show details of harbours charted by Louis Duperry and James Herd, and the general outline of New Zealand is a good match with Cook's first chart.

Following page
STOKES' CHART OF COOK STRAIT, 1876

The first settlers to New Zealand had to rely upon charts that were scant on detail and in places downright unreliable. But once a properly organised administration had got under way, it was deemed essential that the coastline and its harbours were properly charted, in the interests of facilitating commerce but just as importantly so that the serious business of bringing migrants to the new colony could be done as safely as possible. The man chosen for this job was John Lort Stokes, who had been involved in performing survey work aboard HMS *Beagle* (some of it with Charles Darwin). Stokes had already performed a similar job on the Australian coastline with distinction: he was promoted to captain and given the command of a paddle-wheel steamer, the *Acheron*, in 1847. By the time Stokes had completed his tour in early 1851, vast swathes of the New Zealand coastline held few secrets. The density of inshore soundings on the incredibly convoluted waterways of the Marlborough Sounds and the lower North Island is a testament to his diligence: each of those soundings would have been taken with a lead line—literally dropping a lead weight over the side and paying out the line, counting the knots that were tied at measured intervals, in order to read the depth of water. The weight itself commonly had a hollow at the bottom which would sample the quality of the ground—whether mud, sand, shells or gravel—and this information, which helped ensure safe anchorages, can be seen in places on the chart, abbreviated to 'm', 's', and so on. The precision, together with the artistry of their execution (the delicate hachures with which the topography of the land was depicted) make the *Acheron* charts some of the most visually interesting in New Zealand cartography.

NEW ZEALAND – MIDDLE ISLAND

COOK STRAIT ANCHORAGES
SHEET 2.
CROISILLES HARBOUR, PELORUS SOUND, PORT GORE,
QUEEN CHARLOTTE SOUND, TORY CHANNEL,
& PORT UNDERWOOD.

SURVEYED BY CAPTᴺ J.L. STOKES, COMMANDER B. DRURY,
and the Officers of H.M.S. Acheron & Pandora.
1849-53.

SOUNDINGS IN FATHOMS.

PELORUS SOUND
GUARDS BAY
Motu Ngara
Alligator Hd.
C. Lambert
WAITUI BAY
Cape Jackson
Walker Rock
Puzzle Peak
Deep Bay
PORT GORE
QUEEN CHARLOTTE SOUND
Cockle Bay
Gannet Pt.
Mt. Furneaux
Ship Cove
MOTUARA
C. Koamaroo
Brothers
Cook's Rk.
Gilbert Bay
EAST BAY
Pickersgill I.
ENDEAVOUR INLET
Mt. Stokes 3000
Beatrix Bay
HIKURAKI SOUND
WHAKAMAWAHI
MAMARO SOUND
KAREPO SOUND
Edgecumbe Pt.
BLUMINE or PIG I.
Patten Passage
Hawes Rk.
Mt. Chatters
Surgeons Bay
Jackson Bay
Famin Bay
ALAPAWA ISLAND
Wellington Head
East Head
TORY CHANNEL
Henderson Bay
Bay of Many Coves
Acre Bay
Bull Pt.
Boot Cove
Oyster Bay
Jordy Rocks
COOK STRAIT
Heavy Tide Ripplings
PICTON
Waitohi
Waikawa Bay
Treble Mount
Mt. Robertson
Oyster Cove
Ocean B.
Robin Hood Bay
PORT UNDERWOOD

COAST OF NEW ZEALAND AFTER STOKES AND DRURY, 1858

When John Stokes and the *Acheron* were paid off in 1851, there was still an amount of work to be done to complete the hydrographic survey of New Zealand, principally in the North Island. The replacement chosen was Captain Byron Drury, commanding a sailing vessel named the *Pandora*. At the mercy of the winds, Drury was understandably slower in his work than Stokes had been in his paddle-wheeler—his far less extensive survey took four and a half years—but he was no less meticulous. The legacy of these two expert hydrographers was a version of the New Zealand coast that was all but complete.

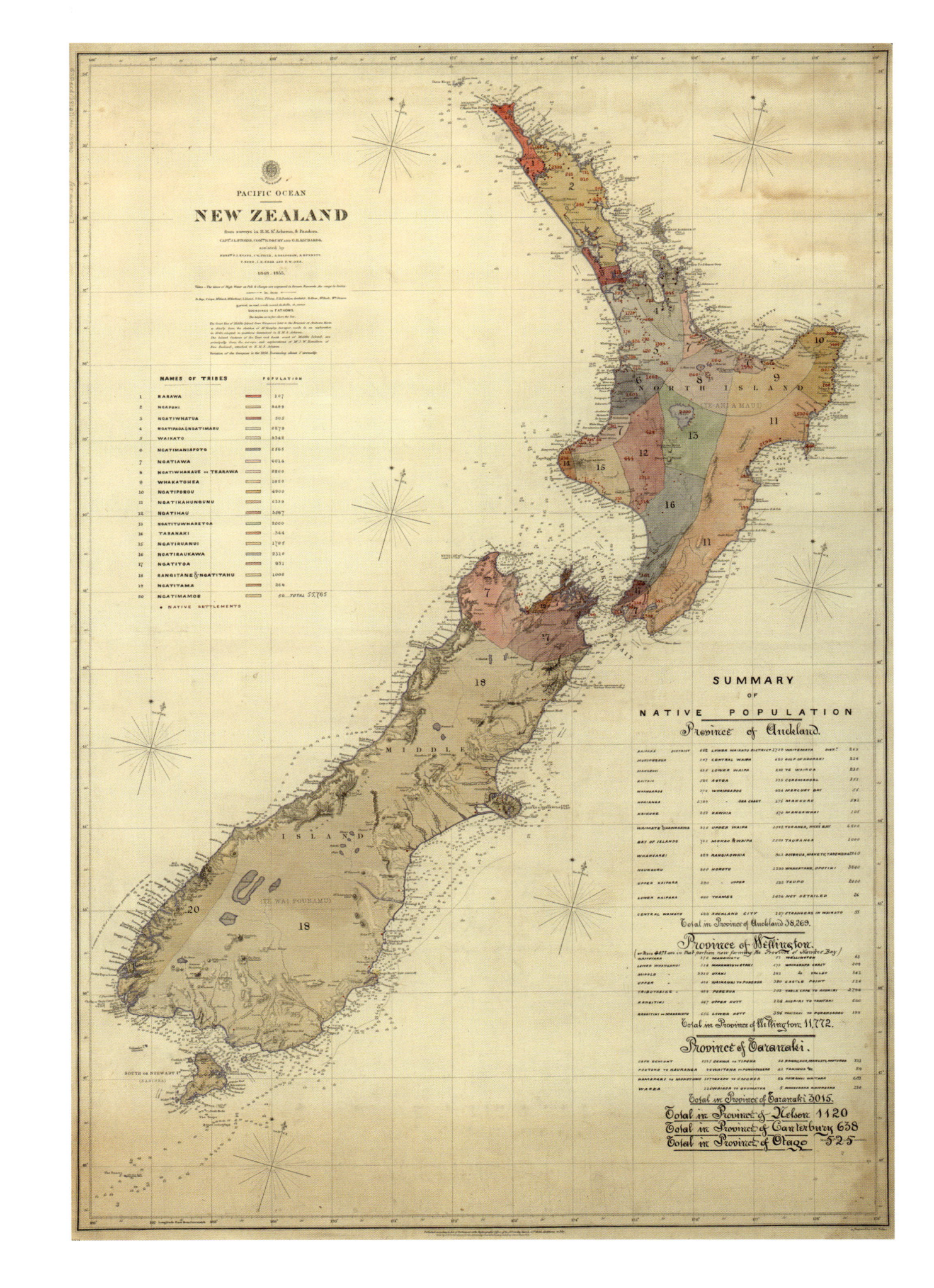

NEW ZEALAND

PACIFIC OCEAN

from surveys in H.M.S.ᵗ Acheron, & Pandora.
Capt.ᵃⁱⁿˢ J.L. STOKES, CONT.ᵈ BY and G.H. RICHARDS,
assisted by
[illegible officer names]
1848 – 1855.

#	NAMES OF TRIBES	POPULATION
1	RARAWA	107
2	NGAPUHI	6493
3	NGATIWHATUA	502
4	NGATIMARU & NGATIPAOA	2579
5	WAIKATO	2340
6	NGATIMANIAPOTO	2505
7	NGATIAWA	6014
8	NGATIWHAKAUE or TEARAWA	2800
9	WHAKATOHEA	1200
10	NGATIPOROU	4900
11	NGATIKAHUNGUNU	6339
12	NGATIHAU	3267
13	NGATITUWHARETOA	2000
14	TARANAKI	344
15	NGATIRUANUI	1705
16	NGATIRAUKAWA	2310
17	NGATITOA	831
18	RANGITANE & NGATITAHU	1000
19	NGATITAMA	264
20	NGATIMAMOE	50

TOTAL 55,765

● NATIVE SETTLEMENTS

SUMMARY OF NATIVE POPULATION

Province of Auckland

Total in Province of Auckland 38,269.

Province of Wellington
(or those 4871 are in that portion now forming the Province of Hawkes Bay)

Total in Province of Wellington 11,772.

Province of Taranaki

Total in Province of Taranaki 3015.

Total in Province of Nelson 1120
Total in Province of Canterbury 638
Total in Province of Otago 525

PART TWO

—

INTERIOR

E M A T A H

PRO

Pt Stanley
CUSTOM HOUSE

RESERVED FOR PUBLIC QUAY

Pt Fisher

Sec 19
Sec 20
Sec 18
Sec 17

BLENHEIM ST
Sec 21
Sec 16

Sec 23
Sec 26
HOBSON SQUARE
VICTORIA

Sec 24
ELIZA PLACE
Sec 22
Sec 15

Sec 33
Sec 14

Sec 27
WELLINGTON SQUARE
RUSSELL PLACE

Sec 35
Sec 36

PYT STREET
Sec 45
Sec 46

Sec 34

Sec 28
Sec 37

SIX

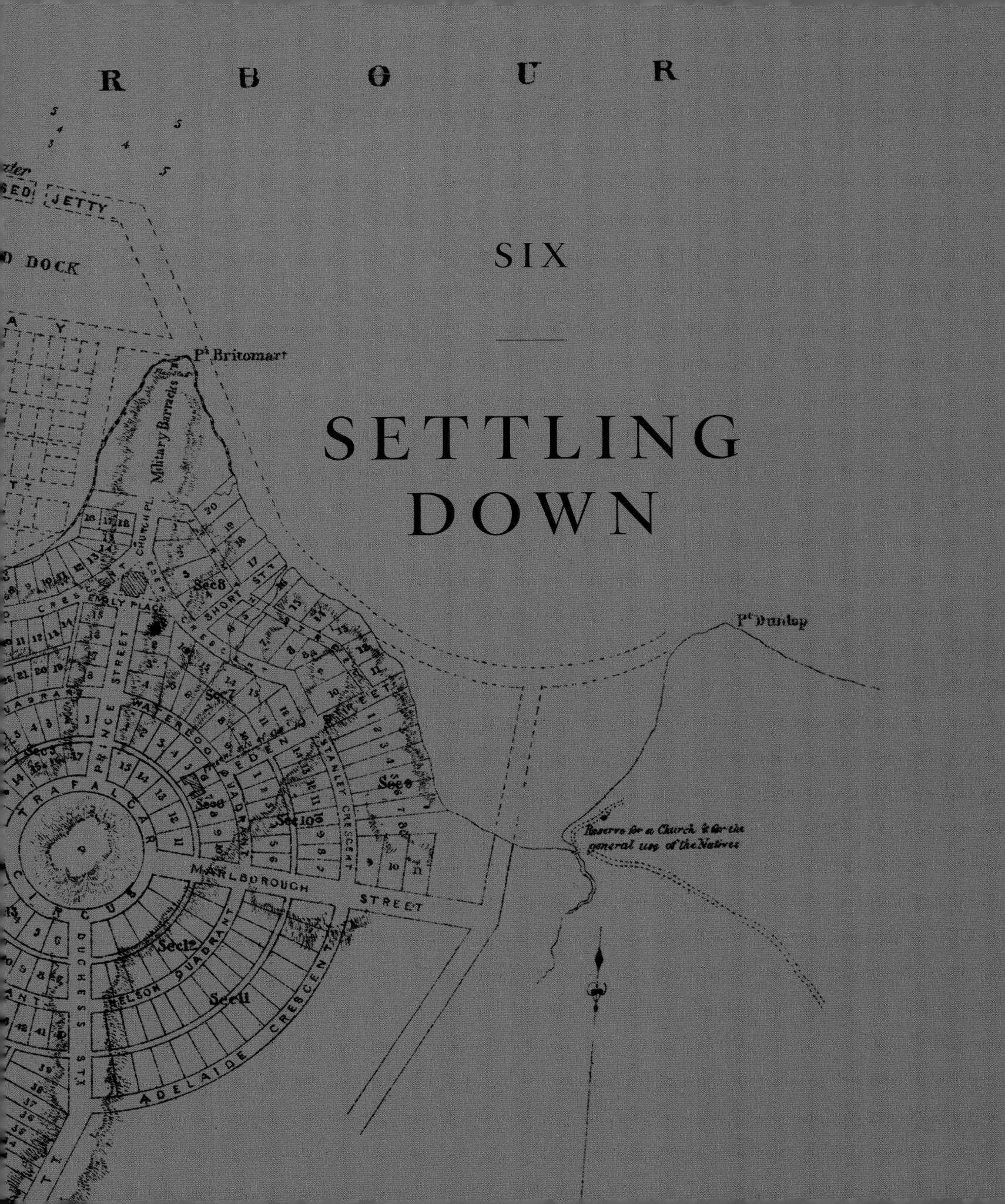

SETTLING DOWN

The first European settlements in New Zealand were little more than camps. They generally came about when sealers, whalers, timbermen or flax cutters found it expedient to establish a base on shore. Needless to say, these encampments were very much at the grace and favour of the tangata whenua, who tolerated them while there were trade advantages, and pushed them back into the sea when there were not. At the turn of the eighteenth and nineteenth centuries, there were a number of Europeans living among the Māori who were more or less acculturated—so-called 'Pākehā Māori'. There were shore whaling stations, from which hardy souls kept lookout for passing whales and rowed out and attacked them in open boats. There were rugged entrepreneurs—traders in provisions for visiting ships and in commodities such as timber and flax outwards, and iron goods— especially muskets—inwards. And from 1814, when the Church of England's Samuel Marsden first set foot ashore, there were missionaries, intent on living amongst the Māori and getting them to see the error of their heathen ways.

The first permanent settlement of any description was that at Riverton on the Southland south coast, closely followed by Kororāreka in the Bay of Islands (now known as Russell, but known to most in its day as the 'Hell Hole of the Pacific', on account of its lawlessness). As ever, Māori tolerated these alien footholds so long as the flow of trade goods was maintained—but the most traded and sought-after commodity of all was already beginning to change their world. Ngā Puhi, an alliance of a number of northern iwi, were the first to acquire an arsenal of firearms, and the first to set off with them on a mission to settle old scores. The great taua they launched to Auckland and Hauraki in 1818 were the beginning of a two-decades-long conflagration that saw the pre-European social order swept away. Whole hapū were wiped out, and many, many more forced off their ancestral lands; the map of te ao Māori was redrawn forever (see p. 127).

And that was just the beginning of what has been called the 'fatal impact' of European colonisation.

———

The first attempts to found British colonies in New Zealand were the result of private enterprise. Seeing the demand from the hundreds of thousands of people who had few or no prospects in stagnating, overcrowded England, the architects of the first New Zealand Company proposed to supply a solution in the form of a planned settlement—a small group of colonists and a small security force—on the other side of the world. The British government was lukewarm on the idea, but the company's founder, John George Lambton, first Earl of Durham and known to his contemporaries as 'Radical Jack', didn't let that stop him. In 1825, he commissioned Captain James Herd to perform an exploratory sweep of New Zealand for potential settlement sites. Herd obliged, running south to north, considering and discarding Rakiura/Stewart Island and the site of present-day Dunedin. He was more impressed with Whanganui-a-Tara, today the site of Wellington, and he also surveyed and set out to buy several tracts of land in the vicinity of 'Shoukianga' (Hokianga). In the end, however, he unilaterally decided that a colony in New Zealand would never be economically viable. He returned to England to tell his masters as much.

There the venture may have rested, had news of it not reached the ears of Edward Gibbon Wakefield, who was cooling his heels in London's Newgate prison for the abduction of a fifteen-year-old heiress in 1826. Shortly after Herd returned to England, Wakefield published the first of a number of pamphlets setting out his views on how to do colonisation properly (emigration being very much on his mind, given how thoroughly he had soiled his nest in England). He was an advocate of 'systematic' settlement rather than the inefficient, haphazard form that was under way in Australia. Central to his idea was the notion of what he called the 'sufficient price' of land: it ought to cost enough to buy land in your new colony to attract wealthy buyers, but not so much that someone working for them for wages couldn't dream of also buying land in some not-so-distant future. This (so he thought) would prevent land becoming locked up in the kinds of vast estates there were in Australia; it would also ensure a steady supply of labour, from those who were too poor to afford land of their own but who could expect, through working hard for landowners, to save enough to buy some.

Wakefield was taken seriously, and at the time was ranked amongst such luminaries of political economy as John Stuart Mill, Thomas Malthus and even Karl Marx, all of whom were trying to nut out a solution

FAIRBURN'S CHART OF THE MISSION STATION AT PAIHIA, 1833

While their countrymen and others were busily exploiting the whales, seals, timber and flax resources of New Zealand, the great work of a different class of Englishman, as they saw it, was to bring civilisation to the Māori. This work was well advanced by 1833, if this pleasant little sketch map is anything to go by. By that date, they had brought not only Christianity—the Anglican Church Missionary Society (CMS) had begun evangelising in 1814—but also cricket: a wicket is marked at the end of Horotutu Beach in the northwestern corner of the map and it was here, according to the map's creator, that the first game in New Zealand was played.

The CMS mission was established at Paihia in 1823 by Henry Williams, whose wife Marianne could see little future in trying to spread the Good Word across the water in the 'Hell Hole of the Pacific', the whaling port Kororāreka. She chose this site, and it was here that New Zealand's first church was built, as was the printing press on which the first Māori version of the Bible was produced. Here, too, Edward Fairburn, the apparent artist of this sketch and the grandfather of the poet A. R. D. Fairburn, was born in 1827, in the house belonging to his parents along the road from the Williamses. The map was not made at the time: instead, it was a reminiscence, and this version itself states that it was a copy. It's not known when the original or the copy were done—or why it was that Fairburn chose 1833 as the moment in time he wanted to chart.

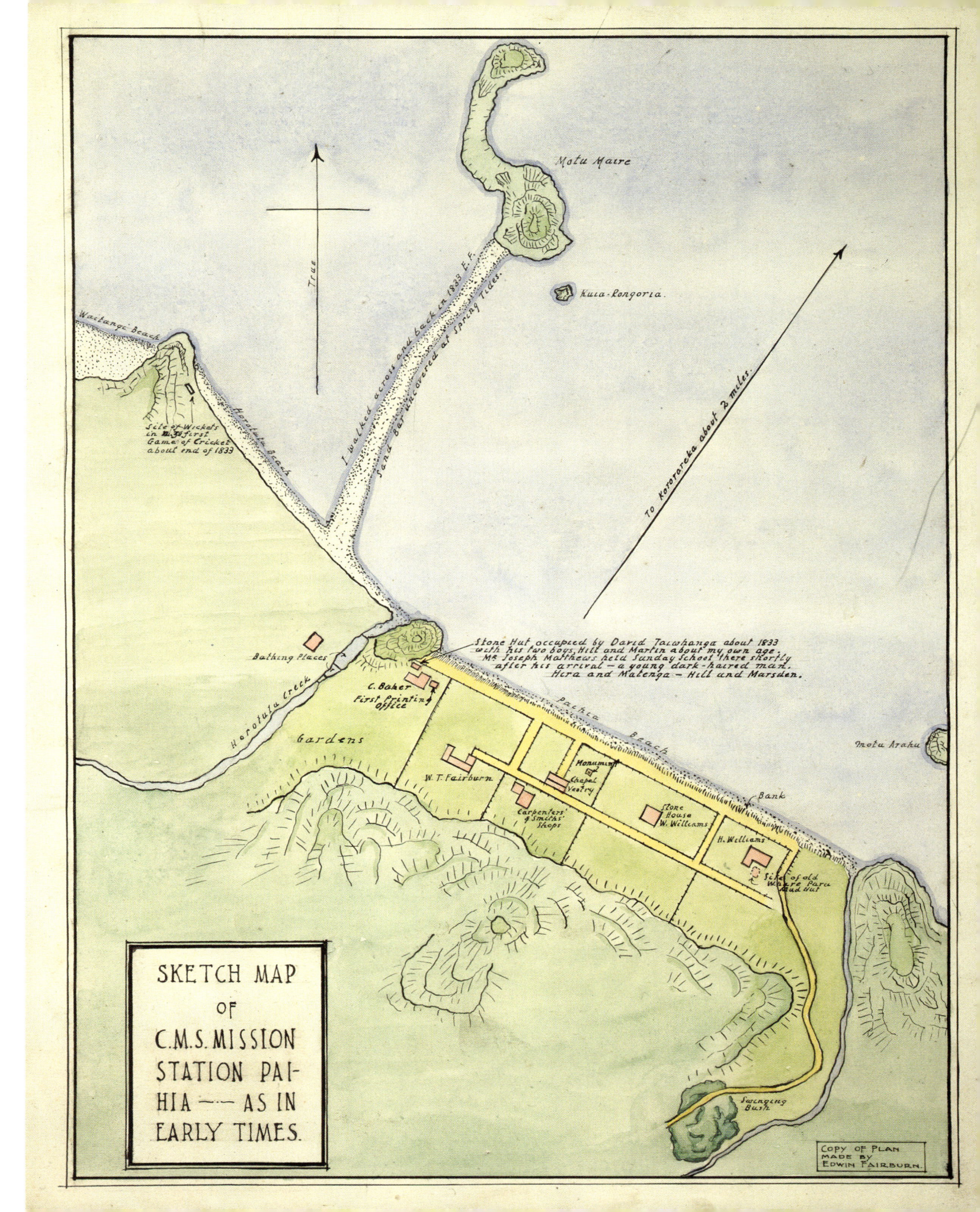

SKETCH MAP OF C.M.S. MISSION STATION PAIHIA — AS IN EARLY TIMES.

Copy of plan made by Edwin Fairburn.

- Motu Maire
- Kuia-Rongoria
- Motu Arahu
- Waitangi Beach
- Site of Wickets in the First Game of Cricket about end of 1833
- I walked across and back in 1833 E.F. Sand bar uncovered at Spring Tides
- True (North)
- To Kororareka about 2 miles.
- Horotutu Creek
- Bathing Places
- C. Baker First Printing Office
- Stone Hut occupied by David Tawhanga about 1833 with his two boys, Hill and Martin about my own age. Mr Joseph Matthews held Sunday School there shortly after his arrival — a young dark-haired man. Hira and Matenga — Hill and Marsden.
- Gardens
- Paihia Beach
- W. T. Fairburn
- Carpenters & Smiths' Shops
- Chapel Vestry
- Monument
- Stone House W. Williams
- H. Williams
- Bank
- Site of old Whare Paru Mud Hut
- Swinging Bush

to Britain's woes, too. Once Wakefield was released from prison, he was instrumental in the launch of a scheme to settle South Australia. His involvement in its execution was minimal, but in 1837, he managed to obtain a royal charter for the colonisation of New Zealand. 'Radical Jack' Lambton was an associate in this scheme, which didn't immediately get off the ground, but in 1838, a revitalised New Zealand Company was floated. Lambton invited Wakefield to join, even as rumours were abroad that New Zealand was to be made an official colony of Britain.

Wakefield's time had come. He urged his fellow directors to proceed with their plans to establish a private colony forthwith, on the grounds that the British government wouldn't interfere with a fait accompli. A ship, the *Tory*, was purchased and promptly despatched in August 1839, with the company's principal agent, William Wakefield (brother of Edward), aboard. Another, the *Cuba*, sailed a month later, carrying a team of surveyors under the leadership of the company's principal surveyor, William Mein Smith. With the company's initial public offer of plots of land selling like hot cakes, both William Wakefield and Smith had very important jobs to do: they had to see, respectively, to the purchase and survey of the land that was needed to make good on company promises.

A mere month after they had sailed, and with no news of how they might have got on expected for a couple of months more, the first of five ships full of bright-eyed, bushy-tailed colonists who had believed the company's slick advertising hype departed for New Zealand. The dangers and discomforts they were prepared to endure are eloquent of how poor they saw their prospects to be in the Old Country—and how glittering the vista set to open up for them on the other side of the world. On the face of it, you could understand their optimism. Each had purchased the title to a 'package' of land—a one-acre 'town' plot and a ten-acre 'country plot', the idea being that the proceeds of working the country plot productively would finance a comfortable lifestyle in town. The money they had paid over to the company, they were assured, would be used to fund infrastructure and to recruit and send out the labourers who would do the actual work. Well, that sounded like a sweet deal. And they had even seen drawings of the town, a tidy grid of streets laid out on either side of a river, not at all unlike the new city of Adelaide in the Wakefield-influenced colony of South Australia. It was going to be called Britannia.

———

It's unlikely the truth of the saying 'It is better to travel hopefully than to arrive' has ever been more thoroughly borne out than when the *Aurora*, the first of the five ships, dropped anchor in Whanganui-a-Tara, or Port Nicholson—named by James Herd for the Sydney harbourmaster, John Nicholson—in early January 1840. The four-month voyage had included a brief stopover across Cook Strait in Port Hardy on D'Urville Island, where the immigrant ships had been directed to rendezvous in order to learn where exactly their passengers' new lives were to begin. But the settlers soon found that the New Zealand Company was behind in its work. *Very* behind. It had not yet finalised details of the purchase of the land for the new arrivals from Māori, let alone surveyed it and parcelled it up into neat plots. What's more, whereas the prospect was in some ways promising—a broad tract of flat land lay behind the dunes and flax of the foreshore at the head of the harbour, and it did indeed look as though a town might be sited there, once the mature forest was removed—there was also cause for anxiety, in that it was obvious there wouldn't be room adjacent to the Hutt River (named for Sir William Hutt, chairman of the New Zealand Company) for the town of Britannia *and* everyone's country plots. The rest of the general area was steep, scrub-covered and forbidding. Perhaps most unsettling of all was that it looked very much as though the site were already occupied. There were Māori pā visible, and extensive cultivations. Nonetheless, the Māori welcomed the settlers who, after a landing on the long, sandy beach at Pito-one (the name means 'end of the long sandy beach'), got on with it, building huts and establishing gardens and such essential services as a flour mill and a newspaper press.

Whereas the chief surveyor, William Mein Smith, had been instructed to establish Britannia around the harbour (on the present-day site of Wellington), he had unilaterally decided that the Hutt Valley was a much better fit for the plans he had been given to execute. He was reasonably well advanced in his work when William Wakefield arrived at the end of an extensive land acquisition tour of New Zealand. The company's principal agent was not at all happy to find his orders being flouted, and he was also of a sufficiently vindictive cast of character to be mightily pleased when Smith's settlement was washed away, along with most of the settlers, by a flood of the Hutt River in April 1840.

Looking around himself and noting all of the features of the valley that indicated floods were a regular occurrence, Smith faced facts and relocated his activities to Lambton Harbour after all. The new site was named Thorndon (after the Essex country seat of Baron William Petre, director of the New Zealand Company), but the basic town plan didn't change much. Despite the highly unconducive terrain, Smith still endeavoured to lay everything out in a neat grid, partly because it was faster and cheaper to proceed with a running survey that used squares and rectangles to measure and divide land areas than to perform the triangulation more commonly used for the purpose of establishing legal boundaries: after all, speed and economy were of the essence for the New Zealand Company. This task must have been frustrating enough, but far worse was Wakefield's refusal to properly resource or support Smith. This was to be the pattern. For although Wakefield had no training in surveying whatsoever, he laid claim to some knowledge of it—Edward senior, the father of the colonising Wakefields, had been a surveyor— and his style was a difficult mix of micro-managing and dictatorial. When friction between the men rose to intolerable levels, Wakefield engineered Smith's dismissal and replaced him with Samuel Brees. He soon alienated Brees, too, and still another surveyor, Alfred Wills, took up the poisoned chalice.

―――

Meanwhile, things in general were turning against the New Zealand Company project. Disturbed by the complaints it was hearing (mostly from scandalised missionaries) about the behaviour of British subjects on New Zealand shores, and spooked by the possibility that France might try to steal it from under its very nose, the British government made good on its occasional threats to annex New Zealand in early 1840. We became a department of the colonial government of New South Wales and a naval officer,

COBHAM'S PLAN OF WELLINGTON, 1839

Robbie Burns once wrote about what happened to the best-laid schemes of mice and men. Who knows how it works out for mice, but the collision of the vision of New Zealand Company town planner Samuel Cobham with the reality of the site where his settlement was to be realised is as fine an example of things 'gang agley' as you could ask for. Cobham's town was laid out with a view to a surveyor's convenience: it is a patchwork of perfectly uniform plots of land defined by a regular grid of straight streets (each 45 feet wide and paved with wood). Civic amenities are thoughtfully placed: the government buildings, presidential palace and law courts in a cluster around the horticultural market (but not too close to the fish market); the prison next to that other refuse bin, the cemetery; the arsenal and battery next to the river, presumably in case of fire; the abattoir also on the river, to facilitate the discharge of waste. Outside the town precincts, the designer firmly states that there will be 1100 farms of 10 acres each.

If the New Zealand Company at large can be likened to present-day wide-boy property developers, then Cobham was that kind of architect whom builders dread to deal with: impractical and with a cavalier disregard (in this instance, born of ignorance) for site realities. Poor old William Mein Smith, the company's chief surveyor, was the man charged with executing this plan on the banks of the Hutt River even as the first ships full of colonists rolled and heaved their way towards him from the other side of the world. No pressure! He gave it a good shake, until a major flood of the Hutt River put him out of this misery. The site of the principal settlement was forthwith shifted around the harbour.

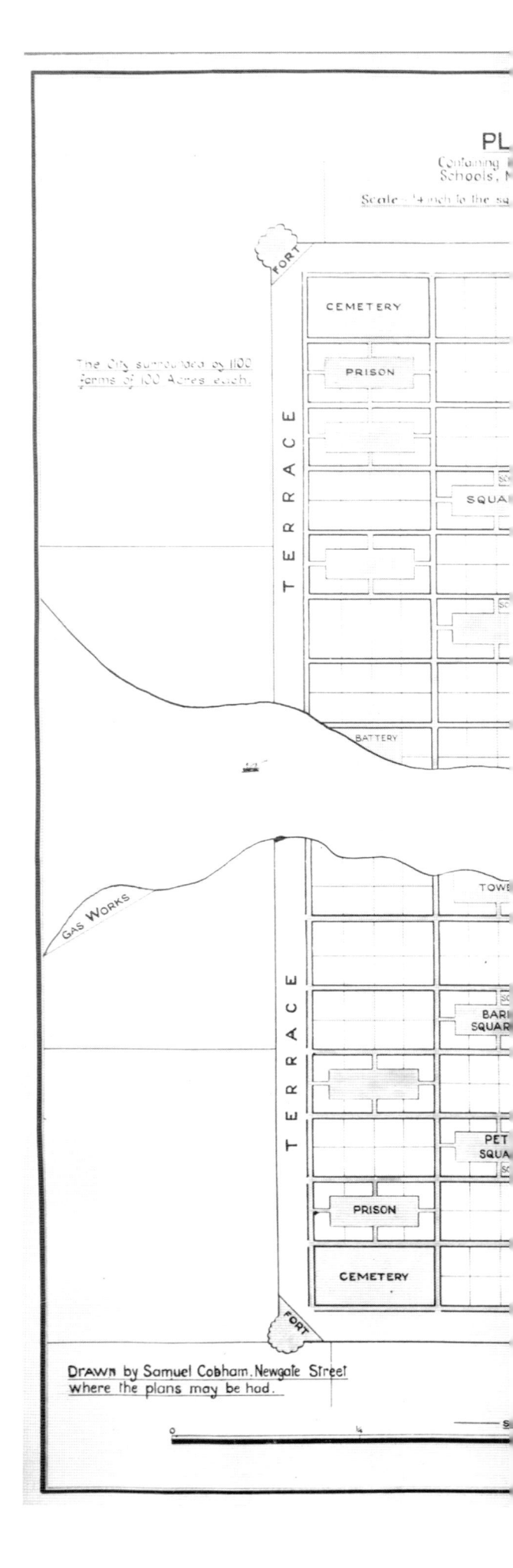

A PROPOSED
the CITY of WELLINGTON in the first Settlement in NEW ZEALAND founded 1839-40

exclusive of Streets & Terraces round the Town, thus allowing 261 Acres for Government purposes, Squares, Public Buildings, Hospitals, Wharfage, etc etc and 1100 Acres for the colonists for Building purposes etc etc.

Streets 45 feet wide & paved with wood

TERRACE

- CEMETERY
- ALDERMAN SQUARE
- SCHOOL
- ELLIOTSON SQUARE
- SCHOOL
- MECHANICS INSTITUTION
- THOMPSON SQUARE
- SQUARE
- HOSPITAL
- HOSPITAL
- PUBLIC BATHS ETC
- LEADENHALL MARKET
- COVENT GARDEN THEATRE
- PUBLIC BATHS LIBRARY ETC
- SOAMES SQUARE
- POLICE OFFICE
- WELLINGTON
- COVENT GARDEN MARKET
- SCHOOL
- SCHOOL
- SCHOOL
- ROYAL EXCHANGE
- ARSENAL BARRACKS & BATTERY
- GOVERNMENT DOCK YARD
- CUSTOM HOUSE
- DOCKS
- POST OFFICE
- HUNGERFORD FISH MARKET

Tunnel or Bridge

- ABBATOIR
- BILLINGSGATE FISH MARKET
- SMITHFIELD MARKET
- MOLESWORTH
- RUSSELL SQUARE
- DURHAM SQUARE
- CAMPBELL SQUARE
- SQUARE
- SCHOOL
- DOCKS
- GOVERNMENT OFFICES
- DRURY LANE THEATRE
- NEWGATE MARKET
- COLLEGE OF PHYSICIANS
- SCHOOL
- PUBLIC BATHS ETC
- HOSPITAL
- GOVERNMENT OFFICES
- POLICE OFFICE
- HORTICULTURAL MARKET
- MUSEUM ETC
- HOSPITAL
- PUBLIC BATHS ETC
- HOUSES OF LEGISLATURE
- PUBLIC RECORD OFFICE
- COLLEGE OF SURGEONS
- SCHOOL
- GOVERNMENT OFFICES
- GUILDS OF LAW
- SCHOOL
- PRESIDENTS PALACE
- SCHOOL
- CEMETERY

TERRACE 70 Yards wide round the city.

ONE MILE · ¾ · 1 MILE

Cemeteries having an area of 8 Acres each
Each blank Square such as the Post Office, Royal Exchange & having 3 Acres Area

William Hobson, was appointed lieutenant-governor. Hobson and others drafted a treaty between the British Crown and Māori that was signed by himself and 45 chiefs at Waitangi in the Bay of Islands on 6 February 1840. Copies were subsequently sent on tour for further signatures.

One of Hobson's first acts was to proclaim an enquiry into pre-treaty land acquisitions by Europeans, the New Zealand Company chief among them. If William Wakefield was to be believed, he had bought up practically half of mainland New Zealand. The new New Zealand government wasn't so sure he *could* be believed, and was cool on the company's ambitions to press ahead with establishing other settlements. Nevertheless, in 1841, it granted consent for the company to develop a new town at the top of the South Island to be known as Nelson (after Vice-Admiral Horatio Nelson). Three immigrant vessels arrived later that year to find the town laid out in the company's trademark neat grid, with wooden pegs at the corner of each plot and even some huts and sheds established as amenities.

But the Nelson scheme was problematic from the start. Few of the immigrants who arrived were in a position to buy land: most were looking for little more than a steady job, and because the town site was nearly as constrained as Wellington, there was little adjacent land for agriculture. Within a couple of years, many of those who had intended settling in Nelson had drifted away. Yet another settlement had been established in the shadow of Taranaki, where British trader Richard 'Dicky' Barrett had been living amongst Māori since 1828. With his mana and his fluency in te reo, Barrett was instrumental in many of the New Zealand Company's negotiations with Māori, and it was he who prevailed upon Taranaki chiefs to sell land for the new site. The first settlers arrived at the end of March 1841 and found their new township neatly pegged out in—you guessed it—a grid pattern. And around the same time, in an effort to supply some of the Wellington settlers with their promised 'country' plots of land to go with their town plots, Edward Gibbon Wakefield's son Edward Jerningham Wakefield had aggressively negotiated what he thought was the full and final sale of 40,000 acres of land adjacent to the Whanganui River. A nice, grid-shaped township named 'Petre' (after Baron Petre) was established there.

By 1843, despite Edward Gibbon Wakefield's boasts that the New Zealand Company was now cosily established as the government's agent in the colonial enterprise, it faced financial difficulties. Its own work on planned colonisation slowed down, and its hunger for land had also brought it into conflict with Māori (see chapter eight). Nevertheless, Wakefield was a prime mover in the establishment of two further planned settlements. The first of these was at Dunedin, where there had long been whaling, sealing and trading operations and where, in 1848, an initiative of the Free Church of Scotland saw a settlement founded.

The man responsible for selecting the site and laying it out was Frederick Tuckett, the New Zealand Company's man who had been responsible for creating Nelson. In his search for suitable land, he had considered but rejected (on the grounds that it was too poorly drained) the area adjacent to Banks Peninsula, which was already being farmed. This site was eventually (in 1850) selected by another religious settlement outfit, the Canterbury Association, a kind of joint venture between Wakefield and John Godley, an Irish-born politician and mainstay of the Church of England. Wakefield and Godley had initially been interested in situating their new town in the Wairarapa, but when this was rejected, a site to north of Port Cooper (soon to be named Lyttelton, after Baron Lyttelton, chair of the Canterbury Association) was selected instead to be the site of the main township, to be named Christchurch after Christ Church, Godley's old Oxford University college.

———

Alongside the initial flurry of 'systematic' colonisation by private interests, there was a small amount of official settlement going on, too. Understandably reluctant to establish his capital in a place known as the 'Hell Hole of the Pacific', Hobson commissioned his acting surveyor general, Felton Mathew, to draw up plans for a new township a little down the road, at a place named Okiato (which he renamed Russell, for Lord John Russell, Secretary of State for the Colonies). American trader (and the first US consul) James Clendon had been living there for a couple of years. A tent city sprang up to house the machinery of government, but within a year, Hobson (now fully fledged Governor Hobson, following the devolution of self-government from New South Wales) decided to up sticks and relocate to a site a couple of hundred kilometres further south, on the Waitematā Harbour. The land in these parts had been largely depopulated by the twin depredations of the musket wars and epidemics of European diseases to which Māori had no natural immunity. Hobson acquired the land necessary to found his new capital—1215 hectares bounded by the Waitematā and a boundary that ran from Hobson Bay (the name came later) to Mount Eden and thence to Cox's Creek—for the bargain price of fifty blankets, some clothes and bolts of cloth, some tobacco, sugar and flour, twenty-six iron pots, twenty hatchets and just over £50 in cash. To Mathew fell the honour of laying out the town. Meanwhile, with the relocation of some of Hobson's government officials up the road, the name 'Russell' began to be used in relation to Kororāreka, the principal port. The change was made official in 1844. As with the Okiato plans he drew up, Mathew's grand design for Auckland (which Hobson named after George Eden, first Earl of Auckland) was never realised, either, although traces of how it was conceived can be detected in the town as it was eventually constructed.

———

The general pattern of settlement after the formalisation of British colonial rule tended to follow in the wake of economic progress and the development of communications. Farms were established in areas such as the Wairarapa and on the Canterbury Plains, and villages (later towns) to service these enterprises sprang up. Harbours adjacent to areas being exploited for their timber or (later) gold resources soon developed into townships. And as friction increased between land-hungry European colonists and the tangata whenua, garrisons were established (see chapter eight).

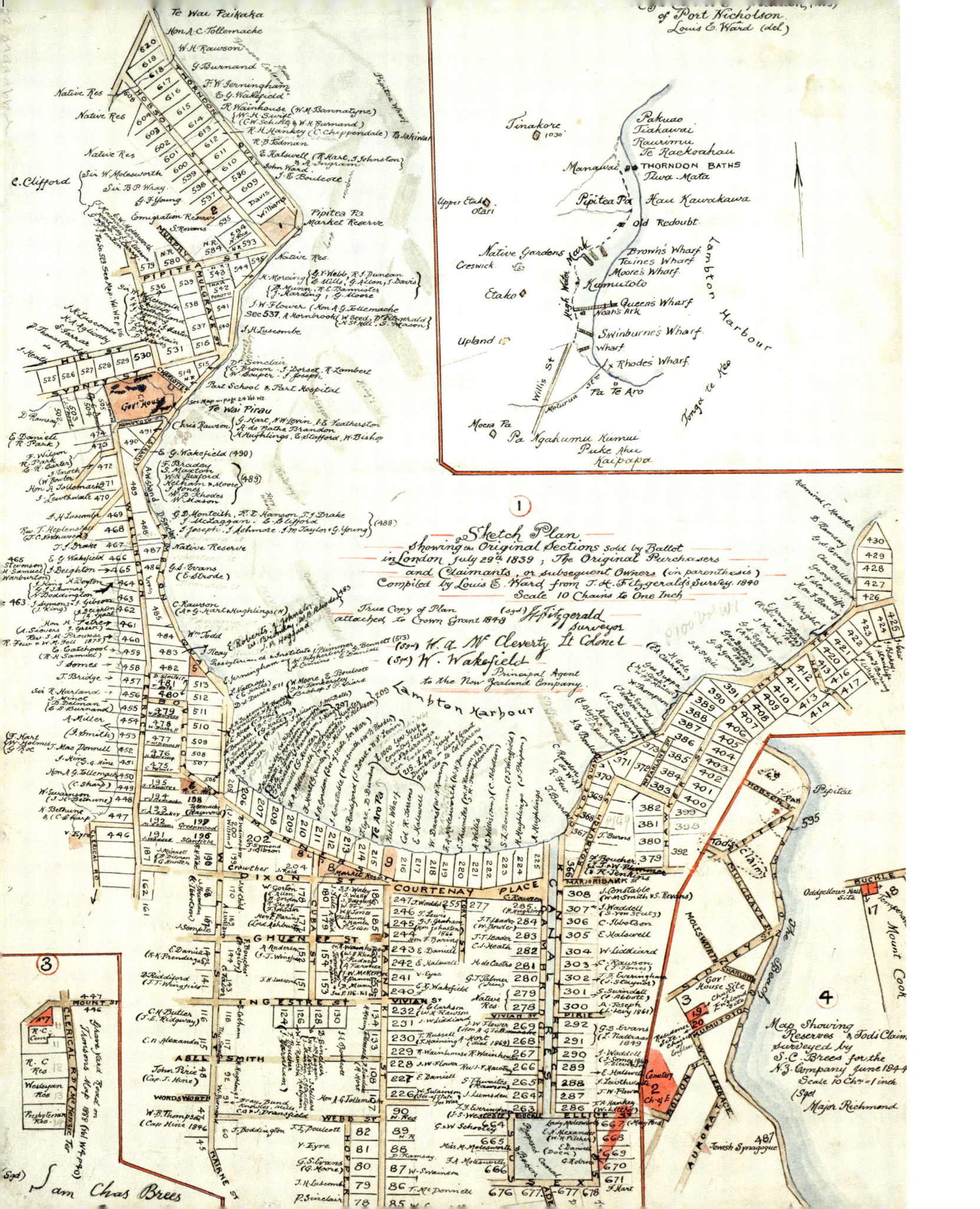

Sketch Plan
Showing the Original Sections sold by Ballot
in London July 29th 1839; The Original Purchasers
and Claimants, or subsequent Owners (in parenthesis)
Compiled by Louis E. Ward from J.H. Fitzgerald's Survey, 1840
Scale 10 Chains to One Inch

True Copy of Plan
attached to Crown Grant 1849 (sgd) J.H. Fitzgerald
Surveyor
(sgd) W. M. Cleverty, Lt Colonel
(sgd) W. Wakefield
Principal Agent
to the New Zealand Company

Map Showing
Reserves & Todd's Claim
Surveyed by
S.C. Brees for the
N.Z. Company June 1844
Scale 10 Chs = 1 inch
(Sgd) Major Richmond

FITZGERALD'S ORIGINAL BALLOT PLAN OF WELLINGTON, 1839

Once it had been decided to establish Wellington (as it came to be known later) on its present-day site, a survey took place under the supervision of William Mein Smith's former apprentice, Thomas Henry Fitzgerald, and so began the task of accommodating the 1100-odd settlers to whom land had been sold in a ballot. This sketch shows the names of those balloted alongside their plots: it's a far cry from Cobham's version, but it got the job done—or half of it, at least, as there was still the matter of finding 'country' plots to go with these 'town' plots. Many of the names will ring bells with modern-day Wellingtonians, not least because many of them became street names as the city expanded into its largely precipitous hinterland. Other names associated with stories in this book feature: Edward Gibbon Wakefield's name is next to lots 217 and 615. E. S. Halswell's name is next to lots 289 and 610. Walter Mantell seems to have bought lot 389—a prime bit of dirt on Oriental Bay—from a man who later went on to survey Auckland, George Duppa. Samuel Cobham's own name appears beside plot 118.

There are other interesting features on this map, too. Where the Basin Reserve is now was an actual basin, a low, swampy area that Ernest Louis Ward (the draughtsman) identifies as a potential shipping basin, communicating with the harbour via a canal (to be constructed). Notable by their scarcity are Māori lands: according to Wakefield's deal with Te Ātiawa, a tenth of all land purchased by the company was to be reserved for Māori.

Wellington City Council has enabled an online copy of this map to be layered with more recent maps and aerial photographs, a fascinating way of relating the present-day city to its somewhat shambolic past.

Following page
CARRINGTON'S PLAN OF THE COUNTRY SECTIONS LAID OUT ON THE WANGANUI, 1841

Wanganui (now Whanganui) came about in practically the reverse of the usual pattern: instead of a town becoming established as a beach-head of settlement and creeping inwards, it was originally conceived as a rural district with a town added as a necessary accoutrement. With too little flat land available in the Wellington district, the New Zealand Company felt obliged to look further afield for land with which it could fulfil its obligations to its stockholders. Nearly 40,000 acres were purchased from Māori in 1840, then surveyed and parcelled into blocks by the company's assistant surveyors, Wellington Carrington and Joseph Thomas. The plan allows a site for a proposed town, which was to be called Petre, after Baron Petre, one of the New Zealand Company directors: it seems significant that very many of the blocks have already been dibsed by Carrington.

The town that was eventually built came to be known as Wanganui, but its early years were somewhat precarious: the original land purchases were disputed by those supposed to have sold it, particularly those Māori who lived upriver. The company was obliged to make another payment to secure its position, and even then, there was the constant threat of conflict.

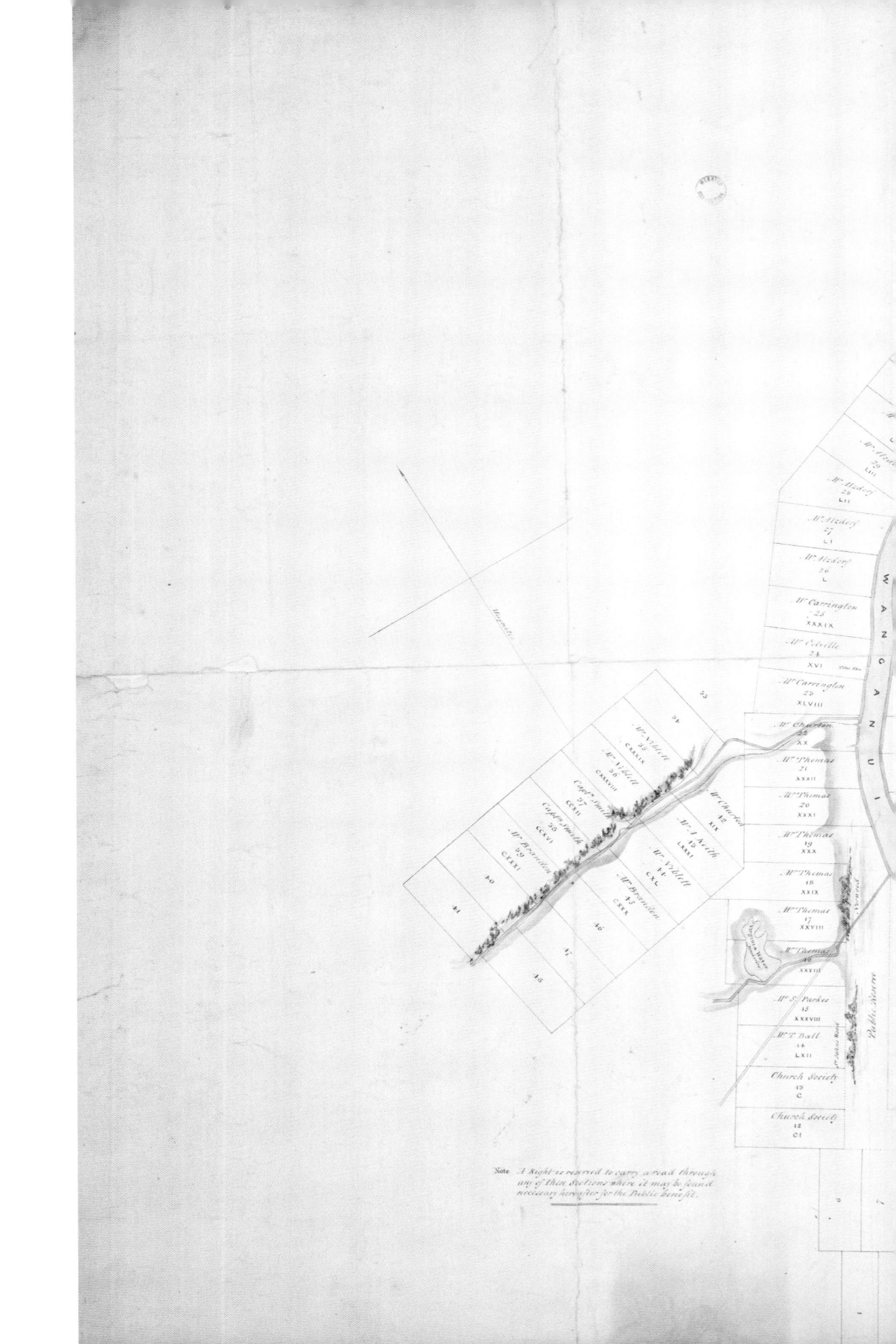

Note. A Right is reserved to carry a road through
any of these Sections where it may be found
necessary hereafter for the Public Benefit.

PLAN
of the
— COUNTRY SECTIONS —
LAID OUT ON THE
— WANGANUI —
1841

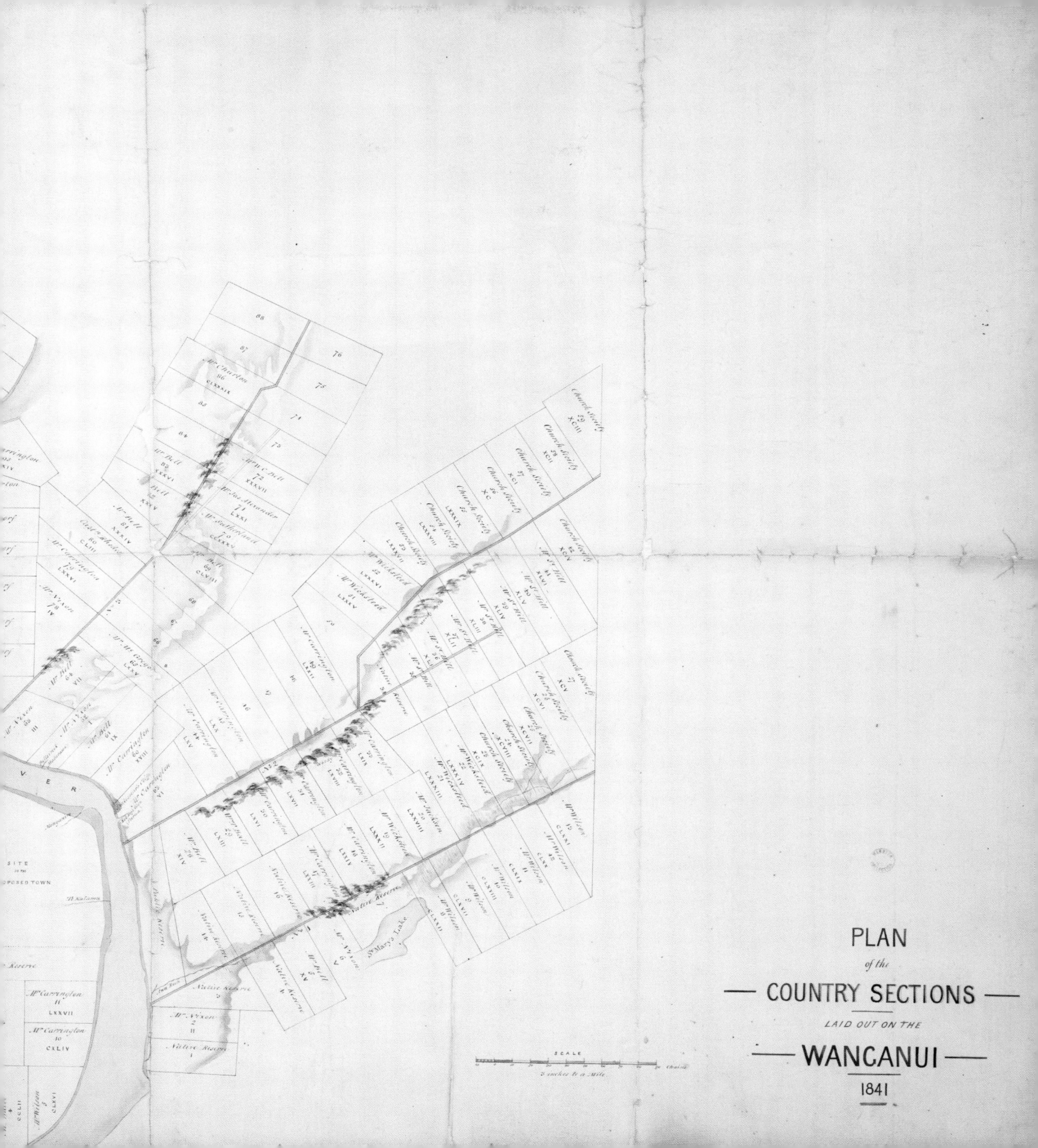

MEIN SMITH'S PLAN OF THE TOWN OF WELLINGTON, 1840

Before he was sacked by his boss, William Wakefield, and replaced by Samuel Charles Brees, William Mein Smith had completed the not-inconsiderable task of laying out the new town of Wellington on the unpromising terrain. Some of the street orientations didn't survive into the final draught: Brees claimed Smith's work was shoddy, and tinkered with it in many respects. Some of the place names will be unfamiliar to Wellingtonians today, such as Ingestre Street, John Abel Smith Street, Sussex Square and Warri Pori Street; and of course, the sight of the water lapping the edge of Lambton Quay comes as a mild shock. The reconfiguration of the shoreline by earthquake and reclamation lay many years in the future. Native Reserves are shaded in green, including the Te Aro and Kumutoto pā at either end of the foreshore.

MOUNT ALBERT

MOUNT VICTORIA

MOUNT COOK

Pah To Aro

Public Wharf

Roman Catholic Cemetery

Hilly Country covered with Timber

PLAN
OF
THE TOWN OF
WELLINGTON
PORT NICHOLSON
the First and Principal Settlement
of the
NEW ZEALAND COMPANY
14th August
1840

Scale

The Upper Figures in the respective Acres show the Numbers denoting the Orders of Choice, as drawn at the Ballot in England.
The Lower Figures show the Positions of the Acres selected in respect of the Ballot Numbering.
The Dotted Lines mark the extent of the Land around the Town, reserved for the enjoyment of the Public and not to be built upon.
The Sections tinted Green are Native Reserves. Those tinted Grey are the Church Missionary Stations, and those tinted Pink are reserved for Public Buildings &c.

W. M. Smith Captain
Royal Artillery
Surveyor General

MATHEW'S PLAN OF RUSSELL, 1840

When New Zealand's brand-new lieutenant-governor William Hobson decided to establish his administration in the Bay of Islands in 1840, it didn't take him long to reject the idea of basing himself at the place that we know as Russell today, but which was known then variously as Kororāreka (the name translates as 'sweet penguins') or the aforementioned Pacific hell hole. Instead, he looked a little up the road (or where a road would one day be) at Okiato. He charged his acting surveyor general, Felton Mathew, who had not long before turned down a similar role at Port Philip (now Melbourne), to lay out the new colony's capital. This map was the result, although very little of what Mathew envisaged ever came to pass. Hardly had sheds been built and tents pitched on the site than a decision was made to shift south to Auckland, which was growing in size and economic importance. The name 'Russell' came, through usage, to be associated with Kororāreka, until it eventually supplanted it. Meanwhile, the name of the sometime capital of the nation reverted to Okiato.

CORRESPONDENCE RESPECTING THE COLONY OF NEW ZEALAND

PLAN
OF
RUSSELL
BAY OF ISLANDS
NEW ZEALAND
Surveyed by
Felton Mathew Esqre Surv.^r Genl
1841

Scale of Chains

569 Ordered by The House of Commons to be Printed 12th Augt 1842

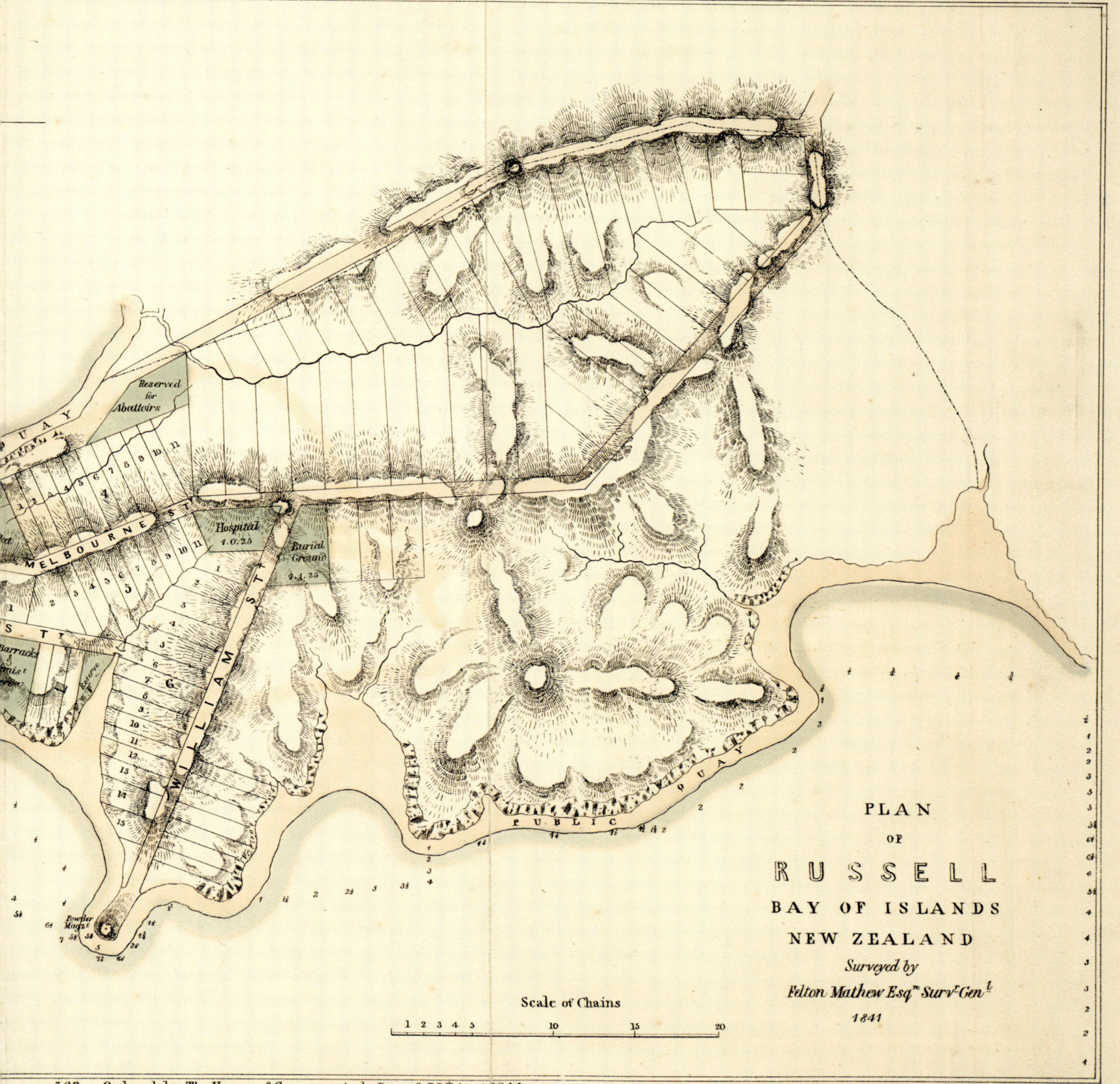

James & Luke J Hansard Printers

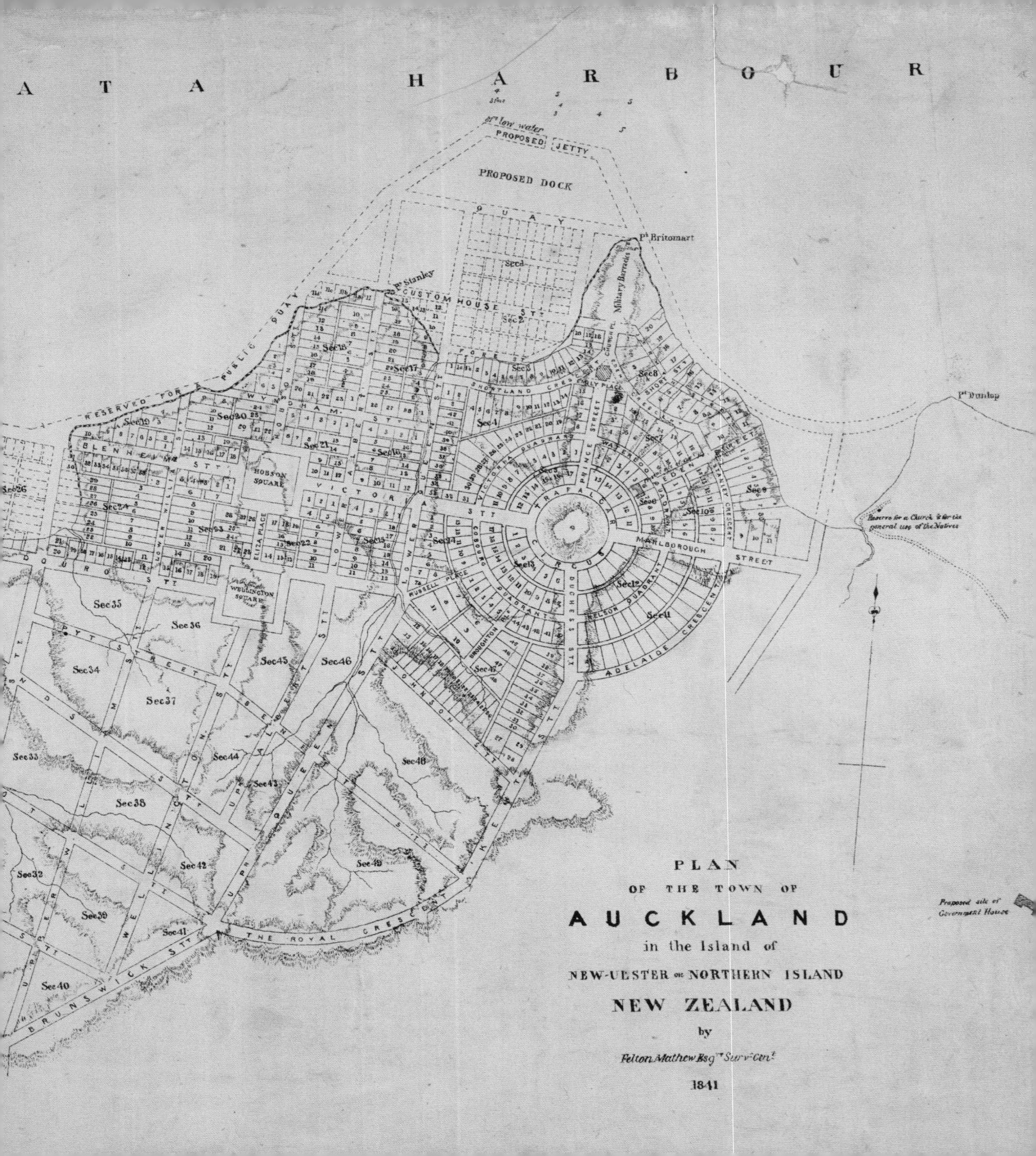

PLAN
OF THE TOWN OF
AUCKLAND
in the Island of
NEW-ULSTER or NORTHERN ISLAND
NEW ZEALAND
by
Felton Mathew Esq'r Surv'r Gen'l
1841

MATHEW'S PLAN OF AUCKLAND, 1841

If Felton Mathew had had his way, New Zealand's largest city would have looked very different. You can only imagine the traffic congestion as Aucklanders grappled with the etiquette involved in a roundabout the size of Trafalgar Circus, the most striking feature of his plan for the elegant town that never was. It would have been a circus, all right. There are some vestigial elements of the Circus, which would have been sited roughly where Albert Park is now, still to be seen in Auckland: there is a Waterloo Quadrant and an Eden Terrace. Shortland Crescent has become Shortland Street, and many of the other streets—Victoria Street, Albert Street, Wyndham Street—are more or less as drawn. Some streets never made it, such as Vandalour Street, William Street and Marsden Street, and nor did Wellington or Hobson squares. The reclamation of the bay between Point Britomart and Point Stanley (known then as Commercial Bay) is projected; it's interesting to note that Mathew would have reserved much of Parnell for the Church of England and 'for the general use of natives'. That didn't happen, either.

Following page
SKETCH MAP SHEWING THE SITE OF CHRISTCHURCH (CREATOR UNKNOWN), 1849

This beautiful map was made at a time when Christchurch was merely a twinkle in the eye of Joseph Thomas, the Canterbury Association's chief surveyor, and a small brown square on the map, little larger than the square representing the proposed town of Lincoln. Much else is different. The Avon is known as the 'River Shakespeare', the Waimakariri is known as the 'River Courtenay' (and a pencil notation beneath it gives an alternative, Waikirikiri), Diamond Harbour is 'Port Victoria', to go with Port Albert (Port Levy), and Riccarton is shown as a bush area to the west of the proposed city. Roads, according to the map, are still under construction, hence the numerous notes indicating the limits of small boat navigation, and the location of a place for landing stores and people at the entrance to the Heathcote estuary. Until the rail tunnel from Lyttelton was pushed through in 1867, communication between Christchurch and its port at Lyttelton was either around Banks Peninsula by small sailing craft or via the steep track on the Port Hills, which came to be known as the Bridle Path, due to the need to lead horses by the bridle here. Notations in ink indicate the presence of gold and copper in the Malvern Hills, and pencil notes across the top of the map record the first public market to be held in Christchurch, on Saturday, 18 May 1853, and the presence of a seam of good-quality coal on Motunau, an island up the coast in Pegasus Bay.

1st public Market held at Christch— on Saty 18 May 53 — 874 —

Sketch Map Shewing the Site of the CANTERBURY SETTLEMENT.

SCALE OF MILES

London Decr 1849. Reduced and Drawn by A Wills late Assistant Surveyor from the Original Map by—

NOTES.
Proposed sites of Towns ☐
The Egyptian Figures denote the
Population of the Native Settlements (N.S)
Total 359.

Estimated Extent of Land — Acres 2,035,000

Wood Land — Acres
Harewood Forest — 60,000
Alford Forest — 40,000
Wilberforce Plain — 1,100
Banks Peninsula 134,000 Goulburn 2000 — 136,000
Total Wood Land — 237,100

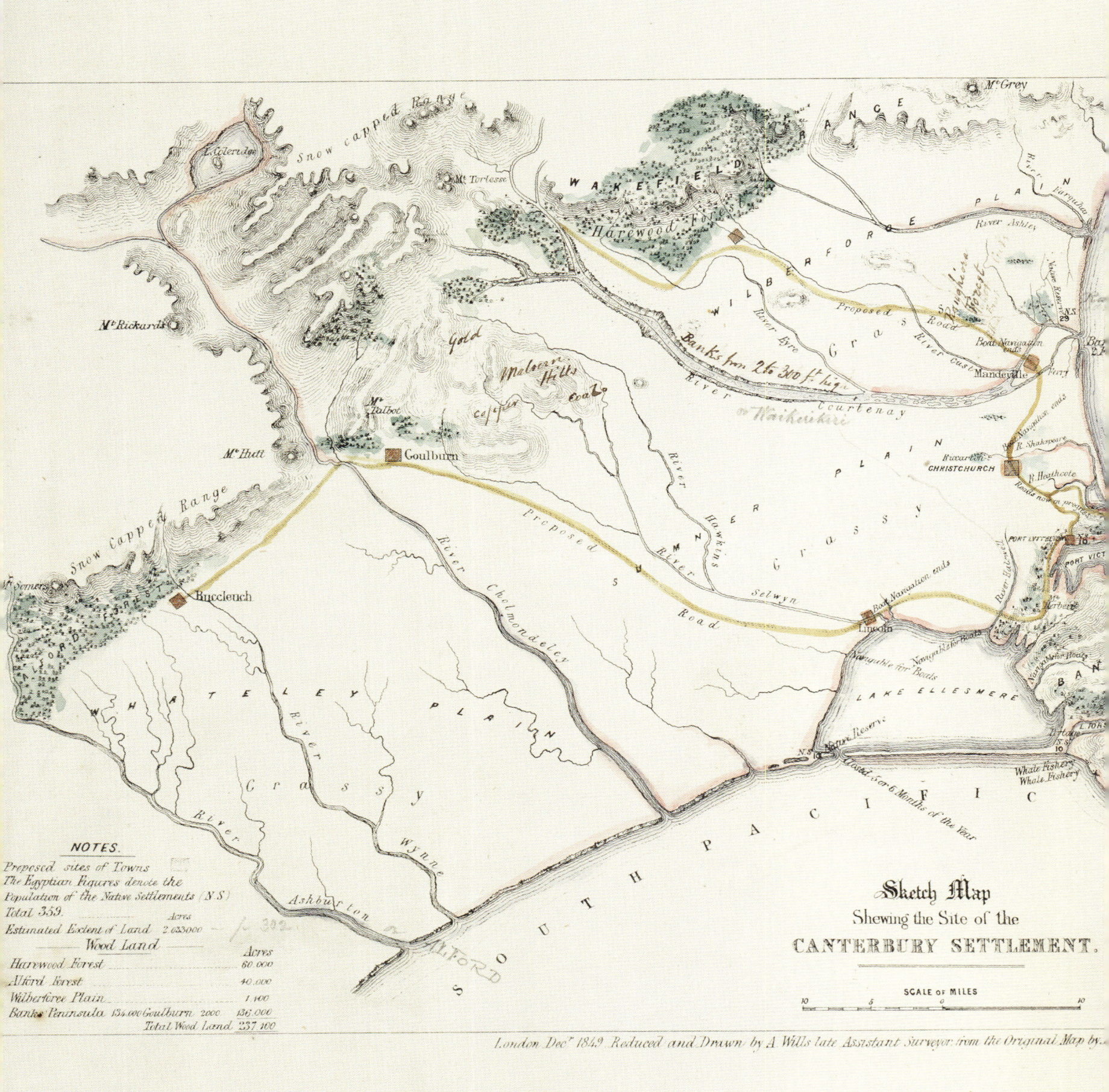

34.44a/1849/Acc 29307

Motunau or Cook's Table Island – a Seam of Cannel Excellent Coal found 1½ miles long 18 to 36" deep
17 Apl 51

ISLANDS OF NEW ZEALAND.

SCALE OF ENGLISH MILES

SOUTH PACIFIC OCEAN

AUCKLAND

NORTHERN ISLAND
OR NEW ULSTER

New Plymouth

Nelson
Wellington
C. Campbell
Waimakariri
Wainui
Ohauru
Waiautoa
Kaikoura

MIDDLE ISLAND
OR NEW MUNSTER

Double Corner
CANTERBURY
PORT VICTORIA
BANKS'
PENINSULA

Timaru

GREAT

Moerangi
Port Otago
Otago

SOUTHERN OCEAN

SOUTHERN ISLAND
OR NEW LEINSTER

"The Double Corner"

True / Magnet

Landing Place
Godley Head
Adderley Head
Pigeon Bay
PENINSULA
Okains Bay
French S
AKAROA HARBOUR

300,000

Standidge & Co. Litho. Old Jewry, London

Esq'r Chief Surveyor to the Canterbury Association.

Mr Godley resigned Dec'r 1, 1852

TUCKETT'S PLAN OF NELSON, 1842

When William Wakefield wanted something, he generally got it. The man who had been selected to lay out the New Zealand Company's new settlement (to be called Nelson, after Horatio, hero of the Battle of Trafalgar) didn't think the town should be sited where he'd been told it was going. Colonel Wakefield directed him to think again. So Frederick Tuckett dutifully set out surveying the site and laying out the town according to this pretty ink-and-wash plan. His next job wasn't so easy. He was charged with finding the vexing 'country' plots to go with the 'town' plots the new Nelsonians were taking up, and the district wasn't notable for its flat land. His search took him as far as the Wairau River valley, where he and his fellow surveyors were confronted by Ngāti Toa under the leadership of Te Rauparaha and Te Rangihaeata. Things soon escalated and the rest, as they say, is history, although Tuckett kept himself well out of the confrontation out of religious conviction (he was a Quaker and dedicated to non-violence). Thus, he lived to help with the establishment of the Free Church settlement at Otago, too.

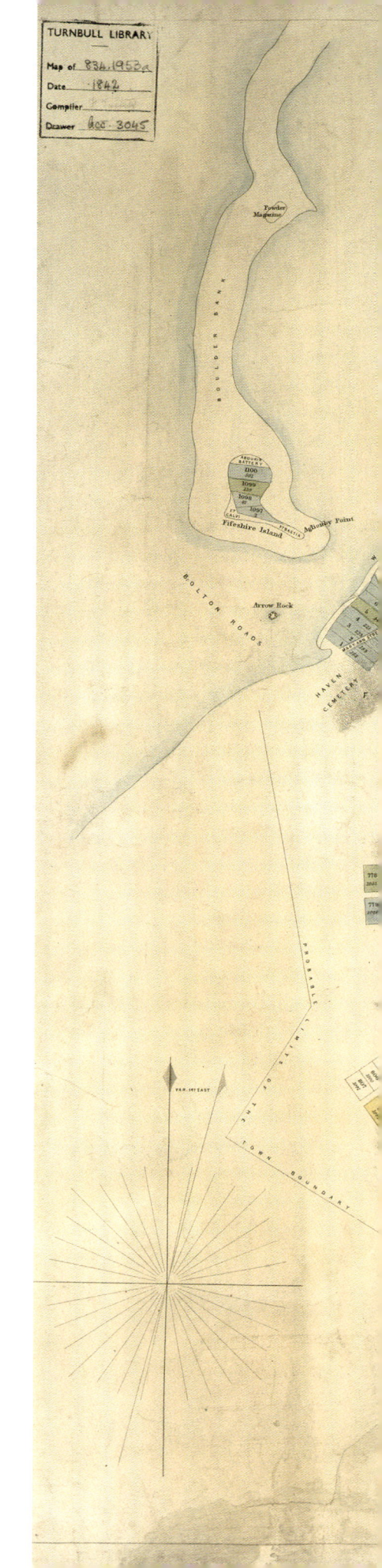

Plan of the Town of Nelson

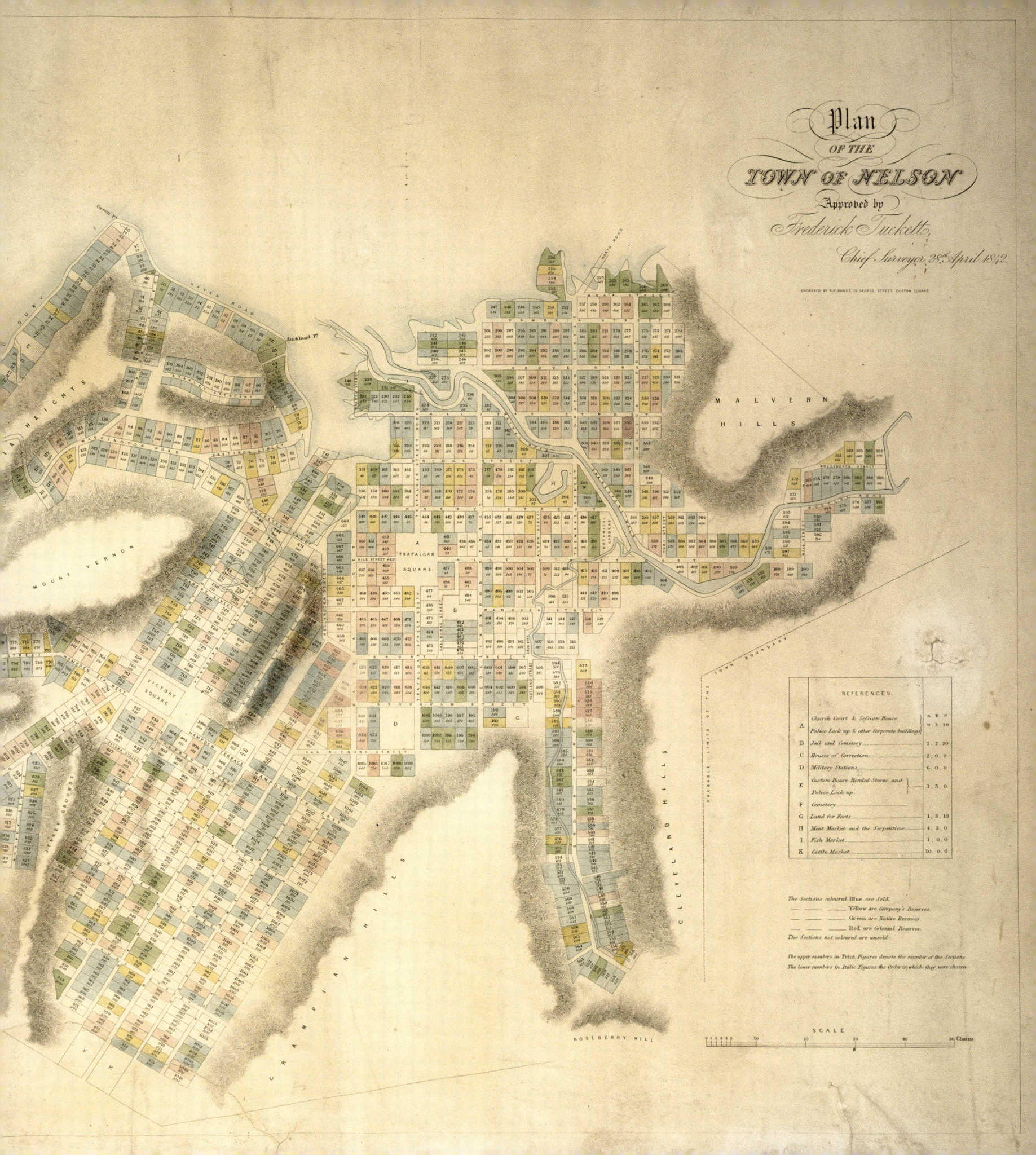

Approved by *Frederick Tuckett,*
Chief Surveyor, 28th April 1842.

ENGRAVED BY R.R. SMOGE, 15 GEORGE STREET, EUSTON SQUARE.

	REFERENCES.	A. R. P.
A	Church Court & Session House	0. 2. 20
	Police Lock up & other Corporate buildings	
B	Jail and Cemetery	7. 2. 30
	House of Correction	2. 0. 0
C	Military Stations	6. 0. 0
D	Custom House Bonded Stores and Police Lock up	1. 3. 0
E	Cemetery	
F	Land for Forts	1. 3. 10
G	Meat Market and the Serpentine	4. 2. 0
H	Fish Market	1. 0. 0
I	Cattle Market	10. 0. 0
K		

The Sections coloured Blue are Sold.
Yellow are Company's Reserves.
Green are Native Reserves.
Red are Colonial Reserves.
The Sections not coloured are unsold.
The upper numbers in Print Figures denote the number of the Sections.
The lower numbers in Italic Figures the Order in which they were chosen.

SCALE
10 20 30 40 50 Chains

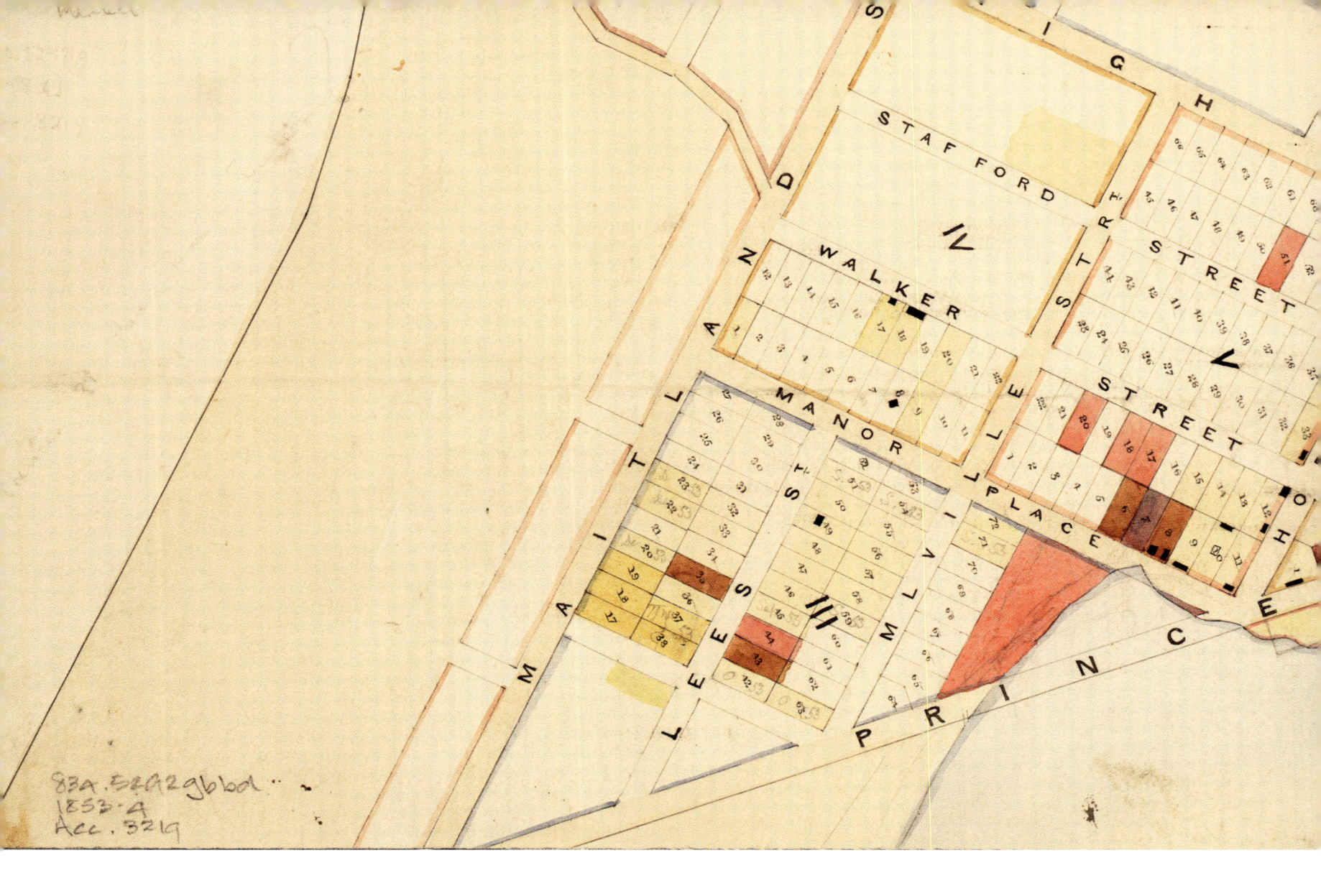

ROUGH MAP OF DUNEDIN (CREATOR UNKNOWN), 1853

The town of Dunedin was founded in 1848 on the initiative of the Free Church of Scotland. Its name comes from the Gaelic name for Edinburgh, and even now the city is known as 'the Edinburgh of the South'. It's not known who drew this partial 'rough map' in 1853: it doesn't seem to have been the town's original planner, Charles Kettle, although it clearly depicts the main features of Kettle's design, most notably the Octagon. The First Church isn't yet there, of course (although the site is marked 'XV'), and nor are many of the grand buildings that came only later, as the gold rushes enriched the region and Dunedin in particular. In fact, looking at the plan, very few buildings of any consequence (marked in black) are in evidence at all.

You'll notice that the foreshore is very close to the line of Princes Street. Much of the apron of land extending from the Octagon through Queen's Gardens to the present-day port is the former Bell Hill, which stood between the Octagon and the swamp that occupied much of the present commercial district. From the 1860s, this was systematically demolished and used for much of the reclamation work.

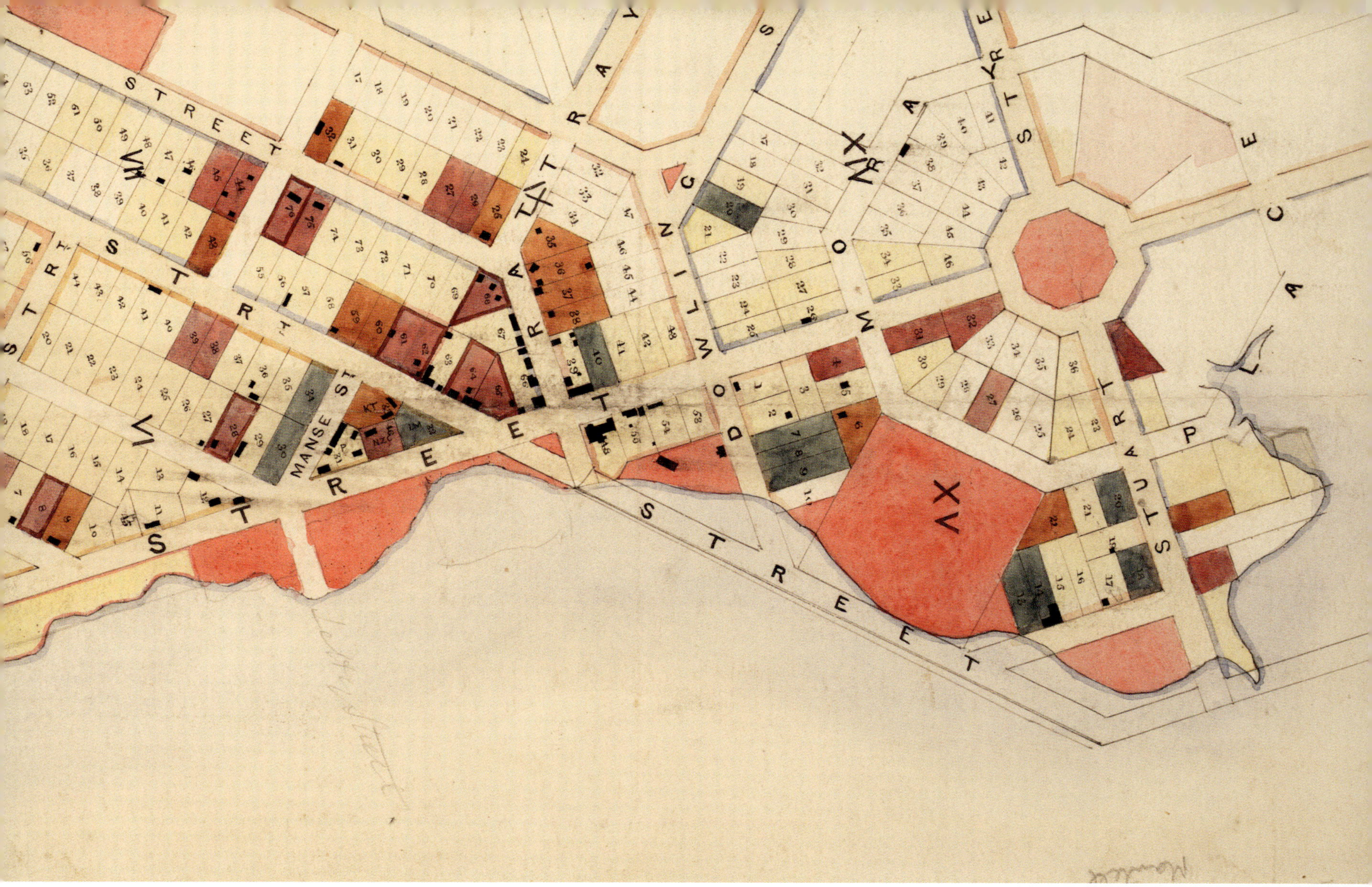
STREET
MANSE ST
STUART PLACE
XV

CARRINGTON'S PLAN OF NEW PLYMOUTH, 1842

When the New Zealand Company set about choosing a site for a settlement to accommodate the people who had signed up to the Plymouth Company (a kind of subsidiary enterprise), they were quick to take advantage of the local knowledge and influence of trader Dicky Barrett, who had lived in Taranaki between 1828 and 1833. Barrett helped broker the deal with local Māori, and the surveyors duly arrived to begin laying out the town. The surveyors in question were three brothers, Frederic, Octavius and Wellington Carrington, all of whom worked for the New Zealand Company. The neat, orderly plan belies the scale of the task the first settlers faced of rendering the tract of bush that occupied the plain habitable; and needless to say, many of those settlers weren't happy when they arrived to confront it. The Huatoke Stream that runs through the city kept its name (albeit spelt Hua Toki), but the Waiwhakaiho was to have been called the Enui, a mishearing, it seems, of He Nui, the big river. Many of the streets Frederic Carrington named have kept those names, including the slightly crooked one running through the lower middle of the map named Carrington Street.

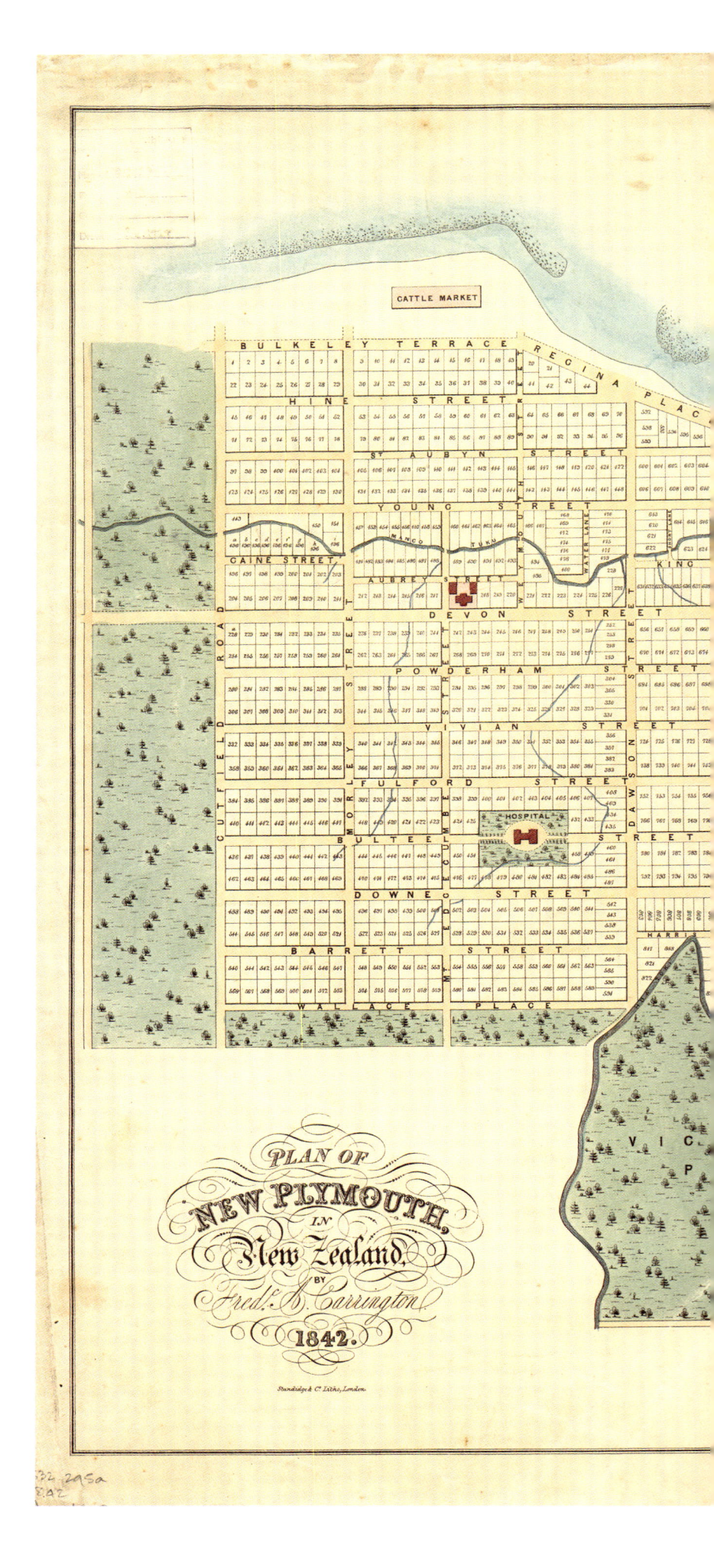

Low Water Mark

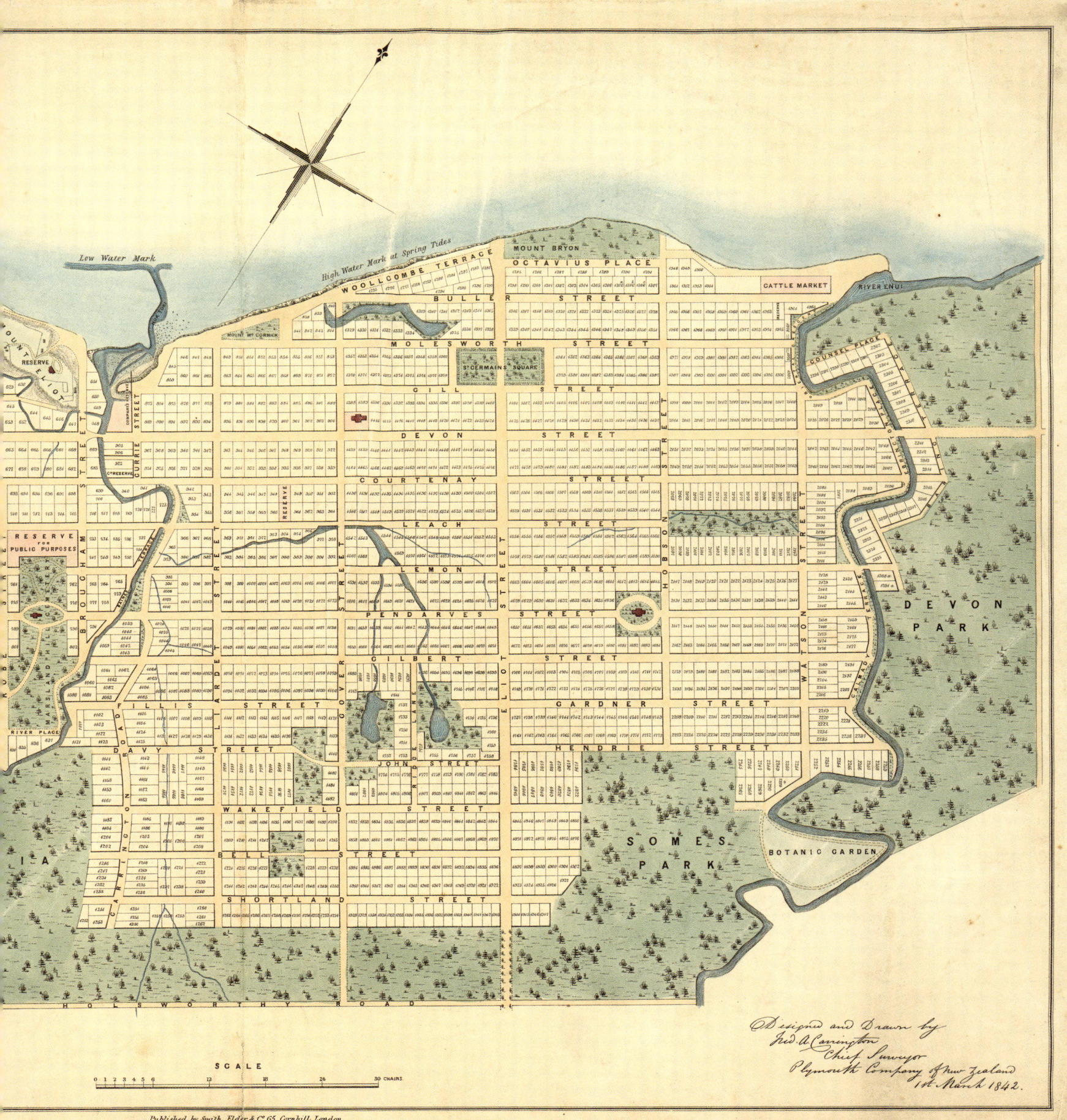

High Water Mark at Spring Tides

MOUNT BRYON

WOOLLCOMBE TERRACE OCTAVIUS PLACE

MOUNT RESERVE

MOUNT McCORMICK

BULLER STREET

CATTLE MARKET

RIVER ENUI

MOLESWORTH STREET

ST GERMAINS SQUARE

COUNSEL PLACE

COMPANYS QUAY

GILL STREET

CURRIE STREET

DEVON STREET

COURTENAY STREET

RESERVE FOR PUBLIC PURPOSES

LEACH STREET

BROUGHAM STREET

LEMON STREET

PENDARVES STREET

DEVON PARK

HOBSON STREET

WATSON STREET

GILBERT STREET

LIARDET STREET

DOVER STREET

FILLIS STREET

GARDNER STREET

RIVER PLACE

DAVY STREET

HENDRE STREET

JOHN STREET

WAKEFIELD STREET

SOMES PARK

BOTANIC GARDEN

BELL STREET

SHORTLAND STREET

HOLSWORTHY ROAD

SCALE
0 1 2 3 4 5 6   12   18   24   30 CHAINS

Designed and Drawn by
Fred. A. Carrington
Chief Surveyor
Plymouth Company of New Zealand
1st March 1842.

Published by Smith, Elder & Co. 65, Cornhill, London.

Brunn
Ara
Okitika R.

Bold Head
Parimata

Waita R.

Cliffy Head

Haze Hill

Wanganui R.

Abut Head

Kaohaihi P.

Yellow Cliffs
Parapara

Makawiho P.

Titihai Head

Mt Cook 12,200 ft
13,200 ft

S O U T H E R N   A L P S

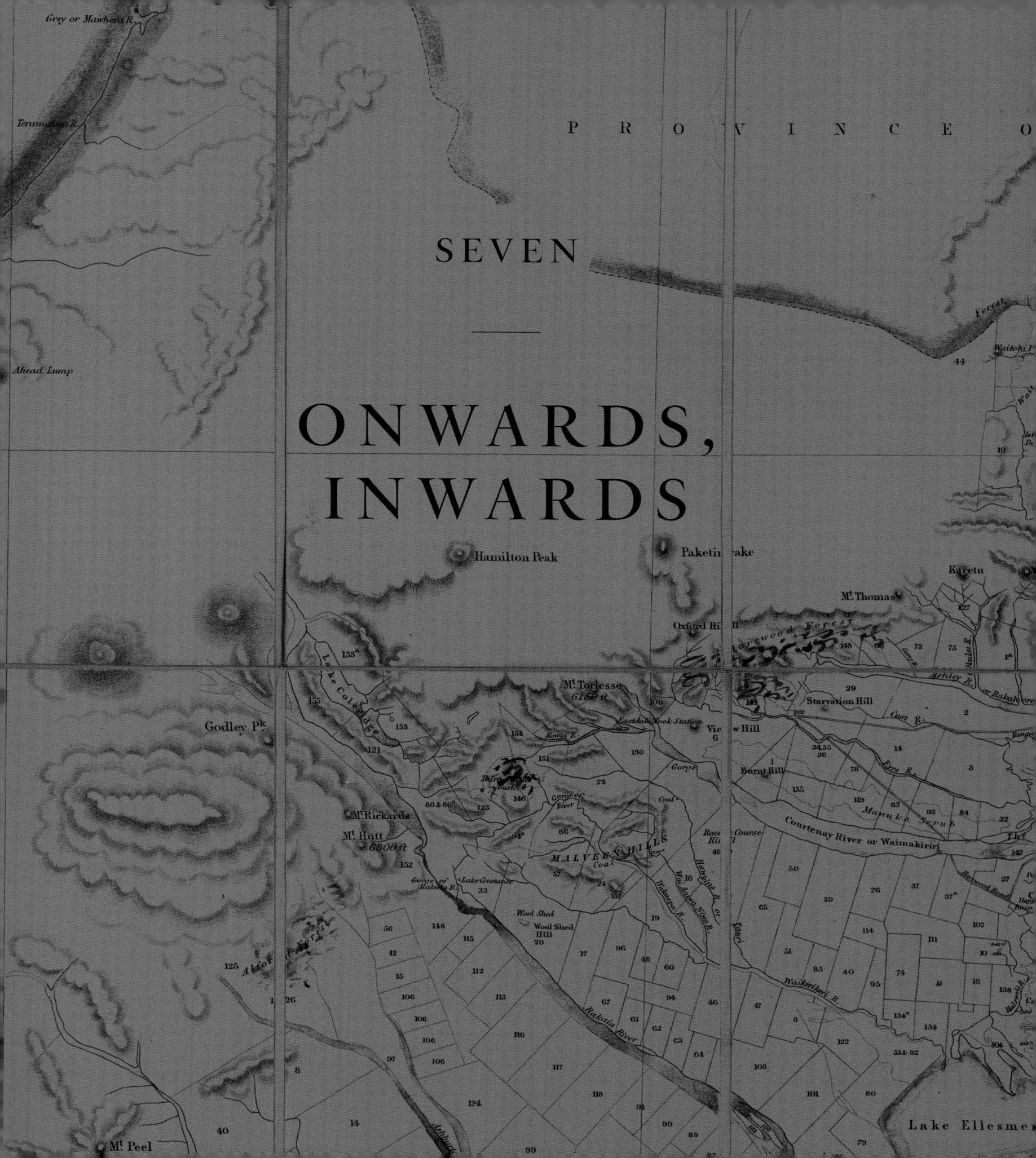

SEVEN

ONWARDS, INWARDS

The initial impetus to explore inland from the coast came from the grandees of the New Zealand Company, who—prisoners of their own rhetoric—felt obliged to find broad tracts of arable land to furnish the ten-acre 'country' blocks that were promised with the one-acre 'town' blocks. This prompted the exploration of the lower North Island, and the top and (soon enough) the west of the South. The colonial government, meanwhile, was despatching surveyors from Northland and Auckland whose job it was to explain to Māori the point of having a government but who, incidentally, were noting the features and promise of the land they were traversing. And when, in 1853, the six provinces were inaugurated, the provincial governments each despatched surveyors to acquire a grasp of the bounty with which their territory was endowed.

The experiences of those exploring the North Island were very different from those who opened up the South. The North Island was densely populated by Māori (and by the middle of the 1850s, these centres of population had attracted missionaries of one stripe or another). Consequently, tours of districts such as the Waikato, the Central Plateau and Taranaki were initially relatively straightforward matters, with Pākehā explorers guided by Māori and made welcome and fed and provisioned in their kāinga and pā. In 1857, Stephenson Percy Smith made a long journey as a seventeen-year-old from Taranaki (at the mouth of the Mōkau River), inland to Taupō and then on to Lake Rotomahana where he viewed the Pink and White Terraces. He was guided every step of the way, and was the beneficiary of the hospitality of the tangata whenua. Because his guides were unavailable to take him back the way he had come, his return journey was made through the rugged watershed of the Whanganui River and back out to the farmland on the coast. He had been away seven weeks.

Two decades later, however, as Smith was engaged in the triangulation of the Hawke's Bay and Urewera districts, the business of exploring had changed. There were now political hazards to be negotiated. After erecting a trig on a high point in the Urewera rainforest—crowned, as a joke, with an empty 50-pound biscuit tin—Smith and his party were hungry and weary. They located a Māori village thanks to the smoke plumes from its cooking fire, and while they were well aware that the mood had turned against Pākehā in recent years, they decided to throw themselves on the mercy of the locals. Their reception was hostile: in an impassioned speech delivered on the paepae, the chief told them that there had been a party of toa scouring the bush to stop them from completing their work. But the people had seen the biscuit tin glinting in the sun and had realised that the trig station had already been established. Well, the surveyors would be fed—even the dogs got fed—but in the morning, they would be shown on their way so that the land could be cleansed. Meanwhile, with the threat of war between tangata whenua and settlers hanging in the air, there was a need for military roads and defensive positions to be surveyed.

Because the South Island was that much more rugged and less populous, the early European explorers brought back much better work stories. The New Zealand Company had learned from Māori that there were supposedly vast arable plains somewhere to the southwest of the company settlement at Nelson. This was welcome news, given what had lately happened to the southeast in the Wairau Valley (see chapter eight). William Fox (the company's agent at Nelson), Thomas Brunner (surveyor) and Charles Heaphy (draughtsman and, being accomplished in watercolours, propagandist) set out to investigate, and penetrated as far as the confluence of the Maruia and Buller rivers in 1846. No flat land here. Less than a month later, having rested and resupplied back in Nelson, Heaphy, Brunner and a Māori guide, Kehu, set off again, this time pushing down the course of the Buller to the coast and making it as far south as the site of present-day Hokitika before returning. It was a five-month epic—still no flat land to speak of—but it was nothing compared with what Brunner did next.

After another couple of restorative months back in Nelson, Brunner, Kehu and another Māori guide, Pitewate, and the two guides' wives set off on 3 December 1846, in an attempt to walk the length of the West Coast and then, if possible, to cross via a fabled alpine pass to Canterbury. It was no walk in the park, and food was so hard to come by that the group was forced to kill and eat Brunner's little fox terrier, Rover, to avoid starvation. After months of hard slog and privation, they reached their farthest south at Paringa in South Westland, where Brunner sprained his ankle. Once he had recovered, they began the return journey, scouting inland for a route through to Canterbury. Kehu and Pitewate were opposed to attempting a crossing of the alps, however, and they pressed on north to the Buller. On their way up the course of the river, Brunner seems to have suffered a stroke. As he lay paralysed in his tent, he heard Pitewate arguing that he was as good as dead and ought to be abandoned. He and his wife did leave, but Kehu refused. Who knows what it was—whether, as seems likely, it was the bond of a mateship forged through sharing months of adversity, or whether Kehu simply knew that he would have some awkward questions to answer if he walked out of the bush without his Pākehā employer: either way, he stayed and nursed Brunner back to a state where they were able to complete the great journey, reaching Nelson fully 550 days after setting out. Brunner's (and Kehu's) exploits did the nineteenth-century equivalent of going viral, being reported in newspapers all over the world, and he (Brunner, not Kehu) was honoured by both the Royal Geographical Society of England and the French Société de Géographie for the feat. Brunner made a partial recovery from his debilitation, sufficient that he and Kehu should ride again, this time looking for an easy route from Golden Bay to the Wairau Valley in 1848. Later still, as chief surveyor and commissioner for native reserves, he was partly responsible for laying out the new towns of Westport and Greymouth—only this time, he travelled to the Buller district by ship.

Other explorations were made in the name of agriculture. Edward Jollie and 1800 head of sheep pioneered a route from the Tophouse in the Nelson district through to North Canterbury in 1852 (Jollie had begun his career in New Zealand as a cadet surveyor working under time pressure and the supercilious regard of William Wakefield across in Wellington; later, he would lay out central Christchurch, and become a Member of Parliament). Similarly, Samuel Butler and John Baker were in search of fresh pastures when they penetrated far up into the alps at the headwaters of the Rakaia River in 1861. Indeed, they crossed far enough over the Main Divide to determine that here was a route to the West Coast, but didn't pursue the issue. That was left to John Whitcombe and Jakob Lauper, who made the full crossing two years later, only for Whitcombe to drown in the Taramakau River once they had stumbled, exhausted and half-starved, onto the coast.

Another pass had been discovered from the Nelson region to the Buller district by Henry Lewis in 1861, and a Prussian geologist, Julius von Haast, had 'discovered' yet another route from the Otago lakes district to South Westland around the same time (although Māori had been using it for centuries). Haast was at that time employed as a geologist by the province of Canterbury, but he had originally come to New Zealand on a commission to investigate its suitability for a German settlement. Upon arrival in Auckland, he was introduced to an Austrian geologist named Ferdinand von Hochstetter, who invited him to tag along as he and Charles Heaphy performed a survey of a potential coalfield south of Auckland. It was the beginning of many years' fruitful collaboration on the exploration of New Zealand and its geology. As a geologist, Haast was first-rate. As an explorer, however, he was held in less high regard by the hard men of South Island exploration. One surveyor wrote that you always knew where the 'jolly old picnicker' had camped, because the site would be littered with jam and biscuit tins. His more illustrious legacy lay in founding Canterbury Museum.

The need to find a convenient pass from Canterbury to the West Coast had become acute after the discovery of gold in the Buller district in 1859. It dawned on the Canterbury Provincial Council that with the difficulty of access (Lewis Pass was too far north, Haast Pass was too far south, Whitcombe Pass was too hard), the West Coast was more easily communicated with from Melbourne than Christchurch. Accordingly, the council promised to richly reward anyone who could discover a useful pass. That pass, linking Canterbury with the Ōtira River catchment, was discovered in 1864 by Arthur Dobson, for whom Arthur's Pass is named.

John Baker (who had explored the Rakaia with Samuel Butler) made a journey of discovery up through the Waitaki River valley to the Mackenzie Country and the vicinity of Lake Pūkaki, before pushing south over what became the Lindis Pass to the Otago lakes in 1862. But more thorough explorations of the lakes district were made by the chief surveyor of Otago, John Turnbull Thomson, in 1857-58 (it was he who named the Lindis Pass, after Lindisfarne in England), and by James McKerrow, who followed the Waiau River up to lakes Manapouri and Te Anau and explored the Southland region between 1861 and 1864.

Meanwhile, the West Coast was becoming intimately known through the work of Charles 'Mr Explorer' Douglas, who forged a forty-year career working on both a voluntary and a paid basis for the survey department, often alone, often collaborating with a who's who of surveyors and explorers in filling in the blanks on maps of some of the most rugged country on Earth. In many ways, Douglas epitomises those early surveyors, as it is plain from their journals, their sketchbooks and even their maps that getting the job of surveying done was not their sole or even their primary motivation. It was more the spirit of exploration for its own sake—the solitude, the grandeur and, yes, even the hardship and the danger. It was not just a case of measuring the land: for many, it was a primal wish to measure one's self against it.

———

It's hard to conceive of just how difficult the life of a pioneering surveyor was, particularly in the South Island, where one had to be as self-sufficient as possible. That meant carrying, on top of the tools of the trade—compass; sextant; the brass theodolite in its sturdy wooden case; the ash or hickory tripod; staff and ranging rods; the Gunter's chain (a chain comprising 100 regular iron links and measuring exactly 20.1 metres, 'one chain'); a set of iron arrows to be laid on the ground at the point where the chain ended and from which it was to be laid out again; a slasher, saws, axe and sharp knife (for clearing sight lines and making wooden survey pegs and trig stations); your field book and writing implements—food, shelter and clothing and firearm, powder and shot for provisioning purposes. Of course, the surveyor rarely travelled alone: he had a gang that often comprised chain men, a cook, cadets (for doing the real donkey work) and, more often than not, Māori guides. Gangs would often live under canvas for months at a time, out by day under rain, hail, snow or shine, traversing steep, broken or swampy ground, afflicted with sandflies by day and mosquitoes by night . . . It was an impossibly tough, poorly paid job, and little wonder those who performed it did it for reasons other than the money.

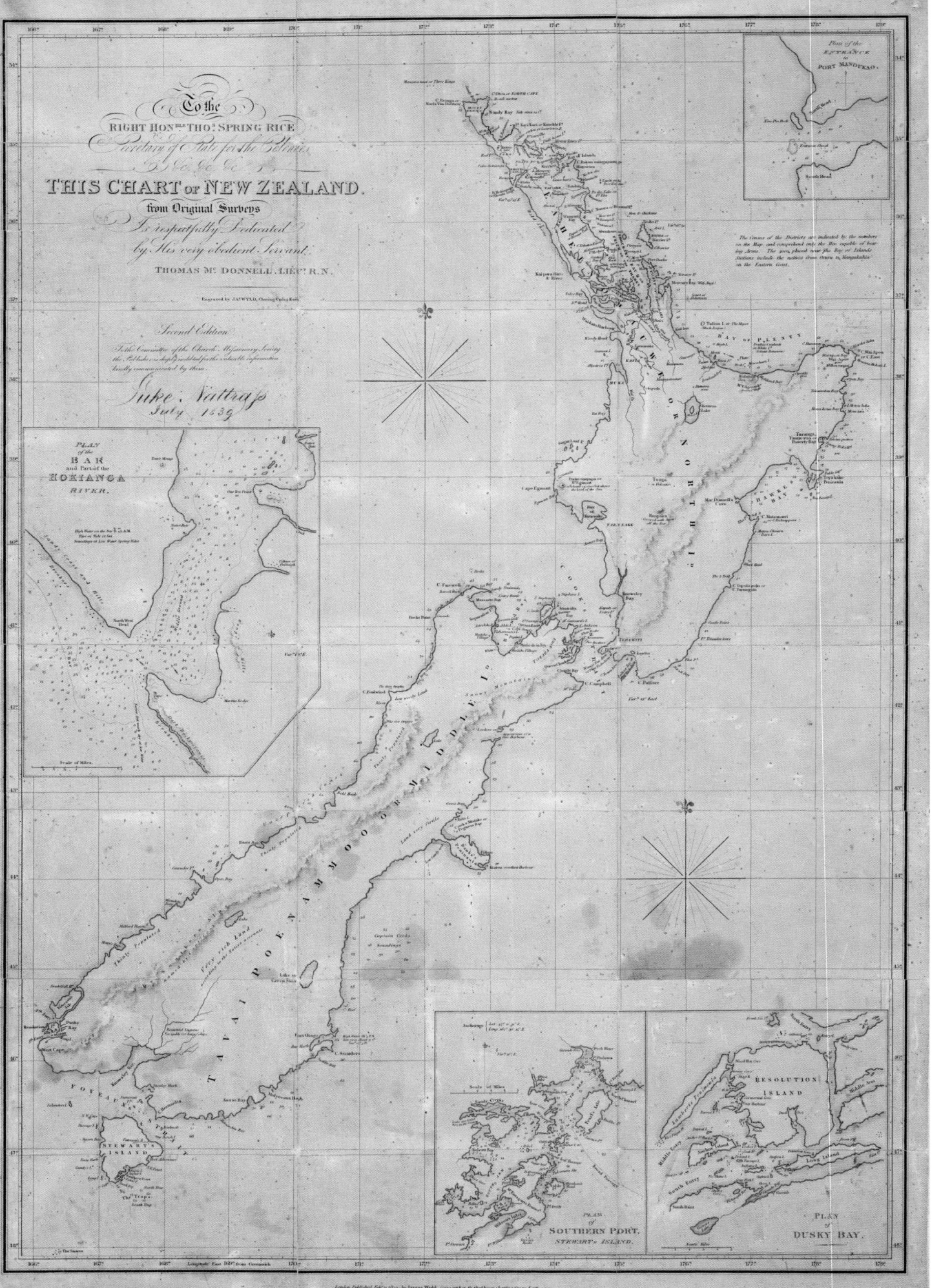

THIS CHART OF NEW ZEALAND.

from Original Surveys
Is respectfully Dedicated
by His very obedient Servant,

THOMAS McDONNELL, A.J.P. R.N.

Engraved by J. & WYLD, Charing Cross East.

Second Edition

To the Committee of the Church Missionary Society the Publisher is deeply indebted for the valuable information kindly communicated by them.

Luke Nattrass
July 1839

PLAN of the BAR and Part of the HOKIANGA RIVER.

Plan of the ENTRANCE to PORT MANUKAO.

PLAN of SOUTHERN PORT, STEWART's ISLAND.

PLAN of DUSKY BAY.

London, Published Feb. 9. 1839, by James Wyld, Geographer to the Queen, Charing Cross East.

WYLD'S CHART OF NEW ZEALAND, 1839

Spring Rice was not, as you might suppose, an exotic takeaway dish, but the Secretary of State for the Colonies in 1839, when this chart was dedicated to him by 'his very obedient servant' Lieutenant Thomas McDonnell. It was published by James Wyld, who had inherited his father's map-making empire three years before. Wyld quickly built a reputation for printing maps of newly discovered territories 'as soon as they were discovered, if not before', and this map has the hallmark of a slightly rushed job. There are a number of fairly obvious errors in his depiction of New Zealand: the south coast of the South Island is deeply indented by the non-existent Knowlsley River, Banks Peninsula looks more pedunculated than it actually is, a rather withered Taranaki features a commodious harbour, and Cape Rēinga is conflated with Cape Maria van Diemen. But the value of this map is that it accurately shows the state of European knowledge of the interior of both islands on the eve of the era of systematic settlement. Apart from the hazily drawn Main Divide, the major ranges of the lower North Island and a strikingly accurately drawn Lake Rotorua, the area encompassed by the coastlines is blank. Even Lake Taupō is conspicuous by its absence. This was all to change, and fast.

N

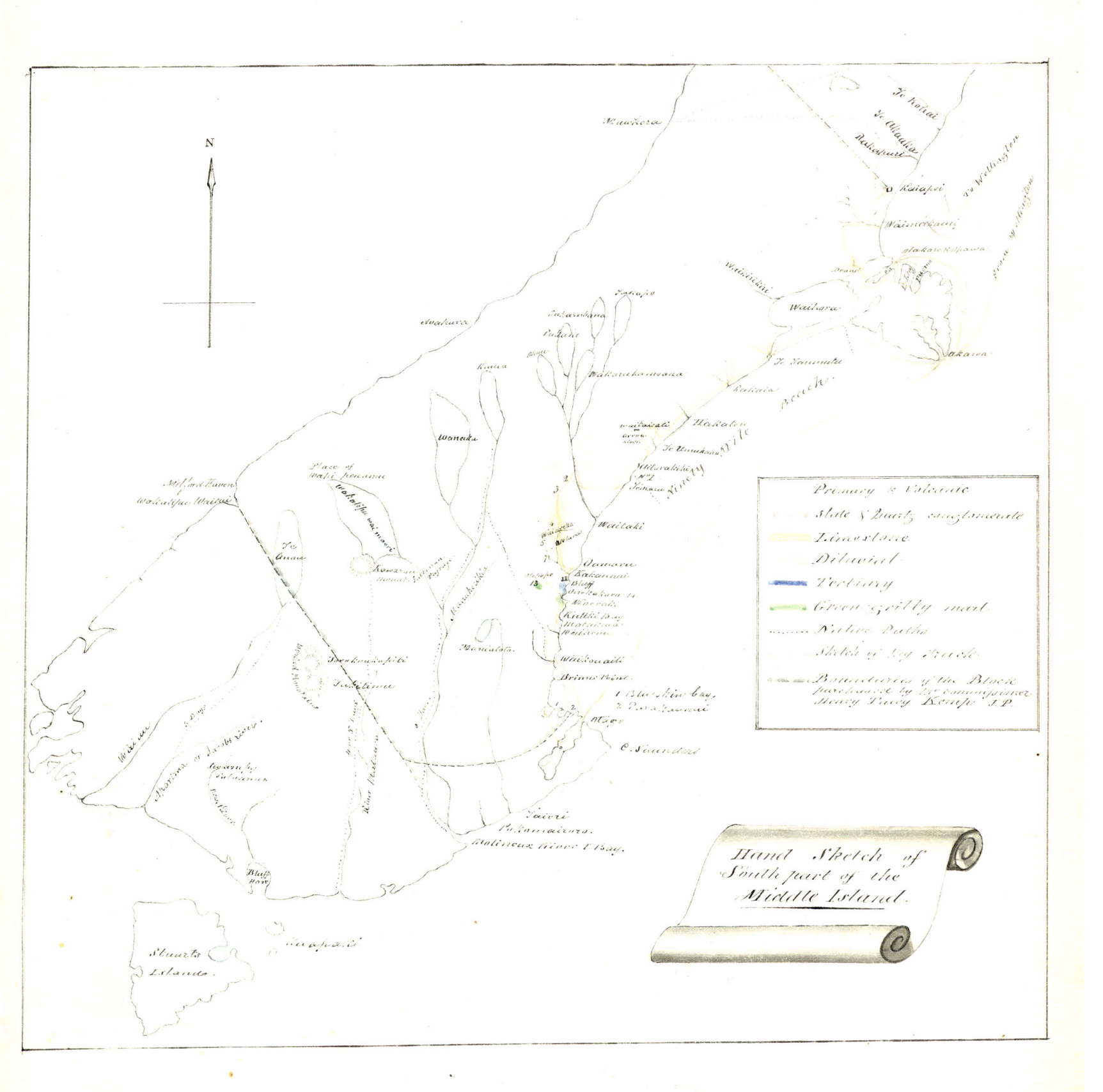

Primary & Volcanic
Slate & Quartz conglomerate
Limestone
Diluvial
Tertiary
Green Grilly marl
Native Paths
Sketch of My Track
Boundaries of the Block purchased by the commissioner Henry Tacy Kemp J.P.

Hand Sketch of South part of the Middle Island

Mawhera
Te Kohai
Te Whachia
Rakahurst
Kaiapoi — To Wellington
Waimokana
Okakarokipawa — Road to Wellington
Avakarve
Waitiekiei
Waihara
Tapuapo
Pakaahana
Pukaki
Rauru
Te Taumutu
Wakarukamoana
Kaiaia — Beach
Waitaiati
Hakatea
Te Umukaha Mile
Wanaka
Wilovakihi
Place of wahi pounamu
No 1
Sawan
Ninety
Midland Haven
Wakatipu Waitipu
Wakotihi wai-mari
Waitaki
Waitareka
Te Anau
Kowarau mouth takau pass
Oamaru
Papakanui
Bluff
Onokakara
Manuhereka
Moerabi
Katiki Bay
Matainan
Waikonu
Manialata
Waikouaiti
Pruchnukapiti
Primis Point
Tahetiena
1 Blueskin bay
2 Purakaunui
Waiau
Otago
Openizu of Lands River
C. Saunders
Agarby
Pukarnes
Waiwen
Taieri
Pukamairus
Molineux River & Bay
Bluff Harr

Stuarts Islands
Ruapuki

MANTELL'S SKETCH OF PART OF THE MIDDLE ISLAND, CIRCA 1848

Just as Edmund Halswell acquired a deep respect for Māori and interest in their knowledge of the land as he conscientiously toured the country enquiring into the justice of their claims to alienated land, so too did the man who in 1848 was appointed to the rather dismally entitled office of Commissioner for the Extinguishment of Native Title. This was Walter Baldock Durrant Mantell, the son of the great British geologist Gideon Mantell. Along with an enquiring mind, Mantell possessed considerable facility with a pen and paintbrush: this attractive map shows the fruits of a journey he made down the east coast of the South Island soon after arriving in the colony. It depicts his best guess as to the location and size of the high-country lakes based on the information given him by Te Wharekorari and others (see p. 32). Blushes of colour indicate geological features, and the map also shows the lines slashed across the South Island from Kaiapoi to Cape Foulwind and from the mouth of the Molyneux (Clutha) River to Milford Haven (Milford Sound), representing the boundaries of the so-called Kemp Purchase, in which Governor George Grey's land commissioner, Henry Kemp, signed a deed for the alienation of over 20,000 acres of Ngāi Tahu land for £2000. It proved to be a classic illustration of the way in which dealings over land between Māori and Pākehā failed to represent a meeting of minds. The Māori wording of the deed seemed to preserve Ngāi Tahu's usufructuary rights to the block, whereas the Crown, of course, imagined the iwi had transferred to it the right to enjoy it exclusively and in perpetuity, give or take some reserves and the places where Māori were living at that point in time (which Grey directed should be no more than 10 acres per head, concentrated in as few localities as possible). Mantell was also instrumental in finalising the alienation of most of Banks Peninsula and Murihuku, the vast swathe of land south of the Kemp Purchase boundary.

Besides his other gifts, Mantell was endowed with a conscience. The failure of the colonial government to honour promises made to Māori and the low price being paid for land induced him to complain to the imperial government, which did little more than shrug. Mantell resigned his post and returned to England. Meanwhile, Mantell had other claims to fame, too, including as a naturalist. He was an avid collector, and gave his name to the takahē, *Notornis mantelli*.

Following page
STANFORD'S MAP OF THE PROVINCE OF CANTERBURY, 1856

By the time this map had been prepared by an English map-maker (from 'communications with colonists') keen to exploit the appetite for information about the new colony of New Zealand, Christchurch was a little over five years old and the work of settling the surrounding district was well under way. Canterbury had been declared one of the six provinces (there had previously been only three: New Munster, New Ulster and New Leinster), and the fine pastoral land of the Canterbury Plains had been surveyed and apportioned. We don't know who owned this copy of the map, and therefore in whose hand the annotations in red ink were made: they detail the names of the owners of many of the blocks and runs. Red patches indicate land 'reserved for townships': Timaru is projected, as is Ōrari. There is no trace of Ashburton, which arose so suddenly amidst the boom that Canterbury enjoyed in its early days that it was nicknamed 'the mushroom of the plains'. The other notable feature here is the haziness (or absence) of information regarding the lie of the land beyond the plains: the southern lakes are shown as Walter Mantell had guessed them to be, and the Southern Alps are desultorily sketched with hachures.

ENLARGEMENT
of the
NEIGHBOURHOOD
OF
CHRISTCHURCH,
SHEWING THE
FREEHOLD SECTIONS
Ashley or Rakahore River
Ashley R. or Rakahore
Native Reserve
The Island
Courtenay R. or Waimakariri
CHRISTCHURCH
Canal Reserve
Native Reserve
LYTTELTON
PORT VICTORIA
Godley Hd
Quail Island
Charteris Bay
Cass Peak
Arnott Pt
Jackson Bay
Cascade Pt
Barn B.
Seal Rocks
Kaohaihi Pt
Yellow Cliffs
Makawiho Pt
Titihai Head
SOUTH
L. Ohou
L. Whakatipu
L. Hawea
PROVINCE OF OTAG
Scale of English Statute Miles: 69.1136 = 1 Degree.
169°
170°
Additions & Corrections by WALTER MANTELL Esq., R.J.S. HARMAN Esq. and the neighbourhood of Mount Peel by J.B.A. ACLAND Esq.

Map of the
PROVINCE of CANTERBURY,
NEW ZEALAND, SHEWING
FREEHOLD SECTIONS AND PASTURAGE RUNS,
FROM
ADMIRALTY CHARTS AND COLONIAL SURVEYS,
WITH COMMUNICATIONS FROM COLONISTS.

LONDON:
Edward Stanford, 6, Charing Cross.
Agent by Appointment for the Ordnance Maps
and Admiralty Charts.
1856

HEAPHY/BRUNNER MAP OF THE WEST COAST, 1847

Charles Heaphy and Thomas Brunner plainly had the exploring bug when they returned from their first, gruelling journey to the Buller district in 1846, as only a couple of weeks after their return, they were shouldering the sugar-bags containing their provisions and equipment once again.

While the Lands Commissioner, William Fox—a companion on the first jaunt—chose to sit out this one, he was happy to bankroll it, and Kehu, the Māori who had guided them, was willing to do it all again. This time, their objective was to explore the coastline south from the Whanganui Inlet (on the West Coast across Cape Farewell from Massacre Bay, as Golden Bay was then known), reporting on the presence of any exploitable resources—especially flat land—they saw on the way. Heaphy's map traces this expedition, on which they managed to walk as far south as Arahura (north of present-day Hokitika) before turning for home.

The journey in both directions was arduous, the return particularly so. The shortage of food resources saw all three men—Brunner, Heaphy and Kehu—close to starvation at times, forced to rely upon mussels, baked mamaku (tree fern) and the rotting remains of fish cast up on the beaches by the surf.

Next to nothing was known of the parts they were traversing—or at least, not by Europeans. Heaphy and Brunner were told that Māori had not traditionally inhabited the West Coast, but were frequent visitors there, in search of pounamu (greenstone). In recent times, kāinga had been established by enterprising hapū who felt they could make a living gleaning pounamu and trading with others.

Abel Tasman was the first European to lay eyes on the region, which he did at a point off South Westland, and he sailed cautiously up the coast, standing well off and making a desultory chart of it. James Cook was rather more meticulous, but his descriptions of the nature of the coastline—frowning mountains crowding a bleak, shingled beach and with no safe harbours or anchorages in evidence—didn't encourage others to visit, although sealers made more or less regular forays. It was partly to verify the reports of one of these, Joseph Thoms, that Brunner and Heaphy were venturing to the area. In 1844, Thoms had crossed the bar at the mouth of the Buller in his brig, the *Three Brothers*, and sailed several miles upriver, reporting heavily timbered plains on either bank.

Little or nothing of what Brunner and Heaphy found and saw is commemorated in Heaphy's map, which is little more than a wiggly ink line descending the page. There are few place names. It was impressionistic—they were not carrying surveying instruments, nor did they note precise latitudes and longitudes. Instead, it was all done by dead reckoning, with bearings taken on prominent landmarks using a handheld compass, dashed down in Heaphy's journal and combined with estimates of distances covered, with the 'map' then probably drawn from memory using the notes. Yet it is a good fit with the coast it depicts, and it was the first eyewitness indication of what lay over the mountains from the more settled country. In the end, even a single black line is a considerable advance on a blank page.

The image shown opposite is a fragment of the Heaphy/Brunner map.

Rocky Point

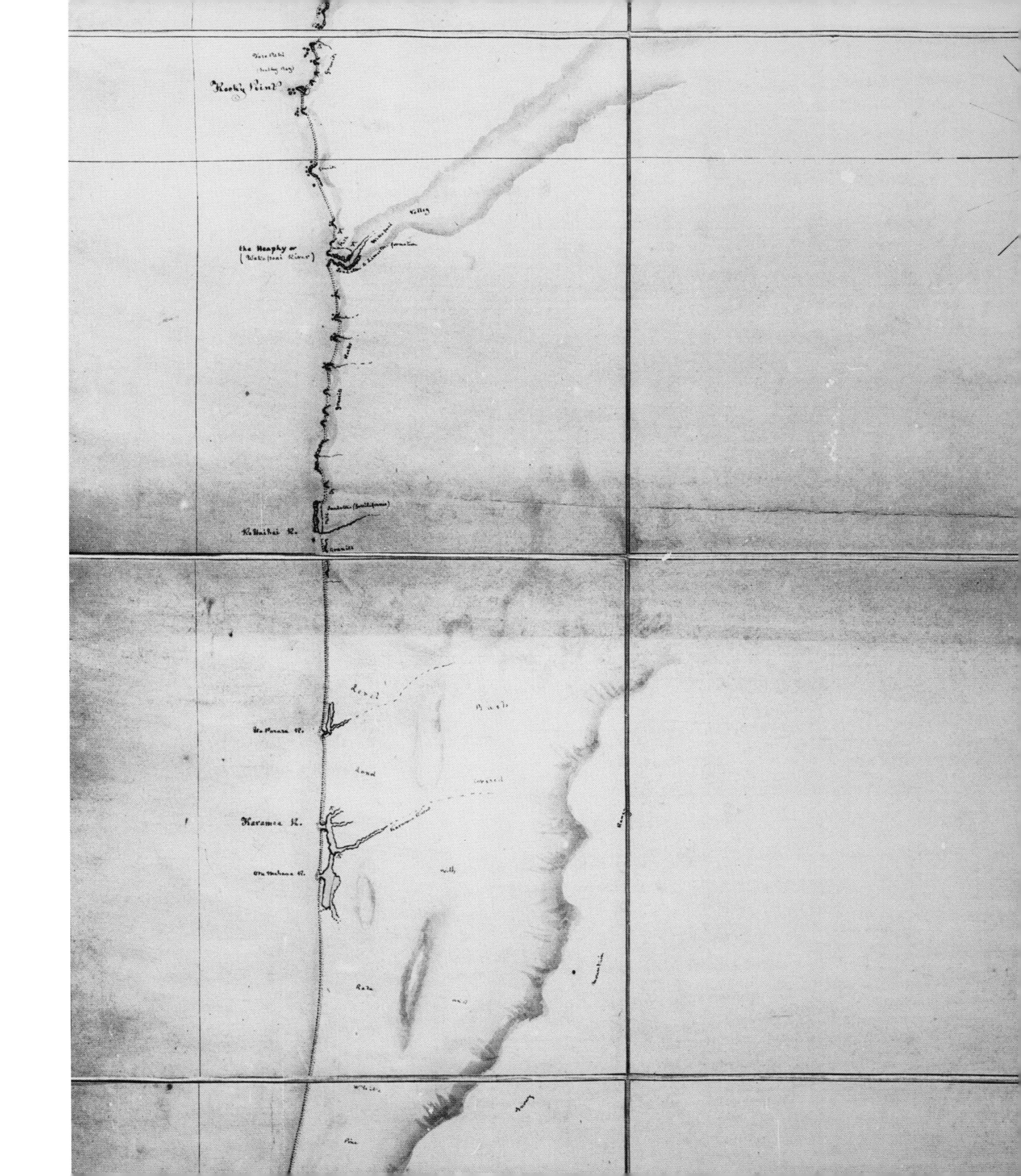

the Heaphy or
(Wakapoai River)

Te Waihei R.

Karamea R.

MCKERROW'S MAP OF THE MERIDIONAL CIRCUITS OF THE PROVINCE OF OTAGO, 1859

James McKerrow, a Scotsman, was appointed district and geodetical surveyor to the Province of Otago in 1859, and got busy. When you consider the territory over which he presided—and over which he dragged his chain and theodolite—while performing the reconnaissance survey, you can begin to imagine how busy.

The work of a geodetical surveyor is to establish the location of points on the landscape with as close to absolute precision as possible, so that these points can be used as references for subsequent surveys. These points are known as meridional circuits. Four years after McKerrow published this masterly map, New Zealand adopted what is known as the Torrens system of land ownership (which creates a state register of 'indefeasible' titles to land, and which crucially relies upon the precise delineation of plots of land): this required each of the provinces to have done the kind of work that McKerrow had already undertaken, but not all of them were up to speed. The new surveyor general, Major H. S. Palmer, noted in 1875 that most were behind in this work. The quality of McKerrow's work, meanwhile, was attracting the favourable attention of the Royal Geographical Society. He later became New Zealand's commissioner for railways.

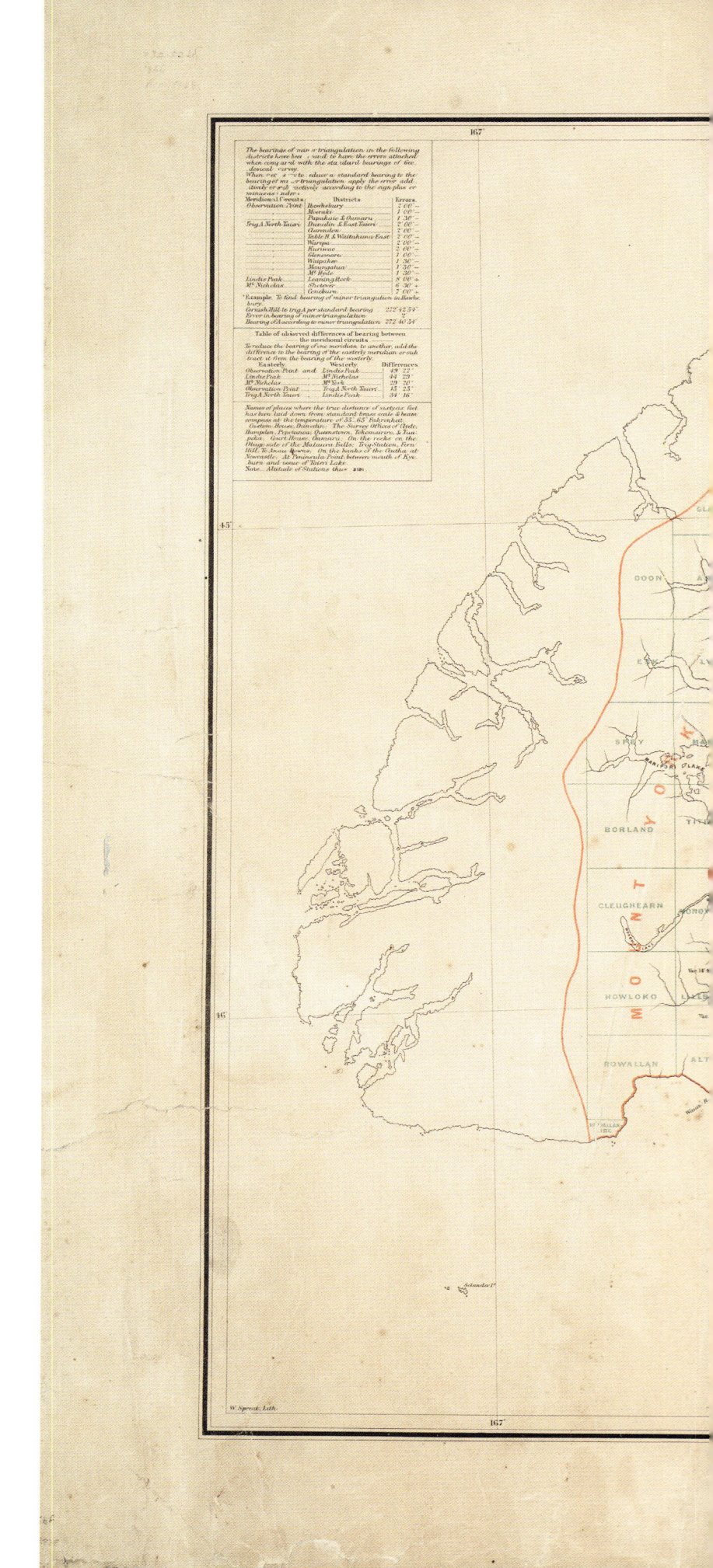

MAP OF
MERIDIONAL CIRCUITS,
PROVINCE OF OTAGO.

J. Mc. Kerrow, Geodesical Surveyor.
1866.

Scale of English Miles.

NOTE. Distances from reduced reconnaissance maps.

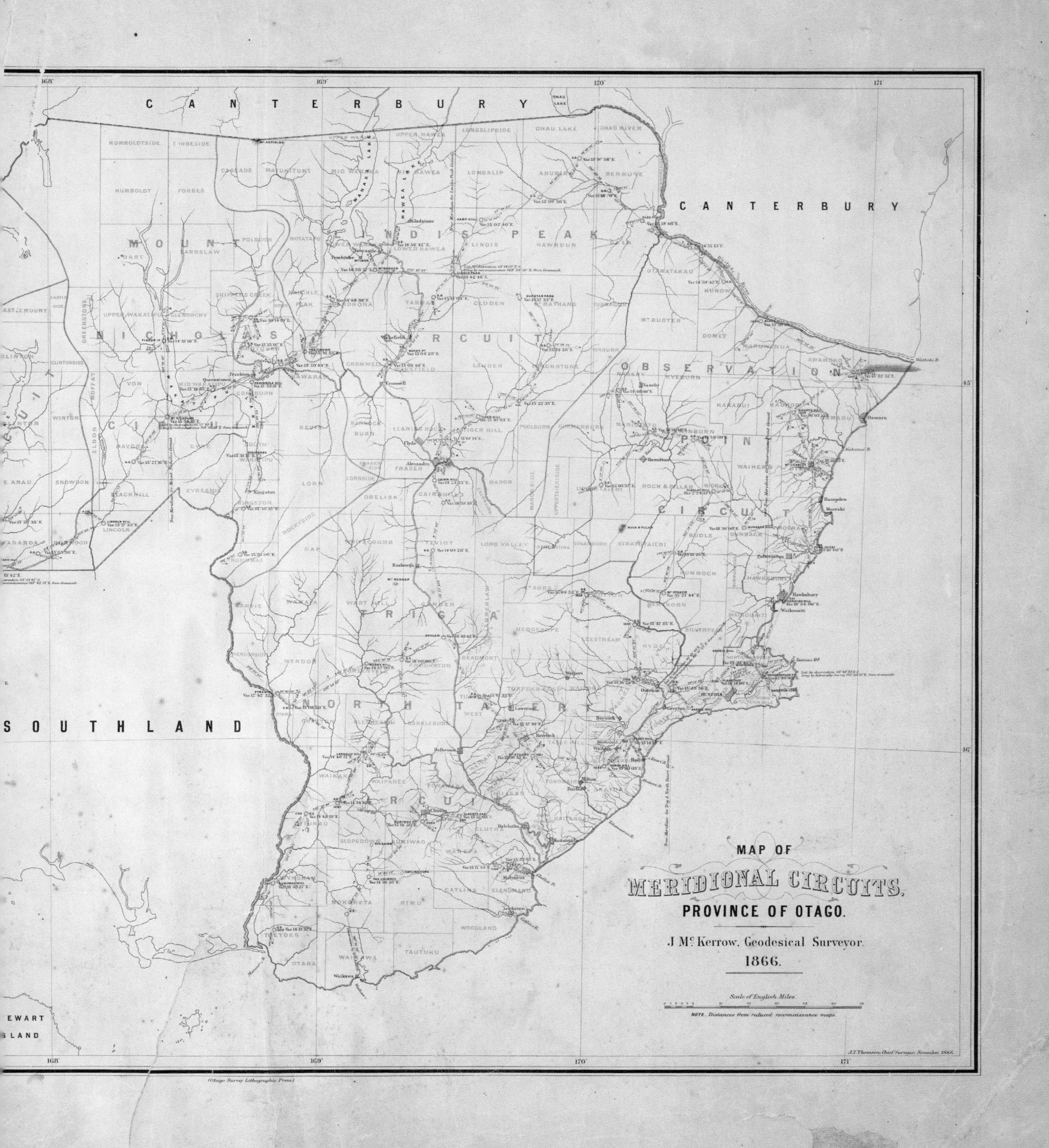

**THOMAS' MAP OF THE GOLDFIELDS OF
THE PROVINCE OF OTAGO, 1864**

There's nothing like the lure of gold to get people scouring the countryside, and the difference in the level of detail on this map and the one produced by James McKerrow is plain to see. Gabriel Read discovered gold 'that shone like the stars of Orion' in May 1861 in a gully that bears his name two or three kilometres north of present-day Lawrence. Gold is one of humanity's oldest get-rich-quick schemes: once the word was out, people flocked from all over the world to see if they could find 'a bit of the colour' for themselves. Most didn't (and many died trying), but plenty did—enough to turn Otago into the richest place in New Zealand and to dismay the sober Presbyterian souls who had settled Dunedin. They labelled the rough-and-ready newcomers the 'New Iniquity', who were in danger of swamping the 'Old Identity' (themselves). Ōamaru, meanwhile, acquired streets full of white stone bank buildings that made it look more like Rome in its pomp than a small provincial town. But it was brief. By 1864, when this map was printed, prospectors were already deserting the paid-out diggings of Otago for the West Coast.

Map of the Gold Fields of the Province of Otago

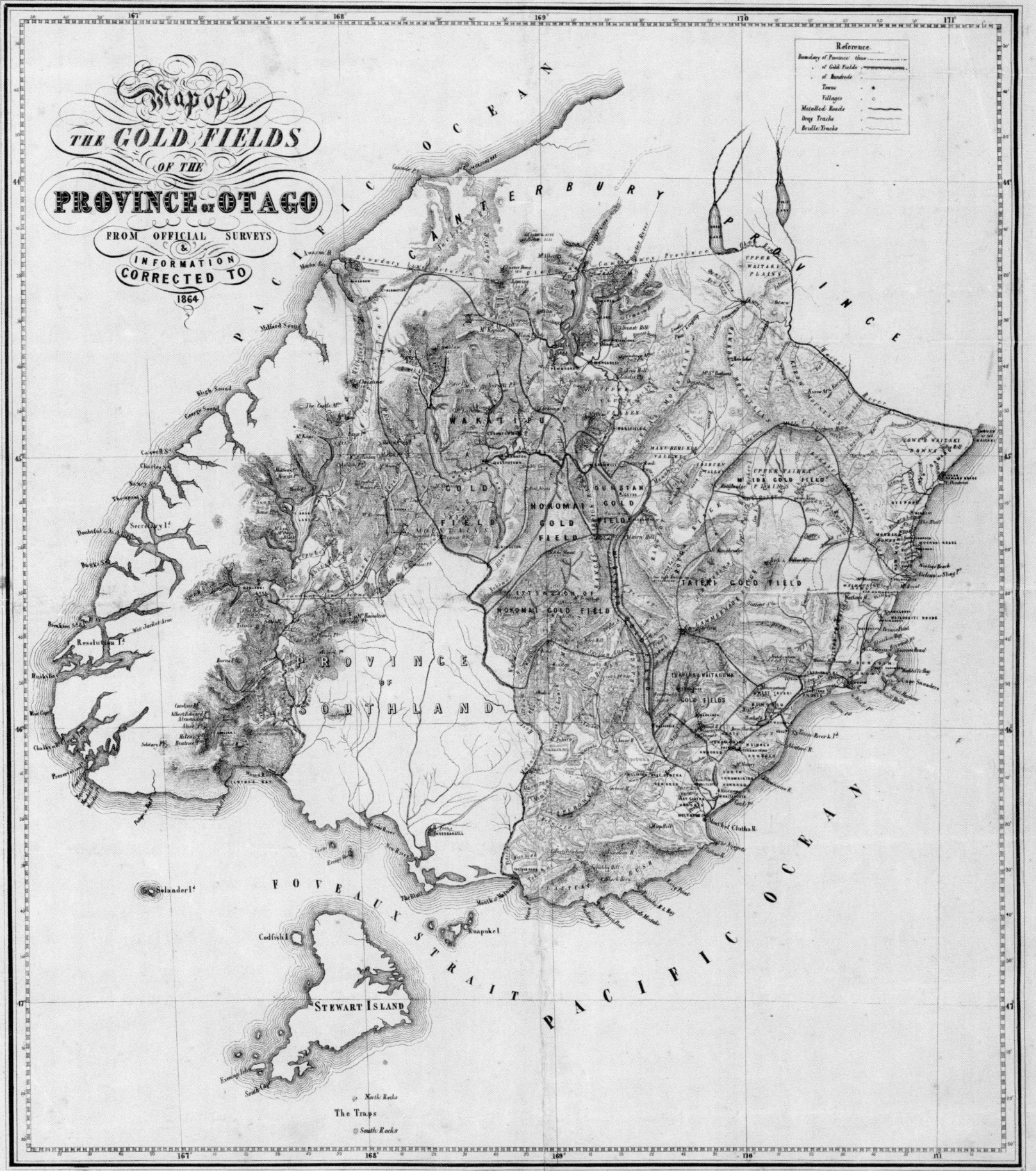

From Official Surveys & Information Corrected to 1864

Reference.
- Boundary of Province
- of Gold Fields
- of Hundreds
- Towns
- Villages
- Metalled Roads
- Dray Tracks
- Bridle Tracks

Drawn on Stone by David Henderson.

(Otago Govt. Survey — Lithographic Press) Price 8/-

Scale 16 inch to an English Mile

J. T. Thomson, Chief Surveyor. January 1864.

MAP OF THE PROVINCE OF OTAGO (CREATOR UNKNOWN), 1871

Modern cartographers use the images acquired by satellites performing multiple sweeps around Earth to compile their maps. The same basic principle was used to create maps and charts a century and a half ago—only the acquisition of the information was infinitely more laborious. The work of a number of different scanners sweeping the Otago district for their own purposes went into the making of this magnificent map in 1871: John Lort Stokes performed the hydrographical survey that fixed the coastline with such precision; James McKerrow put the interior on a sound trigonometrical basis; John Turnbull Thomson, employed by the Otago grandees in 1859 to survey the province for land suitable for freehold, spent two years doing just that, and then from 1861 performed yet another series of surveys to define the goldfields (as depicted in the previous map). Other surveyors and explorers chipped in too, leaving their names on the map as a record of their passing. See how many of the names under the map's title you can find on a modern map of Otago.

MAP OF THE PROVINCE OF
OTAGO,
COMPILED FROM OFFICIAL SURVEYS & EXPLORATIONS.
ADDITIONS TO 1871.

NOTE.— Ruapuke and Solander Groups also Islands adjacent to Stewart Island are not included in the Province of Otago.

Scale of English Miles

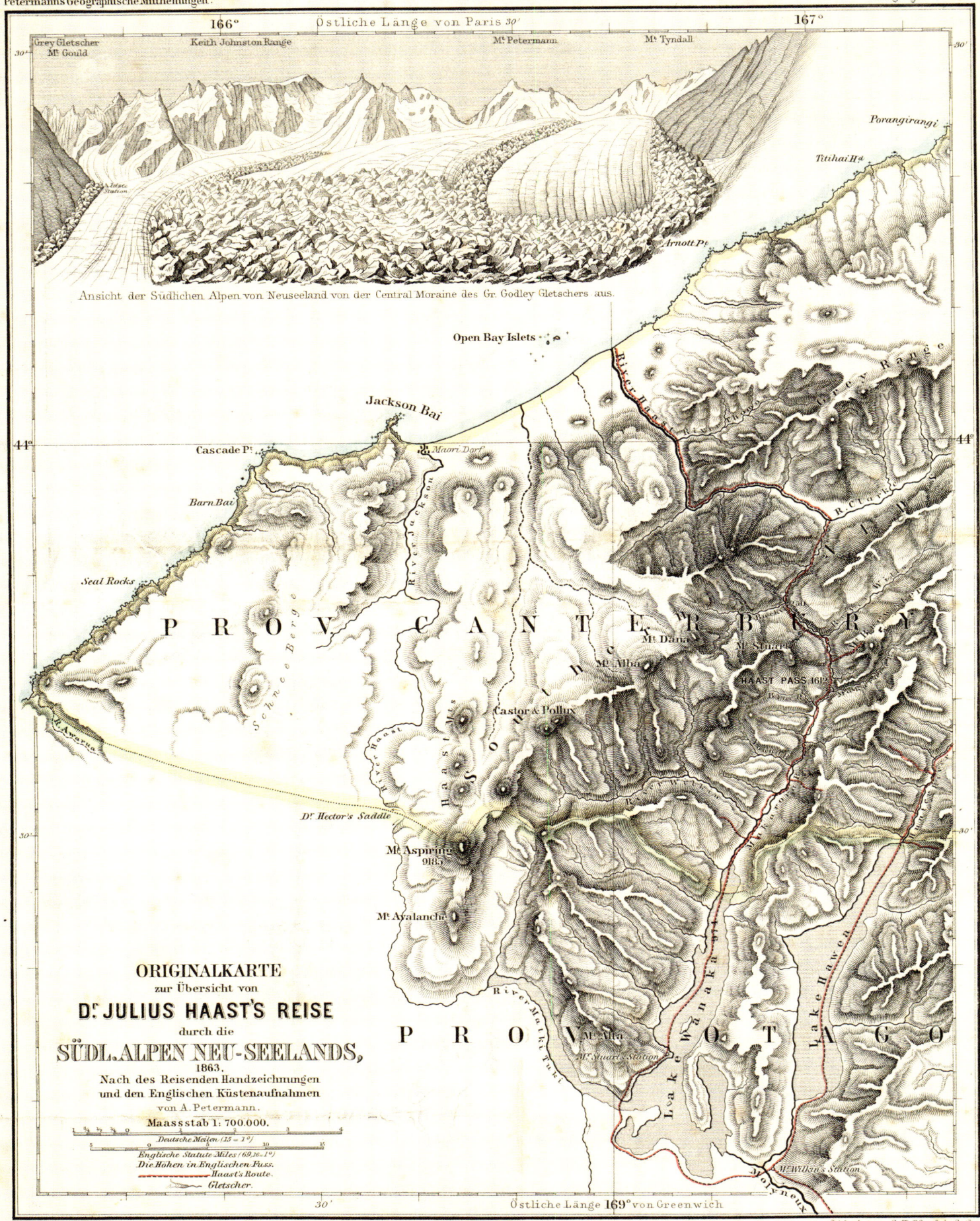

Petermann's Geographische Mittheilungen.   Jahrgang 1863, Tafel 13.

Ansicht der Südlichen Alpen von Neuseeland von der Central Moraine des Gr. Godley Gletschers aus.

ORIGINALKARTE
zur Übersicht von
D: JULIUS HAAST'S REISE
durch die
SÜDL. ALPEN NEU-SEELANDS,
1863.
Nach des Reisenden Handzeichnungen
und den Englischen Küstenaufnahmen
von A. Petermann.
Maassstab 1: 700.000.

Deutsche Meilen (15 = 1°)
Englische Statute Miles (69,16 = 1°)
Die Höhen in Englischen Fuss.
Haast's Route.
Gletscher.

H. Habenicht del.   Lith. Anst. v. C. Hellfarth in Gotha.

GOTHA: JUSTUS PERTHES
1863.

HAAST'S MAP OF HAAST PASS, 1863

Dr Julius von Haast had already helped to survey most of the rest of the country to the north when he arrived in Canterbury. He offered to perform a geological survey of the Southern Alps between Christchurch and the West Coast (then part of Canterbury), and after roping him in to solve the geological difficulties it was having in constructing a rail tunnel between the city and Lyttelton, the provincial council readily agreed.

This map shows the fruits of his exploration in the vicinity of the pass that bears his name, and which is marked in a discreet shade of red; as a bonus, it also shows a view of the Godley Glacier between Mount Wolseley and Mount D'Archiac, deep in the alps at the headwaters of the river that feeds Lake Tekapo. It's a view worth savouring, as the glacier has retreated far back into its valley these days.

Following page
HAAST'S MAP OF THE SOUTHERN ALPS, 1870

If the Southern Alps were represented mostly by blank paper in the map on p. 166, the same was definitely not true by the time Julius von Haast had finished his peripatetic survey in the late 1860s. He named many of the features he described (for Europeans) for the first time: there is a mixture of the usual cronyism (the Moorhouse Range south of Mount Cook, named for William Moorhouse, superintendent of Canterbury) and homage to his peers and illustrious predecessors (the Lyell Glacier, for Charles Lyell, 'the father of geology', and the Agassiz Range for Swiss geologist Jean Louis Rodolphe Agassiz). He discovered stuff that would have endeared him to his provincial masters—notably coal and gold on the West Coast—and, needless to say, the quality of his work earned him many honours: he was elected a Fellow of the Royal Society, and awarded the same august body's Patron's Medal, and was given knighthoods by both Austria and Great Britain. In the year that this map was printed, he was appointed the curator of the Canterbury Museum, the collection of which was a major beneficiary of his activities in the rugged backblocks of New Zealand.

MAP OF THE SOUTHERN ALPS
IN THE PROVINCE OF CANTERBURY
(NEW ZEALAND)

Reduced from the large Map

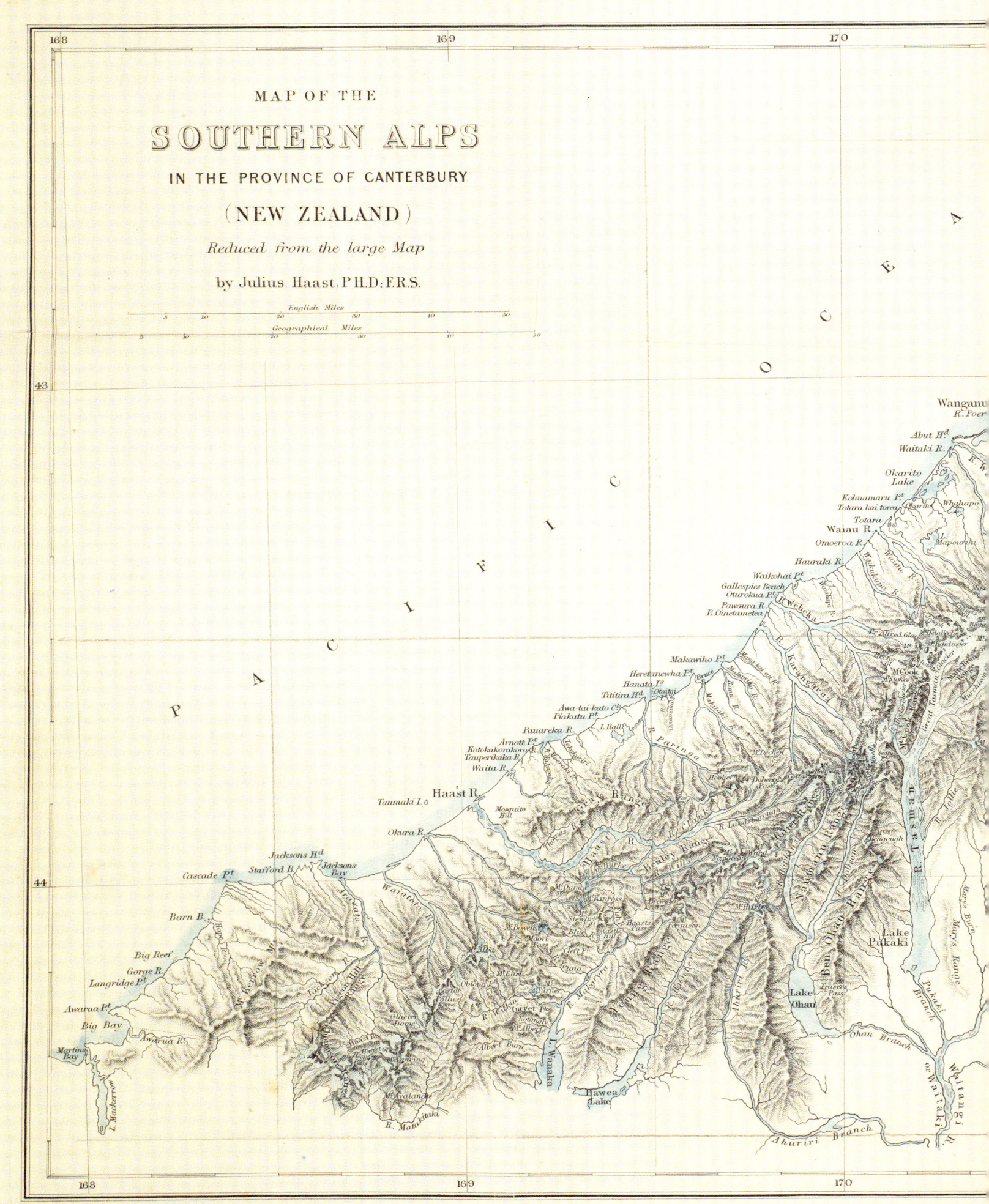

by Julius Haast, PH.D; F.R.S.

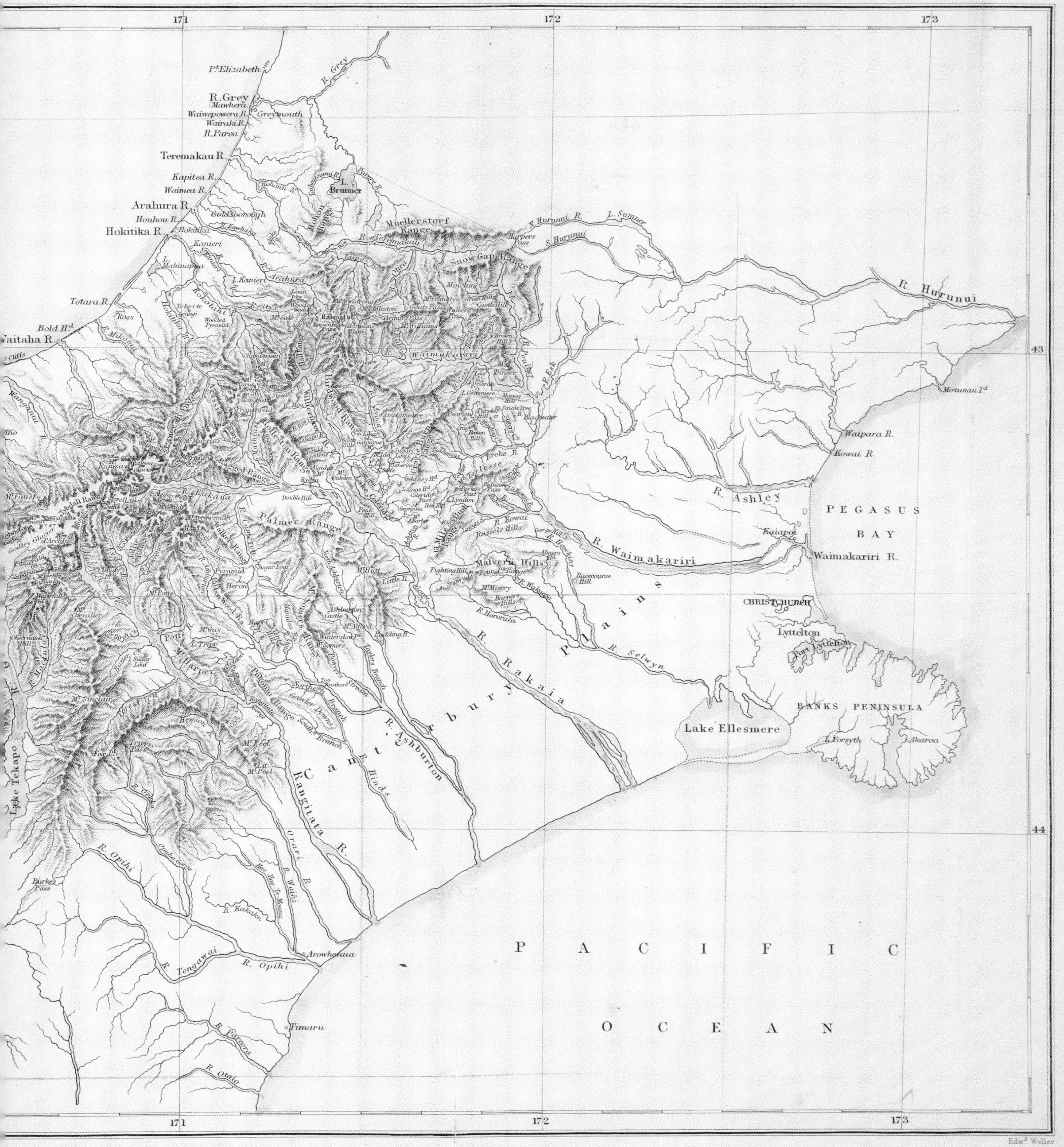

ographical Society by John Murray, Albemarle Street, London 1870.

Edwd Weller

HOCHSTETTER'S MAP OF THE PROVINCE OF AUCKLAND, 1863

It's not often that an invitation to perform a whirlwind geological survey of a new country comes your way, but that's exactly how German geologist Ferdinand von Hochstetter came to produce a geographical atlas of New Zealand. Hochstetter had been on a world tour with like-minded geologists when he met Sir George Grey, governor of New Zealand, on their Cape Town stopover. Grey waxed lyrical about Auckland's volcanic field, and that was all a real-gone rockhound like Hochstetter needed to hear for his interest to be piqued. The Auckland Provincial Council got wind of him, and asked if he wouldn't mind popping down to Drury to inspect a coalfield that had been found there: his report so impressed them that they asked him to stay on and perform a proper study of the entire province.

Hochstetter was assisted in this work by Julius von Haast, and together they swiftly acquired a working knowledge of the mud, rocks and stones that comprise the North Island to produce this striking map. Interestingly, it was in the course of their survey of the hot lakes (depicted here in the black-and-white inset) that Hochstetter fixed the position of the Pink and White Terraces with sufficient accuracy to inform recent expeditions, which may well have rediscovered them beneath Lake Rotomahana, under which they were swamped following the 1886 eruption of Mount Tarawera.

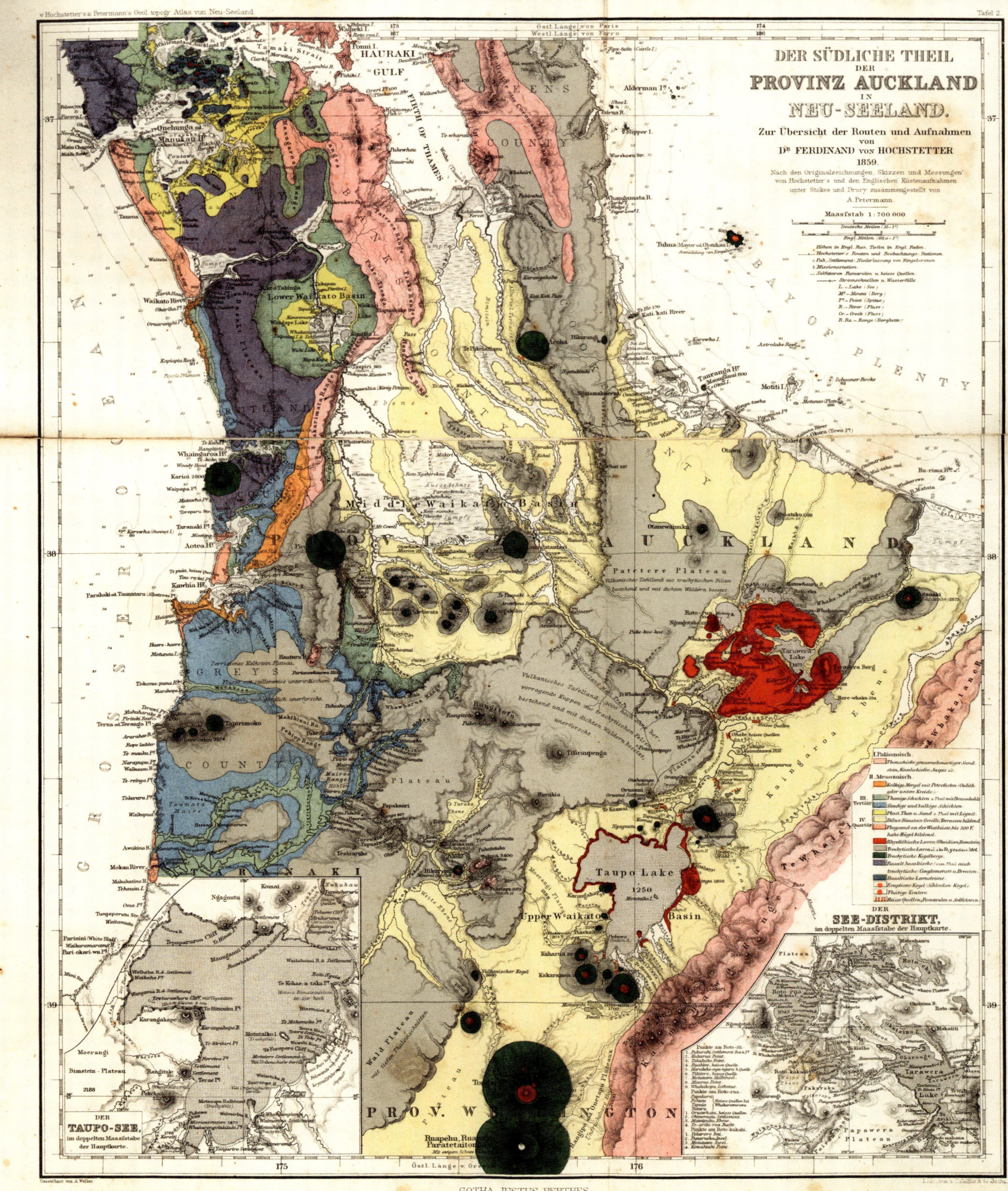

DER SÜDLICHE THEIL DER PROVINZ AUCKLAND IN NEU-SEELAND.

Zur Übersicht der Routen und Aufnahmen von D.r FERDINAND VON HOCHSTETTER 1859.

Nach den Originalzeichnungen, Skizzen und Messungen von Hochstetter's und den Englischen Küstenaufnahmen unter Stokes und Drury zusammengestellt von A. Petermann.

Maasstab 1:700 000

DER SEE-DISTRIKT, im doppelten Maasstabe der Hauptkarte.

DER TAUPO-SEE, im doppelten Maasstabe der Hauptkarte.

GOTHA, JUSTUS PERTHES 1863.

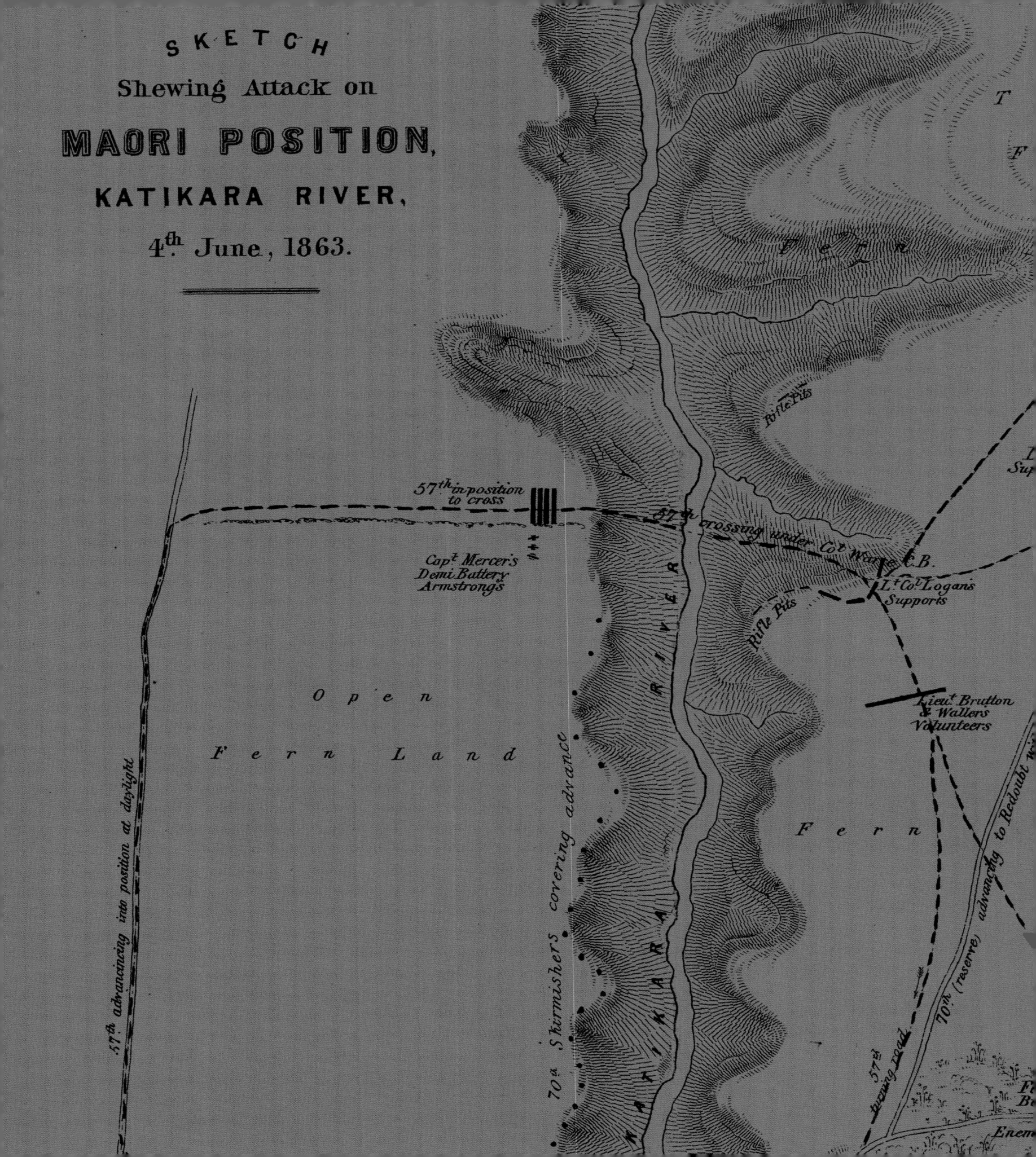

SKETCH
Shewing Attack on
MAORI POSITION,
KATIKARA RIVER,
4th June, 1863.

57th in position to cross

57th crossing under Col. Warre C.B.

Capt Mercer's Demi Battery Armstrongs

Lt Col Logan's Supports

Rifle Pits

Lieut Brutton & Waller's Volunteers

Open Fern Land

Fern

Fern

KATIKARA RIVER

57th advancing into position at daylight

70th Skirmishers covering advance

57th crossing road

70th (reserve) advancing to Redoubt

EIGHT

CADASTRE VS AHI KAA

Down the years, it has often been debated (especially in the forum created more or less for that purpose, the Waitangi Tribunal) how much Māori understood of the European notion of property rights. Te ao Māori had no sense of 'property' at all. For Māori, your entire identity was bound up with the long relationship your hapū and iwi had with tracts of land, which were often the same tracts of land settled by your ancestors at the time of the arrival of Polynesians in New Zealand. Your whakapapa—the song that you sang to establish for others who you were and what your place in the world was—began with the naming of the landmarks that defined your tūrangawaewae, your foothold. And these landmarks were more than mere places: they were just as much tīpuna as your human forebears; they were part of your being, no less than your mother and father, because just as your parents provide for and nourish you, so does the land. When a Māori child is born, their whenua (placenta) is buried in the soil of ancestral land, an act rich in the symbolism of belonging. No less significantly, the Māori word for land is whenua.

So much for the spiritual connection Māori felt to the land. In practical terms, ownership was asserted through ahi kaa, 'fires burning', which can be loosely translated as use and occupation. If an iwi were occupying a territory, their mana whenua—their control over the land—was easy to recognise. But even if there were no dwellings or other apparatus of occupation, they could claim mana whenua merely by using land for the cultivation or gathering of food. If the people were using their land—as signified by blazing cooking fires—then they were the owners.

Needless to say, this didn't mean Aotearoa prior to the coming of Pākehā was a nicely parcelled-up and subdivided paradise, any more than the ubiquity of precise, cadastral surveys has meant that boundary disputes have become a thing of the distant past in European jurisdictions. While there is no definitive explanation for the transition from the kāinga (the relatively peaceable, hunter-gatherer society that the ancestors of the Māori established) to the pā (the bellicose, fortification-building society that the Europeans found), the suspicion is that rising populations and perhaps some climatic shift caused competition for food resources, which in turn set in motion a centuries-long series of tit-for-tat conflicts between iwi. A set of customary sanctions for property violations existed in the form of the codes of tapu and utu; similarly, while warfare could be used to acquire territory, so too could strategic alliances, often reinforced by intermarriage.

When the first Pākehā came to settle in New Zealand, they were often welcomed. Not only was it to the economic advantage of the tangata whenua—it gave them access to European goods—but it also gave them an intermediary in their dealings with other Pākehā. The privileged status of those who were allowed to live amongst Māori was often signified by the throwing of a cloak over their head, a symbolic extension of the mana of the owner of the cloak, conferring protection. They might even be gifted or sold land on which to build a house (or mission, or trading post): it's unlikely such a gift or sale was ever considered to have been in perpetuity, as Māori in this phase of things had no notion of the permanent alienation of land. Many of the early land sales—even some of the major deals, such as William Wakefield's massive buy-up—were probably based on a fundamental misunderstanding. Māori likely imagined they were selling the right to live upon and exploit land (the technical term for such rights is 'usufructuary': literally 'the use of the fruits'), not the land itself. It was closer to the European notion of a lease than to that of a land sale and purchase.

This was a certain recipe for misunderstanding, even before the complications were considered. And the complications were many and varied. Often a European agent anxious to close a deal on a piece of land would wishfully choose to overlook the question of who, amongst the many communal owners of a block of land, had the authority to dispose of it. Sometimes you might be treating with the head of the local hapū rather than with the rangatira of the iwi whose land you were proposing to alienate forever. Or you might be dealing with an opportunist who, with no connection to or interest in the land at all, was quite willing to let on that it was theirs to sell, free and unencumbered. And in plenty of cases, the status of mana whenua over vast tracts of New Zealand had become murky in the wake of the upheavals of the Musket Wars. The people whose cooking fires were burning upon a block of land you were seeking to buy might have been there for only twenty years or so, compared with the centuries-long occupation by the people they had displaced.

All in all, it was the kind of fodder upon which generations of lawyers could—and would—grow fat and very happy indeed.

SKETCH MAP OF HOKIANGA (CREATOR UNKNOWN), 1845

Hōne Heke of Ngā Puhi was initially benevolent towards the increasing European presence in the Bay of Islands. He did nicely out of trade with visiting whalers, and levied a kind of duty on them to boot. But when the new colonial administration shifted its capital south to Auckland, the numbers of visiting ships began to fall away. Symbolically, too, the colours of the United Tribes of New Zealand, adopted amongst the northern iwi at the time of the signing of the Declaration of Independence in 1835 (intended to discourage French attempts at annexation), had been taken down from the flagstaff on the hill above Kororāreka and the Union Jack hoisted instead. Heke became susceptible to the whispers of American whalers who warned that the Treaty of Waitangi had been a deception, and as soon as the British were strong enough, they would seize all Māori land. In late 1844, Heke cut down the flagstaff. He did it twice more in early 1845, and even sacked Kororāreka, whereupon British warships shelled the occupied town.

Action then shifted inland, to the district covered by this sketch map, drawn by an unknown hand. It has been made with a martial eye for terrain. Battles were fought at Heke's pā (shown at the southern end of the green-shaded hill country to the north of Lake Ōmāpere), and then at the pā belonging to Heke's ally, Te Ruki Kawiti (practically the last feature on the top left corner of the map). The route of the British troops is marked, as is the camp they established to mount an assault on Kawiti's pā on 24 December 1845, and the pā occupied by the Ngā Puhi rangatira, Tāmati Wāka Nene, who fought on the side of the British. Heke and Kawiti inflicted a defeat on the British at Ōhaeawai, before a siege took place further south at Ruapekapeka in early 1846.

[ca. 1845]

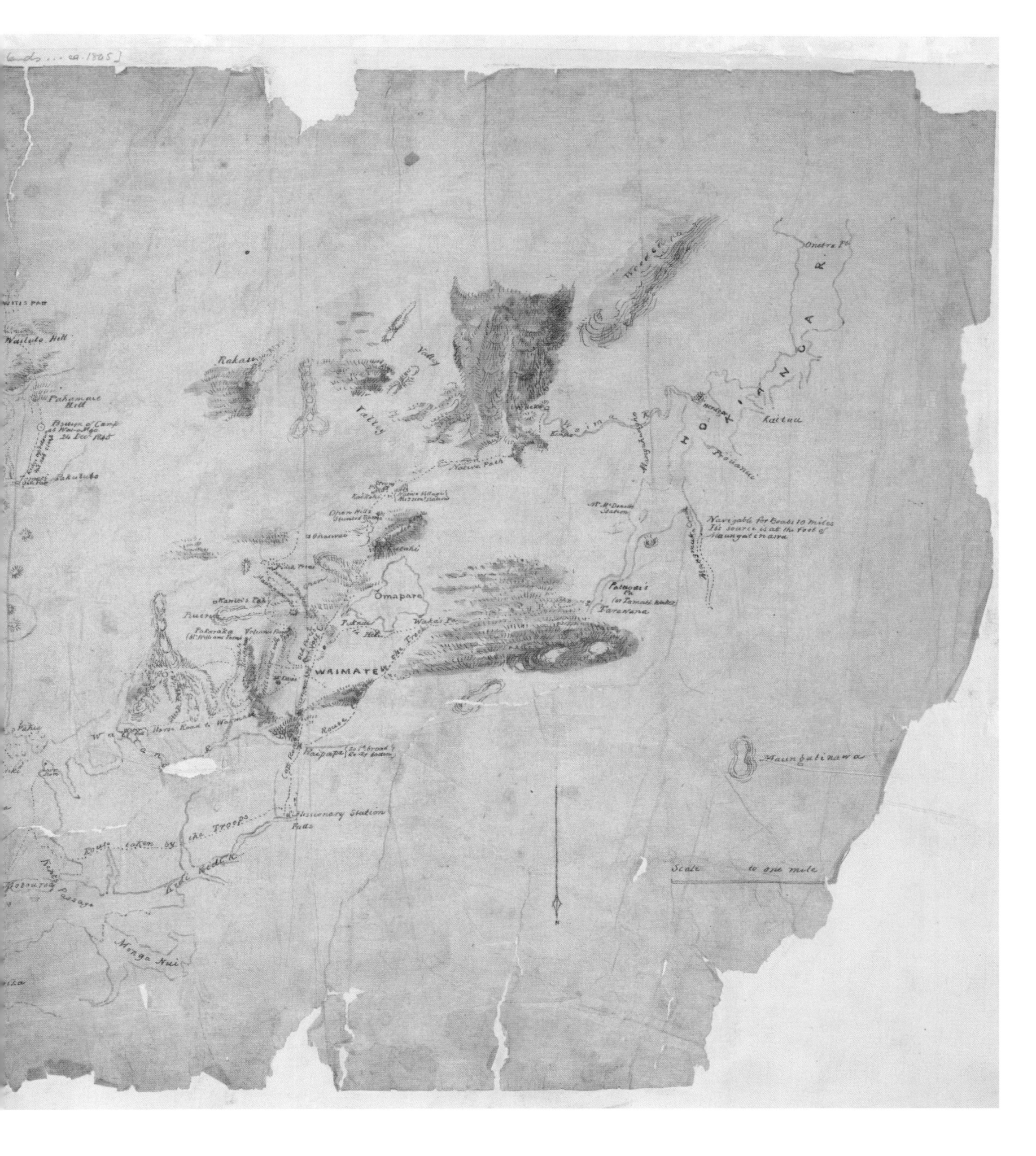

Waitiri Pah
Waitoto Hill
Pakemare Hill
Position of Camp at Wai-Pae 24 Dec 1845
Pakutuko

Rakau

Onetea Po

Waiteteria

Valley

Kororareka

Kaitua

Pouhanui

Nerve Path

Kaikohe
Native Village & Mission Station

Mt McDonald Station

Open Hill Stunted Trees

Navigable for Boats 10 miles Its source is at the foot of Maungatiniwa

Puke Tree

Omapere

Puero
Waimate
Pakaraka (M. Williams Farm)
Volcanic Peaks
Tutao Hill
Waka's Pa

Pationi's Pa (or Tamati Waka's) Tarawana

Route taken by the Troops

Horse Road to Wai___

Waitangi

Raipapa 30 ft broad Rocky bottom

Maungatiniwa

Missionary Station Pah

Route taken by the Troops

Keri Keri R.

Scale to one mile

Hororoa Passage

N

Monga Nui

For as long as European settlement was confined to the coasts, Māori were happy enough. But as Pākehā numbers grew and the new arrivals showed every sign of settling in for the long haul, Māori disquiet grew. And as more and more lean, extravagantly bearded figures toting theodolites, chains and field books began to crop up in the interior, the significance of the colonial enterprise began to dawn upon them. Most of those who signed the Treaty of Waitangi probably believed in Hobson's promise that this symbolic act would bring the full force of the British Crown to bear in sorting out disputes over land dealings and protecting the tangata whenua from the depredations of land-hungry colonists. But this faith was short-lived. The ink was barely dry on the document when the first stirrings of resistance began.

In early 1843, the Ngāti Toa chiefs Te Rauparaha and Te Rangihaeata arrived in Nelson to make it clear to the New Zealand Company that their surveyors were trespassing on their land in the Wairau River valley, inland from the site of present-day Blenheim. Arthur Wakefield (younger brother of Edward and William) maintained that he had bought the block, fair and square, from the widow of a whaler named Blenkinsopp, who had purportedly bought it from Te Rauparaha himself. Te Rauparaha disputed the sale—the deed that Blenkinsopp had drawn up stated that it related to 26,500 acres of land, whereas Te Rauparaha insisted that he had only ever agreed to sell rights to wood and fresh water—and vowed never to sell the land in question: he called upon the native lands commissioner, William Spain, to mediate the matter.

Spain was too slow to give it his attention. Wakefield sent surveyors to the block; Te Rauparaha and Te Rangihaeata politely yet firmly escorted them off again, burning the huts they had built and uprooting their survey pegs. Wakefield enlisted the support of a magistrate, armed forty-odd settlers and set off for Tuamarina to sort the matter out.

On 17 June 1843, the two parties faced one another across the Tuamarina Stream. Words were exchanged, peremptory on the part of the Pākehā, defiant on the side of the Māori. The special constables were ordered forward, and whether it was accidentally or deliberately, a musket discharged and Te Rangihaeata's wife fell dead. Volleys of musket fire were exchanged. The Pākehā broke and ran, but were overtaken. Many were killed even after they surrendered. In the final analysis, 22 Pākehā, including Wakefield and the magistrate, Henry Thompson, died, as did up to nine Māori.

The fledgling colony was electrified by the news. Te Rauparaha and Te Rangihaeata were arrested, and the new governor, Robert FitzRoy, arrived to pass judgement on the case. He found in favour of Ngāti Toa, whether because he genuinely believed the basis of the New Zealand Company's claim to the land was without merit, or because he recognised the precarious position of the settler population, heavily outnumbered as it was by Māori. Either way, the predictable response of settlers was outrage, and in their reaction you can plainly see the sense of entitlement that arose from the Pākehā conviction of the superiority of their culture. It arose from the same engrained belief that was expressed in the New Zealand Company's 'tenths' provision for Māori—that land under European use was ten times more valuable than it was in the rude and uncivilised hands of its indigenous occupiers. The Wairau Affray (it was once named the Wairau Massacre) was a watershed in the history of Māori–Pākehā relations. More and more settlers were arriving by the day, and the numerical imbalance was growing less. The demand for the transfer of land from Māori to Pākehā was intensifying. Little wonder the maps of the next four decades featured fortifications, the routes of marches, battle sites.

The cadastre—the word derives from a register kept in ancient times upon which a poll tax was based—is the official, legal set of definitions of the boundaries, descriptions and titles of land (the 'metes and bounds', to use the technical term). It is the job of surveyors to determine the metes and bounds, by measuring land as precisely as they can. There are differing ways of doing this, but by the nineteenth century it was generally done by triangulation: the determining of distances and directions to two or more points whose geospatial location has been fixed. The mathematics involved in this is spherical trigonometry, which is why those black-and-white wooden structures on prominent hilltops near you are called 'trig' stations. The cadastre was very much a product of the modern European—that is to say, capitalist—estimation of the value of land. To the European mind, land was something to be owned and exploited exclusively, more often than not by individuals: the term in English law is 'freehold' or 'fee simple' over 'an estate in land'.

The tearing out and casting aside of wooden pegs was a symbolic rejection by Māori of the cadastral net that surveyors were casting across the land. Te Rauparaha and his party did it. Surveyors were banned from the territory of the iwi that launched the movement to establish a Māori king, equivalent to the British monarch, in 1850. And the removal of survey pegs and the ploughing of land was the method employed in the final major resistance to the wholesale alienation of Māori land, led by Te Whiti o Rongomai and Tohu Kākahi at Parihaka. The message was twofold: the pou that you have planted do not belong here, and we are using—we own—this land.

Survey gangs were regarded with almost superstitious dread by Māori, who recognised that some arcane knowledge was being used to deprive them of their land. Many surveyors recorded Māori referring to their theodolites as 'taipō', a word for a demon or malign spirit that afflicts people in the night. Little wonder: all it took was for a surveyor and the strange little brass and wooden being to put their heads together and the land was soon carved up and ceased to belong to the tangata whenua. Once the theodolite had swept its cold, glassy regard across the terrain, the land became visible to Pākehā judges, who were deaf to the names and the songs.

Once the dust had settled on the first round of the New Zealand Wars in the early 1860s, the business of transferring land from Māori to Pākehā began in earnest. Some of the measures employed by the settler government were decidedly unsubtle: Waikato and Taranaki iwi were punished for their part in the wars with the confiscation of their land (a process known to Māori as raupatu). It didn't escape their notice that the lands chosen for confiscation were amongst the most fertile and promising for European agriculture: the poor, isolated territory of Ngāti Maniapoto, who had also been combatants, was left alone. Some of the measures were rather more underhand. A Native Land Court was established by the 1865 Native Lands Act, the aim of which was to convert the communal title of Māori land to individual title, which would greatly facilitate its sale. Whether intended or not—and there is no reason to believe it was unforeseen—a major consequence of the process (which demanded applicants bear the costs of preparing their case and attending mandatory court hearings) was that Māori landowners racked up enormous debts, which they could generally only settle by selling their land.

Little wonder those iwi who were still substantially in control of their lands took a leaf out of the Kīngitanga movement's book and banned survey gangs, road-builders and Native Land Court examiners from their territories.

A second round of armed conflict took place in the mid- to late 1860s, with the Pai Mārire and Ringatū movements centred around the prophets Te Ua Haumēne and Te Kooti Arikirangi respectively. Both claimed religious inspiration from the Old Testament, which for the most part is a story of the exile and restoration to their rightful estate of God's chosen people. Pākehā New Zealand looked on anxiously, afraid that Tāwhiao, the Māori king, might mobilise his followers in the cause. But Tāwhiao did not. He preferred to pursue peaceful resolution to Māori grievances over land, petitioning Queen Victoria herself, one monarch to another, to stop the shenanigans being done in her name and to put things right. His plea, like the prayers of the prophets, fell on deaf ears.

Following page
MAP OF NORTH TARANAKI (CREATOR UNKNOWN), 1866

The same process that was used to transfer land from Ngāi Te Rangi to Europeans can be seen at work in this pretty map, which depicts a block of land (just north of present-day Urenui) confiscated from Taranaki iwi and surveyed and allocated to 'the officers, non-commissioned officers and 46 of the men of Captain W. B. Messenger's Company of Military Settlers'. William Bazire Messenger was an accomplished soldier, and featured in just about every conflict that involved New Zealand from the 1860s to the South African War of 1899–1902, in which he also participated. He had some hand in just about every action of the Taranaki campaigns, was in command of the force that overran Parihaka (where his old adversary, the 'Māori Napoleon', Tītokowaru, was living), and was even in command of the force that eventually apprehended the rebel prophet Te Kooti Arikirangi.

The 'military settlers' of whom he was in command at the time this map was drawn was a force of mercenaries (mostly former goldminers) from Melbourne. Most took up the farms allocated to them in the survey that gave rise to this map, as did Messenger, who is here allocated 300 acres. The map notes that much of the land exhibits signs of abundant cultivation from years before, and describes a large tract of it as 'fine open country, the resort of herds of cattle, the soil rich and deep'. Its abundance of water is noted, along with the 'spontaneous growth of clover', as is the fact that the ranges terminate at the boundary of the block, through which 'the Maories' [sic] doubtless found their way from the south through some 'devious track'.

Pages 198–199
MAP OF THE TRIANGULATION OF WANGANUI (CREATOR UNKNOWN), 1869

It wasn't long after the signing of the Treaty of Waitangi that the future became clear to Māori. Not only were Pākehā here to stay, but also they were arriving in increasing numbers. And not only did those who had purchased land from Māori expect it to be theirs forever, but every new arrival expected their own plot, too. The emblem of this encroachment was the survey, where lines of triangulation were extended over the face of the land from trig to trig, and pegs were hammered into the earth. The cadastre—the system of establishing precisely measured plots of land that might be owned exclusively and in perpetuity—was fundamentally at odds with the notion of ahi kaa: occupation by the people with mana whenua.

Whanganui was unsettled right from the start. The New Zealand Company was obliged to pay iwi from up the river a sum nearly equal to the price it had originally paid for the land upon which the town (first known as Petre) and the settlers' country plots were laid out. There was tension in the wake of the Wairau Affray, when it appeared to Pākehā that the flare-up on 17 June 1843 might spread and see a general uprising of Māori against the settler population. There was actual violence in the mid-1840s, with a Pākehā farmer and his family murdered in reprisal for the death (supposed to have been accidental) of a local chief. And Whanganui was a hot-spot of the more general violence that is now known as the New Zealand Wars. A lot of blood was shed before it was possible for James Mitchell to spread the ethereal net of the cadastre over the whenua of the Wanganui District in 1869.

M[AP]

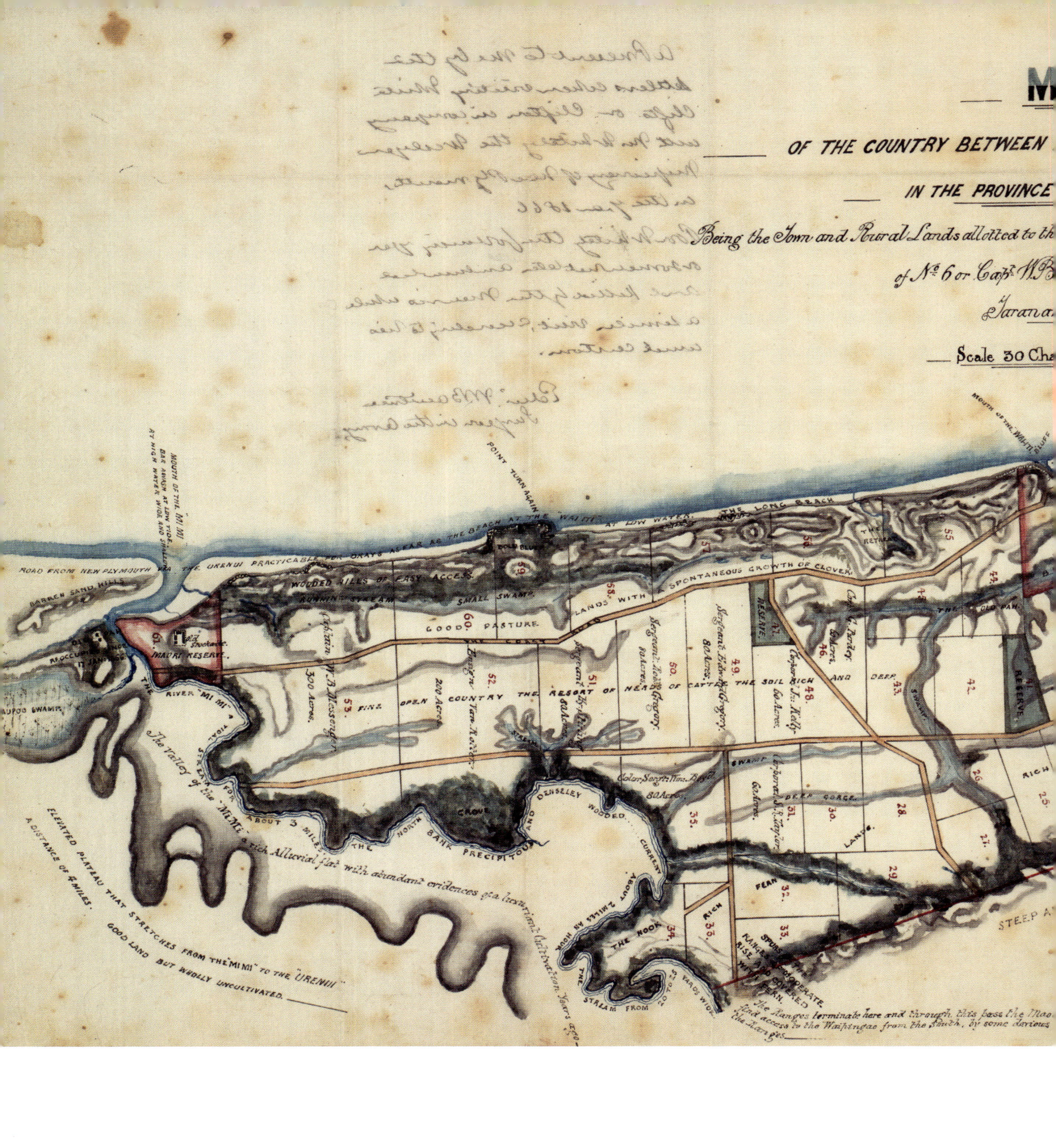

OF THE COUNTRY BETWEEN

IN THE PROVINCE

Being the Town and Rural Lands allotted to th[e]
of No. 6 or Capt. W. B[...]

Taranak[i]

Scale 30 Cha[ins]

...ver "MIMI" AND PUKEARUHE
...ARANAKI N.Z.
... Non Comm.d Officers and Forty six of the Men
...nger's Company
...tary Settlers
...n inch.

NOTABILIA

The Redoubt at Pukearuhe is said to be
distant from New Plymouth .... 32 Miles
Urenui from the Redoubt 11
The Mimi by the Coast road from the same ... 7
Do. by the long beach around Point
"Turn again" from do. 5/8
The greatest length of the block in a straight
line 6
Its greatest breadth 1/8
Area in Acres .... about 4100

EVERY SWAMP HAS A RUNNING STREAM OF PURE
WATER. SPRINGS ALSO ARE VERY NUMEROUS, WHILE THE
NATURAL FACILITIES FOR SURFACE DRAINAGE ARE VERY
GREAT.

Compiled from recent Surveys by George Hadley Esq.re
and the Topographical features of the Country surveyed and filled
in by

Wm G.y Burgoyne
Clifton
15th February 1866

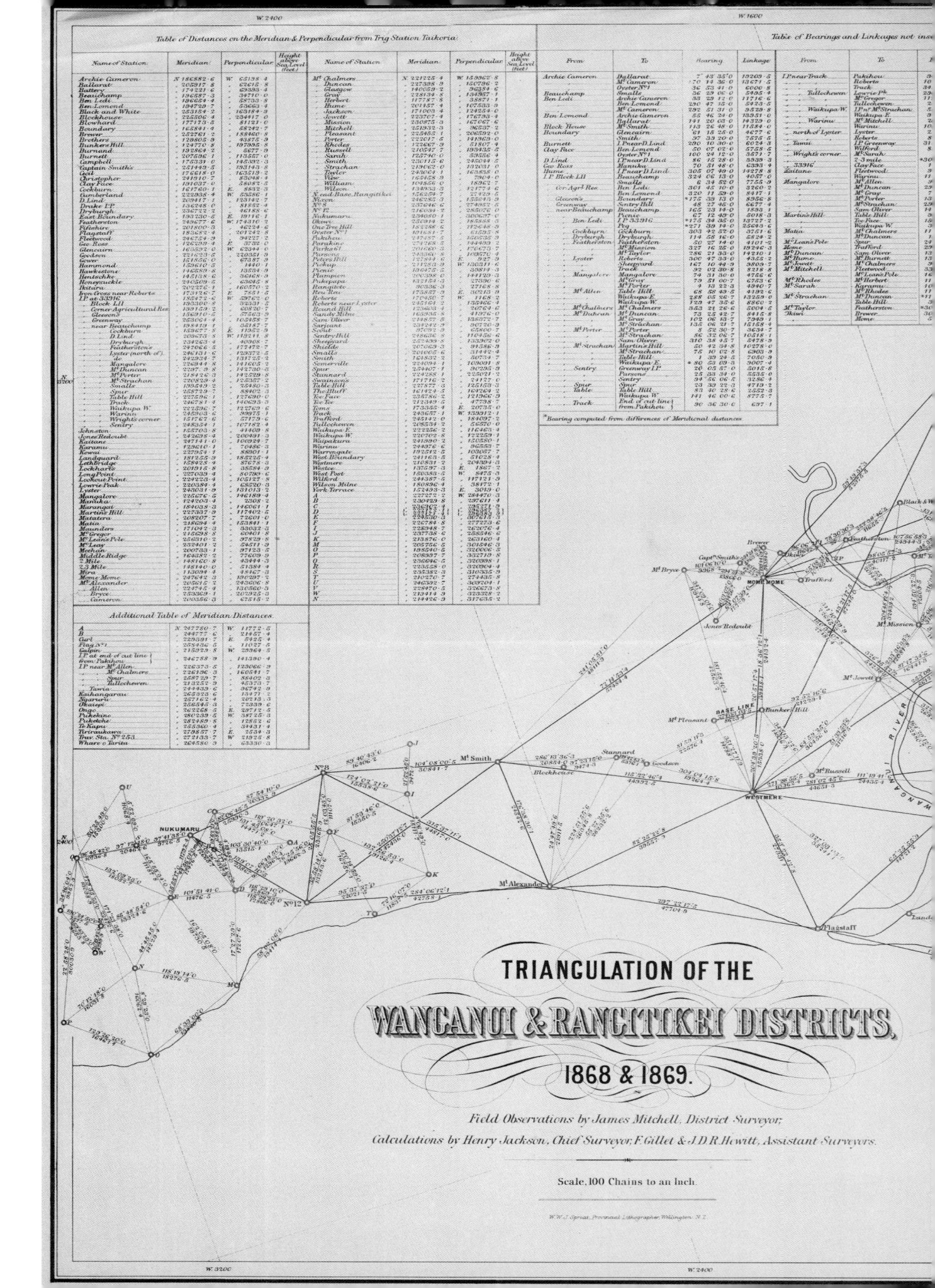

TRIANGULATION OF THE
WANGANUI & RANGITIKEI DISTRICTS,
1868 & 1869.

Field Observations by James Mitchell, District Surveyor;

Calculations by Henry Jackson, Chief Surveyor; F. Gillet & J.D.R. Hewitt, Assistant Surveyors.

Scale, 100 Chains to an Inch.

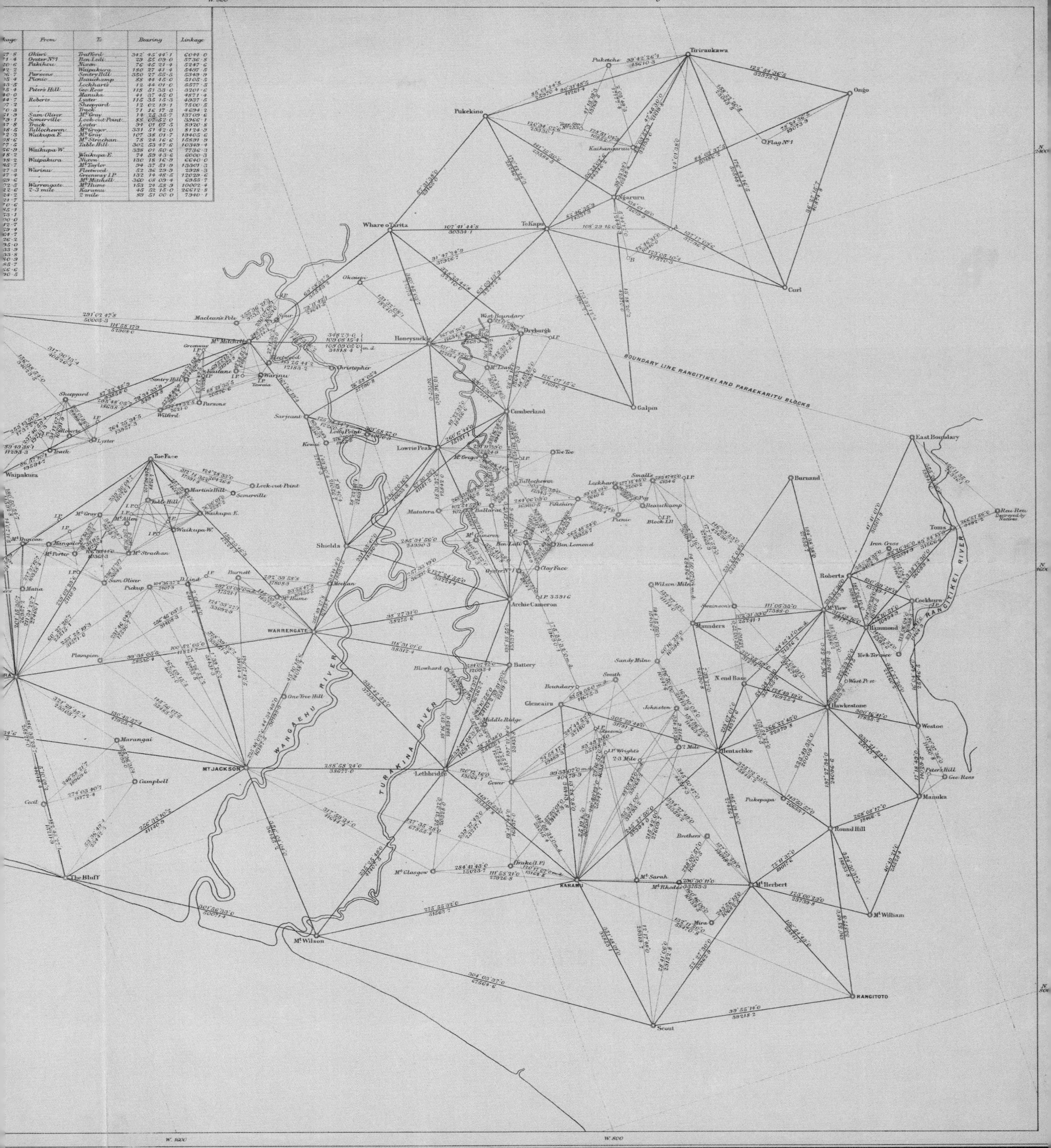

...kage	From	To	Bearing	Linkage
7·8	Okiwi	Trafford	342° 45′ 44″·1	6044·0
1·4	Oyster No. 1	Ben Ledi	29 55 09·0	5736·8
20·6	Pakihou	Nixon	76 46 21·4	5247·6
42·2	"	Waipakura	180 27 41·4	5497·5
06·7	Parsons	Sentry Hill	350 27 55·5	5349·9
05·4	Picnic	Beauchamp	88 44 45·0	5105·5
43·5	"	Lockharts	12 44 01·0	6577·5
15·4	Peter's Hill	Geo. Ross	118 51 33·0	3201·6
40·0	"	Manuka	41 37 45·0	4871·4
44·7	Roberts	Lyster	115 35 15·3	4937·5
07·2	"	Sheepyard	12 02 19·1	7500·5
70·3	"	Track	71 16 17·3	4694·2
51·3	Sam Oliver	Mt. Gray	14 25 35·7	13709·6
79·1	Somerville	Look-out Point	88 07 52·0	3966·1
37·8	Track	Lyster	94 01 07·5	8920·8
38·5	Tullochewen	Mc. Gregor	331 51 42·0	8124·3
92·3	Waikupa E.	Mt. Gray	107 38 01·7	19405·6
98·6	"	Mt. Strachan	78 24 16·6	15891·9
77·5	"	Table Hill	302 53 47·6	10349·4
56·9	Waikupa W.	"	338 01 50·6	7736·3
18·2	"	Waikupa E.	74 59 43·6	6000·3
98·2	Waipakura	Nixon	130 18 16·9	6640·0
85·7	"	Mt. Taylor	94 37 51·9	13301·3
27·3	Warinu	Fleetwood	52 36 29·9	2928·3
47·4	"	Greenway I.P.	132 14 48·5	12029·6
59·6	"	Mt. Mitchell	360 08 09·4	6955·7
02·5	Warrengate	Mt. Hume	153 24 58·9	10002·4
22·6	2-3 mile	Karamu	45 52 15·0	26612·8
24·2	"	2 mile	89 51 00·0	7940·1
21·7				
70·6				
85·1				
53·1				
00·0				
12·7				
69·4				
64·7				
26·2				
95·0				
33·9				
33·8				
80·9				
85·7				
56·6				
90·5				

Major Rookes Division of the Wanganui Militia District

Major Marshall Division of the [...]

R. WAITOTARA
R. WANGANUI
R. WANGAEHU
R. TURAKINA
R. RANGITIKEI
R. MANAWATU

River Mangawhero[?]

MAP OF MILITIA DISTRICTS, WANGANUI (CREATOR UNKNOWN), 1860S

It's hard to think of modern-day Whanganui as a military centre, but that's what the settlement was for much of the 1860s. The 'First Taranaki War' (the name is controversial, as some argue there was only one war, with more than one phase) was sparked by a dodgy land deal at Waitara, where a minor Ātiawa chief, with questionable authority, sold a block of land for the siting of a township. The sale was vetoed by Wiremu Kīngi, the rangatira, but the government was determined to see the sale enforced. Surveyors were sent, along with soldiers who built a fort to house them and protected them as they worked. This sparked a series of armed conflicts and pitched battles, which at its height threatened to involve the King Movement (and therefore the iwi of much of the central North Island), and which ended in an inconclusive truce in 1861. The Second Taranaki War was precipitated by the government's confiscation of land, purportedly from the belligerents, starting from 1863. No obvious distinction was made between those who had fought against the Crown and those who had either remained neutral or fought alongside the British; and when resistance was offered, the heavy-handed (and opportunistic) response was to burn Māori settlements and cultivations and confiscate that land, too.

The residents of Whanganui, meanwhile, spent much of the 1860s understandably jittery, on a war footing. Most able-bodied men joined the militia, divided, as this map shows, under the commands of majors Charles Cecil Rookes and John Marshall. Many of the militiamen were, like Rookes himself, veterans of British campaigns in India. This map shows the militia districts and subdistricts, with a dotted line delineating the land purchase that established Whanganui (which bears that name rather than the original 'Petre') and district.

Following page
SKETCH MAP OF COUNTRY AROUND GATE PĀ (CREATOR UNKNOWN), 1864

It is not known who drew this sketch of the battles in the vicinity of what is now Tauranga in 1864, but whoever they were, they certainly seem to have been in the thick of the action. The map depicts a 'scouting track', which measured a forty-mile round distance between a marked house and Gate Pā, where Bay of Plenty Māori inflicted a humiliating defeat on a vastly larger British force on 29 April. It also shows Te Ranga, where the Māori force, having abandoned their sophisticated fortification at Gate Pā, were in the process of building another when they were surprised by their vengeful foe. These, and other actions, are marked on the map with crossed swords rendered in red ink.

The Māori defenders of Gate Pā are remembered for having shown great gallantry to the British wounded in the battle: the same can't be said of the settler government, which, having defeated Ngāi Te Rangi at Te Ranga, set about depriving them of their land, whether by enforced sale or out-and-out confiscation. The land was surveyed and allocated to 'military settlers'.

Page 203
SEWELL'S MAP OF THE NORTH ISLAND, CIRCA 1865

The policy of the aggressive expansion of settler interests under Thomas Gore Brown, governor of New Zealand from 1855 to 1861, and then George Grey (in his second term, from 1861 to 1868) can be seen in the game of noughts and crosses on this map, drawn in the middle of a decade of conflict between Māori and Pākehā. The red circles represent proposed military settlements (where soldiers—many or most of them lured from the goldfields of Otago and from Australia with the promise of grants of land—were settled on blocks newly confiscated from Māori), while the black crosses represent Māori populations, with each cross representing '100 souls'. Critical to the enterprise of 'opening up' the land was the building of roads: red lines on this map represent roads that were to be built, and brown lines roads that might be built at some future date. The iwi of the southern Bay of Plenty and East Cape and Poverty Bay had not yet shown any resistance to government policy: hence, no roads, and no military settlements.

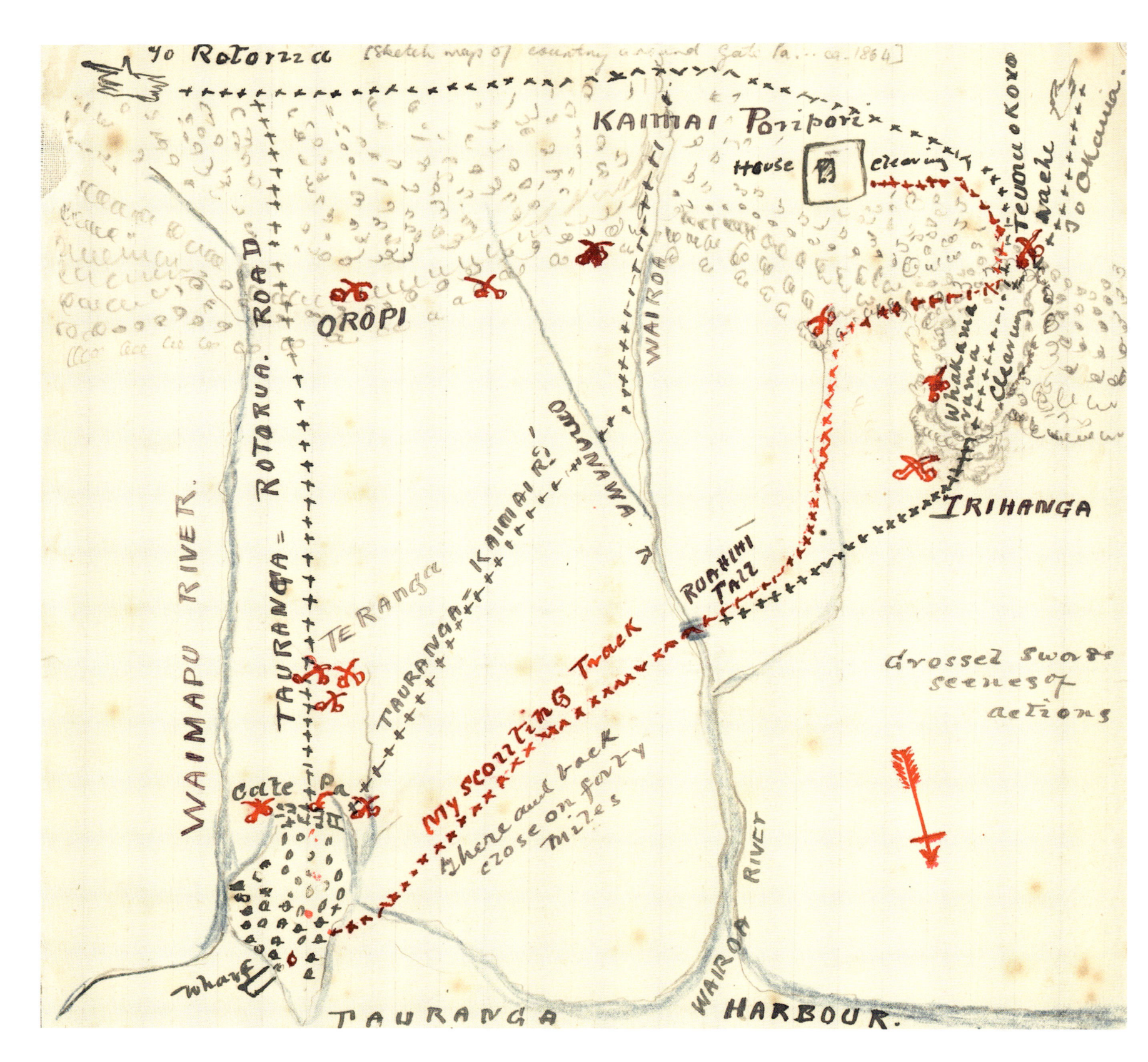

To Rotorua [Sketch map of country around Gate Pa — ca. 1864]

KAIMAI Poripori
House — Clearing — Te Umu o Koro
Waeli
To Ohawa

OROPI

Whakamarama
Clearing

WAIMAPU RIVER

TAURANGA = ROTORUA ROAD

TE RANGA

TAURANGA = KAIMAI Rd

OMANAWA R.

WAIROA

RUAHIHI FALL

IRIHANGA

My scouting track
there and back
close on forty
miles

Crossed swords
scenes of
actions

Gate Pa

Wharf

TAURANGA HARBOUR

WAIROA RIVER

Lines of Road proposed to be made - red
Local position of Military Settlements - red circles
Lines of Road to be made at a future period - brown
The crosses (black) represent the distribution of the
Native Population approximately, each cross
representing about 100 souls.

PLAN OF THE ATTACK ON KATIKARA (CREATOR UNKNOWN), 1863

Even as he was making plans to return the disputed Waitara Block to Te Ātiawa, Governor George Grey moved to occupy and fortify a block of land at Tātaraimaka, around twenty kilometres south of New Plymouth. He was probably secretly hoping this would provoke Taranaki Māori to some action that would provide him with an excuse for holding on to the Waitara land, too.

Then something did happen. On 4 May 1863, a small group of British soldiers was ambushed and killed at Ōakura. The British response was swift and devastating: a force of nearly 900 soldiers marched on a lightly defended pā on the Katikara River, supported by artillery and cannon fire from the steamship *Eclipse*, from the deck of which Grey had a grandstand view of the action as the pā was sacked by the 57th Regiment. Most of the defenders fled, but those who didn't were killed. It was the beginning of the so-called Second Taranaki War, and is memorialised in the clean lines and cheery colours of this somewhat self-congratulatory plan of the attack.

In 2002, a memorial to mark the mass grave where around 28 Māori were buried was unveiled as a joint venture between the Crown and Ngā Māhanga a Tairi, the local hapū.

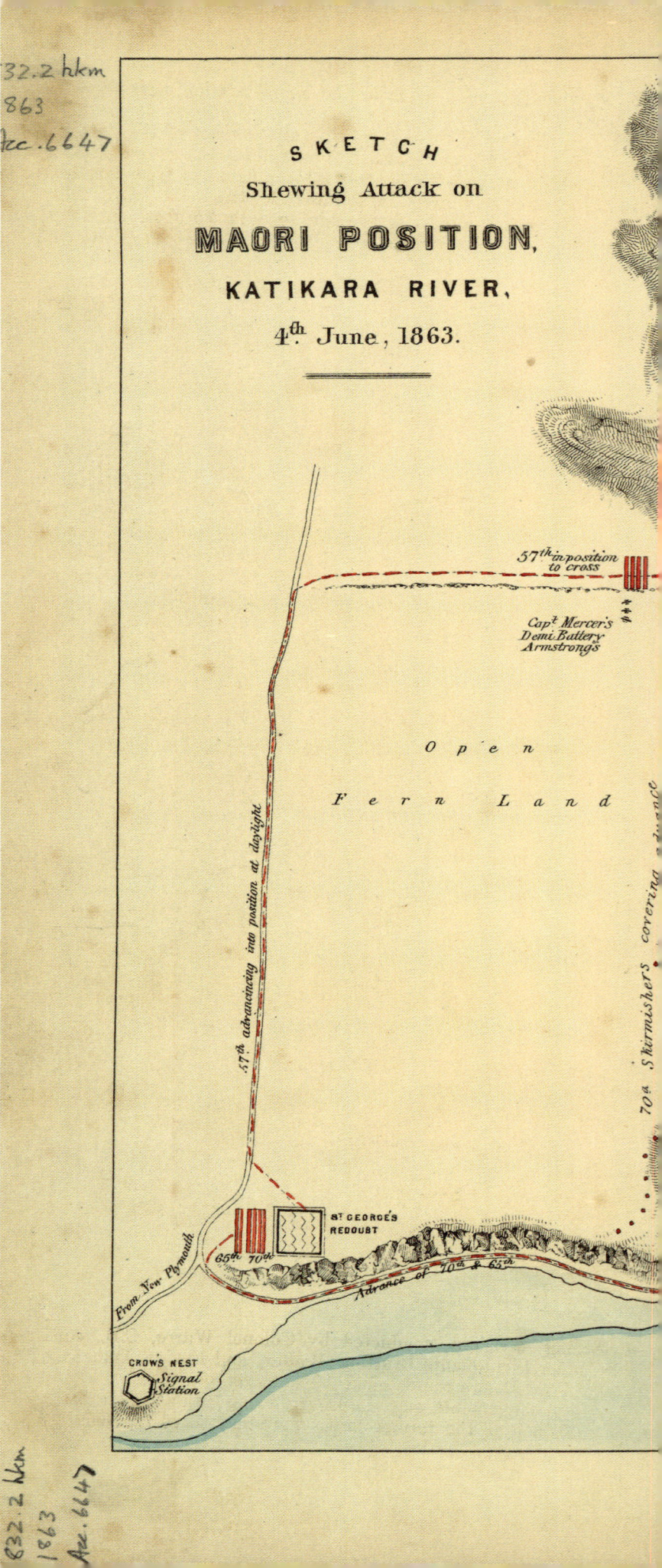

Nº 4.

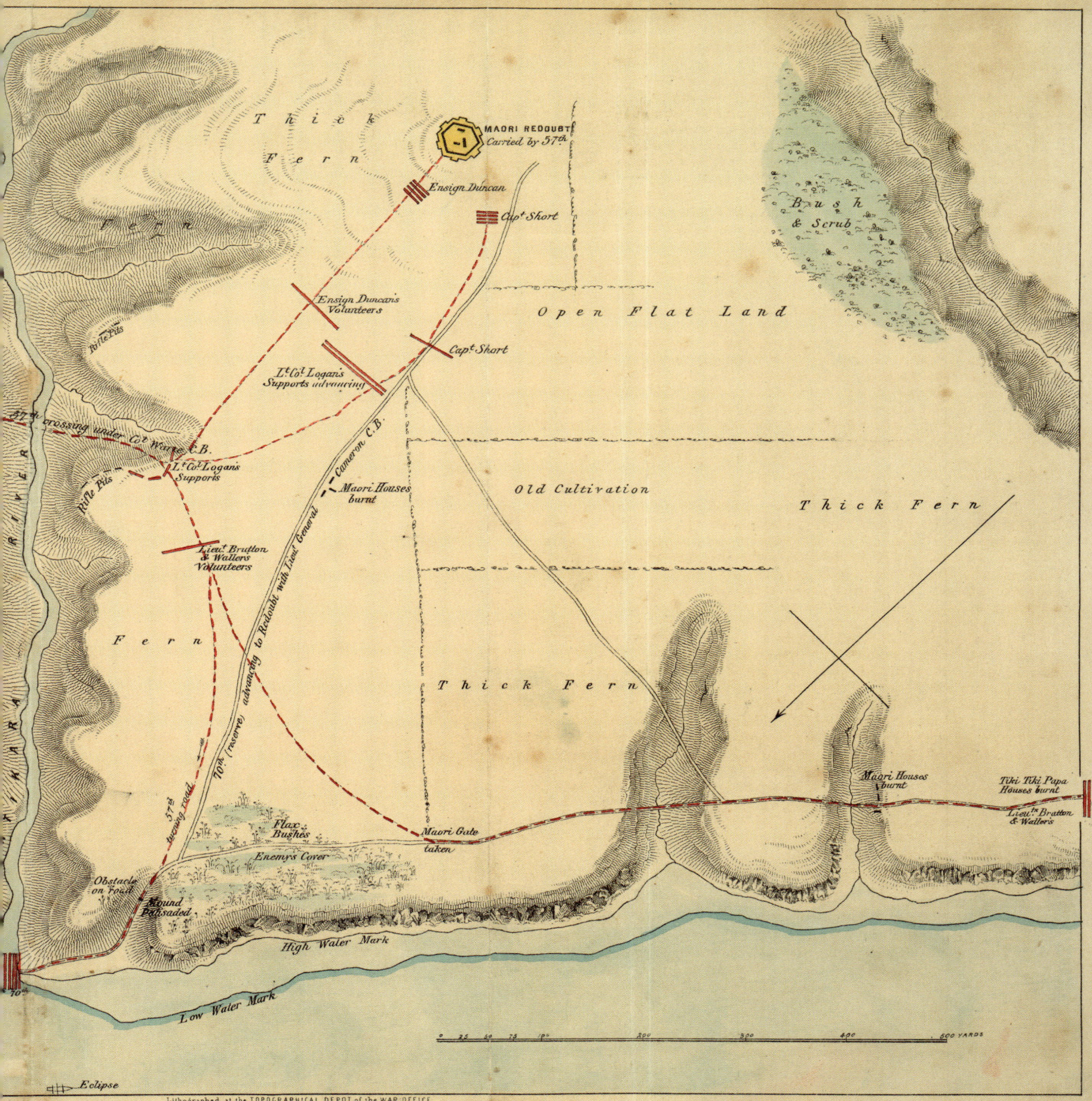

MAORI REDOUBT
Carried by 57th

Ensign Duncan

Capt Short

Thick Fern

Fern

Ensign Duncan's Volunteers

Lt Col Logan's Supports advancing

Capt Short

Open Flat Land

Bush & Scrub

57th crossing under Col Waite C.B.

Rifle Pits

Lt Col Logan's Supports

Cameron C.B.

Maori Houses burnt

Old Cultivation

Thick Fern

Lieut Brutton & Waller's Volunteers

Rifle Pits

70th (reserve) advancing to Redoubt with Lieut General

Thick Fern

57th by-way road.

Flax Bushes

Enemy's Cover

Maori Gate taken

Maori Houses burnt

Tiki Tiki Papa Houses burnt

Lieutt Brutton & Waller's

Obstacle on Foot

Mound Palisaded

High Water Mark

Low Water Mark

70th

WAITIKARA RIVER

Eclipse

0 25 50 75 100 200 300 400 500 YARDS

Lithographed at the TOPOGRAPHICAL DEPOT of the WAR OFFICE,
under the Superintendence of Major A.C. Cooke R.E.
COLONEL SIR HENRY JAMES, R.E. F.R.S. &c. DIRECTOR.
1864

MAP OF THE PROVINCE OF HAWKE'S BAY NEW ZEALAND

COMPILED AND DRAWN FROM OFFICIAL SOURCES
BY A. KOCH, WELLINGTON.
April 1874.

REFERENCE

Boundary of Province
Boundaries of Native Blocks, surveyed ... shown thus
Government Purchases partly sold
Townships
Native Reserves
Native Land
Native Land, not passed the Court
Government Purchase under Native Land Act
Native Reserves out of same
Lands ceded to Government by Natives
Metalled Roads and Dray Tracks
Bridle Tracks
Railway Line
Numbers of Native Crown Grants
Heavy Bush

The line of Telegraph leading south from Napier follows along the Te Aute Road to Eparaima, and thence towards the coast to the Boundary of the Province.
From Napier to Auckland via Taupo and Tauranga by Taupo Road.
From Napier to Poverty Bay via Clyde (Wairoa) along the Coast Road.

ABBREVIATIONS
R. River. C. Creek. S. Stream. I. Island. L. Lake.

Scale, 4 Miles to One Inch.

Published under Authority of the Provincial Government of Hawkes Bay
BY ROBERT BURRETT, PUBLISHER &c., WELLINGTON, N.Z.

SCHEDULE OF BLOCKS OF LAND WHICH HAVE PASSED THE NATIVE LAND COURT.

KOCH'S MAP OF THE PROVINCE OF HAWKE'S BAY, 1874

There's something about a masterfully drawn map that gives the impression of orderliness and calm. This gorgeous piece of work was by Augustus Koch (not to be confused with another masterful map-maker of the same name who was active at the same time in America), who went to sea but chose to settle in New Zealand in 1858 after meeting and falling in love with a woman who was en route to New Plymouth. He bought one of the country's first lithographic presses and became one of our leading map-makers, and certainly one of the most accomplished.

The Hawke's Bay that Koch depicts here was neither calm nor settled. In February 1858, it had seceded (through a majority vote of the district's settlers) from the province of Wellington. Thanks to a chaotic surveying effort, the land within the fledgling province comprised a mish-mash of blocks whose status was uncertain: there are names printed authoritatively over many of the tracts—George Whitmore, in retirement from waging the New Zealand Wars, was one; Henry Stokes Tiffen, one of the early surveyors to come out with the New Zealand Company and sometime commissioner of Crown lands, was another. Tiffen imposed some kind of order on the Hawke's Bay land situation, but where dispute arose, he tended to decide in favour of the European.

HEAPHY'S MAP OF THE NORTH ISLAND SHOWING NATIVE AND EUROPEAN TERRITORY, 1861

Charles Heaphy was many things—surveyor, explorer, artist, Victoria Cross-winning soldier, cartographer. Whether wittingly or not, he was also a politician. This map has been compellingly described by historians as a tool of the 'invasion of the Waikato' by the settler government. Note how clean and tidy the areas shaded in red (European settlements) are by contrast with the undefined 'Native Lands' (which are colourless) and the hazily defined green 'Districts that have fed the war'. The war in question was the war in Taranaki, and the great untruth that this map utters is that all of those areas with a tinge of green were in some way complicit in the Taranaki rebellion. Another untruth, implied by the neat lines and the bold red defining European settlement, is that the native and bellicose districts are somehow holding back the tide of progress and civilisation. Only the most sanguine European resident of the area that is now Raglan would feel secure viewing this map, noting how close to their little enclave the greenish tinge was creeping, or the number (330) of Māori resident at the head of Aotea Harbour. It's easy to see how, waving this map, Governor George Grey was able to enlist the support of a majority of settlers for military incursion into the King Country. This began in July 1863 when a force of British soldiers crossed the Mangatāwhiri Stream (declared an 'aukati', or do not cross line by Tāwhiao, the Māori king), precipitating a short, bitter conflict that led to the defeat of the Kīngitanga movement. There is no coincidence in the fact that most of the more fertile parts of the territory coloured green were soon subject to raupatu—confiscation and forfeiture to the Crown.

A MAP of the NORTH ISLAND of NEW ZEALAND shewing NATIVE AND EUROPEAN TERRITORY

REFERENCE

- NATIVE LANDS ...... WHITE
- EUROPEAN Do ...... RED
- DISTRICTS THAT HAVE FED THE WAR ...... GREEN

The figures indicate the numbers of the Maoris in each locality.

By Charles Heaphy. Auckland. March 1861

Note. The European Lands are compiled here from Official Maps in the Native Land Purchase Department and elsewhere.

The figures are taken from an Official Map entitled "Summary of Native Population" by Andrew Sinclair Govt Surveyor. 1860

C.H.

Martin & Kinloch Litho. Auckland. N.Z. July, 1861

N1 Native & European Territory

CONFISCATED LANDS COMMISSION'S MAP OF TARANAKI LAND DISTRICT, 1927

In 1926, after decades of agitation by Māori, a Royal Commission of Enquiry was established to look into the whole matter of the land confiscations. The chief justice of the Supreme Court, William Sim, presided, and this map was one of those prepared by the Department of Lands and Survey to illustrate the effect of his findings. Sim found that the war in Taranaki had been without legitimate foundation, and that a grave injustice had therefore been done. Some land was returned (shaded yellow here), some was not, but the Sim commission ordered that compensation in the form of an annual sum of £5000 (around half a million nowadays dollars) be paid to a trust representing Taranaki iwi. Elsewhere, Sim found that the Waikato confiscations were partly justified, and the Bay of Plenty confiscations almost fully justified. It was a major admission on the part of the Crown that grievous wrongs had been done, but the redress failed to satisfy iwi.

CONFISCATED LANDS COMMISSION
1927

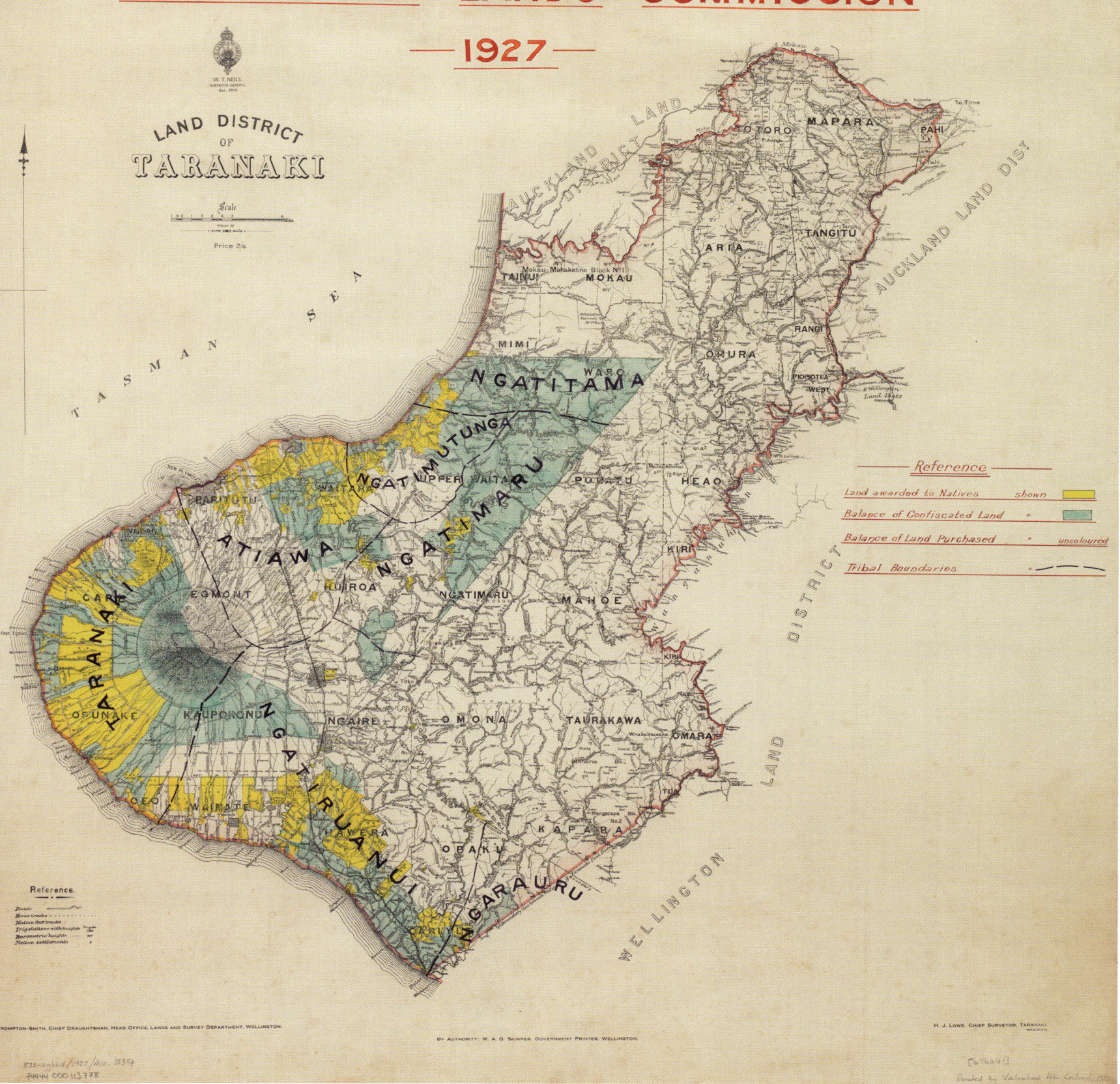

LAND DISTRICT OF TARANAKI

Reference
- Land awarded to Natives — shown yellow
- Balance of Confiscated Land — green
- Balance of Land Purchased — uncoloured
- Tribal Boundaries — dashed

PART THREE

CHANGING VIEWS

British North America.	1851.	Present Time, Latest Returns
Area .. Square Miles	—	8,510,592
Population	2,471,227	4,504,312
Total Trade { Imports, £	7,506,791	35,599,687
Exports, £	5,132,441	20,150,509
Shipping, Entd. & Clrd. tons	3,284,822	9,211,025
Imports from the United Kingdom, 1851		£3,352,897
" " " present time		2,864,058
Exports to " " 1851		2,583,897
" " " present time		9,309,434

DAVIS STRAIT

DOMINION OF CANADA

HUDSON BAY

BRITISH COLUMBIA

QUEBEC TO LIVERPOOL

VANCOUVER — Port Moody — QUEBEC TO PORT MOODY 2330 MILES — Manitoba

VICTORIA

NEWFOUNDLAND

S? Johns

NORTH AMERICA

Quebec

Montreal

NORTH ATLANTIC OCEAN

BY VICTORIA 6180 MILES

San Francisco

New York

Boston

Philadelphia

BERMUDA I.

NORTH PACIFIC OCEAN

New Orleans

GULF OF MEXICO

BAHAMA I.

ABACO

CAT I.

CAICOS

CUBA

S? THOMAS

WEST INDIA ISLANDS

ST THOMAS TO SOUTHAMPTON 3708 MILES

Tropic of Cancer

BRITISH HONDURAS

Belize

JAMAICA

HAYTI

ANTIGUA

DOMINICA

ST LUCIE

BARBADOES

GRENADA

TRINIDAD

CARIBBEAN SEA

ST VINCENT

Panama

Georgetown

BRITISH GUIANA

British West Indies.	1851.	Present Time, Latest Returns
Area .. Square Miles	—	126,374
Population	986,717	1,606,780
Total Trade { Imports, £	4,789,685	9,468,992
Exports, £	4,809,961	9,439,552
Shipping, Entd. & Clrd. tons	1,075,190	6,558,828
Imports from the United Kingdom, 1851		£2,760,281
" " " present time		4,015,644
Exports to " " 1851		5,592,772
" " " present time		4,680,094

BY PANAMA 7501 MILES

SOUTH AMERICA

SYDNEY TO LONDON

Tropic of Capricorn

SOUTH PACIFIC OCEAN

HOMEWARD ROUTE AUSTRALIA TO ENGLAND BY CAPE HORN

NINE

GREATER
NEW ZEALAND

After the proclamation of New Zealand as a colony of Great Britain—something like the international equivalent of a concession to a paternity suit—we officially became part of a greater whole named the British Empire. We were nationally enthusiastic about this, as while it came with certain obligations—contributing to Britain's efforts in overseas conflicts, for example—it also came with a number of perks, not least the Mother Country's protection and a guaranteed market for everything we could produce.

By the turn of the twentieth century, we were deemed to have acquired a certain degree of political maturity, and on 6 September 1907 this was recognised with a proclamation of our status as a dominion (the international equivalent of, say, a thirteen-year-old child). Other changes were happening around the same time. The year after we gained dominion status, the North Island Main Trunk railway was completed. Travelling the length of the North Island landwise was a novel experience for most New Zealanders, and it gave them a new perspective on their country. There was a sense abroad in the first decade of the new century that we were making our mark on the world stage—that we were 'on the map'—by virtue of our participation in the South African wars, and (perhaps even more significantly) the triumphant tour of Great Britain, Ireland and France by a national rugby union team (the 1905 'Originals'). The system of provincial government had been abolished in 1876, but was only now giving way to a sense of national unity. This was further cemented, needless to say, on the battlefields of World War I.

As adolescents will, we began to test our powers around the same time. Largely on the instigation of the New Zealand government, Britain decreed that the Cook Islands and Niue should be officially included within New Zealand's national boundaries. And one of the first military acts of World War I was New Zealand's liberation of the German Pacific territory of Sāmoa on 29 August 1914: around 1400 Kiwi soldiers arrived and pointed their guns at the German colonial administrators, most of whom were the operators of a radio station on the island of Upolu, and none of whom offered any resistance at all. In 1920, New Zealand was rewarded for its faithful discharge of this 'great and urgent service' with a Class C mandate from the brand new League of Nations, which was effectively set up by the victors in the war to divide up the spoils: *viz*, the former colonies and territories of Germany. Class C mandates were granted over the least developed of these. And while we were supposed to be mere administrators on behalf of the League of Nations, it suited the New Zealand temper of the time—we saw ourselves as 'Greater Britain', charged with the noble duty of furthering the Mother Country's interests in our hemisphere—to behave more as a colonial power.

We didn't distinguish ourselves as a ruler of other nations. The most significant event in the time during which we were administering Sāmoa as a British-occupied territory was the 1918 influenza outbreak. A cargo ship from New Zealand carrying passengers suffering symptoms of the flu arrived in Apia Harbour but was not subject to quarantine. In the resulting epidemic, fully a fifth of the Sāmoan population died. This did not endear the New Zealand administration to Sāmoans, but the resentment was overlooked by the administrator, Colonel R. W. Tate, who reported his confidence that the locals 'like children' would get over their sadness if they were treated kindly. In short, they didn't, and an anti-New Zealand resistance movement (known as the Mau) was formed and swiftly gathered support and momentum. This culminated in a violent uprising on 'Black Saturday', 28 September 1929, in which eleven Sāmoans and a New Zealander were killed. This incident earned us the dubious distinction of having been, on a per capita basis, one of the bloodiest colonial powers in history.

Our record in our other offshore territory makes for far easier reading. In 1923, the British government moved to formalise its claim to a piece of the pie that is Antarctica by proclaiming a protectorate over a wedge to the due south of New Zealand, by dint of its discovery by Sir James Clark Ross in 1841. The Ross Dependency was born, and New Zealand became the proud administrator of a vast tract of frozen ocean, rock and ice. This jurisdiction survived the Statute of Westminster in 1931, in which New Zealand effectively came of age, being granted full self-government by the king in parliament. Our claim was subsequently strengthened in two ways: first, we established a permanent presence in Antarctica, in the form of a base to support the Commonwealth Trans-Antarctic Expedition of 1955-58—in the course of which our own Sir Edmund Hillary drove a lightly

CRANE'S MAP OF THE BRITISH EMPIRE, 1886

For much of its history, New Zealand unquestionably regarded itself as part of the British Empire, as depicted in this map, prepared by British illustrator Walter Crane, for the Colonial and Indian Exhibition of 1886. This was arranged as a kind of celebration of the empire just ahead of Queen Victoria's Golden Jubilee the following year. We made it on here, albeit with a rather withered Taranaki, blushing imperial pink beneath a boomerang wielded by a half-nude Australian Aboriginal. It's hard to see where we feature amongst the people and the plenty of the empire in the map's decorative border, unless it's as the sober and industrious-looking couple offering a merino fleece to Britannia from the right-hand corner. There are no identifiable Māori to be seen.

While on the face of it this map projects a portrait of power and justice, it has been pointed out that there are subtle subversive elements. The languid figures of Freedom, Fraternity and Federation wear Phrygian caps, the headgear of liberated slaves in the ancient Roman empire and an emblem of the French Revolution. And look closely at poor old Atlas, straining beneath the weight of an insouciant Britannia atop the globe, and you'll see that the band across his chest features the words 'Human Labour'. Crane was not only a brilliant illustrator, but also a noted socialist.

Supplement to the "GRAPHIC" July 24th 1886.

FRATERNITY   FEDERATION

MAP OF THE WORLD,
SHOWING THE EXTENT OF THE BRITISH TERRITORIES IN 1786.

IMPERIAL FEDERATION,—MAP OF THE WORLD SHOWING THE EXTENT OF THE BRITISH EMPIRE IN 1886.
STATISTICAL INFORMATION FURNISHED BY CAPTAIN J.C.R. COLOMB, M.P. FORMERLY R.M.A. ——— BRITISH TERRITORIES COLOURED RED

MACLURE & Co QUEEN VICTORIA STREET, LONDON

modified Massey-Ferguson tractor to the South Pole in January 1958, becoming the first person to reach it since the ill-starred Sir Robert Falcon Scott in 1912. This grew into a research base in the course of an international collaborative polar research project, the 1957–58 International Geophysical Year, and came to be known as Scott Base (after poor old Sir R. F.). It operates in tandem with the nearby US facility at McMurdo.

Second, under the terms of the Antarctic Treaty of 1959, signed by twelve nations with claims to bits of the frozen continent, Antarctica was declared an international sanctuary for the purposes of peace and science, but claimant nations reserved the right to maintain and pursue their claims. Collectively, New Zealand and its territories—the Cook Islands, Tokelau, Niue and Ross Dependency—are known as the 'Realm of New Zealand'. Who knew?

———

Meanwhile, even as we pretend to a greater degree of importance than our paltry presence in the nether regions of the world might justify, on some maps we struggle to make any impact at all. One of the first acts of Jacinda Ardern in her role as prime minister was to lend her support to a light-hearted media campaign to 'put New Zealand on the map'. This has been a popular phrase down through our nation's history: even the least achievement on the world stage has usually been hailed as an act that will 'put us on the map'. The impetus behind this particular campaign, however, was the fact that New Zealand is left off maps of the world with surprising regularity.

In our very early days, the explanation for this was straightforward: no one knew we were here. Since the days of Tasman, however, that excuse has not been viable. In some cases, it was down to the tendency of a cartographic projection to push us to the limit of view, or even beyond. But in still other cases, there are no excuses. It is simply ignorance of New Zealand's existence, or the failure of the map-maker to care.

In other cases, a choice of projections can give New Zealand an inflated status. If, for example, you abandon the convention that maps should be oriented with north at the top and south at the bottom, then New Zealand can be placed almost literally on top of the world. Alternatively, if you produce a map of the hemisphere with New Zealand at the centre, you would be forgiven for thinking we are all but alone in the world. After all, like other denizens of the Pacific, we grow up with maps where the colour blue predominates. And amongst Pacific islands we are 'last', to borrow from Rudyard Kipling's description of Auckland: 'last, loneliest, loveliest, exquisite, apart'.

Following page
MAP OF NEW ZEALAND AND DEPENDENCIES, 1929

Part of being an enthusiastic lackey state of Great Britain on the other side of the world is that we had the opportunity to project the Mother Country's power. Some of our premiers (later prime ministers) were more enthusiastic about this than others: Julius Vogel was fond, as poet Allen Curnow put it, of 'howling empire from [our] empty shore', for example. It was New Zealand agitation on their behalf that saw the Cook Islands and Niue annexed by Britain, and then brought within New Zealand jurisdiction in 1901. Tokelau was added in 1925 (although the United States recognised our sovereignty there only in 1979), and the Ross Dependency—our slice of Antarctica—was entrusted to us by Great Britain, which claimed it in 1923. This claim isn't universally recognised, but all such disputes with regard to Antarctic territorial claims were put on ice, so to speak, by the Antarctic Treaty, which came into force in 1961.

That leaves Sāmoa. We liberated it from German occupation in 1914 and, following World War I, it was allocated to us as a mandated territory by the League of Nations. It remained that way until 1962, when we finally granted Western Sāmoa its independence.

These days, Tokelau remains a dependency (which means that it is self-governing but its foreign policy is handled by New Zealand). The Cooks and Niue are self-governing nations 'in free association' with New Zealand. Together with the Ross Dependency, the jurisdiction is referred to as the 'Realm of New Zealand'.

Page 223
NEW ZEALAND EXCLUSIVE ECONOMIC ZONE, 1983

Once upon a time, international law considered a nation's territorial waters to extend around three nautical miles from the coast, roughly as far as a shore-based cannon could argue the point with encroaching shipping. This came to be extended to twelve nautical miles by the beginning of the twentieth century.

In 1947, however, Chile and Peru raised the stakes, claiming the right to exploit the resources on and over their continental shelf, which they estimated extended 200 nautical miles from their coastline. This was not universally popular (although most maritime nations, New Zealand included, stood to gain). In 1982, the United Nations Convention on the Law of the Sea adopted the 200-mile Exclusive Economic Zone (EEZ). This map, drawn the following year (and which I remember from a postage stamp that came out that year) illustrates the boon this was to a small country with a big coastline: our EEZ is over four million square kilometres in extent, fully fifteen times our land area. While we don't exploit much of it—we have gas interests off the Taranaki coast, and most of our fisheries are inshore anyway—that's not the point. One day soon, the technology may well exist that will enable us to harvest such bounty as manganese nodules or phosphate from the Chatham Rise, or whatever goodies leach out of 'hot smokers'—undersea volcanoes—way out on our continental shelf.

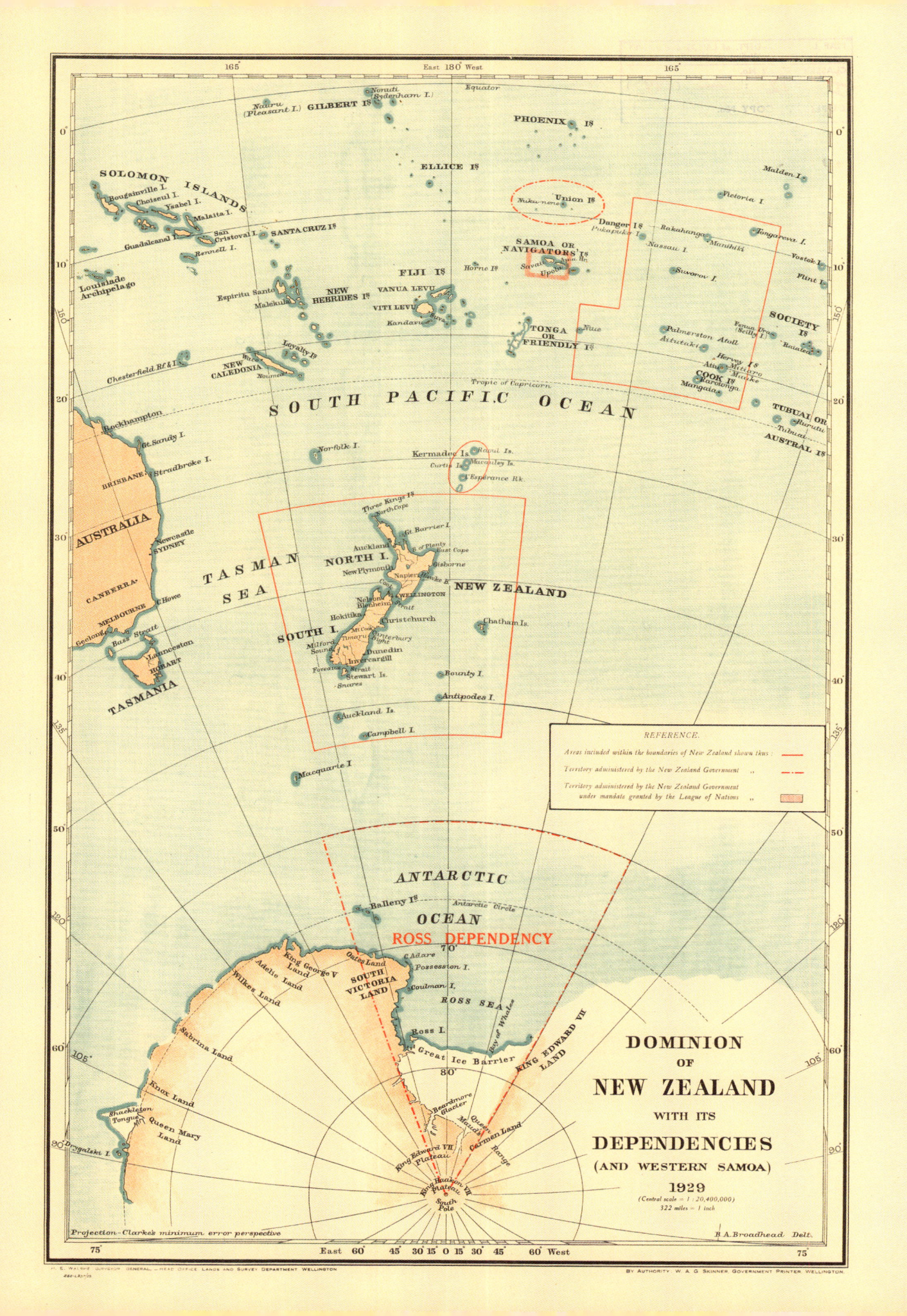

DOMINION OF NEW ZEALAND WITH ITS DEPENDENCIES (AND WESTERN SAMOA)

1929

(Central scale = 1 : 20,400,000
322 miles = 1 inch)

Projection—Clarke's minimum error perspective

B. A. Broadhead, Delt.

REFERENCE.
- Areas included within the boundaries of New Zealand shown thus: —————
- Territory administered by the New Zealand Government: —·—·—
- Territory administered by the New Zealand Government under mandate granted by the League of Nations: ▢

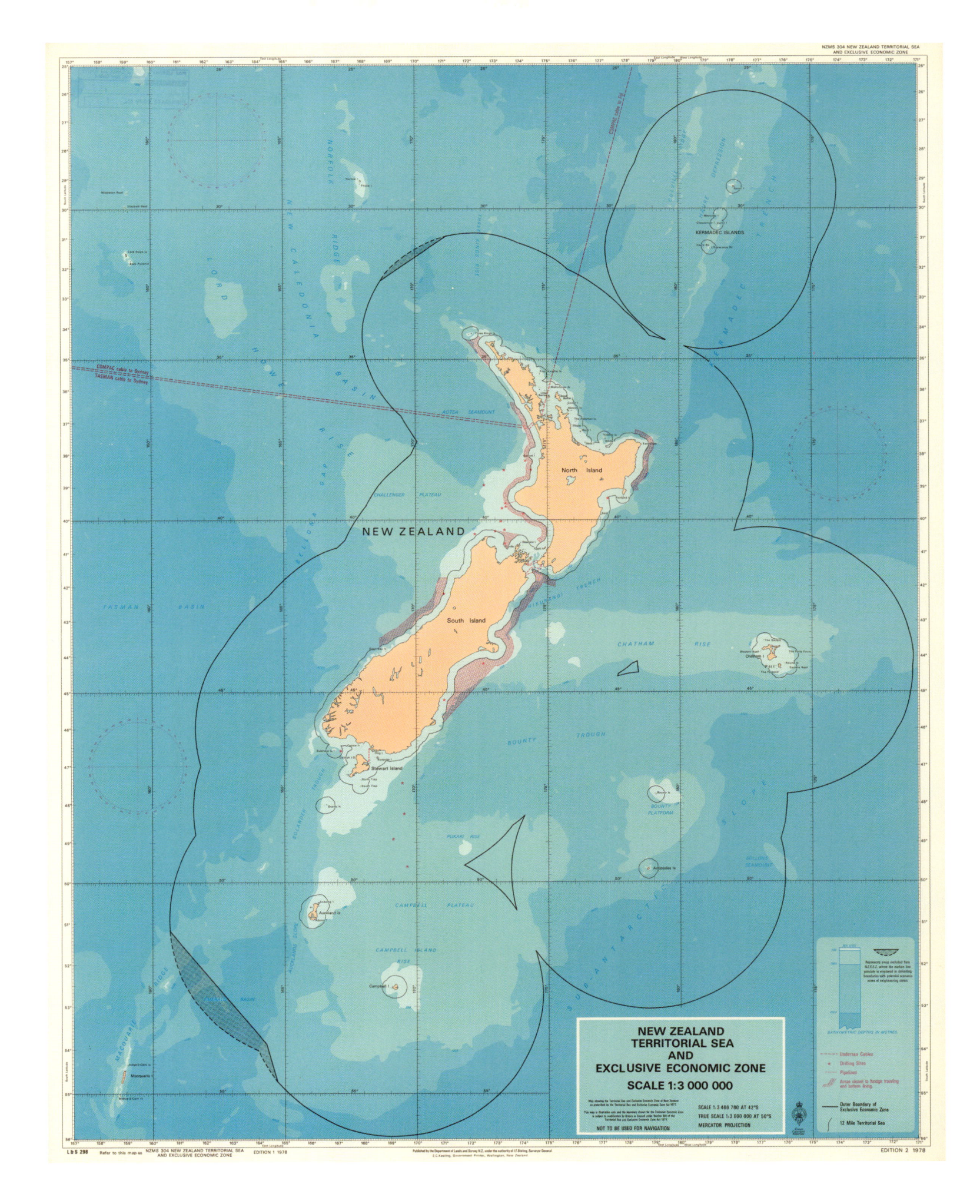

NEW ZEALAND TERRITORIAL SEA AND EXCLUSIVE ECONOMIC ZONE

SCALE 1:3 000 000

SCALE 1:3 468 780 AT 42°S
TRUE SCALE 1:3 000 000 AT 50°S
MERCATOR PROJECTION

NOT TO BE USED FOR NAVIGATION

NZMS 304 NEW ZEALAND TERRITORIAL SEA AND EXCLUSIVE ECONOMIC ZONE

EDITION 2 1978

SUDA BAY WAR CEMETERY

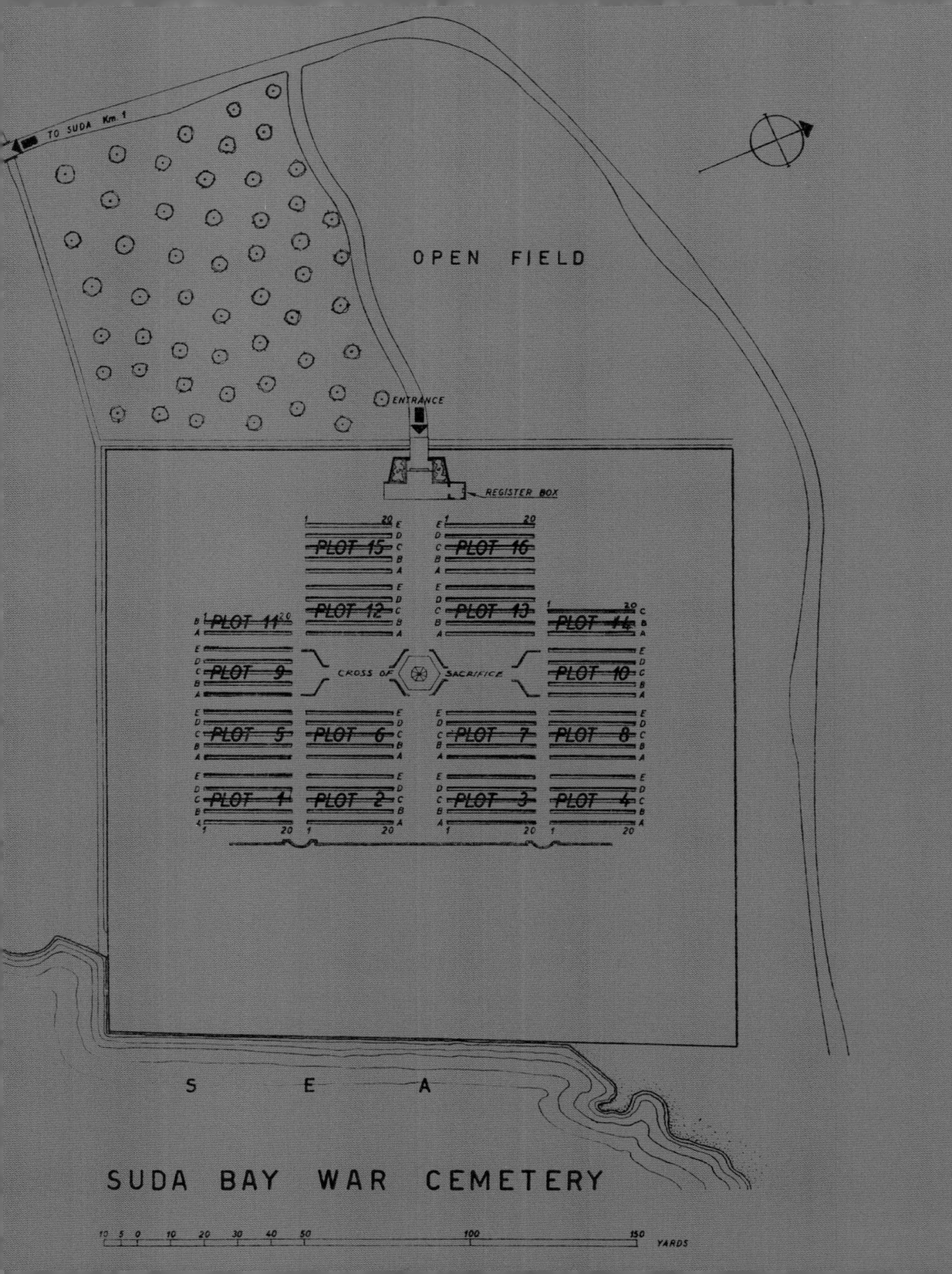

TEN

PLACES
IN THE
HEART

'If I should die,' British poet Rupert Brooke wrote, 'think only this of me: / that there's some corner of a foreign field / that is for ever England.' In Brooke's case, that blessed foreign field is on the Greek island of Skyros, where his troopship was anchored when he died of blood poisoning from an infected mosquito bite while en route to Gallipoli.

If his claim holds true, then there are many corners in many, many foreign fields that are forever New Zealand. One of the more tragic consequences of our political identification with Britain is that we have sent hundreds of thousands of young New Zealanders to enrich the dust of countries in wars that were not of our making. And it's not just Britain. Ever since the Mother Country cut the apron strings of her former colony and we made our own way in the world, we have found reasons to follow other nations into wars overseas. Consequently, a litany of place names in those foreign fields—from South Africa and the Middle East and from Europe to Asia—chimes solemnly in the New Zealand psyche.

MELVILL'S MAP OF LE QUESNOY ACTION, 1917

The northern French town of Le Quesnoy fell to the Germans on 23 January 1914, and it's fair to say the occupiers didn't endear themselves to the locals in the four years they held it. In late 1918, in one of their last actions of World War I, New Zealand soldiers surrounded the ancient walled town and were given the go-ahead by British High Command to take it. It ought to have been easily defensible, as the garrison numbered some 1000 soldiers who had been ordered to hold it, come what may. But when the resourceful New Zealanders found a route into the town via an old sluice gate and over the walls by ladder, the defenders offered little more than desultory resistance.

The town was of vital strategic importance, and its loss opened the way for an Allied advance through Belgium into Germany. The war ended a week after the town fell on 4 November. One hundred and forty New Zealand soldiers died in the action—the last of over 12,000 who fell on the Western Front, more than the entire number who died in World War II. This map belonged to the British major-general Charles William Melvill, who commanded the New Zealanders in the action. Pencilled lines indicate the route of the approach to the town.

GODLEY'S MAP OF GALLIPOLI, 1914

On the face of it, this is a quite unremarkable map. It depicts the Gallipoli peninsula in the vicinity of what came to be known as Anzac Cove. It is a standard 1:40,000 map, which means it is drawn on a scale of 1 inch to every 40,000 inches. But what makes it remarkable is the after-market detail. Terrain and the depth of water adjacent to the shore are indicated with watercolour tints. And then there are annotations. Some of these depict features of the terrain. Others illustrate the disposition of Turkish matériel—artillery, military camps, trenches—as they were known to have been deployed as at 24 April 1915, the night before the New Zealand Expeditionary Force and the Australian Infantry Force landed at Anzac Cove.

Up to this point, according to eminent military historian Christopher Pugsley, who examined it when it was donated to the Alexander Turnbull Library, it's fairly typical of a general's map. But then it suddenly became what Pugsley calls 'a working command map'. There are pencilled grid references out to sea, directly off the point at which the New Zealanders landed amid shell and machine-gun fire. Pencilled lines indicate where Major-General Alexander Godley, the British commander of the New Zealand and Australian Division—whose map this was—understood his troops' positions to be. There are corrections, made as it became plain his initial intelligence was over-optimistic; Pugsley surmised these were added as Godley sat at a table with senior Australian officers beneath a tarpaulin roof erected on the beach on the afternoon of the landings. As he contemplated what he had drawn on this map, Godley apparently sent word to British High Command that he felt their situation was untenable, and asked that his troops be evacuated. The reply came that no evacuation was possible. There was nothing for it but to 'Dig! Dig! Dig!' The rest, as they say, is history.

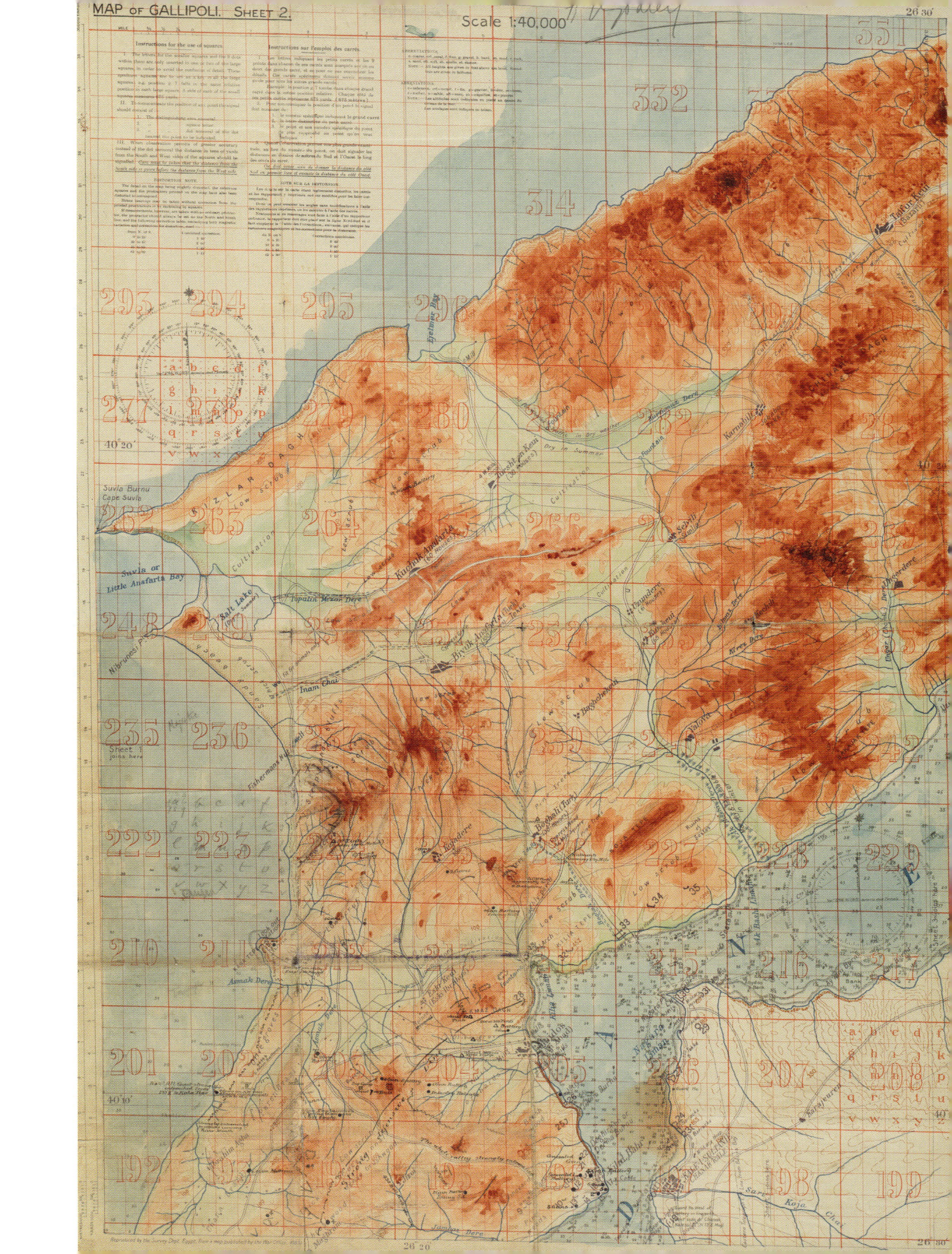

MAP OF GALLIPOLI. SHEET 2.

Scale 1:40,000

BORGES' MAP OF GALLIPOLI, 1915

These maps, titled by their French creator, surveyor Georges Borges, show the landing ('l'étage') of the Australian units on Gallipoli, but the names on the landscape (written in hand in English) resonate with New Zealanders: Chunuk Bair, Hill 60, Shrapnel Valley (aka Shrapnel Gully), Walker's Ridge, Baby 700 . . . Each marked a station of the cross of the suffering of New Zealanders and Australians alike. In the eight months that the ANZACs were on the peninsula, 2779 New Zealanders died—a small number compared with the 87,000 who died fighting on the Ottoman side, but representing around one in six of those from this little nation on the other side of the world who served there. Gallipoli welded our identity with that of Australia (who lost nearly 9000 soldiers), and is supposed by some to have been a coming of age for New Zealand itself, a major step forward in the forging of a national identity separate from that of Great Britain.

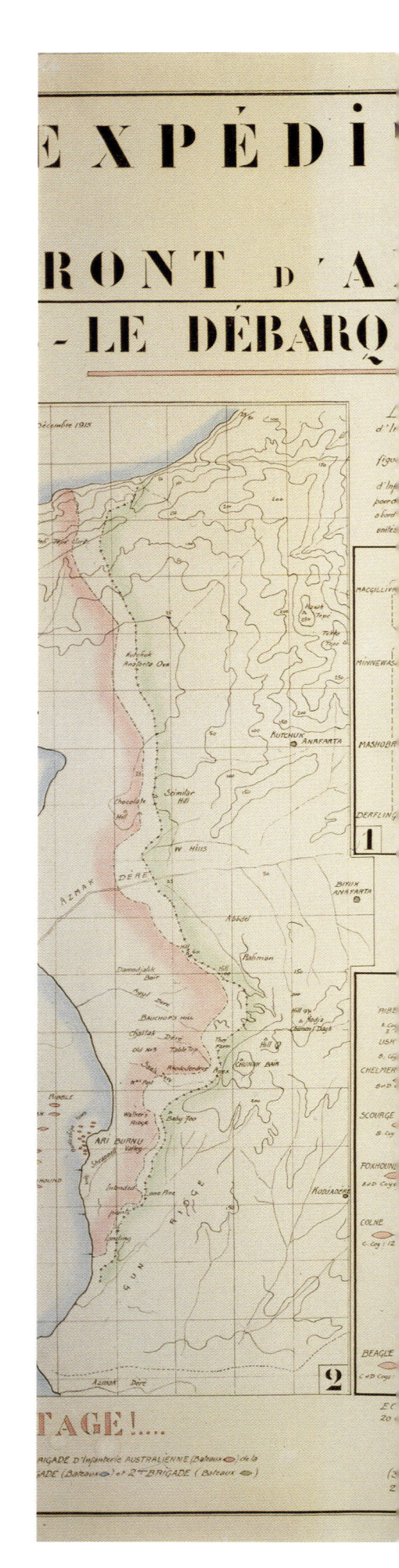

...ION DES DARDANELLES
1915
...ZAC A ARI-BURNU (TURQUIE)

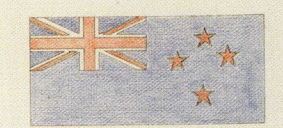

...MENT   **L'ÉVACUATION — 20 DÉCEMBRE 1915**

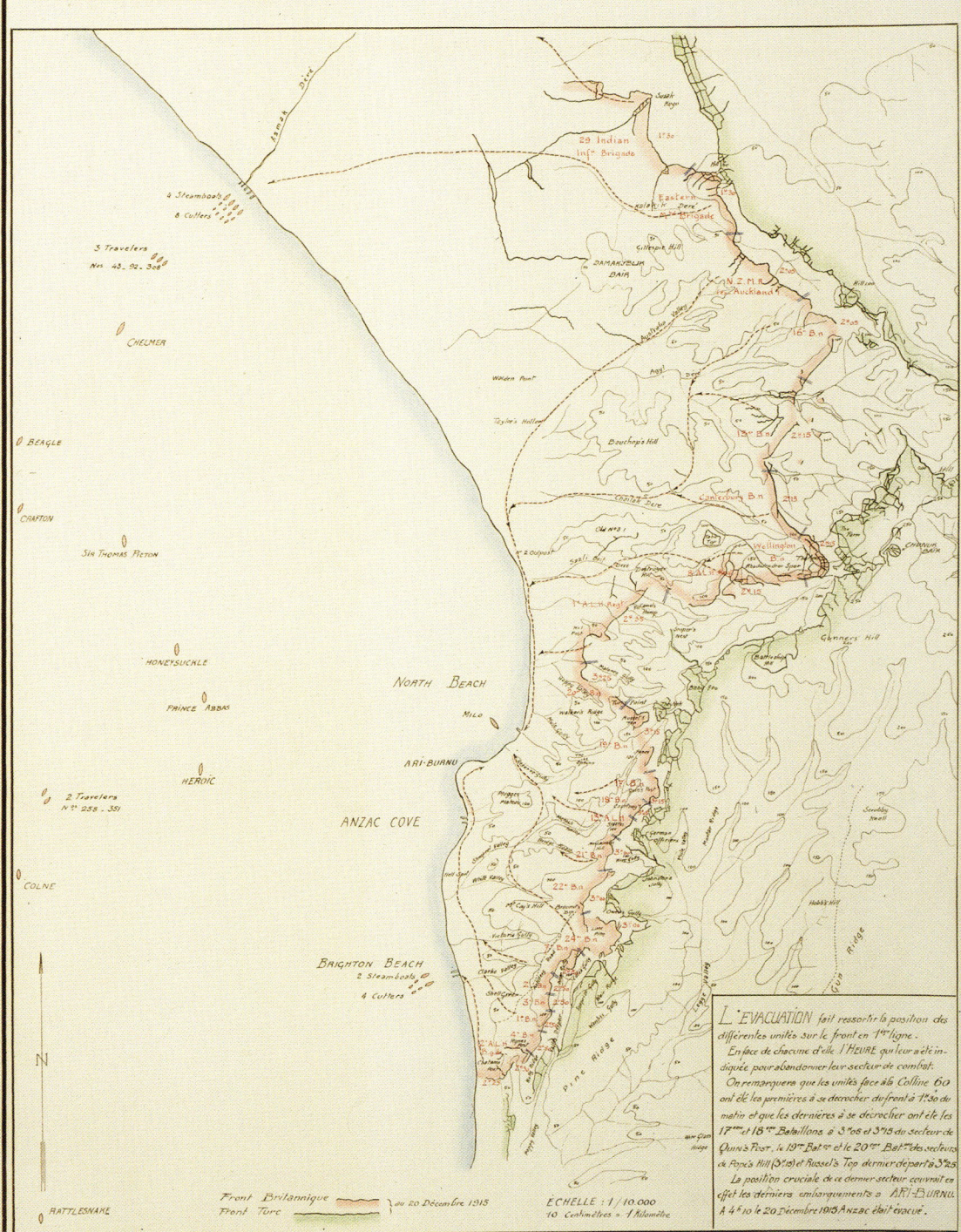

1, **2**, **3** représentent les 3 phases principales du DÉBARQUEMENT de la 1ʳᵉ DIVISION ...ALIENNE à ARI-BURNU.

d'APPROCHE : **1** ne comporte que les principales unités navales transportant les troupes, il n'y ...accompagnement ou de protection (escadrilles de torpilleurs, etc.).

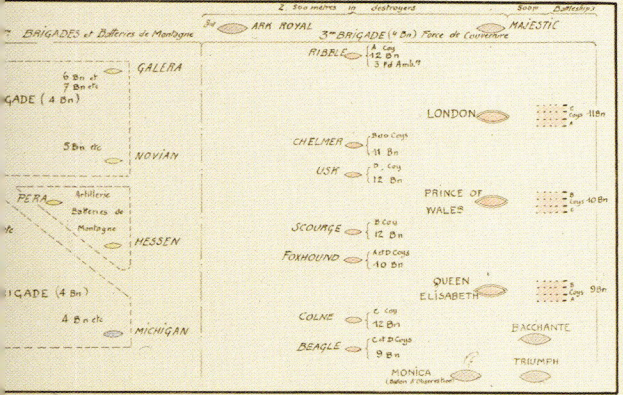

...GE : **2** fait apparaître la position des unités près de la côte ayant amené la force de couverture (3ᵐᵉ BRIGADE ...) Certaines unités transportant parties des 1ʳᵉ et 2ᵐᵉ Brigades d'Infanterie Australienne seront déjà sur la force de couverture ... élément, elles ont passé les Cuirassés : LONDON, PRINCE of WALES, QUEEN ELISABETH, alors que les 4 derniers transports ayant ... la 1ʳᵉ et de la 2ᵐᵉ BRIGADE sont en place pour transverser à leur tour la ligne des cuirassés et amener à la côte les dernières ...

La RUÉE : 3 illustre l'accrochage aux plages et aux Collines.

...ION D'**APPROCHE** VERS ARI-BURNU
...AL DE LA 1ʳᵉ DIVISION D'INFANTERIE AUSTRALIENNE (3 BRIGADES, 12 Bataillons au Total)

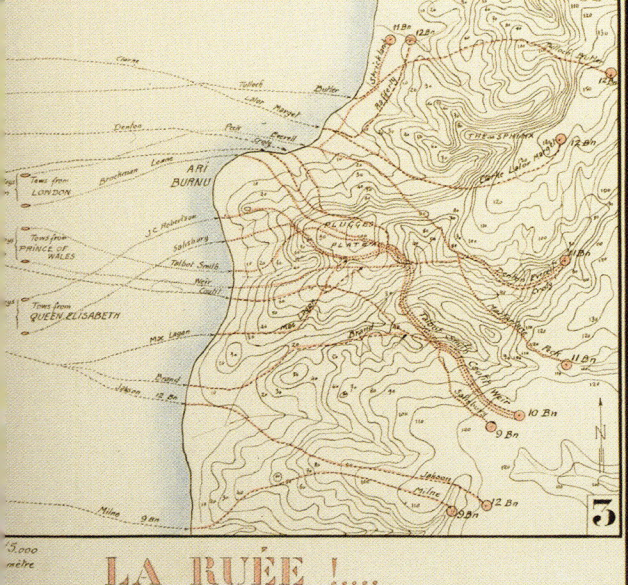

LA RUÉE !....
...ES PLAGES ET DANS LES COLLINES !.... de la Force de Couverture
...Infanterie AUSTRALIENNE) et de la 1ʳᵉ DIVISION d'Infanterie AUSTRALIENNE de 4ʰ30 à 5ʰ30 le...

L'ÉVACUATION fait ressortir la position des différentes unités sur le front en 1ʳᵉ ligne. En face de chacune d'elle, l'HEURE qui leur a été indiquée pour abandonner leur secteur de combat. On remarquera que les unités face à la Colline 60 ont été les premières à se décrocher du front à 11ʰ30 du matin et que les dernières à se décrocher ont été les 17ᵐᵉ et 18ᵐᵉ Bataillons à 3ʰ08 et 3ʰ15 du secteur de Queen's Post, le 19ᵐᵉ Batᵒⁿ et le 20ᵐᵉ Batᵒⁿ des secteurs de Pope's Hill (3ʰ18) et Russel's Top dernier départ à 3ʰ25. La position cruciale de ce dernier secteur couvrait en effet les derniers embarquements à ARI-BURNU à 4ʰ10 le 20 Décembre 1915 ANZAC était évacué.

Front Britannique ━━━ au 20 Décembre 1915
Front Turc ━━━

ÉCHELLE : 1/10.000
10 Centimètres = 1 Kilomètre

MAP OF THE GRAVES OF MOUNTED RIFLEMEN, EAST JORDAN (CREATOR UNKNOWN), 1918

Somehow, it seems all the more poignant when soldiers fall close to the end of the war in which they are combatants. So it is with the six young New Zealanders who were killed in the part of Palestine depicted in this map. Palestine was occupied by the Ottoman Empire in 1917. In March of the following year, the British mounted a major offensive on the strong defensive ground of Gaza. It failed. They tried again shortly afterward, but this push, too, was a failure. It was a case of third time lucky when they took Gaza in November. The New Zealand Mounted Rifles were part of this victory and, unlike during earlier campaigns, they fought on horseback.

Four of the men who occupy the lonely graves on this map probably died during the March raids across the Jordan River. The others fell desperately close to Armistice Day: twenty-one-year-old Trooper Edward Victor Brake, the son of John and Lina Brake of Milford, died only a month before the end of the war, and after victory in the Middle East was all but won. He is commemorated on the Commonwealth War Memorial in Jerusalem. Three of the others are commemorated at Damascus War Cemetery. Of M. J. McRae and F. O. Welsh, nothing beyond what is marked on this map is known.

The map itself is Arabic, and a pencil annotation indicates it was '[t]aken from an Arab Mohamad Tabara at Jis el Dassish'. Extra detail has been overprinted in purple, apparently based on RAF intelligence.

SCALE 1 : 63,360 — **COMPOSITE MAP EAST OF JORDAN (AMMAN)** — 2nd EDITION

Graves Registration — Auckland Mounted Rifles

COMMONWEALTH WAR GRAVES COMMISSION'S MAP OF SUDA BAY CEMETERY, 2019

The rugged hills of Crete reminded many who fought there of New Zealand. There were over 7500 New Zealanders on the island in 1941 when the Germans launched the first ever major assault comprising paratroopers, in May. The Kiwis had been evacuated from Greece as the Germans overran it, and this likely fuelled their determination to put up a good show in the next round of battle. The British, Commonwealth and Cretan forces were under the command of Major-General Bernard 'Tiny' Freyberg, a New Zealander. The Allied forces even had forewarning of the German plans, having decoded Enigma communications relating to the forthcoming aerial assault (the Allies' first significant use of this source of intelligence).

The battle for Crete began on 20 May, with a large German force landing by parachute and glider in the vicinity of Maleme on the northwest coast, where the largest airfield on the island was located. They were repulsed with heavy casualties by New Zealand and Cretan troops but, due to miscommunications, the aerodrome was left undefended and taken by the Germans. This was a turning point, as German reinforcements were landed at Maleme, and the battle soon turned into a fighting withdrawal for the Allies towards Sfakia on the south coast, from which most were evacuated.

It was a demoralising defeat for the British, and something of a Pyrrhic victory for the Germans, who lost up to 20,000 killed or wounded. The British and Commonwealth forces lost a quarter of that number: 671 New Zealanders were killed and 2000 taken prisoner. Others joined Cretan partisans fighting a guerrilla war against the German occupiers. Crete is just one of those places in Europe where the words 'New Zealand' will spark a grin of recognition from locals, an even warmer than customary welcome.

The Suda Bay War Cemetery is home, now, to 343 New Zealanders. This map doesn't do the beauty of the place justice, but nor does the cemetery—with its bleached stones in their green sward against the backdrop of the blue Mediterranean—do justice to the ferocity of the fighting in this vicinity.

Most of the dead fell on or within a few days of 20 May 1941, the day the German paratroopers drifted from the sky. This map is the work of the Commonwealth War Graves Commission, whose job it is to curate and maintain the cemeteries and memorials of those who fell in the service of the British Commonwealth in both world wars.

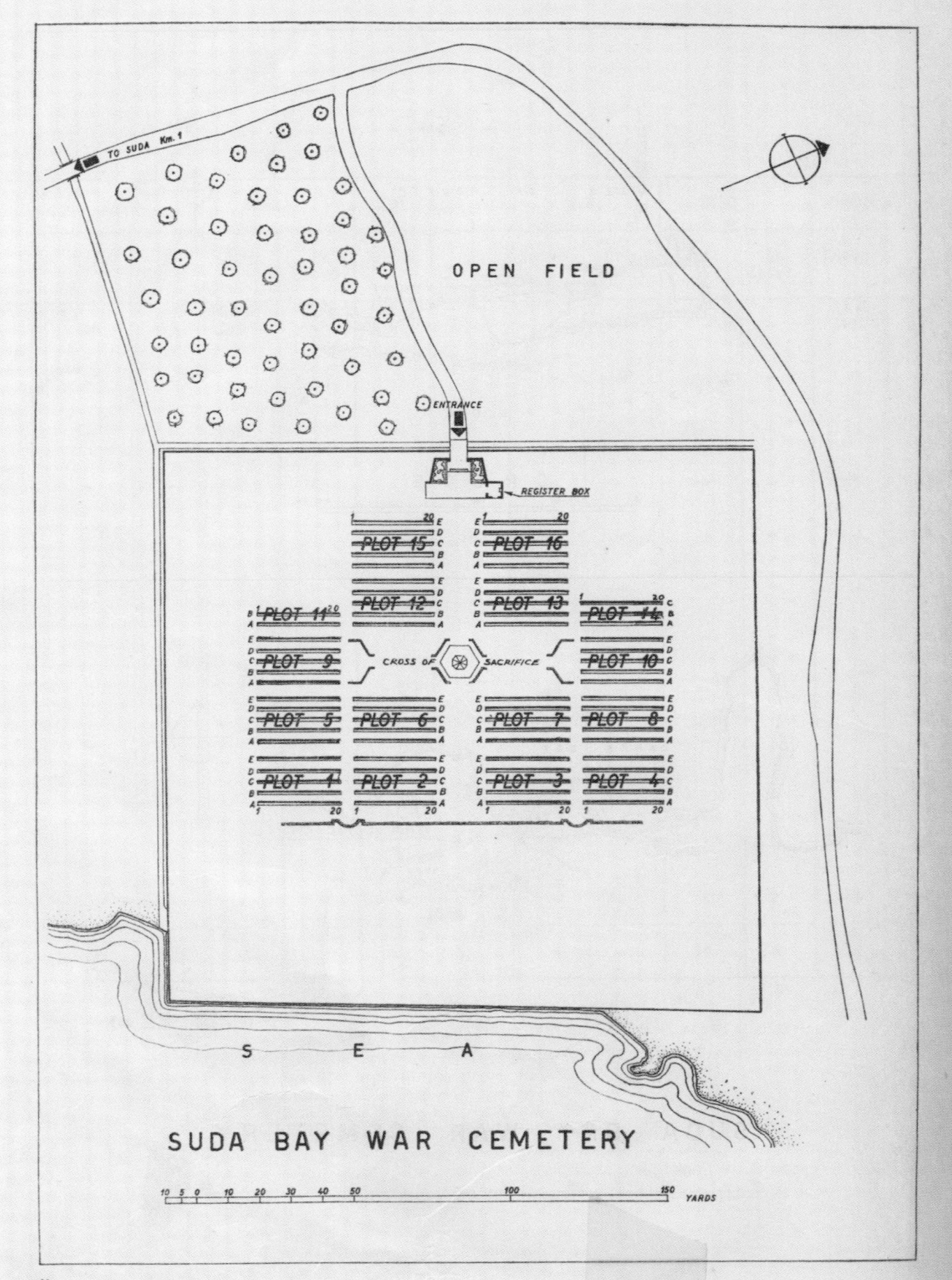

SUDA BAY WAR CEMETERY

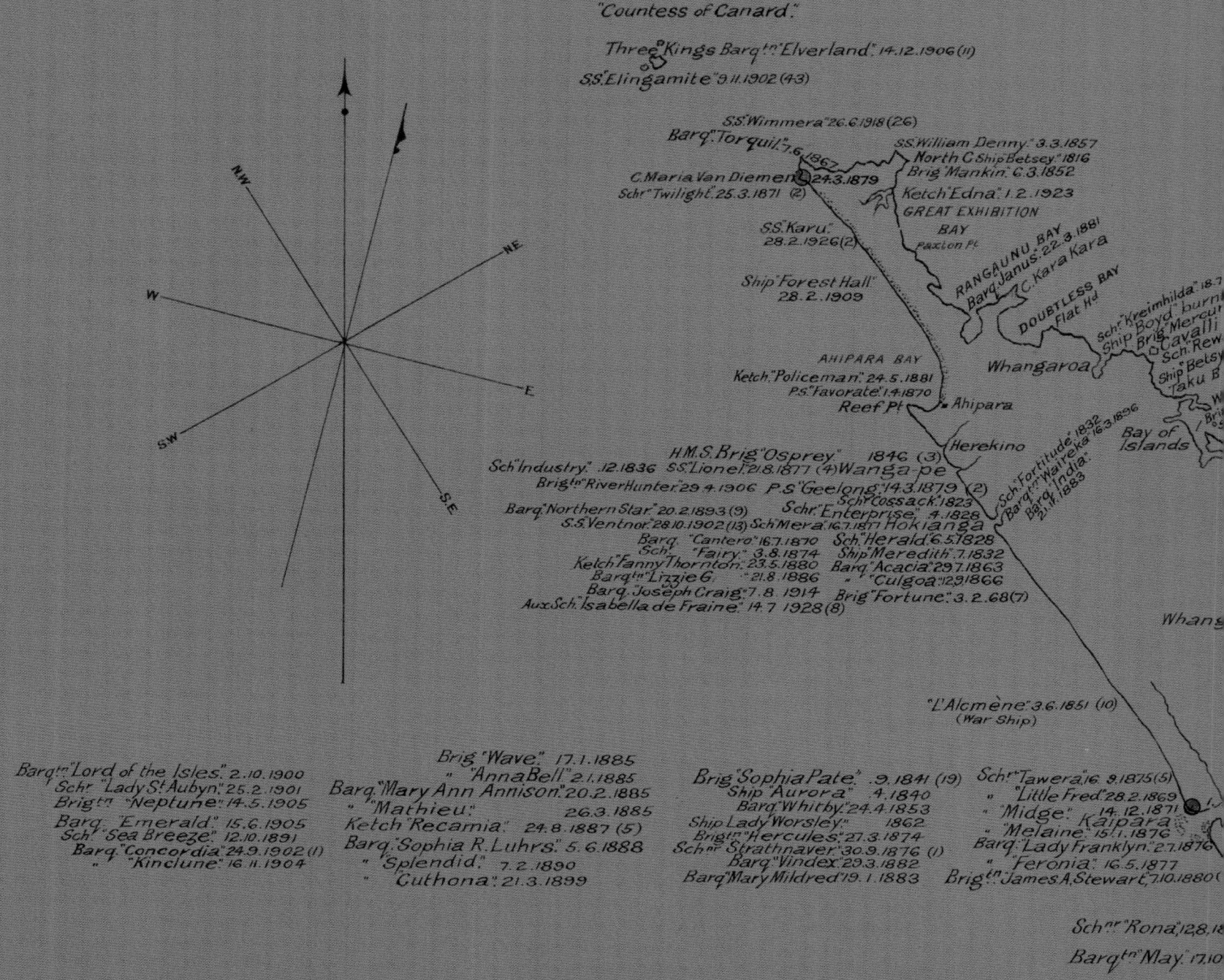

"Countess of Canard."
Three Kings Barqtn "Elverland" 14.12.1906 (11)
S.S. "Elingamite" 9.11.1902 (43)

S.S. "Wimmera" 26.6.1918 (26)
Barq "Torquil" 7.6.1862
S.S. "William Denny" 3.3.1857
North C Ship "Betsey" 1816
Brig "Mankin" 6.3.1852
C. Maria Van Diemen 24.3.1879
Schr "Twilight" 25.3.1871 (2)
Ketch "Edna" 1.2.1923
GREAT EXHIBITION BAY
Paxton Pt
S.S. "Karu" 28.2.1926 (2)
RANGAUNU BAY
Barq "Janus" 22.3.1881
C. Kara Kara
Schr "Kreimhilda" 18.7
Ship "Boyd" burnt
Brig "Mercu
Cavalli
Sch "Rew
Ship "Betsy
Taku B
Ship "Forest Hall" 28.2.1909
DOUBTLESS BAY
Flat Hd
Whangaroa

AHIPARA BAY
Ketch "Policeman" 24.5.1881
P.S. "Favorate" 1.4.1870
Reef Pt — Ahipara
Herekino
Schr "Fortitude" 1832
Barqtn "Waireka" 16.3.1896
Bay of Islands

H.M.S. Brig "Osprey" 1846 (3)
Sch "Industry" 12.1836 S.S. "Lionel" 21.8.1877 (4) Wanga-pe
Brigtn "River Hunter" 29.4.1906 P.S. "Geelong" 14.3.1879 (2)
Barq "Northern Star" 20.2.1893 (9) Schr "Cossack" 1823
S.S. "Ventnor" 28.10.1902 (13) Sch "Mera" 16.7.1871 Hokianga
Barq "Cantero" 16.7.1870 Sch "Herald" 6.5.1828
Sch "Fairy" 3.8.1874 Ship "Meredith" 7.1.1832
Ketch "Fanny Thornton" 23.5.1880 Barq "Acacia" 29.7.1863
Barqtn "Lizzie G." 21.8.1886 — "Culgoa" 12.9.1866
Barq "Joseph Craig" 7.8.1914 Brig "Fortune" 3.2.68 (7)
Aux Sch "Isabella de Fraine" 14.7.1928 (8)
Barqtn "India" 21.11.1883

Whang

"L'Alcmène" 3.6.1851 (10)
(War Ship)

Barqtn "Lord of the Isles" 2.10.1900   Brig "Wave" 17.1.1885   Brig "Sophia Pate" 9.1841 (19)   Schr "Tawera" 16.9.1875 (5)
Schr "Lady St Aubyn" 25.2.1901   " "Anna Bell" 2.1.1885   Ship "Aurora" 4.1840   " "Little Fred" 28.2.1869
Brigtn "Neptune" 14.5.1905   Barq "Mary Ann Annison" 20.2.1885   Barq "Whitby" 24.4.1853   " "Midge" 14.12.1871
Barq "Emerald" 15.6.1905   " "Mathieu" 26.3.1885   Ship "Lady Worsley" 1862   Kaipara
Sch "Sea Breeze" 12.10.1891   Ketch "Recarnia" 24.8.1887 (5) Brigtn "Hercules" 27.3.1874   " "Melaine" 15.1.1876
Barq "Concordia" 24.9.1902 (1)   Barq "Sophia R. Luhrs" 5.6.1888 Schnr "Strathnaver" 30.9.1876 (1)   Barq "Lady Franklyn" 27.1.1876
" "Kinclune" 16.11.1904   " "Splendid" 7.2.1890   Barq "Vindex" 29.3.1882   " "Feronia" 16.5.1877
                                        " "Cuthona" 21.3.1899   Barq "Mary Mildred" 19.1.1883   Brigtn "James A. Stewart" 7.10.1880

Schnr "Rona" 12.8.18
Barqtn "May" 17.10

Brig "Emr
H.M.S. "Orpheus" 6.2.1863 (187) M
S.S. "Pioneer" 24.12.1866 Schnr "Challenge
Cutter "Flora Macdonald" 2.
" "Paku" fnd 1.7.1894 (

hart

ELEVEN

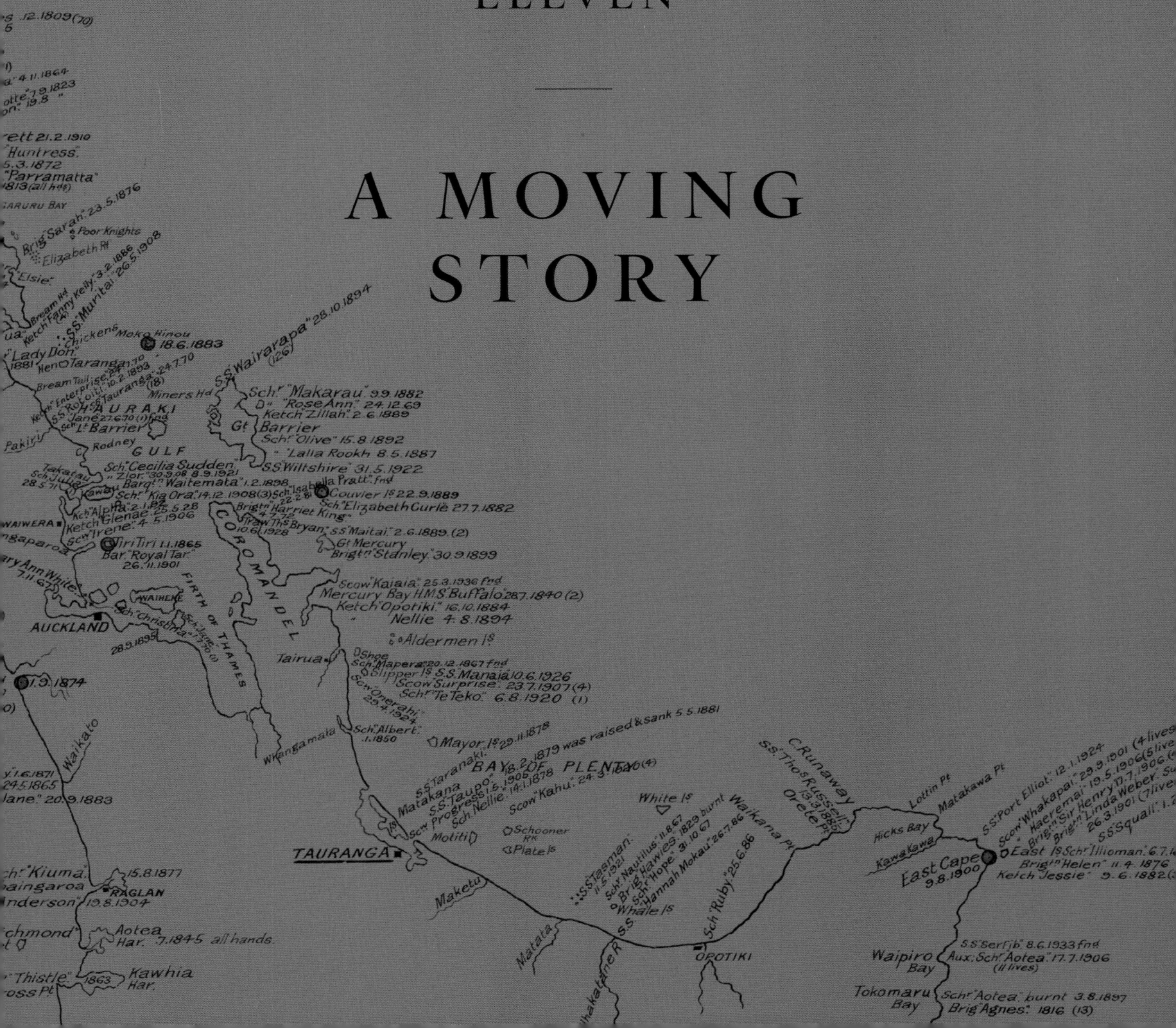

A MOVING STORY

SKETCH TO ACCOMPANY REPORT
OF ACTING ENGINEER IN CHIEF,
(CREATOR UNKNOWN), 1871

People who complain about the state of New Zealand's roads today—you know who you are—wouldn't have had much to complain about in 1871. There simply weren't that many roads to speak of, let alone whinge about, as this report of the acting chief engineer to the House of Representatives indicates. It shows the roads, railways and water races built (or surveyed, or proposed) during the calendar year, and there aren't many of them. Note that while a railway has been surveyed to link with a proposed road into the Waikato, the King Country is still very much a no-go zone (and would be for another ten years).

Railways were regarded as the way forward, as the ratio of blue lines—surveyed railways—to pink for roads on this map indicates. When Sir Julius Vogel became premier two years after this map was drawn, a new emphasis was placed on realising the dream of placing a railhead close to every farm gate. Vogel wanted to take a nationwide approach, and borrowed £10,000,000 to embark on the intensive public works programme required to build roads and railways.

All the same, his vision was compromised by the system of provincial government, which saw transport progress pursued piecemeal. It wasn't until the abolition of the provinces in 1876 that much nationally coordinated progress could be made. Note some of the place names in this map—Ngāruawāhia is known as Newcastle—and the military settlement of Alexandra (Pirongia) is still maintaining its redoubtable vigil on the border with the King Country.

The driving through of the North Island Main Trunk railway achieved two things: one, it was a dagger to the heart of the Kīngitanga movement, and two, it served as a unifying principle for North Islanders and New Zealanders more generally. This is emblematic of the significance of communications for the character of a country. The entire pattern of settlement is determined by it, and the landscape itself is often shaped by it.

When first settled, New Zealand was a distinctly maritime nation. Māori preferred, where possible, to travel long distances by waka; Europeans, too, tended to move coastwise. With the opening up of the interior and the survey and construction of roads, this began to change. Railways came next—the first public passenger line was the Ferrymead railway in Christchurch, opened in 1863—and then, with advances in the technology of motor vehicles, roads began to creep their way across the land. With the Main Highways Act of 1924 providing the political fillip and the Great Depression of the early 1930s providing the manpower, the basis of our modern roading network was laid.

Today, it's practically impossible to imagine what New Zealand would (or did) look like without tarsealed roads and cars.

NORTH ISLAND

SOUTH ISLAND

Reference.

Roads   made
          Surveyed & partly made
          Surveyed
Horse Roads

Railways   at work
    "   being made
    "   Surveys

Water Races Surveys

SKETCH MAP
TO ACCOMPANY REPORT OF
Acting Engineer in Chief
FOR YEARS 1870-71

ŌTIRA TOPOGRAPHICAL MAP, 1997

In 1884, when the first New Zealand topographical map (that is, showing the contours of the landscape) was produced, the process still relied very much upon the work of foot-slogging surveyors with their measuring equipment and their field books filled with trigonometrical data. Contours were usually rendered with shading (sometimes applied in watercolour) and high points indicated, and while the result was usually pretty and a general indication of terrain, it was not particularly accurate. But with the advent of aircraft (and of more portable gear), aerial photography became a tool that could perform in hours what it would have taken a surveying team days, weeks or even months to perform.

The first aerial survey of part of the New Zealand landscape was done in 1931, the subject the broad, braided Waimakariri River. From 1936, a small unit in the Department of Lands and Survey began using photogrammetric equipment (where a map-maker looks at two slightly different aerial views of a piece of terrain through a stereograph to get a 3D impression) to produce topographical maps. Two hand-cranked wheels enabled the operator to trace contour lines on the image, while the machine used a stylus to trace these lines onto a paper copy. The work of surveyors on the ground in the production of topographical maps was now confined to establishing control points and to checking the accuracy of maps produced photogrammetrically.

With the threat of war (and possible invasion) looming at the end of the 1930s, the topography of most of the coastline was mapped. After World War II, the effort was extended to mapping the rest of the country. The results of this work are minutely detailed maps such as this, of the Arthur's Pass region of the Southern Alps. Lives literally depend on the accuracy of such maps, as trampers and pilots routinely use a combination of maps and compasses to determine their location and routes in the back country. The snowline (and bushline) are indicated by shading. The meandering paths of tracks are drawn with dotted lines, and the presence of huts or shelters indicated with symbols. The map is overlaid with a grid that provides an easy method of reporting location.

The orange lines are contours (marking equal altitude). Where these are close together, the terrain is steep; where they are further apart, the gradient is more gentle.

SCALE 1:50 000

1:50 000
Topographic Map 260-K33
OTIRA
Edition 1 1989
Limited Revision 1997

Published under the authority of A. J. Bevin, Surveyor General,
Land Information New Zealand

New Zealand Lighthouse Chart

General Coast and Principal Harbour Lights
1900

SYMBOLS

- Fixed Light
- Flashing Light 10 Seconds
- Revolving Light 30 Seconds
- Revolving Light 1 Minute
- Revolving, Flashes Twice Every 30 Sec. with Intervals of 3" Betw'n Flash
- Group Flashing 2 Flashes in Quick Succession Every 30 Sec.

Enlarged Plan showing the Southern Entrance through Cook Strait

NORTH ISLAND

Locations shown: Three Kings, Cap Maria van Diemen, Hoko Hinau, Cuvier Id., Kaipara, Tiri-Tiri, Auckland, Manukau, Tauranga, White I., East Cape, Gisborne, New Plymouth, Cape Egmont, Patea, Wanganui, Foxton, Farewell Spit, Stephens Island, Nelson, Blenheim, Wairau R., Picton, Brothers, Wellington, Pencarrow, Cape Campbell, Cape Palliser, Napier, Portland Island

SOUTH ISLAND

Locations shown: Cape Foulwind, Westport, Greymouth, Hokitika, Kaikoura, Christchurch, Lyttelton, Akaroa Head, Godley Head, Timaru, Oamaru, Moeraki, Taiaroa Head, Dunedin, Puysegur Point, Centre I., The Bluff, Invercargill, Stewart Id., Nugget Point, Foveaux Strait

REFERENCE

Number of Lighthouse	Name of Lighthouse	Order of Apparatus	Fixed, Flashing, or Revolving	Interval of Revolution or Flashing	Height of Light above Sea	Colours of Light	Distance Visible in Nautical Miles	Colour of Lighthouse
1	Cape Maria van Diemen	1st order dioptric	Revolving	1 minute	530	Red, to show over Columbia Reef	24½	White
2	Moko Hinau	"	Fixed		206	White	26	"
3	Cuvier Island	1st order dioptric	Flashing	10 sec.		White		
4	Tiri-Tiri	2nd " "	Fixed		297	White, with red arc over Flat Rock	24	Red
5	Bean Rock	5th " "	"		40	White, red, green		
6	Ponui Passage	5th " "	"			White and red	12	
7	East Cape	2nd " "	Flashing	10 secs.	362	White flash		
8	Gisborne		Fixed			Red		
9	Portland Island	2nd order dioptric	Revolving	30 secs.	198	Red, to show over Bull Rock	20	White
10	Napier	4th order dioptric	Fixed		180	White	16½	"
11	Cape Palliser	1st " "	"		258	White, intervals of 3 secs. between flash	19	"
12	Pencarrow Head	2nd " "	Fixed		40	White	17	White
13	Somes Island				43	White in mid-channel and Lambton Harbour; red on western and green on eastern shore	8	
14	Manawatu River	Ordinary lamp			45		10	
15	Wanganui River	4th order port light	"		40	White	10	
16	Patea	5th " "	"			Red		
17	Cape Egmont	2nd order dioptric	"		103	White		
18	New Plymouth	5th order port light	"		80	Red		
19	Waitara	"	"			White		
20	Manukau	3rd order dioptric	"		390		26½	Brown
21	Kaipara	"	Flashing	10 secs.	270	White	22	
22	Nelson	5th order port light	Fixed			White, with red arc to mark limit of anchorage	12	White
23	French Pass				13	White and red, with white light on beacon		
24	Stephen's Island	2nd " "	Revolving	Group F.F.R.	608	White	30½	
25	The Brothers	"	Flashing	10 secs.	400	"	25	
26	Tory Channel Leading Lights		Fixed			Red, to show over Cook Rock	14	
27	Wairau River	5th order port light	Revolving	1 minute	45	White		White
28	Cape Campbell	2nd order dioptric	Flashing	75	450	Red	22	
29	Godley Head	3rd " "	"		420		26	White
30	Akaroa Head	"	Flashing		480		19	
31	Timaru	5th order port light	"		34	White and green	11	
32	Oamaru	5th "	"			Red	10	Light stone
33	Moeraki	3rd order dioptric	"		240	White	20	White
34	Taiaroa Head	"	Revolving	1 minute	240	Red	26½	"
35	Cape Saunders	"	"	"	230	"	25	"
36	Nugget Point	"	Flashing	10 secs.	250		20	"
37	Waipapapa Point	"	"		70		19	White & black bands
38	Dog Island	1st order catadioptric	Revolving	30 secs.	120		22	White
39	Centre Island	1st order dioptric	Fixed		293	White, with red arc over western danger	20½	"
40	Puysegur Point	1st " "	"		230	White and red	25	
41	Hokitika	5th order dioptric	"		122		11	"
42	Greymouth	4th order port light				White		
43	Cape Foulwind	3rd order dioptric	Revolving	30 secs.	220		22	
44	Westport	Dioptric combined R.	Flashing	1 minute	90	White, with red arc over Spit end	14	Upper part white, lower part red
45	Farewell Spit	3rd order dioptric	Revolving		100	White		

KOCH'S LIGHTHOUSE MAP, 1900

In its early years, New Zealand was almost exclusively a maritime nation. In the days before air travel (which means to say our entire history before the middle of the twentieth century), our ancestors, Māori and Pākehā alike, arrived by sea. And until we had established rail and road systems, communication between ports and provinces was most easily done by sea, too. This made our lighthouse network of vital importance.

The first lighthouse in New Zealand, at Pencarrow, Wellington, was built from a kitset shipped from England in 1858 and switched on (or rather lit) on 1 January 1859: its first permanent keeper was a woman, Mary Bennett, who took over from her husband when he drowned. This striking 1900 map by Augustus Koch shows 45 lights, together with the range from which they were visible and the colour and pattern of the lights as they would appear from different sectors (for example, some, such as that on Somes Island, shown in the inset, would shine red if you were too far west to enter the harbour safely, but a white light marked a safe passage).

All New Zealand lighthouses were electrified by 1950, and by 1990, when The Brothers light in Cook Strait was automated, the job of keeper was a thing of the past, too.

Following page
GUIDE MAP OF NEW ZEALAND, 1905 (CREATOR UNKNOWN)

Motorcars were something of a novelty in New Zealand when this map was printed in 1905, presumably to help your hunting, shooting, fishing tourist get around. It depicts 'railway, steamer and coach routes' rather than roads as such. What would become the North Island Main Trunk line is discontinuous, with railends at Taumarunui and Mangaweka travelling from the north and south respectively. The route of the ferry that once plied between Lyttelton and Wellington is shown, as are the steamer routes around the country's principal ports. Passenger steamers from Sydney would run around the top of the North Island and down the east coast, departing from Bluff for Hobart. Other points of interest on this map are the overprinted (in red) labels indicating what game is to be had—trout, various species of deer—and the seasons for deer, sporting fish and 'feathered game' are included, along with the legend (in bold type) promising 'Excellent sea fishing'.

Page 245
HALSE'S MAP OF NEW ZEALAND SHIPWRECKS, 1935

Our lighthouses and their intrepid keepers notwithstanding, New Zealand's rugged coastline took a terrible toll on shipping. Indeed, in the early days of the colony, with coastal shipping being the main mode of long-distance travel and the absence of bridges obliging landlubbers to cross our very many unpredictable rivers by fording, punts or ferries, death by drowning was so common that it was known as 'the New Zealand death'. A glance at this map, prepared by retired Survey Department draughtsman Frederick James Halse in 1935, the year before he died, shows every wreck he could learn about 'from official and other sources'. After the name of each vessel and the date of its mishap, inked on in an impeccable hand, he included a figure that indicated the number of casualties. The wrecks are predictably clustered about the principal sites of European settlement (and on the West Coast of the South Island, where there isn't room to mark them all against the spots where they came to grief). Of course, the map does not include the wrecks of the unknown vessels that fetched up along the coastline, and it doesn't include the vessels that met their end on our offshore islands, particularly the Chathams and the Aucklands.

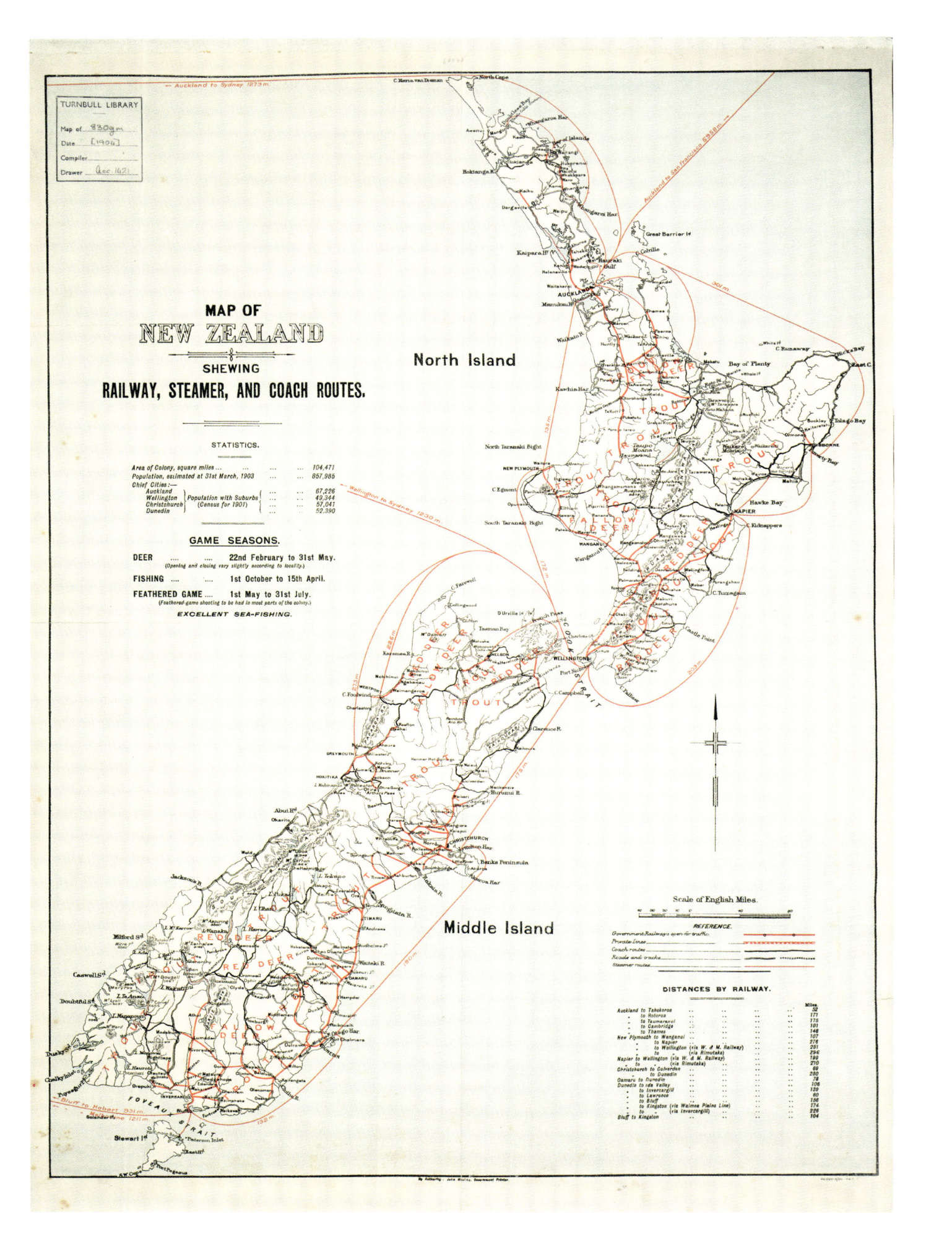

MAP OF NEW ZEALAND

SHEWING RAILWAY, STEAMER, AND COACH ROUTES.

STATISTICS.

Area of Colony, square miles	104,471
Population, estimated at 31st March, 1903	857,985
Chief Cities:—	
Auckland	67,226
Wellington (Population with Suburbs, Census for 1901)	49,344
Christchurch	57,041
Dunedin	52,390

GAME SEASONS.

DEER — 22nd February to 31st May.
(Opening and closing vary slightly according to locality.)

FISHING — 1st October to 15th April.

FEATHERED GAME — 1st May to 31st July.
(Feathered-game shooting to be had in most parts of the colony.)

EXCELLENT SEA-FISHING.

REFERENCE.

Government Railways open for traffic
Private Lines
Coach-routes
Roads and tracks
Steamer routes

DISTANCES BY RAILWAY.

	Miles
Auckland to Tahekoroa	52
to Rotorua	171
to Taumaranui	175
to Cambridge	101
to Thames	148
New Plymouth to Wanganui	107
to Napier	276
to Wellington (via W. & M. Railway)	201
to (via Rimutaka)	296
Napier to Wellington (via W. & M. Railway)	199
to (via Rimutaka)	210
Christchurch to Culverden	69
to Dunedin	230
Oamaru to Dunedin	78
Dunedin to Ida Valley	106
to Invercargill	139
to Lawrence	60
to Bluff	156
to Kingston (via Waimea Plains Line)	174
to (via Invercargill)	226
Bluff to Kingston	104

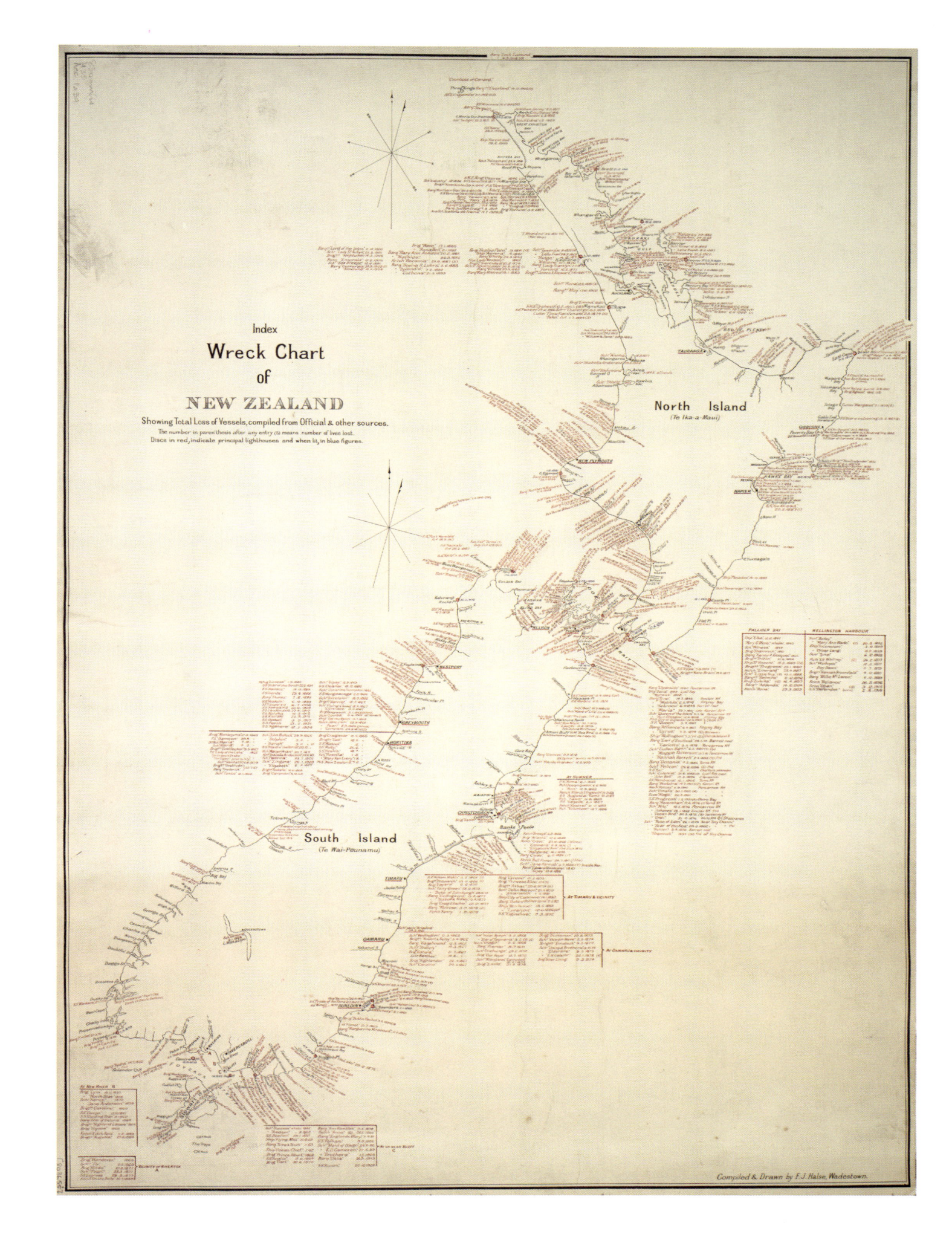

Index
Wreck Chart
of
NEW ZEALAND

Showing Total Loss of Vessels, compiled from Official & other sources.

The number in parenthesis after any entry (6) means number of lives lost.
Discs in red, indicate principal lighthouses and when lit, in blue figures.

North Island
(Te Ika-a-Maui)

South Island
(Te Wai-Pounamu)

Compiled & Drawn by F.J. Halse, Wadestown.

BRADSHAW'S NEW ZEALAND ROUTE GUIDE, 1885

The state of New Zealand's long-distance transport scene in 1885 is captured in this 'Bradshaw Guide', prepared by J. Stewart Reid. George Bradshaw had founded a business empire selling transport guides in the United Kingdom in 1839, and this guide to New Zealand was a late example. The difficulty of getting about is plain to see. A disjointed network of railways was supplemented by coaches in both islands—the lower part of the South Island's east coast is relatively well served, due to the gold rushes, but there are no coach roads through Northland to speak of, and nothing of any description through the King Country or Marlborough, which featured several dangerous rivers. Most travel between settlements was still done by sea, and the distances of the major routes are given.

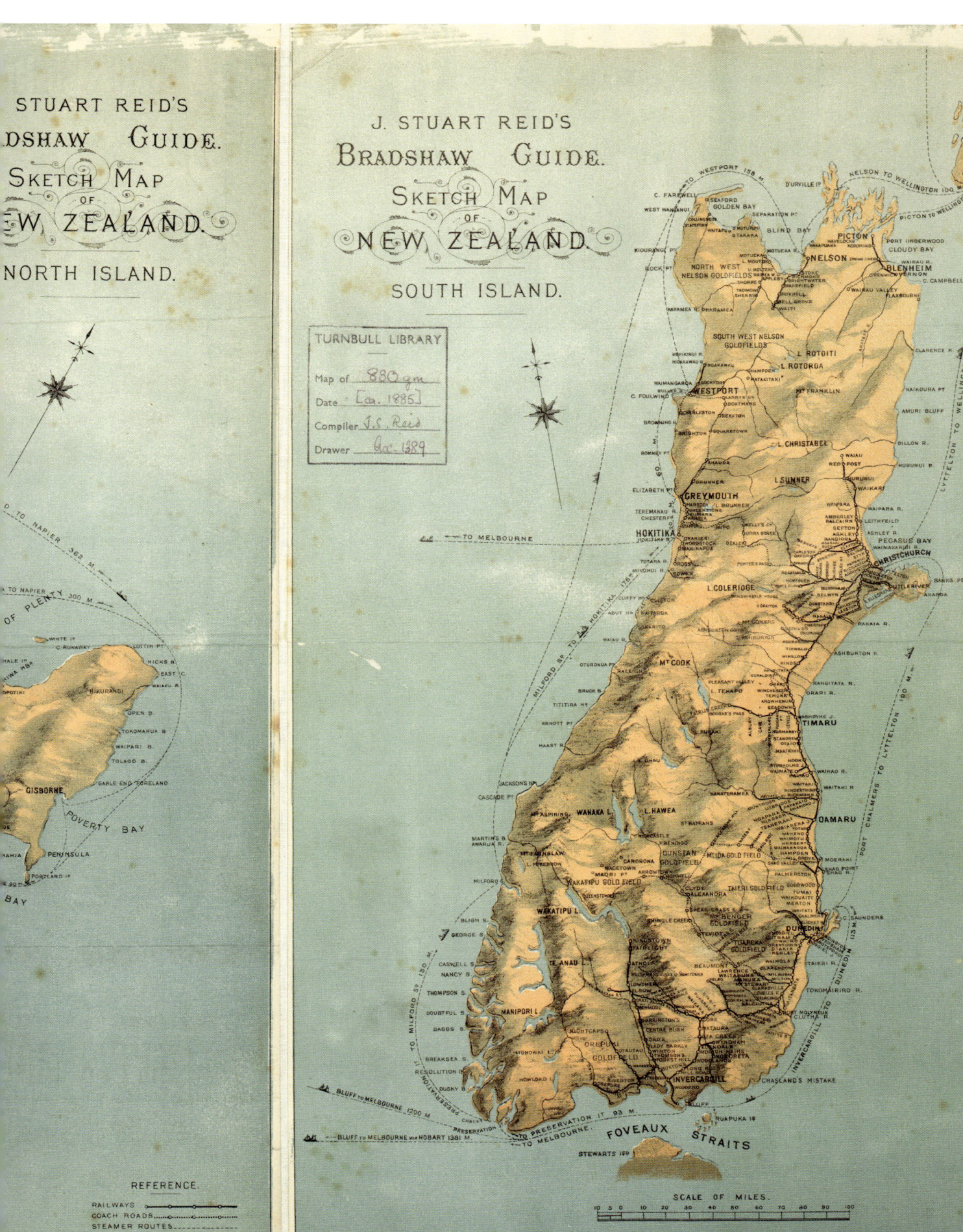

J. STUART REID'S Bradshaw Guide.
SKETCH MAP OF NEW ZEALAND.
SOUTH ISLAND.

TURNBULL LIBRARY
Map of 880 gm
Date [ca. 1885]
Compiler J.S. Reid
Drawer Acc. 1389

SCALE OF MILES.
10 5 0 10 20 30 40 50 60 70 80 90 100

REFERENCE.
RAILWAYS
COACH ROADS
STEAMER ROUTES

NEW ZEALAND RAIL PUBLICITY DEPARTMENT'S RAURIMU SPIRAL MAP, 1929

The North Island Main Trunk Line, as the main railway between Auckland and Wellington is known, was something of a marvel when it was finally completed in 1908—not least on account of the complicated Raurimu Spiral, which provided the altitude necessary for a steam locomotive to get from the township of Raurimu to nearby National Park. The first section of the line was built in Auckland between Point Britomart and Onehunga, and opened in 1873. It was pushed as far south as Te Awamutu by 1880, at which point the chickens of Sir Julius Vogel's big borrowing campaign had come home to roost and New Zealand suffered a severe economic depression.

By the time progress was resumed, a deal had been brokered with Ngāti Maniapoto, who consented to allow the line to pass through the King Country. Construction of the Central Plateau section began when paramount chief Wahanui turned the first sod on 15 April 1885. Meanwhile, a privately owned line from Wellington to Longburn was being constructed by the Wellington and Manawatu Railway Company; the government purchased this in 1908, as work on the line that would link it to the northern section was nearing completion. Having decided the line should pass through Taumarunui, the government found it had bitten off a greater engineering challenge than it had expected to chew. But with the construction of several soaring viaducts and one magnificent spiral—celebrated in this handsome promotional map drawn by the New Zealand Railways marketing department in 1929—the thing was done. A group of politicians, including the premier, Sir Joseph Ward, made the inaugural journey from Wellington to Auckland by rail on 7 August 1908. Of course, with a railway running right through the heart of it, the King Country could never again have quite the same sense of self-containment that had enabled the King Movement to comport itself as a state within a state. It's unlikely this was an unintended consequence.

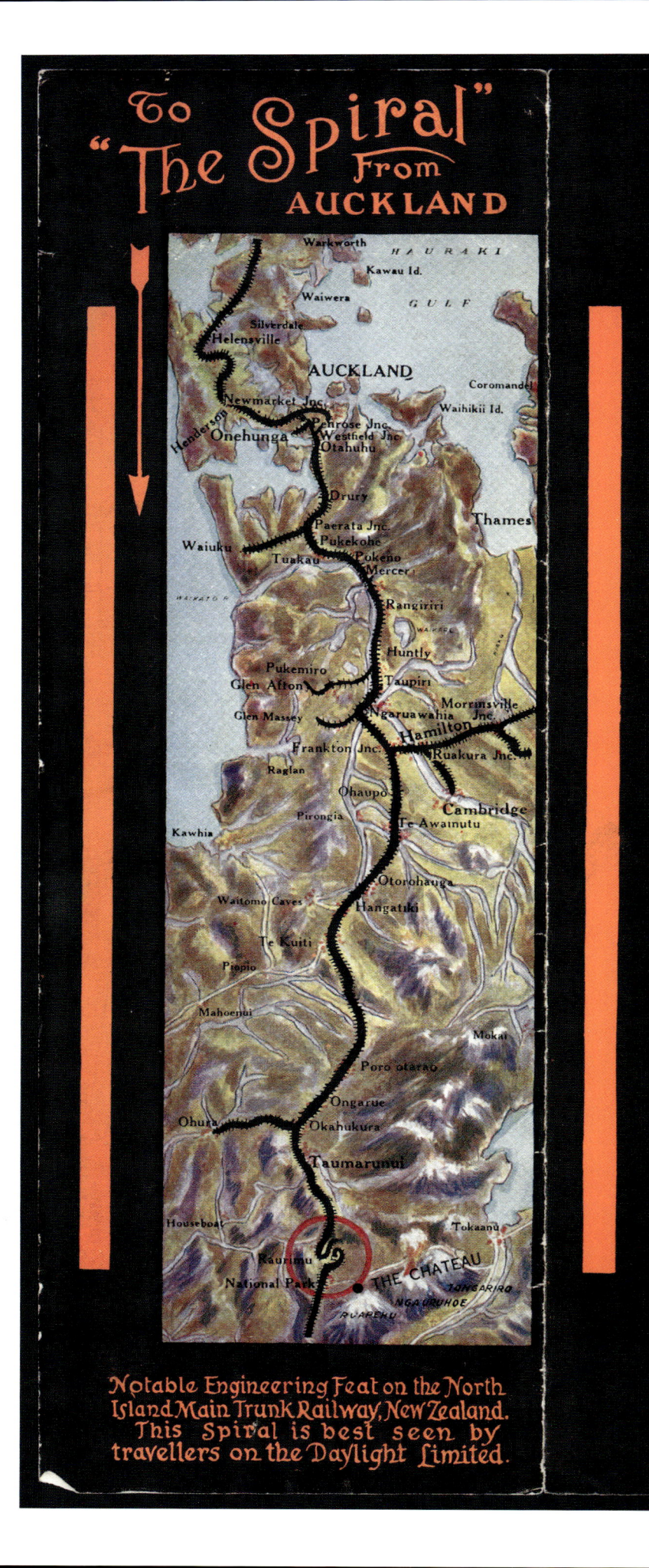

RAURIMU SPIRAL AND NATIONAL PARK
NEW ZEALAND RAILWAYS

The Line rises from Raurimu Railway Station and Township to National Park Station (on the edge of National Park). In the background, the Volcanic mountains, Tongariro (left), Ngauruhoe (centre) & Ruapehu (right) with the Chateau at its base.

To "The Spiral" From WELLINGTON

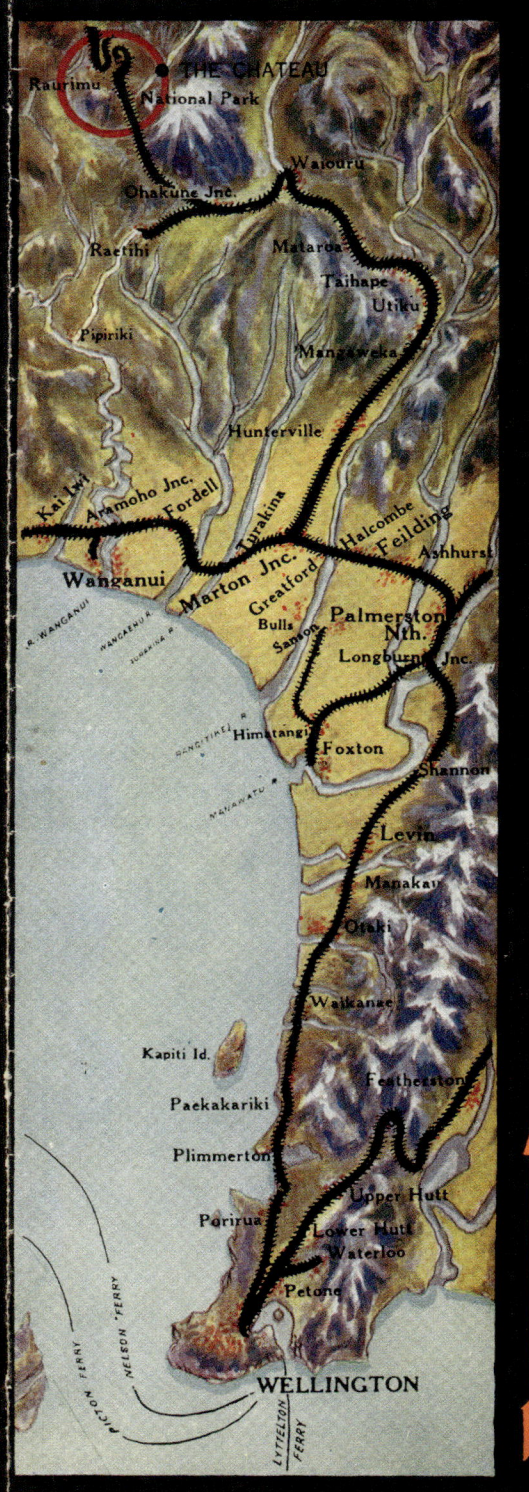

Piopiotea River, tributary of the Retaruke River flowing from plateau crosses, and then accompanies Railway into Raurimu Township

AARD MOTOR SERVICES MAP, CIRCA 1920

It was quite some time into the twentieth century before most New Zealanders could aspire to own any kind of motorcar of their own, let alone a car that was capable of travelling over the poor roads and steep gradients that lay between towns. Until the 1920s, for those who needed to get somewhere that wasn't served by rail, the answer was to endure a coach ride; but from around 1910 onwards, an increasing number of enterprising souls began running 'service cars' over set routes. These started out as contractors to the Postal Department (hence 'service'), and it was the mail that determined the route and timetable. The cars used were usually large touring cars, sometimes modified to seat more passengers in greater comfort (which was a relative thing anyway) than the factory edition offered.

Rupert Rennie ('Dot') Woodcock started out as a Napier taxi driver in 1916, using a 1913 Model T Ford. When he and his business partner decided to expand in 1918, he suggested they rename their company 'AARD Motor Services', not really because 'Aard' means 'earth' in Dutch, but because it would secure them the first entry in the alphabetically arranged *Wise's Business Directory*.

As the business bloomed to cover much of the North Island, his promotional inspiration knew few bounds: he painted the company name on all manner of objects—the Pātangata Hotel's chookhouse acquired a sign reading 'AARD boiled eggs', and he even carved it into the carcass of a whale that washed onto the beach at Napier (he had to hurriedly assure the council that he hadn't claimed it as it began to decompose). Dot obviously also knew the promotional value of a nicely drawn map. The AARD brand continued to appear in *Wise's* long after the brand had been deregistered in 1938: the entry reads 'see New Zealand Rail Road Services'.

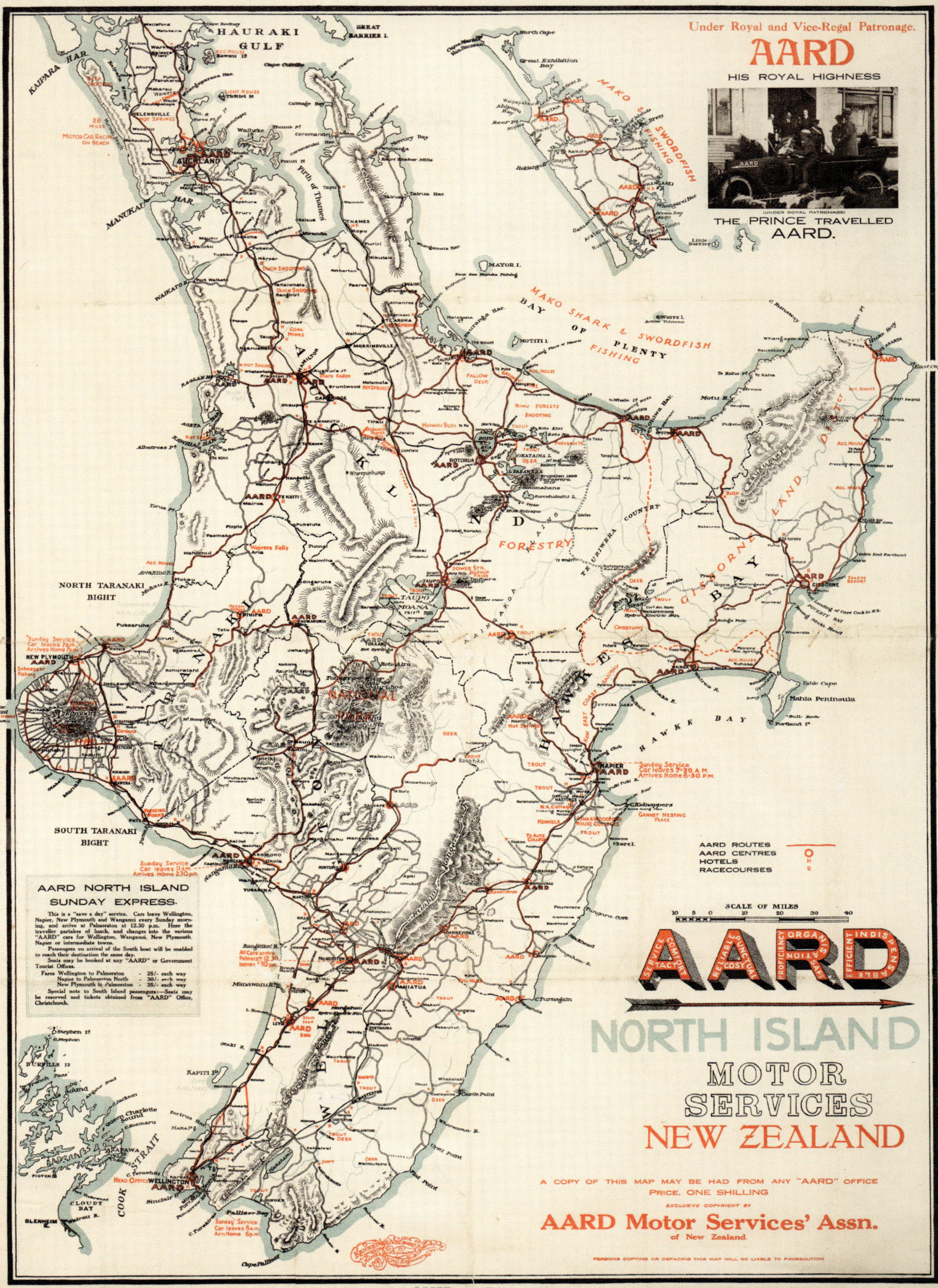

BRETT LITHO. AUCK.

Legend

JET-PROP SERVICES

OTHER NAC SERVICES

ASSOCIATED AIRLINES

NAC FUN MAP OF NEW ZEALAND, 1960

The National Airways Corporation (NAC) was created through the amalgamation of several disparate elements, including the transport arm of the Royal New Zealand Air Force and Union Airways, a private commercial airline established by the Union Steam Ship Company. It was New Zealand's domestic air carrier: the international equivalent was Tasman Empire Air Lines (TEAL), which was established as a wartime service to carry mail, cargo and passengers across the Tasman as the result of a treaty between New Zealand, Australia and the United Kingdom. TEAL was supposed to cease after the war, but in the event it survived until 1961, when the Australian government decided to back its own airline, QANTAS. The New Zealand government did likewise, buying out Union Airways' shareholding in TEAL and creating a national carrier to fly international routes. This was known as Air New Zealand from 1965, and in 1978, NAC merged with it.

From the outset, NAC was as much involved in flying tourists around New Zealand as it was flying New Zealanders. This 'fun map' reflects this, depicting various attractions and leisure activities up and down the country. It can be viewed as a political statement, too: apart from what may be the Treaty House at Waitangi, beneath a large Union Jack, the only Māori aspect of New Zealand shown is a single caricature of a taiaha-wielding warrior, presumably performing a haka, in the vicinity of Rotorua.

MAP OF AUCKLAND AND ENVIRONS, 1957

At first glance, this map of Auckland from the CBD south is familiar. But look more closely and various elements start standing out. There is a flying boat harbour at Mechanics Bay. There is a 'lighter basin', complete with an actual viaduct and lifting bridge, where the Viaduct Harbour is now situated. The Auckland Harbour Bridge is under construction, as is the approach road around St Marys Bay. The railway runs into the old railway station at the bottom of Parnell Rise, and lines run into Quay Street. You only need to go as far west as Massey or as far south as Ellerslie for the grey hatching connoting 'built-up area' to give way to a lighter grey, where there is a smattering of industry: a glass works and milk treatment factory at Penrose, a fertiliser works at Te Papapa and a freezing works at Southdown. There are motorways, but not many of them, and there is not yet a Spaghetti Junction.

Much of Auckland's development had been driven by its tramways, which had seen suburbia spread out like tentacles along the lines from the central city. But by 1954, three years before this map was drawn, Auckland had sold its soul to the motorcar. In 1949, a report into the city's transport options had been commissioned from two British engineers: the choice was between pouring resources into a more extensive, Los Angeles–style motorway system, or into alternatives, such as a better rail network. The report recommended the latter, and the Labour government agreed. After Sidney Holland's National government came to power in 1949, the plan was frozen, and it was decided to tear up the city's tram tracks. Then, in 1954, as Holland won a third term in government, the entire transport policy direction was shoved abruptly into reverse, and it was decided that Auckland would get its motorways. The effect was to spread the urban area far and wide: with prosperity and the increasing availability of private cars, you could live much further out and still commute to town conveniently—at first, anyway.

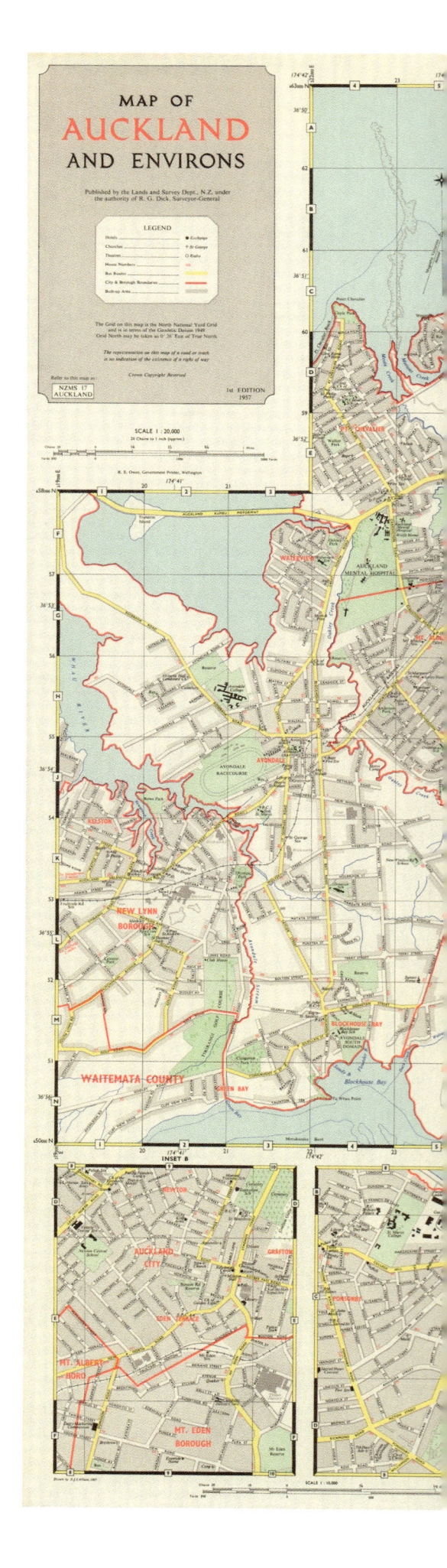

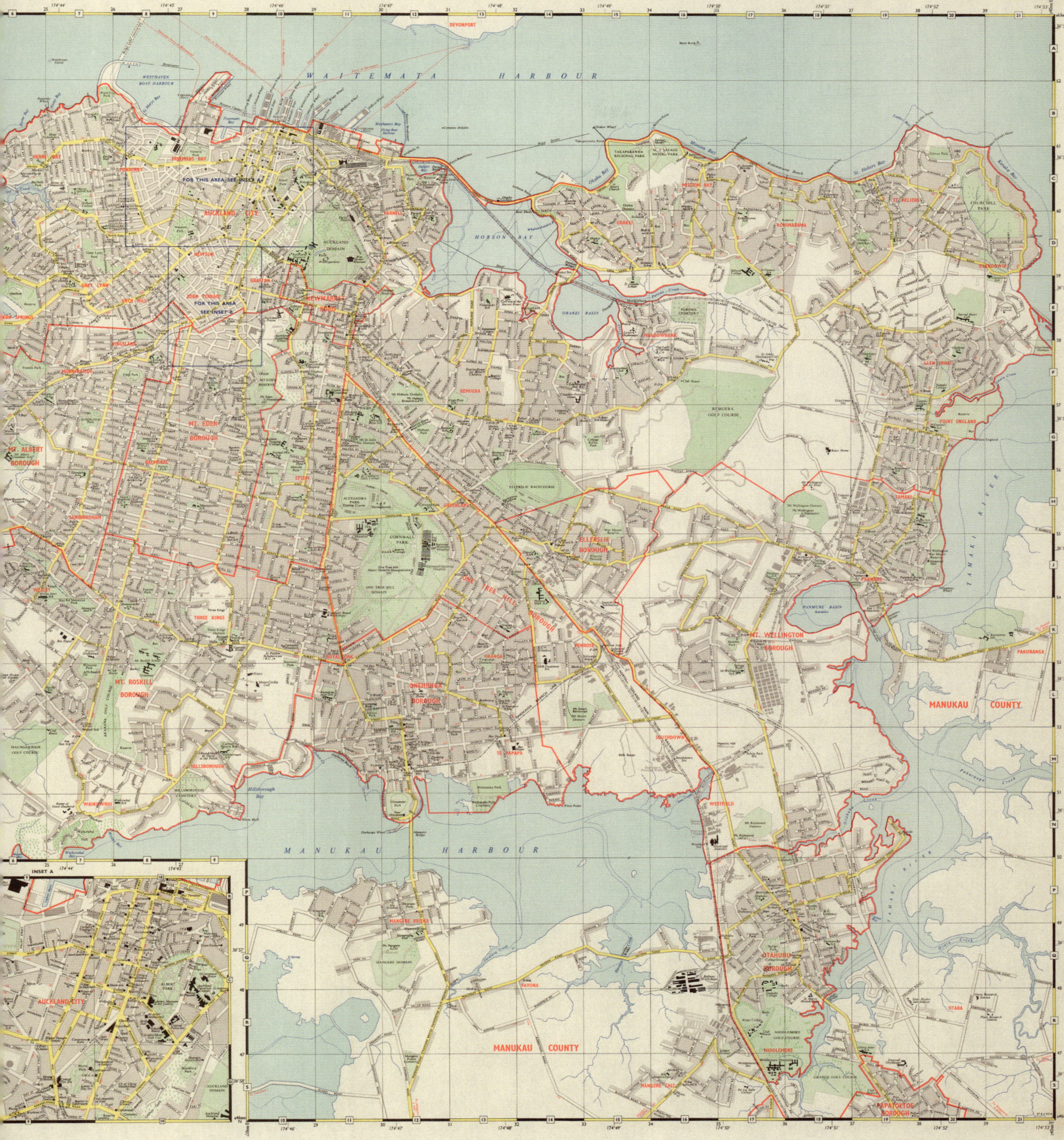

Motukakapo
1379
Wharepuhanga
1943
Tikorangi
2046
Te Ranga
2309
Uraura
1737
RIVER
Kopokorahi Stm
Ranginui
3224
Whangapoa Stm
Whakamaru
2608
WAIMAHANA
Ongaroto
Upper
Parakiri
Waitaranga
MARAEROA PLAIN
Waikino Stm
Mangakino Stm
Pukutu
2231
OHINEARIKI
Waipapa
Titiraupenga
Maraonui
2950
Pureora
3793
Puketapu
Old Pa
WATERFALL
Te Papa
Ngangiho
2155
Puketarata
GEYSERS
Oruanui
Ketemaringi
3082
Waihora Stm
Motumoa
2144
Moturoa
1925
KARAPITI
Huka
Falls
TAUPO
Te Kauae
Whangamata B.
Waihaha Stm
Te Tuhingamata
2202
Tahunatara
Pawharariki
2087
Waihaha Boat Ldg
Ohinetuhua
Waikino Stm
Te Turoa
Boat Landing
Te Wharawhara
LAKE
TAUPO
Waipahihi Stm
Karangahape
2379
Kohaitako
ROTONGAIO
Moutere
3248
Puketurua
2278
Te Putu
2195
Hauhungaroa
Tengarara
Ouaha
2067
Waitotara Stm
Motuwhara
Whareroa Stm
MOTU
TAIKO

TWELVE

SCRUTINY ON THE BOUNTY

Given that maps are a means of communicating what is known (and what is wanted known), it's scarcely surprising that one of the chief functions of map-makers has been to record the location, extent and abundance of resources. The things that we consider to be resources vary over time and according to changes in economic activity: pre-European Māori valued food resources, timber and stone (especially pounamu). Early European visitors noted the abundance of timber, flax, seals and whales. The first Pākehā explorers to push into the interior were (mostly) in search of arable land, but they also recorded such useful items as coal seams and rocks that suggested there might be gold in them thar hills.

As first provincial and then national governments became involved, surveys included the geology, soil types and hydrology of the landscape and, in many cases, the information charted depended upon the technologies deployed to gather it. The advance of science meant that seismology and spectrometry, for example, produced a picture in higher resolution than the geologist's eye and hammer.

And as the demand for new resources opened up, research supplied information as to where they were and in what quantity. As the motor vehicle fleet grew and our consumption of petrochemicals increased, for example, the tantalising possibility of meeting the demand from our own, domestic resources led to more mineral exploration using new and ever better prospecting techniques. And when concerns grew over the impact of the use of all those fossil fuels and a new focus fell upon renewable energy, people began looking for sources of geothermal, hydroelectric and wind power generation. You might have mapped the existence of thermal springs in the nineteenth century because you were the government balneologist (yes, there was a government balneologist), charged with finding hot pools to deliver the supposed therapeutic benefits of naturally heated mineral water. You would never have dreamed the same resource would be of interest to the minister of energy 100 years on. And it would never have occurred to anyone in the 1860s that ferocious river rapids and persistent gales were a resource of any description, or that we might one day need to know where our underground water was coming from and how long it would last.

Some things haven't changed all that much. Our economy continues to be based upon primary industry, but patterns of land use have changed according to technology (refrigerated transport knocked cash-cropping on the head as everyone rushed to run sheep) and global market trends. The most dramatic changes in 150 years came about when Great Britain entered the European Economic Community in 1973 and ceased to be a guaranteed buyer of all the meat, wool and dairy we could produce. First there was a great push for diversification of production: we tried everything from kiwifruit and babacos to *Pinus radiata* and ostriches, in case one such commodity might become the new mutton. There were booms in kiwifruit and forestry: babacos and ostriches not so much. Then dairy swept all before it, and maps reflected the mass conversion of exotic forests to dairy units—and, consequentially, dramatic declines in water quality.

HECTOR'S MAP OF PRINCIPAL MINERAL LOCALITIES, 1886

James Hector was a Scotsman who, although qualified as a doctor, had proven himself as a capable geologist on a field survey of western Canada (for which work he was honoured with fellowships of the Royal Society of Edinburgh and the Royal Geographical Society). When, in 1861, the provincial council of Otago decided it wanted to find out what kind of goodies lay buried in their patch of dirt, they decided Hector was their man.

He did such a good job of the Otago survey that the central government decided to task him with a geological survey of the colony at large. In 1865, he was appointed director of the National Geographical Survey and of the Colonial Museum. For the next twenty years, he and a small staff worked indefatigably on the survey, in the field in the summer and in the office and laboratory in the winter. In the same year this map was produced, he published a report named *Outline of New Zealand Geology*, the foundation of our geological knowledge of our country.

The map indicates gold in many parts of New Zealand, including some quite surprising ones: in Wellington's western hills, in the vicinity of Lake Wairarapa, even at Twilight Beach in Northland. Who knew you could find the chalcogen tellurium at Waihī, or a significant arsenic resource just south of Coromandel township? If you wanted osmium or iridium, then Orepuki Beach was the place: there was petroleum there (in the form of shale sands), as well as at East Cape and Castlepoint.

GEOLOGICAL SURVEY OF NEW ZEALAND
SKETCH MAP
OF
NEW ZEALAND
SHOWING
PRINCIPAL MINERAL LOCALITIES.

BY

JAMES HECTOR.

1886.

SCALE OF MILES

REFERENCE TO DISTINGUISHING SYMBOLS OF MINERALS.

- OSMIUM-IRIDIUM.
- PLATINUM.
- GOLD.
- SILVER.
- TELLURIUM.
- MERCURY.
- COPPER.
- NICKEL.
- IRON.
- LEAD.
- TIN.
- ZINC.
- ANTIMONY.
- ARSENIC.
- MANGANESE.
- TUNGSTEN.
- TITANIUM.
- CHROMIUM.
- COAL MINES.
- COAL MEASURES.
- GRAPHITE.
- PETROLEUM & SHALE.

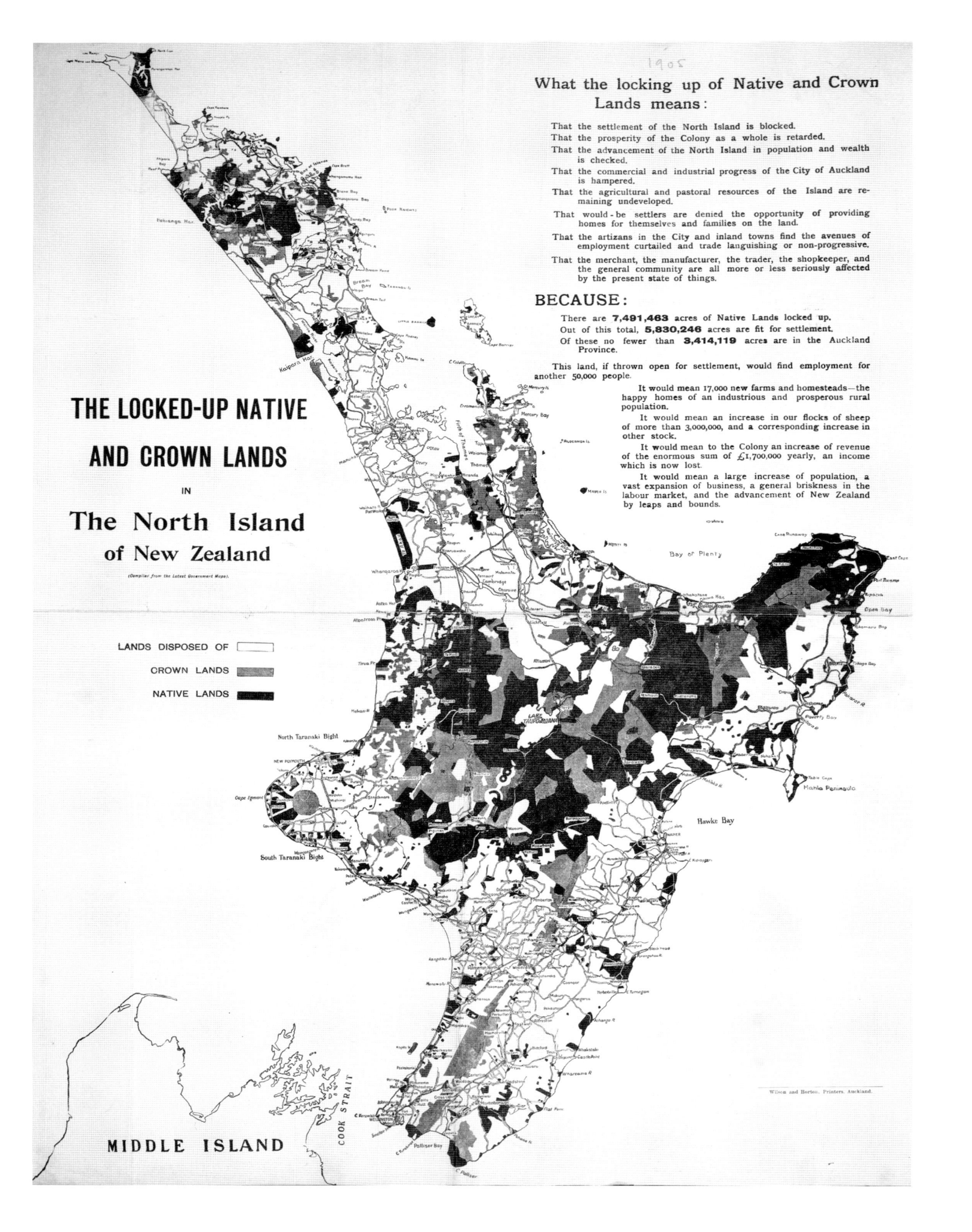

THE LOCKED-UP NATIVE AND CROWN LANDS IN The North Island of New Zealand

(Compiled from the Latest Government Maps)

Legend:
- LANDS DISPOSED OF
- CROWN LANDS
- NATIVE LANDS

What the locking up of Native and Crown Lands means:

That the settlement of the North Island is blocked.

That the prosperity of the Colony as a whole is retarded.

That the advancement of the North Island in population and wealth is checked.

That the commercial and industrial progress of the City of Auckland is hampered.

That the agricultural and pastoral resources of the Island are remaining undeveloped.

That would-be settlers are denied the opportunity of providing homes for themselves and families on the land.

That the artizans in the City and inland towns find the avenues of employment curtailed and trade languishing or non-progressive.

That the merchant, the manufacturer, the trader, the shopkeeper, and the general community are all more or less seriously affected by the present state of things.

BECAUSE:

There are **7,491,463** acres of Native Lands locked up.

Out of this total, **5,830,246** acres are fit for settlement.

Of these no fewer than **3,414,119** acres are in the Auckland Province.

This land, if thrown open for settlement, would find employment for another 50,000 people.

It would mean 17,000 new farms and homesteads—the happy homes of an industrious and prosperous rural population.

It would mean an increase in our flocks of sheep of more than 3,000,000, and a corresponding increase in other stock.

It would mean to the Colony an increase of revenue of the enormous sum of £1,700,000 yearly, an income which is now lost.

It would mean a large increase of population, a vast expansion of business, a general briskness in the labour market, and the advancement of New Zealand by leaps and bounds.

Wilson and Horton, Printers, Auckland.

WILSON AND HORTON'S MAP OF NATIVE LANDS LOCKED UP, 1905

Most maps have a political angle. Some have more of a political angle than others. With the end of armed conflict over land, the dust settled (for the time being) on confiscations by the government, and the methodical work of the Confiscations Commission under way, you'd have thought that Māori might feel their tenure of their own land to be secure. But no. From the 1880s onwards, newspapers up and down the country were peppered with reports of meetings, letters to the editor and editorials arguing that this block or that block of land was lying scandalously idle in Māori hands, and ought to be taken from them and delivered into the ownership of people who would make proper, beneficial use of it: *viz*, European settlers. One of the more vocal agitators for this course of action was the Auckland Chamber of Commerce. In 1905, either it or a group of sympathisers paid the Auckland printing firm Wilson and Horton (which also published the *New Zealand Herald*) to produce this map, depicting native and Crown lands that were 'locked up'—that is, unable to be bought, sold or leased while their status was determined by the Native Land Court or the Confiscations Commission. The text alongside it argues that 'the prosperity of the Colony as a whole is retarded' and 'the commercial and industrial progress of the City of Auckland is hampered' by the fact that five million acres of land is 'doing nothing'. The land would furnish '17,000 new farms and homesteads—the happy homes of an industrious and prosperous rural population' and promote 'the advancement of New Zealand by leaps and bounds'.

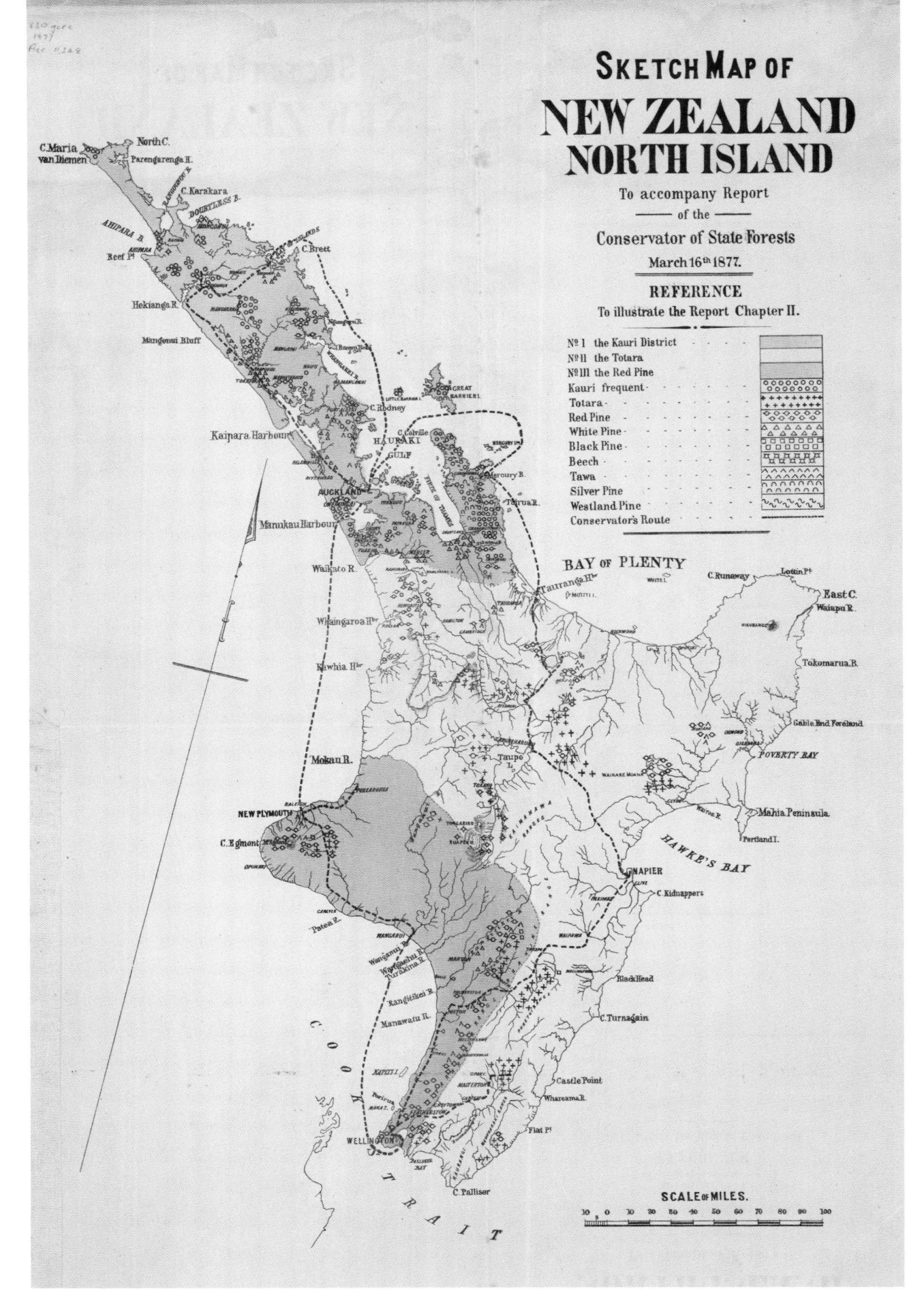

SKETCH MAP OF NEW ZEALAND NORTH ISLAND

To accompany Report
of the
Conservator of State Forests
March 16th 1877.

REFERENCE
To illustrate the Report Chapter II.

- Nº I   the Kauri District
- Nº II   the Totara
- Nº III the Red Pine
- Kauri frequent
- Totara
- Red Pine
- White Pine
- Black Pine
- Beech
- Tawa
- Silver Pine
- Westland Pine
- Conservator's Route

SCALE OF MILES.
10 0 10 20 30 40 50 60 70 80 90 100

SKETCH MAP OF NORTH ISLAND TO ACCOMPANY REPORT OF THE CONSERVATOR OF FORESTS, 1872

It might seem remarkable that we had a conservator of forests as early as 1877. The fact is, however, that the word 'conservation' back then was closer to our term 'sustainable use' than it was to the preservation of natural heritage and biodiversity.

It had not escaped official attention that, by the 1870s, there was very little left of the forests that had originally blanketed the North Island: Sir James Hector stated in Parliament in 1868 that twenty per cent of the original cover had gone. Anything in the way of accessible kauri had been taken in the timber booms of the previous four decades. The lowland podocarp forests—tōtara and kahikatea—had been cleared to put land in pasture. All the same, the prevailing opinion was that such bush as was still there was to supply timber for agricultural and building purposes. The best use of the land, as an MP put it around this time, was to clear it for pasture. Public outrage at cutting down trees was usually stirred up only when timber was exported or used for making railway sleepers or other such 'wasteful' purposes.

This map, which accompanied the report of Captain Campbell Walker, the conservator of forests (appointed under the auspices of the Forests Act 1874), indicates how little was left, and how confined it was to the less accessible parts of the country.

Note, incidentally, the old place names: Shortland and Grahamstown (together, present-day Thames), Newcastle for Ngāruawāhia, and Richmond, close to the site of present-day Matatā, which was surveyed but never really happened.

MCKERROW'S MAP OF THE THERMAL SPRINGS DISTRICT, 1888

This beautiful map was created (under the direction of the New Zealand surveyor general, James McKerrow) at a time of transition both for the region and the resource it depicts. Ever since Europeans had first set eyes on the region, they were fascinated by the burping mud pools, spouting geysers, fizzing springs and hissing fumaroles. The jewels in the crown of the hot lakes district had been the Pink and White Terraces, natural silica formations on the shores of Lake Rotomahana, until they were destroyed in the catastrophic eruption of Mount Tarawera in 1886.

Around the same time, the belief was growing that thermally heated mineral water was not merely therapeutic but also curative of a range of ailments, particularly rheumatism. The government was swift to capitalise, appointing Arthur Stanley Wohlmann to the position of government balneologist in 1902 (there had been a medical officer at Rotorua for ten years previously), whose job it was to construct spa facilities. Rotorua's famous Bath House (now a museum) was his brain-child.

Wohlmann (although he was English, he changed his German-sounding surname to Herbert during World War I) left his job and the country in 1919, but the office of government balneologist wasn't abolished until 1957. By then, however, the hot lakes district's geothermal resource had found another use. A plant was already under construction at Wairākei that generated electricity from the superheated steam issuing from underground. It opened in 1958.

THE CENTRAL THERMAL SPRINGS COUNTRY.

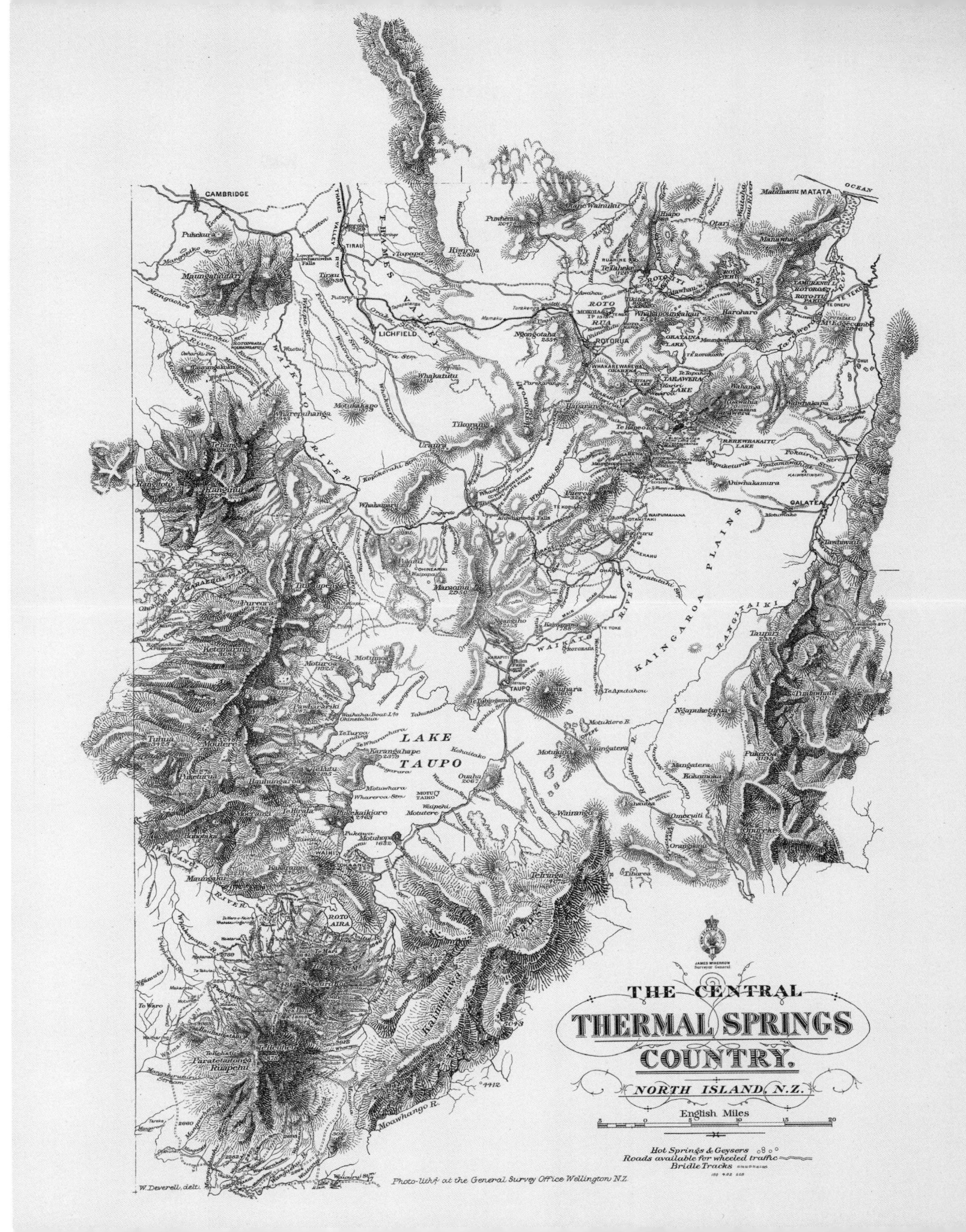

NORTH ISLAND, N.Z.

English Miles

Hot Springs & Geysers
Roads available for wheeled traffic
Bridle Tracks

W. Deverell, delt.

Photo-lith'd at the General Survey Office Wellington N.Z.

James McKerrow, Surveyor General

NEW ZEALAND
Her Natural and Industrial Resources

KEY to SYMBOLS
- Coal
- Oil
- Gold
- Platinum
- Iron
- Tungsten
- Mercury Extraction

NORTH ISLAND

SOUTH ISLAND

THE NEW ERA

The demands of war caused New Zealand to expand her industries and develop new ones. Their conversion to peaceful purposes and the continued production of vital foodstuffs will be used by New Zealand for two purposes—to maintain her own high standard of living and social security and also to contribute to the well-being of the world at large.

MacDonald Gill 1943

PRINTED FOR H.M. STATIONERY OFFICE BY FOSH & CROSS LTD. 51-9214

O P D 39/219/6

NEW ZEALAND: HER INDUSTRIAL AND NATURAL RESOURCES, 1943

In a curious way, this apparently frivolous map crosses and recrosses some of the maps and history covered in the preceding pages. It was created by the famous British illustrator and map-maker Leslie MacDonald 'Max' Gill, who pioneered the use of this kind of pictorial map art in promotion. His career had largely been built upon a bird's-eye view of London commissioned by the Underground Electric Railways Company in 1913 to promote the rail network beneath the city: Gill's *Wonderground Map* of London was a huge hit, and its print run was extended to permit sales to the public. It can therefore be seen as the forerunner to the kind of map shown on p. 252. During World War I, Gill was commissioned to design the lettering used on British imperial war graves and memorials: his stark, declamatory upper-case letters therefore spell the names and dates of many thousands of New Zealanders who lost their lives in the service of the empire.

He was busy during World War II, also. It's unclear who commissioned this particular piece, but it was likely some combination of British and New Zealand government interests, who were looking ahead to the end of the war. Gill had also produced a vast pictorial map for a hoarding on Charing Cross Road in London in 1927 entitled *Highways of Empire*, which encouraged loyal British subjects to buy produce from Britain and its colonies rather than elsewhere, and a map depicting New Zealand's agricultural and fisheries resources in the early 1930s on behalf of the short-lived Empire Marketing Board.

NEW ZEALAND FROM SPACE

So this is what we look like with all the details filled in. This exquisite image was captured by a NASA satellite passing over: it's from such a vantage point that our weather information comes, and all manner of other remotely sensed data streams, too. James Cook would have felt quietly pleased with his work on the coastline, as would John Lort Stokes. James Hector, James McKerrow and Julius von Haast would have recognised their pictures of the Southern Alps in this. Any number of rangatira would have tangied to see the footprint of the cadastre all over the places where the tīpuna trod and the cooking fires burned.

It's a beautiful but also cold and inhuman perspective on our country. We don't live this map, even if many of the satellite-based technologies inform systems and apps such as Fitbit, MapMyRide, GPS, Apple Maps and Google Maps, TomTom and so on. These can only give us the numbers: the altitude, the bearing, the precise location. Our lives are trails across this map, lines that only we can see completely, for all the surveillance made possible by CCTV and smartphone locations. The place we were born, went to school; the places where we fell in love; the places where our children are born; the places where family members triangulate holiday memories, arriving at a more or less contested version of the time and the place and the weather and what kind of time everyone had; the graves of our forebears and loved ones; and, in time, our own graves. We can grasp this image in the same way we grasp the concept of our own deaths: it makes theoretical sense, but has limited existential meaning for us. New Zealand is the sum of the trails of New Zealanders, and the songs of those trails.

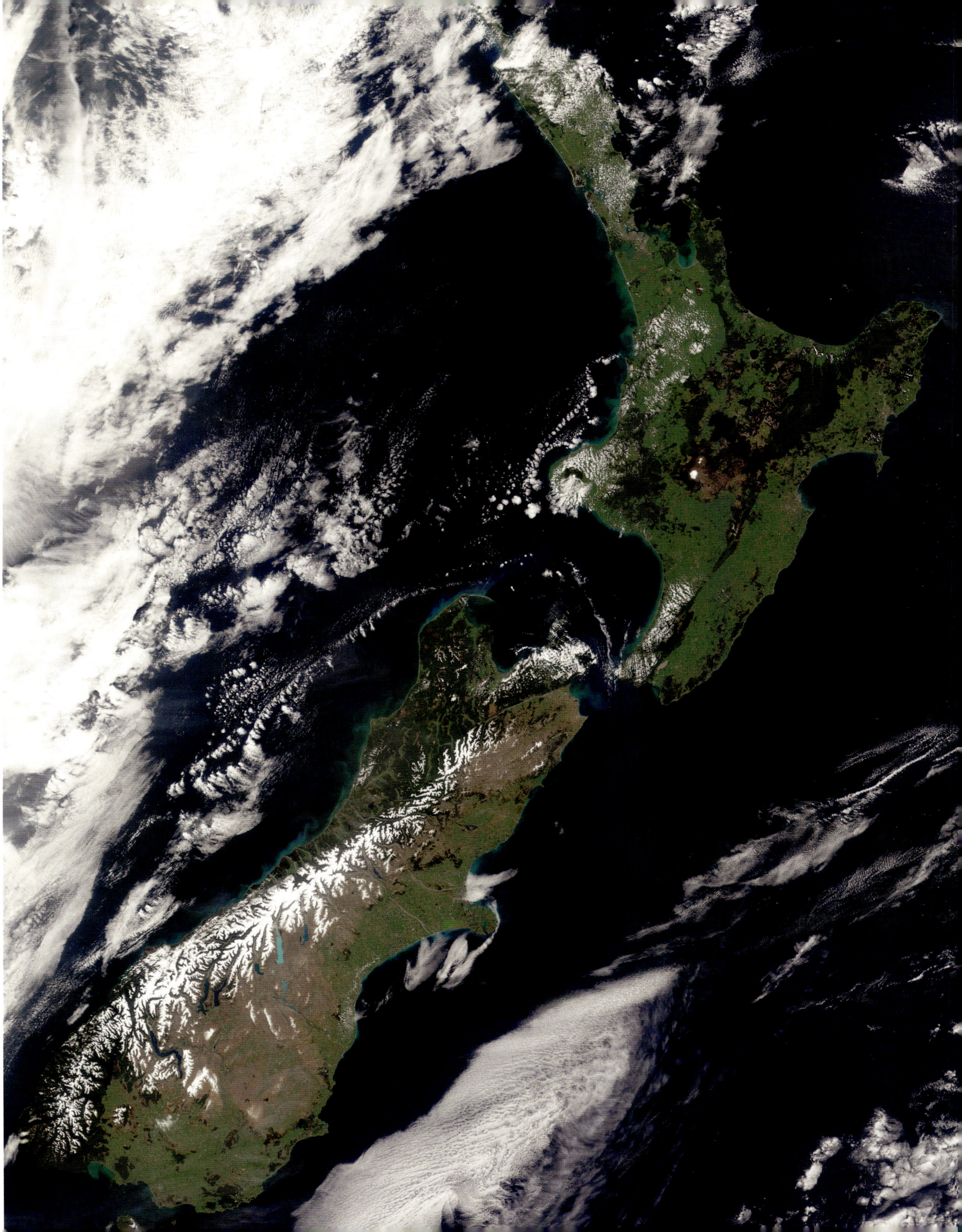

FURTHER READING

I consulted many sources in the course of researching this book. Such is the world we live in, most of these were online, and are too numerous to name. They ranged from Wikipedia to online learned journals, but I can commend *Te Ara —The Encyclopaedia of New Zealand* (www.teara.govt. nz) as a superb resource on New Zealand history.

I read many books and a few journal articles in the course of my research, too, and while the following is not an exhaustive list, it will serve to guide the footsteps of anyone following after, supposing they want to see the same view.

BOOKS

Alexander Turnbull Library, *Map New Zealand: 100 magnificent maps from the collection of the Alexander Turnbull Library*. Auckland: Godwit, 2006.

Anderson, Grahame, *The Merchant of the Zeehaen: Isaac Gilsemans and the voyages of Abel Tasman*. Wellington: Te Papa Press, 2001.

Brooke-Hitching, Edward, *The Phantom Atlas: The greatest myths, lies and blunders on maps*. London: Simon & Schuster, 2016.

Brown, Lloyd, *The Story of Maps* [1949]. New York: Dover, 1979.

David, Andrew, Rudiger Joppien and Bernard Smith (eds), *The Charts and Coastal Views of Captain Cook's Voyages, vol. 1: The Voyage of the* Endeavour, *1768–1771, with a descriptive catalogue of all the known surveys and coastal views and the original engravings associated with them, together with original drawings of the* Endeavour *and her boats*. London: Hakluyt Society, 1988.

Easdale, Nola, *Kairuri: The measurer of land: The life of the 19th century surveyor pictured in his art and writings*. Wellington: Highgate/Price Milburn, 1988.

Garfield, Simon, *On the Map: Why the world looks the way it does*. London: Profile Books, 2012.

McKinnon, Malcolm (ed.), *New Zealand Historical Atlas*. Auckland: David Bateman, 1997.

Maling, Peter, *Historic Charts and Maps of New Zealand, 1642–1875*. Auckland: Reed, 1996.

Monmonier, Mark, *Drawing the Line: Tales of maps and cartocontroversy*. New York: Henry Holt, 1995.

Robson, John, *Captain Cook's World: Maps of the life and voyages of James Cook, R.N.* Auckland: Random House, 2000.

Sadler, Donald, *Man Is Not Lost: A record of two hundred years of astronomical navigation with the nautical almanac, 1767–1967*. London: HM Stationery Office, 1968.

Simmons, David, *The Great New Zealand Myth*. Wellington: A. H. & A. W. Reed, 1976.

Wilford, John, *The Mapmakers: The story of the great pioneers in cartography—from antiquity to the space age*. London: Junction Books, 1981.

ARTICLES

Barton, Philip, 'Maori Cartography and the European Encounter', in David Woodward and G. Malcolm Lewis (eds), *Cartography in the Traditional African, American, Arctic, Australian, and Pacific Societies*. Vol. 2.3 of *The History of Cartography*. Chicago: Chicago University Press, 1988.

Eckstein, Lars, and Anja Schwarz, 'The Making of Tupaia's Map: A story of the extent and mastery of Polynesian navigation, competing systems of wayfinding on James Cook's *Endeavour*, and the invention of an ingenious cartographic system', *Journal of Pacific History*, vol. 54, no. 1 (2019), pp. 1–95.

Maling, Peter, 'Recording Maori cartographic knowledge: Dr Phil Barton acknowledges Phil Barton's contribution', in *Turnbull Library Record*, no. 33 (2000), pp. 81–84.

Patterson, Brad, '"A Queer Cantankerous Lot": The human factor in the conduct of the New Zealand Company's Wellington surveys', in David Hamer, *The Making of Wellington*. Wellington: Victoria University Press, 1990.

ACKNOWLEDGEMENTS

This book arose from a conversation with the wonderful Jenny Hellen of Allen & Unwin. She was, she told me, interested in producing a book about maps. Since I've had a lifelong interest in maps and charts, this struck an immediate chord with me, and together we roughed out a plan of what the book would cover and look like. We had a destination, and a map.

In the very best traditions of exploration, the journey was far from linear and straightforward. There were plenty of detours, sidetracks, short cuts gone awry, blind alleys and dead ends. There were crossroads and u-turns and quite a bit of going in circles. There were mirages and Fata Morgana. There were moments of plain sailing, and plenty of squalls of the kind of adversity that afflicts any research project. When finally I arrived, I found the destination was 'something different', in the words of one of my favourite poems, Allen Curnow's 'Landfall in Unknown Seas', 'something nobody counted on', but none the less for that.

Along the way, I received advice and assistance from many expert pilots. I benefited from conversations with Mark Bagnall, sometime cartographical curator of the Alexander Turnbull Library, and with Alison Midwinter of LINZ. The staff of the Auckland

Public Library, Hocken Collections Uare Taoka o Hākena, Auckland Museum and the Museum of New Zealand Te Papa Tongarewa all helped where they could. The staff at Archives New Zealand were unwaveringly supportive and efficient, despite logistical difficulties caused by structural work to their facilities that neatly coincided with my demands. And whereas I had entertained grand visions of scouring the length and the breadth of the land for obscure and hitherto unseen cartographic material, I was eventually forced to scale back my ambitions. Happily for me, the cartographic collection at the Alexander Turnbull Library is as rich a resource as I could possibly have hoped for. Thanks to the staff, who were always kind and helpful in mining it for me, despite the gaping hole left in their collective institutional knowledge by their permanent curator's departure.

Making books is a team effort. In this instance, I relied far more heavily upon my team than I had any right to do, and no words can adequately express my gratitude to Jenny Hellen, Leanne McGregor and Sarah Ell for bringing the project home. The book looks as good as it does thanks to Megan van Staden's attractive design. Megan will have suffered as much at the unforgiving intersection of time and space as any New Zealand Company surveyor: thanks hardly seem enough. I have worked with any number of excellent editors in my time, who have saved me from my fallible self on more occasions than I care to admit, but even in their august company Matt Turner stands out. He has the eagle eyes essential for the trade, but also brought to this project a rare sympathy and a vast depth of knowledge. Several of his gems illuminate these pages. Thank you, Matt.

Last, as always, but as ever, far from least, thank you to my family. When James Cook set off on his three voyages of exploration, he left behind his wife, Elizabeth, and a growing number of children. Likewise, my own voyages of exploration have only ever been possible because of the indulgence of my partner, upon whom (along with my children) the burden fell while I was off poring over maps. Thank you, Madeleine, now and always.

For Hugh and Nell, adventurers

IMAGE CREDITS

Alexander Turnbull Library, Wellington, New Zealand: cover (detail) and pp. 246–247 (Alma MMSID: 9918215273602836), pp. 12–13 (detail) and 28–29 (830ap [1793] 1804), pp. 30–31 (MapColl-834.6gbbd/1851/Acc.3261), pp. 32–33 (E-333-036), p. 35 (MapColl-834ap/[1841-2?]/Acc.527), pp. 54–55 (MapColl 910a 1589 35004), p. 64 (Alma MMSID: 9918252368002836), pp. 68–69 (MapColl-910a/1753/Acc.32695), pp. 70–71 (detail) and 92–93 (Alma MMSID: 9918188162102836), pp. 74–75 (MapColl-833aj/1773/Acc.422), pp. 76–77 (MapColl-832.1aj/[1769]/Acc.12471), pp. 78–79 (MapColl-832.15aj/1769/Acc.2014), pp. 82–83 (Alma MMSID: 9918182973002836), pp. 86–87 (Alma MMSID: 9918572170102836), pp. 88–89 (MapColl-834.6aj/1773/Acc.32024), p. 90 (PUBL-0120-17), pp. 98–99 (800a 1776), pp. 100–101 (detail) and 104–105 (MapColl-835aj/1806/Acc.92), pp. 108–109 (MapColl-835at/[1813]/Acc.425), pp. 114–115 (MapColl-832.3aj/1837/Acc.419), p. 116 (832.11aj 1836), p. 118 (MapColl-832.47aj/1826/Acc.379), p. 121 (830ecd 1858?), p. 122 (MapColl-832.11aj/1822-27/Acc.384), pp. 124–125 (Alma MMSID: 9918144169702836), p. 127 (834.2aj 1876), pp. 130–131 and 150 (detail; MapColl-832.1291bje/1841/Acc.415), p. 135 (MapColl-832.11a/1833/Acc.39923), pp. 138–139 (1/2-051659-F), p. 142 (MapColl-832.4799gbbd/1840-1916/Acc.16123), pp. 144–145 (MapColl-832.41gbbd/1841/Acc.15388), pp. 146–147 (Alma MMSID: 9918158671402836), pp. 148–149 (Alma MMSID: 9918571073202836), pp. 152–153 (Alma MMSID: 9918575666802836), pp. 154–155 (Alma MMSID: 9918158671502836), pp. 156–157 (MapColl-834.5292gbbd/[1853-4]/Acc.3217-9), pp. 158–159 (Alma MMSID: 9918158671602836), pp. 160–161 (detail) and 170–171 (Alma MMSID: 9918218262402836), p. 166 (Alma MMSID: 9918185773502836), p. 168 (MapColl-834caq/[ca.1848]/Acc.23675), p. 173 (detail; MapColl-834.1atc/[1846]/Acc.46948-53), pp. 174–175 (Alma MMSID: 9918217336402836), p. 177 (Alma MMSID: 9918218273202836), pp. 178–179 (Alma MMSID: 9918218244402836), p. 180 (Alma MMSID: 9918252348402836), pp. 182–183 (834.4atc 1870), pp. 186–187 (detail) and 204–205 (Alma MMSID: 9918577173302836), pp. 190–191 (MapColl-832.11a/[ca.1845]/Acc.414), pp. 196–197 (MapColl-c832.2gbbd/1866/Acc.54588), p. 200 (MapColl-832.41hkcf/[186-?]/Acc.1165), p. 202 (MapColl-832.16hkm/[ca.1864]/Acc.1869), p. 203 (MapColl-832gmbd/[1865]/Acc.6172), p. 206 (832.3 fb 1874), p. 211 (MapColl-832.2gbbd/1927/Acc.35354), p. 222 (828a 1929), p. 223 (830faa 1983), p. 227 (MapColl-240hkm/1914-18/Acc.47105), p. 229 (MapColl-388.7hkm/[1915]/Acc.48724), pp. 230–231 (MapColl-r388.7hkm/1915/Acc.37274), pp. 236–237 (detail) and 245 (Alma MMSID: 9918215259802836), p. 239 (830 cba 1977), pp. 240–241 (Alma MMSID: 9918575666702836), p. 242 (Alma MMSID: 9918252368302836), p. 244 (MapColl-830gmfw/1935/Acc.1439), pp. 248–249 (Eph-B-RAIL-1930-01-front), p. 251 (Alma MMSID: 9918145366602836), p. 252 (Eph-C-AVIATION-NAC-1960-01-map), pp. 254–255 (832.1291gmbd 1957), p. 261 (MapColl 830gbc 1886 1397), p. 262 (Eph-D-POLITICS-1905-01), p. 264 (830gcrc 1877), p. 268 (MapColl 830ap 1943 50106); **Alexander Turnbull Library (sourced from LINZ; Crown Copyright reserved)**: pp. 198–199, pp. 256–257 (detail) and 267; **Archives New Zealand/Te Rua Mahara o te Kāwanatanga**: pp. 38–39 (CH765/17; R19034451), p. 233 (AAAA 21573 W5617 4/R17582352); **Auckland Libraries Heritage Collections**: p. 209 (NZ Map 2562); **British Library Board**: pp. 22–23 (BL3292585), pp. 40–41 (detail) and 48–49 (BL3297174), pp. 44–45 (BL3294199), pp. 52–53 (BL33137456); **Commonwealth War Graves Commission**: pp. 224 (detail) and 235; **Cornell University—PJ Mode Collection of Persuasive Cartography**: pp. 214–215 (detail) and 218–219 (1095.01); **Ferdinand von Hochstetter, from p. 4 of** *Hochstetter's Atlas*, published c. 1863: p. 185; **NASA Earth Observatory**: p. 271 (TMO2002296); **National Library of Australia**: pp. 96–97 (MAP NK 2456/22), pp. 112–113 (MAP RM 627); **State Library of New South Wales**: pp. 56–57 (detail) and 60–61 (M ZSafe 1/72), pp. 66–67 (M2 800/1643/4), p. 110 (M2 982.42/1809/1).

First published in 2019

Text © John McCrystal, 2019
Imagery as credited opposite

All rights reserved. No part of this book may be reproduced or transmitted in any form or by any means, electronic or mechanical, including photocopying, recording or by any information storage and retrieval system, without prior permission in writing from the publisher.

Allen & Unwin
Level 3, 228 Queen Street
Auckland 1010, New Zealand
Phone: (64 9) 377 3800
Email: info@allenandunwin.com
Web: www.allenandunwin.co.nz

83 Alexander Street
Crows Nest NSW 2065, Australia
Phone: (61 2) 8425 0100

A catalogue record for this book is available from the National Library of New Zealand.

ISBN 978 1 76063 359 2

Design by Megan van Staden
Set in Galaxie Copernicus, National and Heldane
Printed in Malaysia for Imago
10 9 8 7 6 5 4 3 2 1